WIPO ARBITRATION RULES:

COMMENTARY AND ANALYSIS

Juris Publishing

JurisNet

Juris Publishing
JurisNet LLC
Executive Park
One Odell Plaza
Yonkers, New York 10701

DEDICATION

This volume is dedicated to Vratislav Pechota who, since joining the Columbia Law School community in 1984, has been in the vanguard of our endeavors in the field of international commercial arbitration. As Co-Editor-in-Chief of *The American Review of International Arbitration* and the moving force behind our publications on international arbitration, including the *World Arbitration Reporter*, the *Guides to International Arbitration*, the *Roster of International Arbitration and Arbitrators*, and the *International Bibliography on International Arbitration*, he has indefatigably and immeasurably contributed to the resources available to academia and the practicing bar alike. It is most fitting that we acknowledge his contributions and honor him on the occasion of his formal retirement from Columbia, although, most fortunately, not from the work of our Center, where he continues to be the Director of Research.

Vratislav Pechota was born in Czechoslovakia in 1928. Educated in law, both at the famous Charles University in Prague and in Russia, he rose to become Legal Advisor to the Czech Ministry of Foreign Affairs and member of the International Law Department at Charles University. He represented Czechoslovakia in international bodies, including the United Nations, and was elected Chairman of the Prestigious Sixth (Legal) Committee of the U.N. General Assembly.

Having chosen the side of Dubcek in the Czech efforts to free itself from Soviet domination, he became *persona non grata* when the Communist regime was reinstated by the Soviet Army. Due to the efforts of Professor Oscar Schachter, then the Deputy Head of the U.N. Institute for Training and Research, Professor Pechota and his family were able to come to the United States. Shortly thereafter, we were fortunate to persuade him to come to Columbia to work in the area of international arbitration.

While working on many aspects of international arbitration, Vratislav Pechota taught two offerings on East European law, first in collaboration with Professor John N. Hazard, and, after Professor Hazard's retirement, alone. For use in these offerings, Professor Pechota collected a great many primary and secondary sources, which in time were published in three collections, one on the Soviet Union, the second on the Commonwealth of Independent States, and the third on the Russian Federation. His efforts to encourage research in East European Law led to publication of the *Survey on East European Law* and, subsequently, of the *Journal on East European Law*, a law review devoted to the study of Russian and East European Law. All the while, Professor Pechota also took on the continuation of the *Szladits Bibliography on Foreign and Comparative Law*.

Professor Pechota's contributions to making Columbia Law School the predominant law school in the United States in the areas of international arbitration and East European legal studies are truly exceptional.

We owe him a great debt and are grateful for having this opportunity to do him homage.

December 1999

Hans Smit
Stanley H. Fuld Professor of Law
Director, Center for International
Arbitration and Litigation Law
Columbia University

WIPO ARBITRATION RULES: COMMENTARY AND ANALYSIS

INTRODUCTION

The technological revolution is proceeding apace and with it the need to resolve fairly and expeditiously disputes that inevitably attend it.

The World Intellectual Property Organization is ideally situated to provide the proper structure to accommodate these developments. It plays a pivotal role in assuring proper protection for intellectual property rights worldwide under a number of international agreements. And, in 1994, it promulgated the WIPO Arbitration and Expedited Arbitration Rules.

These articles provide analytical comments on each of the articles of the new WIPO Arbitration and Expedited Arbitration Rules, as well as the WIPO Emergency Relief Rules and WIPO's recommended clauses and agreements. It constitutes the only article-by-article commentary on the WIPO Rules in print. The authors of these contributions are practitioners and scholars with extensive experience in the fields of intellectual property and arbitration. The WIPO Arbitration Rules are among the most recent comprehensive institutional arbitration rules to be promulgated. They contain novel rules on such subjects as confidentiality, interim relief, expert evidence, and expedited arbitration. The application of these Rules is likely to contribute greatly to developments in international arbitration. The Center for International Arbitration and Litigation Law is proud to present this volume as an integral part of its publications in the area of international arbitration.

Hans Smit
Stanley H. Fuld Professor of Law
Director, Center for International
*   Arbitration and Litigation Law*
Columbia University

GENERAL COMMENTARY ON THE WIPO ARBITRATION RULES, RECOMMENDED CLAUSES, GENERAL PROVISIONS AND THE WIPO EXPEDITED ARBITRATION RULES

Articles 1 to 5; Articles 39 and 40

*Robert H. Smit**

The Arbitration Center of the World Intellectual Property Organization commenced operations in October 1994 as an international center offering mediation, arbitration and other services for the resolution of international commercial disputes involving intellectual property.[1] For parties wishing to arbitrate their intellectual property disputes, the Center has issued two sets of arbitration rules: its general purpose WIPO Arbitration Rules ("WIPO Rules") and its WIPO Expedited Arbitration Rules ("WIPO Expedited Rules") for disputes requiring and amenable to expeditious resolution. While those sets of Rules have yet to be tested in practice (as of the date of this writing), it may fairly be said that they offer one of the best regimes available for institutional arbitration of international intellectual property disputes.

This commentary examines the following aspects of the WIPO Rules and Expedited Rules:

    1.   WIPO's recommended arbitration clauses and agreements, by which parties may adopt the WIPO Rules to resolve their intellectual property disputes;

    2.   Articles 1 through 5 of the WIPO Rules — entitled "General Provisions" — which define certain of the terms used in the Rules and deal with the scope of application of the Rules, notices, periods of time, and documents to be submitted to the Center under the Rules;

    3.   Articles 39 and 40 of the WIPO Rules, governing the place and language of the arbitration; and

---

* Partner, Simpson Thacher & Bartlett, New York City.
[1] The WIPO Arbitration Center and its services were the subject of a Worldwide Forum in 1994 organized by WIPO and the American Arbitration Association. The papers presented at that Forum are published in Volume V of *The American Review of International Arbitration* (1994). On the arbitration of international intellectual property disputes generally, *see* Jennifer Mills, Note, *Alternative Dispute Resolution in International Intellectual Property Disputes*, 11 OHIO ST. J. ON DISP. RESOL. 227 (1996); Camille A. Laturno, Comment, *International Arbitration of the Creative: A Look at the World Intellectual Property Organization's New Arbitration Rules*, 9 TRANSNAT'L LAW. 357 (1996); Ewell E. Murphy, Jr., *Taking IP and ADR International: Arbitration as the Key to Effective Management of Transnational Intellectual Property Disputes*, 8–3 INT'L Q. 439 (1995); William Grantham, Comment, *The Arbitrability of International Intellectual Property Disputes*, 14 BERKELEY J. INT'L L. 173 (1996); M. Scott Donahey, *Enforcement of Injunctive Relief and Arbitration Awards Concerning Title to and Enforcement of Intellectual Property Rights in Asia and the Pacific Rim*, 19 HASTINGS INT'L & COMP. L. REV. 727 (1996).

4. The WIPO Expedited Rules in their entirety, with particular emphasis on the ways in which they differ from the general WIPO Rules.

I. WIPO'S RECOMMENDED ARBITRATION CLAUSES AND AGREEMENTS

Before turning to the arbitration provisions recommended by WIPO for parties who choose WIPO arbitration to resolve their intellectual property disputes, it is worth reviewing some of the primary factors to be considered by parties in making that choice.

A. *Arbitration of International Intellectual Property Disputes Generally*

The advantages of arbitration of international commercial disputes have long been recognized.[2] In recent times, there has also been a growing sentiment that intellectual property disputes in particular may be especially well-suited for resolution by arbitration.[3] Indeed, it is precisely that conviction that inspired the creation of the WIPO Arbitration Center. As the Director of the Center has written:

> The underlying reason for the establishment of the Center was a belief in the specificity of intellectual property as a subject matter, and, thus, of disputes concerning intellectual property, coupled with the conviction that arbitration and other dispute resolution alternatives offered particularly suitable means of accommodating the specific characteristics of intellectual property disputes.[4]

While advice is plentiful on the factors to consider generally in deciding whether and how to arbitrate, certain of those factors assume particular importance in the intellectual property context in determining (1) whether to arbitrate intellectual property disputes; (2) whether to use institutional or *ad hoc* arbitration; and (3) which arbitration rules to adopt.

1. *Whether to Arbitrate*
The potential advantages of arbitration of intellectual property disputes are numerous:[5]

---

[2] *See, e.g.*, ALAN REDFERN & MARTIN HUNTER, LAW AND PRACTICE OF INTERNATIONAL COMMERCIAL ARBITRATION 22–26 (2d ed. 1991); Sir Michael Kerr, *International Arbitration v. Litigation*, J. BUS. L. 164 (1980).

[3] On the advantages of arbitration of intellectual property disputes, *see generally* Bryan Niblett, *The Arbitration of Intellectual Property Disputes*, 5 AM. REV. INT'L ARB. 117, 118–19 (1994); Mills, *supra* note 1, at 230–31; Murphy, *supra* note 1, at 454–56; Laturno, *supra* note 1, at 369–71; Tom Arnold & Willem G. Schuurman, *Alternative Dispute Resolution in Intellectual Property Cases*, *in* PATENT LITIGATION 1991, at 437, 441–61 (PLI Patents, Copyrights, Trademarks, and Literary Property Course Handbook Series No. 321, 1991).

[4] Francis Gurry, *The WIPO Arbitration Center and Its Services*, 5 AM. REV. INT'L ARB. 197 (1994).

[5] A WIPO brochure entitled THE SERVICES OF THE WIPO ARBITRATION CENTER (WIPO Publication No. 445(E)) enumerates some of the most important advantages. *See also supra* note 2.

- First, intellectual property disputes often involve highly technical subject matter that is more suitable for resolution by an arbitrator handpicked by the parties for his or her specialized competence than by a national court judge or jury with little or no prior knowledge or experience in the field.[6] The arbitrator's specialized competence may enhance not only the quality of the decision-making but also the efficiency with which the proceedings are conducted.

- Second, because intellectual property is a time-wasting asset, arbitration with its limited discovery and appeals offers a potentially faster means of resolving intellectual property disputes than does litigation. Disputed patents and technology can become obsolete, or the market saturated with infringing materials, while a case awaits adjudication on a crowded court docket or makes its way through judicial trial and appeals.[7]

- Third, the privacy of the arbitration process provides superior protection for the confidentiality of the intellectual property rights at issue.[8] While litigation may be conducted *in camera* and protective orders concerning confidentiality may be available, the inherent privacy and confidentiality of arbitration arguably provides superior safeguards against unwanted publicity.

- Fourth, arbitration may be better suited to preserve the long-term relationships contemplated by the license and technology transfer agreements that give rise to many intellectual property disputes.[9]

- Fifth, arbitration provides a single neutral forum in which intellectual property disputes involving different national markets and parties from different countries can be resolved.[10] In fact, neither party is likely to want to litigate in

---

[6] This is especially true in patent cases involving novel subject matter as well as in copyright matters involving computer programs. The types of technical disputes that commonly arise in intellectual property cases are described in Niblett *supra* note 3, at 118; Julian Lew, *The Arbitration of Intellectual Property Disputes*, 5 AM REV. INT'L ARB. 110, 111–12 (1991).

[7] The horror stories of interminable intellectual property litigations are legion. *See, e.g.,* Arnold and Schuurman, *supra* note 3, at 441–43.

[8] Intellectual property disputes may involve confidential know-how, customer lists, challenges to intellectual property rights and difficulties with licensees. A publicized dispute over title to a copyright, for instance, could be devastating to the success of the product at issue. On the advantages of the confidentiality of the arbitration process for intellectual property disputes, *see* Lew, *supra* note 6, at 115–16; Gurry *supra* note 4, at 198; Niblett, *supra* note 3, at 118.

[9] *See, e.g.*, Niblett, *supra* note 3, at 118; Laturno, *supra* note 1, at 371; Murphy, *supra* note 1, at 454–56.

[10] *See e.g.*, Gurry, *supra* note 4, at 197–98; Niblett, *supra* note 3, at 118. The availability of a neutral forum may be particularly important for disputes pitting nationals from developing countries against nationals from developed countries in light of the disparate approaches of developing and developed countries towards intellectual property protection. On that disparate approach, *see* Mills, *supra* note 1, at 229–32; Laturno, *supra* note 1, at 359; Marshall A. Leaffer, *Protecting United States Intellectual Property Abroad: Toward a New Multilateralism*, 76 IOWA L. REV. 273, 275 (1991). On the other hand, parties from developing countries may also harbor reservations about the impartiality of international arbitral tribunals. *See* Laturno, *supra* note 1, at 366–67; Mauro Rubino-Sammartano, *Developing Countries vis-à-*

the other party's courts, and a single forum may be preferable to a multiplicity
of national court actions for disputes involving different national and regional
intellectual property titles covering the same subject matter.

- Sixth, one of the most important advantages of international arbitration
  generally, and of intellectual property arbitration in particular, is that arbitral
  awards are readily enforceable world-wide as a result of the ratification by
  over one hundred countries of the New York Convention of 1958, whereas the
  enforceability of national court judgments is not similarly enhanced by any
  international treaties of comparable scope.

- Finally, arbitrators may be better able than judges to fashion private remedies
  for intellectual property disputes involving issues at the cutting edge of the law
  where legal principles have yet to be fully developed.[11] One advantage of
  arbitration in that connection is that the private remedy devised by the tribunal
  can be tested in practice without far-reaching legal consequences.

Countervailing considerations exist too, however, and each party's decision as to
whether to agree to arbitrate potential intellectual property disputes should take into
account the particular circumstances of the transaction and that party's anticipated
strategic objectives. Those countervailing considerations may include the following:

- First, some countries have specialized courts, such as patent courts, with
  particular expertise in intellectual property matters, making resort to an
  arbitrator with specialized competence unnecessary; the fact that national court
  decisions are generally public also offers a greater predictability of result than
  that available to parties choosing arbitration.[12] In any event, the need for an
  adjudicator with specialized intellectual property competence can be overstated: in the contractual context in which the choice between arbitration and
  litigation is made, detailed technical knowledge (as opposed to a general
  familiarity with the language and concepts of intellectual property) may be

---

vis International Arbitration, 13(1) J. INT'L ARB. 21 (1996). This may be particularly true of WIPO
arbitration in light of its stated purpose in the 1967 Convention establishing WIPO to "promote protection
of intellectual property." It should be noted, however, that an important aspect of WIPO's activities
consists of promoting respect for intellectual property within developing countries and in their
international relations. *See* BACKGROUND READING MATERIAL ON INTELLECTUAL PROPERTY (WIPO
Publication No. 659(E)), at 40 (1988).

[11] Intellectual property law may benefit from the development of a *lex arbitralis* in the subject matter.
See Gurry, *supra* note 4, at 198 (noting that technological innovation and change in the intellectual
property arena often out-pace legislative solutions or precedents in judicial decisions); Niblett, *supra* note
3, at 118–19.

[12] On the advantages of resort to the German Federal Patent Court rather than to arbitration, *see* Jochen
Pagenberg, *The Arbitrability of Intellectual Property Disputes in Germany*, 5 AM. REV. INT'L ARB. 44
(1994). It remains true, however, that national courts with specialized expertise in intellectual property
may not also be sensitive to the specificity of the *international* context in which the parties' dispute arises.

less important than broad international commercial experience and simple common sense.[13]

- Second, horror stories of interminable and costly proceedings are not unique to intellectual property litigation; intellectual property arbitration has its share of such horror stories as well.[14]
- Third, a private global resolution of the parties' intellectual property dispute in a single neutral forum may not always be the property holder's preferred means of dispute resolution. A licensor whose intellectual property has been licensed in several different countries, for example, may prefer to reserve its right to bring suit in the markets of its choice, believing that the publicity generated by those suits will effectively discourage breach or infringement of its intellectual property rights in other markets.[15]
- Fourth, arbitration of intellectual property disputes raises several important issues of enforceability: (i) the arbitrability of intellectual property disputes, and hence the enforceability of arbitration agreements and awards encompassing those matters, remains limited and/or uncertain in various parts of the world;[16] (ii) arbitration agreements and awards encompassing intellectual property matters do not bind and are not enforceable against non-parties to the arbitration agreement and proceedings;[17] and (iii) the availability of effective

---

[13] Several commentators have recommended that arbitrators in intellectual property disputes should be chosen not only for their substantive expertise in intellectual property but also for their general commercial perspective and experience in international arbitration. *See e.g.*, James H. Carter, *The Selection of Arbitrators*, 5 AM. REV. INT'L ARB. 84, 91–92 (1994); Lew, *supra* note 6, at 113.

[14] Two particularly egregious examples — *Pilkington PLC v. PPG* and *Intel v. Advanced Micro Devices, Inc.* — are described in Tom Arnold, *Why ADR? Booby Traps in Arbitration Practice and How to Avoid Them*, 5 AM. REV. INT'L ARB. 179, 187 (1994).

[15] *See* Pagenberg, *supra* note 12, at 44–45. Maintaining the right to sue in various jurisdictions also avoids placing all of one's eggs in a single basket: an unfavorable result in one jurisdiction may not preclude a second bite at the apple in another jurisdiction.

[16] On the arbitrability of intellectual property disputes, *see generally* Robert Briner, *The Arbitrability of Intellectual Property Disputes with Particular Emphasis on the Situation in Switzerland*, 5 AM. REV. INT'L ARB. 28 (1994); David W. Plant, *Arbitrability of Intellectual Property Issues in the United States*, 5 AM. REV. INT'L ARB. 11 (1994); Donahey; *supra* note 1, at 731–37; Pagenberg, *supra* note 12; Grantham, *supra* note 1, at 179–99. Public policy objections to the arbitrability of intellectual property matters may be raised under three of the grounds listed in Article V of the New York Convention for opposing enforcement of arbitration awards: (i) the arbitration agreement is not valid under the law chosen by the parties, and if the parties have not made such a choice, under the law of the country where the award was made (Article V(1)(a)); (ii) the subject matter of the award is not arbitrable under the law of the state in which enforcement is sought (Article V(2)(a)); (iii) the award is against the public policy of the state in which enforcement is sought (Article V(2)(b)). Convention on the Recognition and Enforcement of Foreign Arbitral Awards, New York, *opened for signature* June 10, 1958, *entered into force* June 7, 1959, 21 U.S.T. 2517, 330 U.N.T.S. 38 (1959) [hereinafter New York Convention].

[17] On the other hand, in some jurisdictions non-parties may be able to take advantage of any arbitral decisions unfavorable to an intellectual property holder by virtue of the doctrine of collateral estoppel. *See* Aufderhar v. Data Dispatch, Inc., 452 N.W.2d 648 (Minn. 1990) (non-party to prior arbitration may

interim relief, which is often vital in intellectual property disputes, is limited in arbitration.[18]

• Finally, some may argue that the development of intellectual property jurisprudence will be stunted by arbitration, in which solutions to cutting-edge issues are privately formulated behind closed conference room doors rather than out in the open for the benefit of the international public eye.

Indeed, some of the foregoing considerations and constraints on the enforceability of arbitration agreements and awards help to explain why arbitration has yet to be fully exploited as a means of resolving intellectual property disputes.[19]

2. *Institutional Versus Ad Hoc Arbitration*

Parties who decide to arbitrate their intellectual property disputes must choose between *institutional* and *ad hoc* arbitration. The general merits and demerits of each have been widely debated;[20] how those considerations apply in intellectual property disputes in particular has received less attention. In fact, institutional arbitration would appear to enjoy three significant advantages as far as intellectual property disputes in particular are concerned. First, an arbitral institution such as the WIPO Arbitration Center can play a useful role in assisting parties in drafting arbitration clauses for their intellectual property-related contracts. The institution may also act as an intermediary between parties negotiating submission agreements for their patent, trademark and copyright infringement disputes in which the parties are generally not contractually

---

invoke collateral estoppel to preclude the claimant in that arbitration from relitigating issues decided against it in the arbitration); *see generally Collateral Estoppel and Arbitration*, 8 AAA LAW. ARB. LETTER, March 1984, at 1.

[18] As a practical matter, a high proportion of intellectual property disputes are determined at the preliminary injunction stage. The need for interim relief therefore ordinarily arises at the outset of the parties' dispute, before the tribunal has been constituted and, thus, before it is in a position to award interim relief. *See* Richard Alan Horning, *infra* at 155; Niblett, *supra* note 3, at 120; Lew, *supra* note 6, at 113–16; PROPOSED WIPO SUPPLEMENTARY EMERGENCY INTERIM RELIEF RULES, *Consultation Document Prepared by the International Bureau,* at 1–2 (Apr. 19, 1996). Moreover, the courts in various jurisdictions have refused to recognize an arbitrator's right to grant interim relief, have denied enforcement of arbitral orders of interim relief on the ground that they are not final orders, and/or have themselves refused to grant judicial interim relief on the ground that the parties' arbitration agreement precludes them from doing so. *See generally* CONSERVATORY AND PROVISIONAL MEASURES IN INTERNATIONAL ARBITRATION (ICC Publishing 1993).

[19] *See* Gurry, *supra* note 4, at 199.

[20] Depending on the institution administering the arbitration, institutional arbitration will generally provide an experience-tested set of arbitration rules, administrative services and/or supervisory functions such as scrutiny of the arbitrators' awards, a buffer between the parties and the arbitrators with respect to delicate issues concerning arbitrators' fees and challenges to arbitrators, and enhanced acceptability of the arbitral process. *Ad hoc* arbitration, on the other hand, may provide more flexible procedures which can be tailored to the specific needs of the dispute and avoids the administrative costs and sometimes unwelcome bureaucratic procedures that plague institutional arbitration. The need for recourse to the court looms ever-present in *ad hoc* arbitration, however. For a useful discussion of the pros and cons of institutional versus *ad hoc* arbitration, *see* Marc Blessing, *Drafting Arbitration Clauses*, 5 AM. REV. INT'L ARB. 54, 57–58 (1994); *see also* Laturno, *supra* note 1, at 387.

bound.[21] Second, institutional arbitration may be better suited to handle uncertainties concerning the arbitrability of intellectual property disputes, which often form the basis for jurisdictional objections prior to the constitution of the tribunal.[22] It is useful to have the support of an arbitral institution to keep the proceedings moving towards the constitution of the tribunal, notwithstanding such jurisdictional objections, without need for recourse to the courts. Finally, an arbitral institution, and the WIPO Center in particular, is generally better suited than a national court (acting as the appointing authority in an *ad hoc* arbitration) to designate competent arbitrators for an international intellectual property arbitration.

3. *The Choice Among Arbitration Institutions and Rules*

If institutional arbitration is preferred, the parties must then choose from among the various institutional arbitration rules available.[23] In doing so, they should consider both the quality and experience of the arbitral institution and the extent to which its arbitration rules are suited to resolve intellectual property disputes. Considerations in choosing the arbitral institution should include its history, neutrality, reputation, role in the proceedings and experience in intellectual property matters. While the WIPO Arbitration Center has been operating only for a relatively short time, the World Intellectual Property Organization of which it forms a part has functioned as an inter-governmental organization for over 110 years.[24] Moreover, unlike the AAA and the LCIA, which are national institutions generally associated with the countries in which they are located, WIPO is a specialized agency of the United Nations, staffed by an international secretariat of approximately 500 people drawn from over 60 countries, and located in Geneva, Switzerland, a country with a long tradition of neutrality. As far as the Center's role in the arbitral proceedings is concerned, its primary function is to assist in the constitution of the tribunal, leaving the conduct of the ensuing proceedings to the parties and the arbitrators.[25] In that connection, the Center has gone to great lengths to identify arbitrators with extensive experience both in intellectual property

---

[21] *See* Michael F. Hoellering, *The Institution's Role in Managing the Arbitration Process*, 5 AM. REV. INT'L ARB. 121, 121–22 (1994); Gurry, *supra* note 4, at 198–200 (describing the WIPO Center as a resource center for parties considering arbitration of their intellectual property disputes).

[22] *See* Hoellering, *supra* note 21, at 124.

[23] The leading institutional arbitration rules include the International Chamber of Commerce's Arbitration Rules ("ICC RULES" — the new 1998 version, in force as from January 1, 1998, unless otherwise specified), the American Arbitration Association's International Arbitration Rules ("AAA INTERNATIONAL RULES" — as amended and effective on April 1, 1997, unless otherwise specified), and the London Court of International Arbitration's Arbitration Rules ("LCIA RULES" — the new 1998 version, effective from January 1, 1998, unless otherwise specified).

[24] On the history and constitution of WIPO, *see* Francis Gurry, *Introduction to the 1994 Worldwide Forum on the Arbitration of Intellectual Property Disputes*, 5 AM. REV. INT'L ARB. 1 (1994); Mills, *supra* note 1, at 235; Laturno, *supra* note 1, at 371–74.

[25] The ICC Court, by contrast, plays a more interventionist role in the proceedings by virtue of, among other things, its scrutiny of the arbitrators' Terms of Reference and award. *See* Robert H. Smit, *An Inside View of the ICC Court*, 10 ARB. INT'L 53 (1994).

and in international arbitration.[26] Finally, while the Center has yet to administer any arbitrations, its pedigree in intellectual property is without peer among the leading arbitral institutions.[27] For all of these reasons, arbitration administered by the WIPO Center would appear to offer most of the advantages of institutional arbitration without the bureaucracy or inflexible procedures for which other forms of institutional arbitration have been criticized.

As far as the actual rules of the various arbitral institutions are concerned, parties are well-advised to examine those provisions likely to be of particular importance to intellectual property disputes, such as rules providing for the expeditious resolution of the dispute, the availability of interim relief, and the confidentiality of the proceedings.[28] The WIPO Rules, while heavily influenced by the arbitration rules of the United Nations Commission on International Trade Law ("UNCITRAL Rules") and the AAA International Rules, were tailored to accommodate the specific characteristics of intellectual property disputes.[29] They therefore contain innovative provisions designed to expedite the proceedings, protect the confidentiality of the proceedings, and ensure the availability of effective interim relief.[30]

---

[26] The WIPO Arbitration Center maintains, but does not make publicly available, a list of over 500 arbitrators along with resumes detailing their experience in intellectual property and international arbitration.

[27] While case load statistics are not available for each of the leading institutions, intellectual property disputes generally represent a relatively small percentage of the arbitrations administered by those institutions. For example, approximately 14.5% of all ICC arbitrations commenced in 1996 involved intellectual property. *1996 Statistical Report*, ICC INT'L CT. ARB. BULL., May 1997, at 6, 7, 9.

[28] *See* HANS SMIT & VRATISLAV PECHOTA, A CHART COMPARING INTERNATIONAL COMMERCIAL ARBITRATION RULES (1998). The Chart is a useful tool in comparing specific provisions of the major arbitration rules.

[29] For a discussion of how particular WIPO Rules reflect the specificity of intellectual property disputes, *see* Gurry, *supra* note 24, at 2–4. While other arbitration rules specifically designed for intellectual property disputes exist, *see, e.g.*, AAA PATENT ARBITRATION RULES; CENTER FOR PUBLIC RESOURCES (CPR) RULES FOR NON-ADMINISTERED ARBITRATION OF PATENT AND TRADE SECRET DISPUTES, those rules are generally intended for use in domestic as opposed to international arbitrations. Accordingly, they are patterned on general domestic arbitration rules and provide for partisan party-appointed arbitrators and unreasoned awards, both of which are disfavored in international arbitration.

[30] The WIPO Center is considering offering a new procedure for obtaining emergency interim relief prior to the constitution of the tribunal, and has circulated draft Supplementary Emergency Interim Relief Rules for comment. *See* Richard Alan Horning, *infra* at 155. [EDITOR'S NOTE: The WIPO Emergency Relief Rules are expected to be approved in December 1999.] A similar procedure was introduced by the ICC in 1990 with its ICC Pre-Arbitral Referee Procedure, and emergency interim relief procedures are under consideration by the AAA and LCIA as well. For a commentary on the ICC Pre-Arbitral Referee Rules, *see* Hans Smit, *Provisional Relief in International Arbitration: The ICC and Other Proposed Rules*, 1 AM. REV. INT'L ARB. 388 (1991). Like the ICC Pre-Arbitral Referee Rules, the proposed WIPO Supplementary Emergency Interim Relief Rules would only apply if expressly chosen by the parties in their arbitration clause or submission agreement. Unlike the ICC Pre-Arbitral Referee Rules, the proposed WIPO Supplementary Emergency Interim Relief Rules would be integrated (at the parties' option) with the conventional arbitration procedure under the WIPO Rules, and the Tribunal would be constituted from a stand-by panel of arbitrators to ensure appointment on twenty-four hours' notice. *See* PROPOSED WIPO

B. *WIPO's Recommended Arbitration Clauses and Agreements*

The WIPO Center has published standard clauses and submission agreements by which parties may choose to resolve their future or existing disputes by:

- Mediation under the WIPO Mediation Rules;
- Arbitration under the WIPO Arbitration Rules;
- Expedited arbitration under the WIPO Expedited Arbitration Rules; or
- Mediation under the WIPO Mediation Rules, followed, in the absence of a settlement, by arbitration under the WIPO Arbitration Rules.

While the advisability of resort to mediation, and an analysis of the WIPO Mediation Rules in particular, are beyond the scope of this commentary, the potential benefits of mediation can hardly be ignored.[31] Its rate of efficacy in resolving commercial disputes, as well as the relative dearth of mediation horror stories, makes mediation a promising means of achieving creative solutions and preserving long-term relationships created by intellectual property-related agreements. On the other hand, the risk that mediation may be misused solely as a tool of discovery and the fact that mediation does not result in a binding decision may explain the relatively infrequent resort to mediation to resolve major international commercial disputes.[32] Because mediation is a non-binding procedure, parties who do provide for WIPO mediation should generally also provide for WIPO arbitration in the event the mediation fails to resolve the dispute. In that connection, an issue of enforceability is raised by the compulsory nature of mediation under WIPO's mediation-followed-by-arbitration clause because only arbitration agreements, not mediation agreements, qualify for summary enforcement under the New York Convention; some courts may therefore hesitate to compel arbitration or stay litigation until the condition precedent — the obligation to mediate — is performed.[33]

SUPPLEMENTARY EMERGENCY INTERIM RELIEF RULES, *supra* note 18. The Proposed WIPO Emergency Interim Relief Rules represent a significant and desirable addition to the arbitration services it currently offers.

[31] On the mediation of intellectual property disputes, *see* Sir Laurence Street, *Mediation*, 5 AM. REV. INT'L ARB. 149 (1994); Toshio Sawada, *Conciliation — Japan's Experience — Prospects of Success in International Transactions*, 5 AM. REV. INT'L ARB. 162 (1994); Tom Arnold, *Advocacy in Mediation*, 5 AM. REV. INT'L ARB. 169 (1994); Mills, *supra* note 1, at 231–35; Arnold and Schuurman, *supra* note 3, at 462–79.

[32] Since the new ICC Conciliation Rules came into force, for example, the ratio of Requests for Conciliation to Requests for Arbitration has been less than 3%. Eric A. Schwartz, *International Conciliation and the ICC*, ICC INT'L CT. ARB. BULL., Nov. 1994, at 5.

[33] *See* Lord Mustill's opinion in Channel Tunnel Group Ltd. v. Balfour Beatty Constr. Ltd., [1993] App. Cas. 334, 354 (1993), *reprinted in* 8 MEALEY'S INT'L ARB. REP. E-1, at E-8 (Feb. 1993) ("If the English legislation had followed the Convention, as strictly speaking it should have done, it would have been hard to resist the conclusion that the duty to stay does not apply to a situation where the reference to the arbitrators is to take place, if at all, only after the matter has been referred to someone else."); *cf.* GARY B. BORN, INTERNATIONAL COMMERCIAL ARBITRATION IN THE UNITED STATES 409 (1994) (U.S. courts generally refuse to inquire as to whether contractually-stipulated procedural steps prior to arbitration were properly taken, reasoning that the issue is one for the arbitrator).

C. *WIPO's Recommended Arbitration Clause*

WIPO's recommended arbitration clause provides:

> **Any dispute, controversy or claim arising under, out of or relating to this contract and any subsequent amendments of this contract, including, without limitation, its formation, validity, binding effect, interpretation, performance, breach or termination, as well as non-contractual claims, shall be referred to and finally determined by arbitration in accordance with the WIPO Arbitration Rules. The arbitral tribunal shall consist of [three arbitrators] [a sole arbitrator]. The place of arbitration shall be . . . . The language to be used in the arbitral proceeding shall be . . . . The dispute, controversy or claim shall be decided in accordance with the law of . . . .**

WIPO's standard clause differs from other standard arbitration clauses in at least three respects. First, it appropriately makes explicit what other standard clauses only imply: that the scope of the parties' arbitration agreement encompasses "non-contractual" claims as well as contractual claims relating to the parties' underlying agreement.[34] The express inclusion of non-contractual claims is particularly important with respect to intellectual property disputes in which parties frequently assert infringement claims cast in tort rather than in contract as well as statutory antitrust-related defenses.

The second difference between WIPO's recommended arbitration clause and the standard ICC, AAA and UNCITRAL clauses is that the WIPO clause does not merely *suggest* that the parties consider agreeing on (i) the number of arbitrators, (ii) the place of arbitration, (iii) the language of the arbitration, and (iv) the law to be applied, but instead affirmatively incorporates those choices into the parties' arbitration agreement.[35] While it may not always be possible or desirable to agree on such provisions before a dispute arises and its scope and circumstances become known, it is generally preferable that the parties agree on those matters in advance in order to avoid procedural disputes and delays once the dispute arises.[36]

---

[34] U.S. courts have reached inconsistent results in determining whether agreements to arbitrate claims "arising out of" or "relating to" the underlying contract encompass related tort claims. *See* BORN, *supra* note 33, at 406–07 (canvassing the relevant case law).

[35] The WIPO Rules governing the appointment of arbitrators, the designation of the seat and language of the arbitration, and the law to be applied, provide for the event that the parties do not make those selections in advance. *See* WIPO RULES, art. 14 (number of arbitrators), art. 39 (place of arbitration), art. 40 (language of the arbitration) and art. 59 (applicable law). For a useful discussion of additional provisions that may be included in an arbitration clause, *see* Blessing, *supra* note 20, at 65–80; W. LAWRENCE CRAIG, WILLIAM W. PARK & JAN PAULSSON, INTERNATIONAL CHAMBER OF COMMERCE ARBITRATION, chs. 7–8 (2d ed. 1990).

[36] Indeed, for these reasons it has been suggested that the ICC amend the current *"reminder"* in its standard clause that *"it may be desirable for"* parties to stipulate as to those matters to contain more emphatic language that *"it will normally be desirable"* or *"it will invariably be necessary"* that the parties so stipulate. *See* Richard H. Kreindler, *Impending Revision of the ICC Arbitration Rules: Opportunities and Hazards for Experienced and Inexperienced Users Alike*, 13(2) J. INT'L ARB. 45, 51 (1996). That suggestion was not ultimately incorporated in the ICC's revised Rules of Arbitration, in force

Third, unlike the UNCITRAL and AAA standard clauses, the WIPO clause includes a choice-of-law provision. An advantage of incorporating the choice-of-law provision in the arbitration clause rather than including it as a separate provision in the underlying agreement is that it is made clear that the chosen law is intended to govern *all* claims in the arbitration, including any non-contractual tort or statutory claims. A separate choice-of-law clause which provides, for example, that "this agreement shall be governed by the law of _____ " is susceptible of being construed not to apply to extra-contractual claims. On the other hand, a possible disadvantage of including the choice-of-law provision in the arbitration clause is that, in context, it may be misconstrued to designate the applicable procedural law as well as (or, rather than) the applicable substantive law.[37] Finally, it bears noting that the reference to "law" in WIPO's recommended clause is not intended to limit the parties' choice to the law of any particular country; Article 59(a) of the WIPO Rules expressly provides that parties may choose either "law or rules of law," presumably encompassing *lex mercatoria*, to govern their dispute.[38]

II. THE PLACE AND LANGUAGE OF THE ARBITRATION

Articles 39 and 40 of the WIPO Rules govern the consequences of the parties' choice of, or failure to choose, the place and language of the arbitration, respectively.

A. *Article 39: The Place of Arbitration*

Article 39 of the WIPO Rules provides:

> (a) **Unless otherwise agreed by the parties, the place of arbitration shall be decided by the Center, taking into consideration any observations of the parties and the circumstances of the arbitration.**
>
> (b) **The Tribunal may, after consultation with the parties, conduct hearings at any place that it considers appropriate. It may deliberate wherever it deems appropriate.**
>
> (c) **The award shall be deemed to have been made at the place of arbitration.**

Like all of the major international arbitration rules, WIPO Article 39(a) authorizes the parties to select the situs of the arbitration. The place of arbitration is critically

---

as of January 1, 1998. On the pros and cons of designating the number of arbitrators, language and place of arbitration in the arbitration agreement, *see* Robert H. Smit, *The Center for Public Resources Rules for Non-Administered Arbitration of International Disputes: A Critical and Comparative Commentary*, 2 AM. REV. INT'L ARB. 411, 413 (1991).

[37] Article 59 of the WIPO Rules, which distinguishes among the laws applicable to the substance of the dispute, the arbitration proceedings and the arbitration agreement, should be sufficient to avoid any such confusion. While Article 59 provides for the application of the law chosen by the parties to govern the arbitration agreement and the arbitration procedure, WIPO's recommended clause does not expressly include any such choices. *Cf.* LCIA RULES Recommended Arbitration Clauses.

[38] A similar provision in the AAA INTERNATIONAL RULES (Article 28) (denominated article 29 prior to 1997 revisions) has been praised. *See* Hans Smit, *The New International Arbitration Rules of the AAA*, 2 AM. REV. INT'L ARB. 1, 26–27 (1991).

important for a number of practical, procedural and legal reasons, and therefore should be designated in the parties' arbitration agreement whenever possible.[39] As a practical matter, the place of arbitration may affect the nationality of the sole or presiding arbitrator ultimately appointed, the need to retain local counsel and incur travel and other expenses, and (last but not least) the availability of fine restaurants, hotels and conference facilities. As a legal matter, the law of the arbitral situs will or may determine the arbitrability of the intellectual property dispute, the validity of the arbitration agreement, the procedures that may or must be used in the arbitration, the availability of interim relief from the arbitrators or local courts, the availability of particular types of relief (such as punitive damages), the nature and extent of judicial intervention in the proceedings, the procedural recourse for confirming, enforcing and vacating the award, and the enforceability of the award in other countries.

Like the ICC Rules and the AAA International Rules, Article 39(a) authorizes the Center to designate the place of arbitration absent agreement of the parties.[40] However, in light of the importance of the arbitral situs the Center is directed to afford the parties an opportunity to be heard on the issue before making that designation. While the reference to the "circumstances of the arbitration" provides little guidance as to the specific factors the Center will consider in making its choice, the factors likely to be considered include the desirability of a neutral arbitral forum, the arbitration law at potential arbitration sites, the language and applicable law of the contract, and the convenience of the parties, their counsel and the arbitrators.[41]

Like all of the major international arbitration rules, Article 39(b) authorizes the Tribunal, after consultation with the parties, to conduct hearings and/or deliberate outside the arbitral situs if it deems appropriate.[42] The location of the hearings may be determined not only to suit the convenience of the arbitrators, parties and witnesses, but also to take advantage of the evidentiary assistance or ancillary relief available from the local courts at the hearing sites.[43]

---

[39] On the importance and selection of the place of arbitration, *see* Blessing, *supra* note 20, at 66; Kazuo Iwasaki, *Selection of Situs: Criteria and Priorities*, 2 ARB. INT'L 57 (1986); Howard M. Holtzmann, *The Importance of Choosing the Right Place to Arbitrate an International Case, in* PRIVATE INVESTORS ABROAD — PROBLEMS AND SOLUTIONS IN INTERNATIONAL BUSINESS (1988).

[40] *See* ICC RULES, art. 14; AAA INTERNATIONAL RULES, art. 13(1). Unlike the AAA International Rules, however, the WIPO Rules do not give the Tribunal authority subsequently to change the place of arbitration. *See* AAA INTERNATIONAL RULES, art. 13(1). While remote in practice, the possibility exists that it may be desirable to change the place of arbitration after its initial designation such as when, for instance, the arbitration law of the initially designated seat of arbitration is changed for the worse. *See* REDFERN & HUNTER, *supra* note 2, at 305–06. For the same reasons, the parties should remain free to redesignate the place of arbitration once it has been designated by the Center. *See* BORN, *supra* note 33, at 77.

[41] *See* CRAIG, PARK & PAULSSON, *supra* note 35, § 12.01 (describing the factors considered by the ICC Court in fixing the place of arbitration).

[42] The term "hearings" should be construed to encompass any meeting of the Tribunal for any purpose without being limited to the substantive "hearings" contemplated by WIPO Rules Article 53.

[43] The U.S. Federal Arbitration Act, for instance, authorizes arbitrators to issue subpoenas, and courts to enforce arbitrators' subpoenas, for production of testimony or documents directed at any person within the

Finally, Article 39(c) appropriately provides that the award shall be "deemed to have been made" at the place of arbitration. Indeed, international arbitration awards are frequently "made" in several places when they are circulated for execution to each of the members of a multi-national Tribunal where he or she resides. The WIPO Rules therefore avoid the unfortunate wording in some arbitration rules that appear to require that the award physically be "made" at the place of arbitration.[44]

B. *Article 40: The Language of the Arbitration*

Article 40 of the WIPO Rules provides:

   (a) Unless otherwise agreed by the parties, the language of the arbitration shall be the language of the Arbitration Agreement, subject to the power of the Tribunal to determine otherwise, having regard to any observations of the parties and the circumstances of the arbitration.

   (b) The Tribunal may order that any documents submitted in languages other than the language of arbitration be accompanied by a translation in whole or in part into the language of arbitration.

The practical consequences of the language of the arbitration can hardly be ignored. Perhaps most important, the language of the arbitration will effectively limit both the pool of potential arbitrators and the parties' choice of counsel to those fluent in the applicable language.

WIPO Article 40(a) provides that the language of the arbitration shall be that agreed upon by the parties or, in the absence of such agreement, that of the arbitration agreement, with the proviso that the Tribunal may select another language. It is similar to Article 14 of the AAA International Rules. Like AAA Article 14, its grammatical construction leaves somewhat unclear whether the Tribunal may override the agreement of the parties as to the applicable language; the better construction is that the Tribunal may not, its power to select a language other than that of the arbitration agreement being limited to the situation where the parties have not agreed on the applicable language.[45]

Unlike the AAA International Rules, WIPO Article 40(a) provides that (absent agreement of the parties) the language of the arbitration shall be that of the arbitration agreement, rather than "that of the documents containing the arbitration agreement," as AAA Article 14 provides.[46] This distinction will be of practical consequence only in

---

state in which the arbitrators "are sitting." 9 U.S.C. § 7; *see* Lawrence W. Newman & Michael Burrows, *Subpoenas Under the Federal Arbitration Act*, N.Y.L.J., Sept. 16, 1993, at 3, col. 1.

[44] UNCITRAL RULE 16(4), for example, states that the "award shall be made at the place of arbitration." The legislative history of the Rule, however, makes clear that it was not intended to require that the award be physically rendered in the place of arbitration. *See* STEWART A. BAKER & MARK D. DAVIS, THE UNCITRAL ARBITRATION RULES IN PRACTICE: THE EXPERIENCE OF THE IRAN-UNITED STATES CLAIMS TRIBUNAL 79 (1992).

[45] *See* H. Smit, *supra* note 38, at 14.

[46] The designation of the applicable language as that of the contract or arbitration agreement is particularly useful in fixing the language for the Request for Arbitration and Answer to the Request where

the rare situation where the parties' arbitration agreement is separate from and in a different language than that of the underlying agreement to which it relates. On the other hand, neither the WIPO Rules nor the AAA International Rules deal with the possibility that the arbitration agreement (or the underlying contract) may be in more than one language. AAA Article 14, however, implies by its reference to "language(s)" that more than one language may be used in the arbitration, whereas WIPO Article 40 clearly contemplates the use of a single language — which is the preferable result.[47]

WIPO Article 40(b) properly leaves it to the Tribunal's discretion to determine whether documents submitted in another language should be accompanied by translations;[48] a rigid rule requiring translations of all documents might prove unduly onerous and expensive. When translations are required, the WIPO Rules do not require that such translations be certified, although the Tribunal in its discretion might impose such a requirement.[49]

III.   GENERAL PROVISIONS

The first section of the WIPO Rules, entitled "General Provisions," defines some of the terms used in the WIPO Rules and deals with the scope of application of the Rules, notices, periods of time, and documents required to be submitted to the Center.

A.   *Article 1: Abbreviated Expressions*

Article 1 defines certain terms used in the WIPO Rules. Specifically, it provides:

> **"Arbitration Agreement" means an agreement by the parties to submit to arbitration all or certain disputes which have arisen or which may arise between them; an Arbitration Agreement may be in the form of an arbitration clause in a contract or in the form of a separate contract;**
> **"Claimant" means the party initiating an arbitration;**
> **"Respondent" means the party against which the arbitration is initiated, as named in the Request for Arbitration;**
> **"Tribunal" includes a sole arbitrator or all the arbitrators where more than one is appointed;**
> **"WIPO" means the World Intellectual Property Organization;**

---

the parties have not stipulated the language and the Tribunal has not yet been formed to designate the language. By contrast, under the ICC Rules — which provide only that, absent agreement of the parties, the language of the arbitration shall be determined by the tribunal — the parties may each submit their initial pleadings and correspondence to the administering institution in different languages and without translations. *See* ICC RULES, art. 16.

[47] *See* BAKER & DAVIS, *supra* note 44, at 81 (noting that the dual language provisions of the Iran-U.S. Claims Tribunal Rules proved to be expensive and burdensome in practice).

[48] UNCITRAL RULES, art. 17(2) and AAA INTERNATIONAL RULES, art. 14 are to the same effect.

[49] National laws generally require parties seeking enforcement of an award to supply a certified translation of the award into the language of the country in which enforcement is sought. *See* UNCITRAL MODEL LAW, art. 35(2).

> "Center" means the WIPO Arbitration Center, a unit of the International Bureau of WIPO.
> Words used in the singular include the plural and vice versa, as the context may require.

The only definition that raises any interesting questions is the definition of the "Arbitration Agreement." While the WIPO Rules were designed specifically for intellectual property disputes of an international character, nothing in Article 1's definition of the arbitration agreements to which the Rules apply requires that the disputes to be arbitrated concern either intellectual property or anything international. In that connection, the Director of the WIPO Center has explained:

> [The WIPO Rules] do not seek to confine the competence of the Center, or of any proceedings administered by it, to disputes which purely or even predominantly concern intellectual property. While the Center's services are designed for intellectual property disputes, it was considered that any formal jurisdictional limitation would only serve to invite argument over competence and attempts to excise artificially from the dispute certain elements that might be classified as contractual or otherwise, rather than as intellectual property.[50]

Indeed, the WIPO Rules are arguably sufficiently generic to be used for any kind of general commercial dispute.

Article 1's definition of "Arbitration Agreement" also does not prescribe any requirements as to the form of the arbitration agreement, although a requirement that it be in writing may be implied from the statement that it "may be in the form of an arbitration clause in a contract or in the form of a separate contract."[51] As a result, any requirements as to the form of the arbitration agreement, including any specific writing requirements, should be determined by reference to applicable national law and international treaty.[52]

Article 1 states that the arbitration agreement may take the form either of a clause in the underlying contract or of a separate agreement. The form it takes may in fact have significant consequences. The fact that an arbitration agreement is separate from the parties' underlying agreement may enhance the likelihood that a Tribunal, in the exercise of its authority under WIPO Article 36 to rule on objections to its own jurisdiction, will reject a challenge to its jurisdiction based on a defect in the

---

[50] Gurry, *supra* note 4, at 201. The drafters of the UNCITRAL Rules refrained from defining "international" for similar reasons. *See* JACOMIJN J. VAN HOF, COMMENTARY ON THE UNCITRAL ARBITRATION RULES: APPLICATION BY THE IRAN-U.S. CLAIMS TRIBUNAL 13–14 (1991).

[51] Other arbitration rules expressly require that the agreement to arbitrate be in writing. *See* AAA INTERNATIONAL RULES, art. 1; UNCITRAL RULES, art. 1(1).

[52] WIPO Rules Article 59(c) specifically provides that the arbitration agreement should conform to the requirements concerning form, existence, validity and scope of either the applicable substantive law, procedural law, or law chosen by the parties to govern the arbitration agreement. National laws and international treaties generally require that the agreement to arbitrate be in writing, although that writing need not be signed by the party against whom arbitration is sought. *See, e.g.,* UNCITRAL MODEL LAW, art. 7(2); New York Convention, art. V(e).

underlying agreement. While it is well-established that, under the doctrine of the separability of the arbitration clause, the *invalidity* or *unenforceability* of the underlying agreement does not necessarily negate the arbitration clause embedded in that agreement,[53] it is perhaps less clear whether the parties' arbitration clause can survive a finding that the underlying agreement containing that clause never even came into *existence* because it was never consummated.[54] On the other hand, certain "unilateral" arbitration agreements — agreements which allow one of the parties unilaterally to choose whether to litigate or arbitrate its claims while requiring the other party to arbitrate all of its claims — have been denied enforcement in the United States precisely because they were *not* contained in the underlying agreement and therefore were not found to have been supported by the consideration exchanged in that underlying agreement.[55]

B. *Articles 2 and 3: The Scope of Application of the WIPO Rules*

Articles 2 and 3 of the WIPO Rules dictate which procedural rules will govern the arbitration, either by agreement of the parties or by operation of law.

1. *Article 2: The Parties' Agreement to the WIPO Rules*
Article 2 of the WIPO Rules provides:

> **Where an Arbitration Agreement provides for arbitration under the WIPO Arbitration Rules, these Rules shall be deemed to form part of that Arbitration Agreement and the dispute shall be settled in accordance with these Rules, as in effect on the date of the commencement of the arbitration, unless the parties have agreed otherwise.**

Article 2 incorporates the WIPO Rules into the parties' arbitration agreement. Like the AAA International Rules, the applicable version of the WIPO Rules is the one in effect when the arbitration commences, which should eliminate any confusion should the Center decide to amend any of its Rules.[56] While it is true that the parties

---

[53] *See, e.g.*, REDFERN & HUNTER, *supra* note 2, at 276–79. On the separability doctrine generally, *see* Carl Svernlov, *What Isn't, Ain't: The Current Status of the Doctrine of Separability*, 8(4) J. INT'L ARB. 37 (1991); Jonathan S. Sanoff, *Sojuznefteexport v. Joc Oil Ltd.: A Recent Development in the Theory of the Separability of the Arbitration Clause*, 1 AM. REV. INT'L ARB. 157 (1990).

[54] *Compare* Pollux Marine Agencies, Inc. v. Louis Dreyfus Corp., 455 F. Supp. 211, 219 (S.D.N.Y. 1978) ("[S]omething can be severed only from something else that exists. How can the Court 'sever' an arbitration clause from a non-existent charter-party?") *with* Republic of Nicaragua v. Standard Fruit Co., 937 F.2d 469 (9th Cir. 1991) (finding that the parties' arbitration agreement is binding even if the Memorandum of Intent that contains it is not); *see generally* BORN, *supra* note 33, at 256–57.

[55] *Compare* Lopez v. Plaza Finance Co., No. 95 Civ. 7567, 1996 WL 210073 (N.D. Ill. Apr. 25, 1996) (separate arbitration agreement requiring only one party to arbitrate its claims is unenforceable for lack of mutuality and consideration) *with* Design Benefit Plans, Inc. v. Enright, 940 F. Supp. 200, 206 (N.D. Ill. 1996) (distinguishing *Lopez* in holding a unilateral arbitration clause contained in a valid contract to be sufficiently supported by the consideration exchanged in the underlying contract).

[56] *See* AAA INTERNATIONAL RULES, art. 1(1); ICC RULES, art. 6(1). The 1998 version of the ICC Rules (Article 6(1)) adopted the WIPO and AAA approach to the issue. By contrast, the UNCITRAL Rules do

will not have been aware of any such revisions when they entered into their arbitration agreement, presumably those revisions will only change the Rules for the better.

The final clause of Article 2 is somewhat unclear as to whether it authorizes the parties not only to provide for application of the version of the WIPO Rules in effect at the time of their arbitration agreement, but also to modify specific provisions of the applicable WIPO Rules.[57] That raises the question as to which of the WIPO Rules should be deemed mandatory — or, put another way, ''whose arbitration is it, anyway?'' While the WIPO Rules do not itemize which of its provisions are subject to modification by agreement of the parties, the parties' authority clearly is limited with respect to the Center's role in constituting the Tribunal, administrative fees and arbitrators' fees.[58] Trickier questions include whether the parties may agree to withdraw the Center's authority under Article 4(g) to extend various time limits set forth in the WIPO Rules or whether the parties may agree that the claimant may appoint an arbitrator on behalf of a respondent who fails to do so, notwithstanding the Center's authority to make such an appointment under Article 19.

2. *Article 3: The Application of National Arbitration Laws*

Article 3 of the WIPO Rules concerns the application of mandatory and non-mandatory national arbitration law to govern the arbitral proceedings. That Article provides:

(a) **These Rules shall govern the arbitration, except that, where any of these Rules is in conflict with a provision of the law applicable to the arbitration from which the parties cannot derogate, that provision shall prevail.**

(b) **The law applicable to the arbitration shall be determined in accordance with Article 59(b).**

Article 3(a), which mirrors the parallel provisions in the UNCITRAL Rules and AAA International Rules,[59] provides that any applicable laws from which the parties cannot derogate shall prevail over conflicting WIPO Rules. Although, strictly speaking, this provision is unnecessary since applicable mandatory laws will, in any event, prevail over conflicting contractual or institutional arbitration rules, the provision serves the useful function of giving notice to parties and arbitrators of the potential issue.

---

not contain a comparable provision, leaving the issue up to either the arbitral institution or the tribunal. *See* CRAIG, PARK & PAULSSON, *supra* note 35, § 10.03. While the ICC Rules have been amended on several occasions, the UNCITRAL Rules have yet to be amended since their promulgation in 1976.

[57] The formulation in AAA International Rules Article 1(1) — which provides that the AAA International Rules in effect at the time of the arbitration shall apply ''subject to whatever modifications the parties may adopt in writing'' — more clearly vests the parties with the broader authority to modify the Rules as well as to choose which version of the Rules should apply.

[58] The question of ''mandatory institutional rules'' is undoubtedly more interesting with respect to the ICC Rules, and to the question of the parties' authority to dispense with the National Committee procedure for selecting arbitrators, the Terms of Reference, and the ICC Court's scrutiny of awards.

[59] *See* UNCITRAL RULES, art. 1(2); AAA INTERNATIONAL RULES, art. 1(2).

It also raises several questions. First, to what types of "law" from which the parties cannot derogate does the Article refer? Article 3(a) clearly is intended to refer only to applicable national *arbitration* law, not to applicable substantive law; Article 3(b) read in conjunction with Article 59(b) makes this explicit. Moreover, in determining whether the parties may derogate from arguably "mandatory" applicable arbitration law, only those provisions of national arbitration law which reflect *international,* as opposed to merely *domestic*, public policy should prevail over the arbitration rules chosen by the parties.[60] Examples of such mandatory provisions include national laws precluding arbitrators from granting provisional or conservatory measures, requiring witnesses to take oaths, and imposing voting requirements or prohibiting dissents in arbitral awards.[61]

Second, which country's mandatory arbitration laws should apply?[62] Article 3(b), by repeating the phrase "the law applicable to the arbitration" and referring to Article 59(b), suggests that the mandatory laws to which subsection (a) refers are those of the arbitral situs, absent agreement of the parties to a different law. Indeed, it is generally recognized that mandatory laws at the arbitral situs will apply. The interplay between subsections (a) and (b) of Article 3 may be problematic, however, to the extent they are construed to allow the parties to avoid a mandatory law at the arbitral situs by choosing a foreign arbitration law; clearly, the parties cannot effectively do so.[63] It also bears noting that if the parties do choose an arbitration law other than that of the place of arbitration, it is uncertain to what extent a mandatory provision of that chosen law should prevail over a conflicting WIPO Rule or procedure adopted by the parties or the

---

[60] For a discussion of the distinction between international and domestic public policy, *see* Pierre Lalive, *Transnational (or Truly International) Public Policy and International Arbitration, in* COMPARATIVE ARBITRATION PRACTICE AND PUBLIC POLICY IN ARBITRATION 257, 261 (Pieter Sanders ed., 1986); Christopher B. Kuner, *The Public Policy Exception to the Enforcement of Foreign Arbitral Awards in the United States and West Germany Under the New York Convention,* 7(4) J. INT'L ARB. 71 (1990).

[61] For a list of potentially mandatory provisions of national arbitration law, *see* Blessing, *supra* note 20, at 58–61.

[62] Choice-of-law complexities relating to the applicable arbitration law are not uncommon. *See* Alain Hirsch, *The Place of Arbitration and the Lex Arbitri,* 34 ARB. J. 43 (1979); Pierre Lalive, *Problèmes Relatives à l'Arbitrage International Commercial,* 120 RECUEIL DES COURS 573 (1967); William W. Park, *The Lex Loci Arbitri and International Commercial Arbitration,* 32 INT'L & COMP. L.Q. 21 (1983); Jan Paulsson, *Delocalisation of International Commercial Arbitration: When and Why It Matters,* 32 INT'L & COMP. L.Q. 53 (1983); Fritz A. Mann, *Lex Facit Arbitrum, reprinted in* 2 ARB. INT'L 241 (1986); Hans Smit, *Substance and Procedure in International Arbitration: The Development of a New Legal Order,* 65 TUL. L. REV. 1309 (1991).

[63] *See* Interim ICC Award of July 16, 1986, 12 Y.B. COM. ARB. 113 (1987) (mandatory provisions of the law of the arbitral situs apply even where the parties have agreed on a foreign curial law); Mann, *supra* note 62, at 245–47; BORN, *supra* note 33, at 177. The proviso in Article 59(b) of the WIPO Rules that the parties may only agree on a foreign curial law if "such agreement is permitted by the law of the place of arbitration" may not clear the confusion since the law at the place of arbitration may permit the parties to choose a foreign curial law to govern their arbitration generally, but nevertheless require application of specific, mandatory provisions of the *lex arbitri.*

arbitrators.[64] Finally, as a practical matter, the mandatory arbitration laws in any country where the award may have to be enforced should also be taken into consideration.

The last question is who determines whether and which potentially applicable mandatory arbitration laws apply to the arbitration. Obviously, the issue cannot be left solely up to the parties to determine whether they can derogate from mandatory arbitration laws. Rather, the question is for the Tribunal to determine in the first instance.[65] In any event, the Tribunal's decision may get revisited by any court in which enforcement of the award is sought, particularly if the mandatory arbitration laws of the country in which that court sits were not applied.

As noted above, Article 3(b) of the WIPO Rules designates the law applicable to the arbitral proceedings by reference to Article 59(b). This is a very useful provision not found in the UNCITRAL Rules or the AAA International Rules. It is useful because, by expressly designating the arbitration law of the place of arbitration as the applicable arbitration law, it avoids any disputes as to the applicable law as well as an inappropriate proliferation of potentially applicable laws. On the other hand, the Tribunal should not be constrained to apply the *non-mandatory* arbitration law at the place of arbitration if it believes a more appropriate rule is preferable. The greatest utility of designating the applicable arbitration law may therefore often lie less in the specific arbitration law chosen than in the exclusion of any doubt as to whether any other arbitration laws should apply.

C. *Article 4: Notices and Periods of Time*

Article 4 of the WIPO Rules deals with the form and transmittal of notices in the arbitration, how the periods of time fixed in the Rules are to be calculated, and the authority of the parties and the Center to modify certain time limits prescribed in the Rules. These provisions are designed to avoid confusion about some of the relatively mundane (but frequently critical) aspects of the arbitration.

1. *Article 4(a) and (b): The Form and Delivery of Notices*

The form and transmittal of notices and communications in the arbitration are governed by the first two subsections of Article 4, which provide:

(a) **Any notice or other communication that may or is required to be given under these Rules shall be in writing and shall be delivered by expedited postal or courier service, or transmitted by telex, telefax or other means of telecommunication that provide a record thereof.**

---

[64] In an unpublished ICC award, for instance, an arbitral tribunal seated in Rome held that its implied power to grant interim relief under ICC Article 8(5) ''superseded'' the prohibition against arbitral awards of interim relief contained in Article 26 of the Swiss Concordat, which was the arbitration law designated in the Terms of Reference to supplement the ICC Rules.

[65] *Cf.* WIPO RULES, art. 62(e) (authorizing the Tribunal to consult with the Center concerning matters of form bearing on the enforceability of the award).

(b) A party's last-known residence or place of business shall be a valid address for the purpose of any notice or other communication in the absence of any notification of a change by that party. Communications may in any event be addressed to a party in the manner stipulated or, failing such a stipulation, according to the practice followed in the course of the dealings between the parties.

Article 4(a) prescribes the form and means of delivery of any notice or other communication in the arbitration. The writing requirement obviously should be construed to apply only to notices or communications specifically referenced in the WIPO Rules, and not literally to "any . . . communication that may . . . be given under these Rules." The means of transmittal prescribed in the Rules serve two ends: to ensure expeditious delivery of the notices and to provide a record of their delivery. Indeed, those ends may explain why delivery by ordinary mail is not even included as a permissible means of delivery. The AAA International Rules, by contrast, permit service by air mail.[66] Article 4(a) also does not give the Tribunal authority to permit other methods of service or to *require* service by only one of the listed methods as do the AAA International Rules.[67] It may be appropriate, for example, for the Tribunal to require that all communications be faxed rather than delivered by expedited postal service in order to accommodate an expedited arbitral schedule.

Article 4(b) prescribes where the notices or communications may be delivered. The order of the two sentences in the subsection might better have been reversed to make clear that, if the parties have agreed to addresses for notification purposes, notices should be sent to those addresses absent reason to believe the stipulated addresses are no longer effective. Certainly, notices delivered to a party's last known residence or place of business should not be deemed effective if the parties have stipulated to different addresses.[68] Article 4(b) should therefore be construed to provide that notices are to be sent to the addresses stipulated by the parties or, failing such stipulation, to a party's last known residence or place of business. The course of the parties' dealings might offer another potential address, although it might also raise uncertainties if that practice has changed over time or if correspondence was addressed to more than one address.

2. *Article 4(c), (d) and (e): Calculating Periods of Time*
The next three subsections of Article 4 govern how periods of time identified in the WIPO Rules are to be calculated, which may assume critical importance in expedited arbitration with its short time limits. They provide:

(c) For the purpose of determining the date of commencement of a time-limit, a notice or other communication shall be deemed to have been received on

---

[66] *See* AAA INTERNATIONAL RULES, art. 18(1). The UNCITRAL Rules, by contrast, do not prescribe specific means of delivery for notices or other communications.

[67] *See* AAA INTERNATIONAL RULES, art. 18(1).

[68] Often, corporate parties have several places of business and therefore stipulate in their agreements to a specific address for notices and communications.

the day it is delivered or, in the case of telecommunications, transmitted in accordance with paragraphs 9(a) and (b) of this Article.

(d) For the purpose of determining compliance with a time-limit, a notice or other communication shall be deemed to have been sent, made or transmitted if it is dispatched, in accordance with paragraphs (a) and (b) of this Article, prior to or on the day of the expiration of the time limit.

(e) For the purpose of calculating a period of time under these Rules, such period shall begin to run on the day following the day when a notice or other communication is received. If the last day of such period is an official holiday or a non-business day at the residence or place of business of the addressee, the period is extended until the first business day which follows. Official holidays or non-business days occurring during the running of the period of time are included in calculating the period.

Article 4(c) governs when the notice is deemed to have been received. If the notice is delivered by postal or courier service, it is deemed received on the day it is "delivered," *i.e.*, when it arrives at its destination. The reference to delivery rather than mere receipt is useful because it covers the situation in which the notice is delivered but the addressee party is not there to receive it.[69] If, on the other hand, the notice is telecommunicated, it is deemed to have been received on the day it was actually transmitted. No doubt, parties will seek to use this provision to their advantage by timing the transmittal of notices or communications to take advantage of differences in time zones that frequently come into play in international arbitration. Neither the AAA International Rules nor the UNCITRAL Rules contain comparable exceptions for telecommunications from the general rule that notice is effective upon receipt.

Article 4(d), which provides that a communication is deemed to have been made on the day it is dispatched, is uncontroversial. The method of calculating periods of time set forth in Article 4(e), on the other hand, merits some comments. Like the UNCITRAL Rules and the AAA International Rules, periods of time begin to run on the day following receipt of notice, regardless of whether the day of receipt or the following day is a holiday at the place where notice is received.[70] Mean-spirited parties will undoubtedly be tempted to time their submissions to fall on holidays. On the other hand, Article 4(e) extends deadlines that fall on an official holiday or non-business day until the first business day which follows, as do all of the major arbitration rules.[71] Those arbitration rules differ, however, as to whether the holiday must be at the residence or place of business of the addressee or at the place the notice

---

[69] Another way to cover the situation is simply to provide that the notice is effective on the day it is received or deemed received. *See, e.g.*, ICC RULES, art. 3(3) ("A notification or communication shall be deemed to have been effected on the day when it was received by the party itself or by its representative, or would have been so received if made in accordance with the preceeding paragraph.").

[70] *See* UNCITRAL RULES, art. 2(2); AAA INTERNATIONAL RULES, art. 18(2). ICC Rules Article 3(4), by contrast, tolls the running of the period of time until the working day following any official holiday.

[71] *See, e.g.*, UNCITRAL RULES, art. 2(2); AAA INTERNATIONAL RULES, art. 18(2); ICC RULES, art. 3(4).

is received; the WIPO Rules opt for the residence or place of business of the addressee.[72] Looking to the place where the notice is duly delivered and received might be preferable in the event the addressee does not reside where the notice is deemed effective. The WIPO Rules, like all of the other arbitration rules, provide that official holidays or non-business days occurring during the prescribed periods of time are included in calculating the period.[73]

3. *Article 4(f) and (g): Authority to Modify Periods of Time*

The last two subsections of Article 4, which authorize the parties and the Center to modify certain periods of time prescribed in the WIPO Rules, provide:

> **(f)   The parties may agree to reduce or extend the periods of time referred to in Articles 11, 15(b), 16(b), 17(b), 17(c), 18(b), 19(b)(iii), 41(a) and 42(a).**
> **(g)   The Center may, at the request of a party or on its own motion, extend the periods of time referred to in Articles 11, 15(b), 16(b), 17(b), 17(c), 18(b), 19(b)(iii), 67(d), 68(e) and 70(e).**

The time limits referenced in subsection (f), which the parties may agree to *reduce* or *extend*, consist of time limits for the Answer,[74] various time limits prescribed for the constitution of the Tribunal,[75] and time limits for the Statements of Claim and Defense.[76] Subsection (g) authorizes the Center to *extend*, but not to reduce, the same time periods for the Answer and the constitution of the Tribunal, but not the deadlines for the Statements of Claim and Defense. The Center is also authorized to extend the time limits for the parties' payment of administrative fees and deposits,[77] time limits which the parties are not authorized to modify for obvious reasons.

Rather than itemizing the specific rules subject to modification by the parties or the Center, it might have been preferable either to incorporate the parties' and the Center's authority to modify time periods within the referenced Rules and/or simply to identify those time limits which are *not* subject to modification by the parties or the Center. A potential problem with the approach adopted is that the parties and/or the Center may be deemed not to have the authority to modify any of the time limits not listed in Article 4(f) and (g). In appropriate circumstances, it would seem that the

---

[72] *Compare* UNCITRAL RULES, art. 2(2) (residence or business of the addressee) *with* AAA INTERNATIONAL RULES, art. 18(2) (the place received) *and* ICC RULES, art. 3(4) (the country where the notification is deemed to have been effected).

[73] *See* UNCITRAL RULES, art. 2(2); AAA INTERNATIONAL RULES, art. 18(2); ICC RULES, art. 3(4).

[74] WIPO RULES, art. 11.

[75] WIPO RULES, arts. 15(b), 16(b), 17(b), 17(c), 18(b) and 19(b)(iii). With respect to Article 15(b), which establishes a forty-five day time limit for the parties to agree upon a Tribunal if the parties themselves have not established a time limit, query whether an agreement of the parties should be necessary to reduce that forty-five day time limit. If one of the parties is unwilling to attempt to agree on the appointment of the arbitrators, or it is otherwise clear that the parties will not be able to agree, either party should be able to request that the Center appoint the arbitrators forthwith, without waiting for the forty-five day period to expire.

[76] WIPO RULES, arts. 41(a) and 42(a).

[77] WIPO RULES, arts. 67(b), 68(e) and 70(e).

parties should be able to reduce or extend the time limits prescribed in the WIPO Rules for any challenges of an arbitrator,[78] the closure of hearings and the final award,[79] and the correction of the award.[80] Similarly, the Center should be authorized to extend those time periods where appropriate, or to shorten the time limits for payment of administrative fees or deposits.

Article 4 does not deal with the Tribunal's authority to reduce or extend time limits prescribed in the WIPO Rules. In fact, the only authority expressly granted to the Tribunal to modify any of the prescribed time periods is found in Article 38(c), which authorizes the Tribunal to extend, but not to reduce, periods of time fixed by the Rules, and only "in exceptional cases." The Tribunal's general power to extend time limits is important to allow it to ensure the parties are afforded an adequate opportunity to be heard. It might also have been appropriate to authorize the Tribunal to shorten certain time limits, such as the deadlines for the Statements of Claim and Defense, whenever necessary to expedite the proceedings. The UNCITRAL Rules, for example, leave the timing of the Statement of Claim and Defense entirely to the Tribunal.[81]

D. *Article 5: Documents Required to Be Submitted to the Center*

The final General Provision of the WIPO Rules — Article 5 — indicates which documents exchanged during the course of the arbitration must be submitted to the Center. It provides:

>   **(a) Until the notification by the Center of the establishment of the Tribunal, any written statement, notice or other communication required or allowed under Articles 6 to 36 shall be submitted by a party to the Center and a copy thereof shall at the same time be transmitted by that party to the other party.**
>
>   **(b) Any written statement, notice or other communication so sent to the Center shall be sent in a number of copies equal to the number required to provide one copy for each envisaged arbitrator and one for the Center.**
>
>   **(c) After the notification by the Center of the establishment of the Tribunal, any written statements, notices or other communications shall be submitted by a party directly to the Tribunal and a copy thereof shall at the same time be supplied by that party to the other party.**
>
>   **(d) The Tribunal shall send to the Center a copy of each order or other decision that it makes.**

In short, the Article requires that any communications made pursuant to the Rules be submitted to the Center until the Tribunal is constituted; after the Tribunal is in place, only its orders, awards and other decisions need be communicated to the Center,

---

[78] WIPO RULES, arts. 25 and 26.

[79] WIPO RULES, art. 63(a).

[80] WIPO RULES, art. 66(a).

[81] *See* UNCITRAL RULES, arts. 18(1) and 19(1).

consistent with the Center's limited role in the ensuing proceedings.[82] The specific provisions of Article 5 are relatively straightforward, provided common sense is brought to bear on their construction. For example, a party challenging an arbitrator under Article 25 should not be required to send the Center copies of the challenge for each of the arbitrators because Article 25 itself requires the challenging party to send its challenge directly to the Tribunal. In addition, in the event the number of arbitrators has not been agreed on by the parties and is to be determined by the Center, the parties should exercise their common sense in determining how many copies of the Request for Arbitration and Answer should be sent to the Center. A more significant ambiguity lies in the nature of the "order or other decision" that the Tribunal is required to send to the Center under subsection (b). Presumably, the Center requires only procedural and substantive orders of some import, such as procedural orders establishing the schedule for the arbitration, any interim orders or awards, and the final award.

IV. THE WIPO EXPEDITED ARBITRATION RULES

A. *Ordinary Arbitration versus Fast-Track Arbitration: Dueling Pathologies?*

Bemoaning the ritualistic process dominated by lawyers that international arbitration has become, Lord Mustill has described the contemporary condition of international arbitration as "pathological."[83] Indeed, one of the most important advantages of international arbitration — speed — is slipping away or has already been lost with the increasing proceduralization of arbitral proceedings.[84] Whatever the causes of that proceduralization, and whatever its benefits as far as the fairness of the proceedings is concerned, users and practitioners of international arbitration no longer expect great savings in time or cost from choosing arbitration rather than litigation.[85] Whether by self-fulfilling prophecy or otherwise, diminished expectations as to the speed and cost of international arbitration are increasingly being realized.

Various solutions have been proposed to expedite international arbitration and change those diminished expectations — to develop a "new psychology of

---

[82] Under the ICC Rules, by contrast, all pleadings and written statements submitted by the parties throughout the arbitral proceedings must be copied to the ICC Secretariat, an often burdensome requirement. *See* ICC RULES, art. 3(1).

[83] Michael Mustill, *Comments on Fast-Track Arbitration*, 10(4) J. INT'L ARB. 121, 123 (1993).

[84] On the causes and effects of the proceduralization of international arbitration, *see* Mustill, *supra* note 83, at 123–25; Arthur W. Rovine, *Fast-Track Arbitration: A Step Away From Judicialization of International Arbitration*, TWELFTH SOKOL COLLOQUIUM, INTERNATIONAL ARBITRATION IN THE 21ST CENTURY: TOWARDS "JUDICIALIZATION" AND UNIFORMITY? 45–47 (Richard B. Lillich & Charles N. Brower eds., 1994) (international arbitration is gradually evolving into an essentially private equivalent of international litigation).

[85] *See* Rovine, *supra* note 84, at 46 n.6 (discussing the results of an AAA Commercial Arbitration Survey indicating that significant percentages of attorneys and their clients now believe that arbitration of a complex commercial dispute is as expensive as or more expensive than litigation); *see also* Michael Segalla, *Survey: The Speed and Cost of Complex Commercial Arbitration*, 46(4) ARB. J. 12, 17, 20–21 (1991).

arbitration," in Lord Mustill's words.[86] Recently, a new solution to the problem of arbitral delay — "fast-track" arbitration — has received considerable attention worldwide as a result of an ICC arbitration (the "Fast-Track Arbitration") in which the arbitral tribunal rendered an award a mere 78 days after the initial filing of the Request for Arbitration.[87] Several calls for international arbitration institutions to adopt fast-track arbitration rules to supplement their current rules followed in the wake of the Fast-Track Arbitration.[88]

At the same time, it has been recognized that not all disputes are suited for resolution by fast-track arbitration and that fast-track arbitral procedures must remain sufficiently flexible to ensure the Tribunal's ability to timely render its award while affording the parties due process. Not surprisingly, fast-track arbitration is best suited for disputes that are capable of being mastered and resolved within a relatively short time, *not* for large complex disputes requiring extensive discovery, witness testimony or lengthy hearings.[89] The time limits and procedures used in fast-track arbitration must also be sufficiently flexible to avoid either having the tribunal's mandate expire before it is able, as a practical matter, to render an award or forcing the tribunal, in order to comply with the time limit, to pay short shrift to a party's opportunity to

---

[86] Mustill, *supra* note 83, at 125. Those solutions have included an international arbitral court of appeal (*see* Mauro Rubino-Sammartano, *An International Arbitral Court of Appeal as an Alternative to Long Attacks and Recognition Proceeding*, 6(1) J. INT'L ARB. 181, 185 (1989)), mandatory preliminary meetings (*see* Leonard Fletcher, *Unrealised Expectations: The Root of Procedural Confusion in International Arbitrations*, 2(2) J. INT'L ARB. 7, 12–13 (1985)), and alternative dispute resolution. *See* Schwartz, *supra* note 32 (discussing the impetus for the ICC's reform of its Conciliation Rules in 1988).

[87] Fast-track arbitration has been defined as arbitration conducted pursuant to an arbitration agreement in which "the parties select a subset . . . of disputes from the universe of potential disputes and agree that, if a dispute in this category arises, it will be resolved within a non-extendable time limit." Benjamin Davis, Odette Legacé-Glain & Michael Volkovitsch, *When Doctrines Meet: Fast-Track Arbitration and the ICC Experience*, 10(4) J. INT'L ARB. 69, 70 n.2 (1993). For descriptions of the Fast-Track Arbitration, *see The 1993 Geneva Global Arbitration Forum: The Drive Towards Speedier Arbitral Justice*, 10(4) J. INT'L ARB. 49 (1993); *ICC Fast-Track Arbitration: Different Perspectives*, 1 ICC INT'L CT. ARB. BULL. 4 (No. 2 1992); *Special Section: Fast-Track Arbitration*, 2 AM. REV. INT'L ARB. 137 (1991).

[88] *See* Hans Smit, *Fast-Track Arbitration*, 2 AM. REV. INT'L ARB. 138, 140–41 (1991); Moses Silverman, *Fast-Track Arbitration: Respondent's Perspective*, 2 AM. REV. INT'L ARB. 154, 156 (1991); Peter J. Nickles, *Fast-Track Arbitration: A Claimant's Perspective*, 2 AM. REV. INT'L ARB. 143, 147 (1991).

[89] The types of disputes amenable to fast-track arbitration have been identified to include disputes arising out of financial transactions — such as loans, securities, banking and broker transactions — which normally involve issues of default that can be resolved relatively quickly, as well as price adjustment disputes in long-term contracts, such as the dispute involved in the Fast-Track Arbitration. *See* Pierre Yves Tschanz, *The Chamber of Commerce and Industry of Geneva's Arbitration Rules and their Expedited Procedure*, 10(4) J. INT'L ARB. 51, 56 (1993); Lawrence W. Newman & Michael Burrows, *Fast-Track Litigation*, N.Y.L.J., May 12, 1994, at 3, col. 1; John B. Ballem, *Fast-Track Arbitration on the International Scene*, 2 AM. REV. INT'L ARB. 152, 153 (1991); Silverman, *supra* note 88, at 156; David Watkiss, *Fast-Track Arbitration: A Contractual Intermediary's Perspective*, 2 AM. REV. INT'L ARB. 150, 151 (1991).

present his case.[90] Indeed, unless properly used, fast-track arbitration may prove to be more "pathological" than the delays in ordinary arbitration it is intended to cure.[91]

B. *WIPO Expedited Arbitration: A Compromise Solution?*

1. *Answering the Call for Institutional Expedited Arbitration*

In promulgating its Expedited Arbitration Rules, the WIPO Center has joined a number of other arbitral institutions that offer expedited arbitration under their auspices.[92] The role of those arbitral institutions in expedited arbitration is particularly important to the viability of the new product to the extent the institutions are available to insure the smooth administration of the arbitral proceedings and to legitimize the proceedings with their imprimatur. WIPO's Expedited Rules may be particularly opportune in light of the special need for speed in intellectual property disputes.[93]

2. *WIPO's Recommended Expedited Arbitration Clause*

WIPO recommends the following clause for parties choosing WIPO expedited arbitration to resolve their disputes:

> **Any dispute, controversy or claim arising under, out of or relating to this contract and any subsequent amendments of this contract, including, without limitation, its formation, validity, binding effect, interpretation, performance, breach or termination, as well as non-contractual claims, shall be referred to and finally determined by arbitration in accordance with the WIPO Expedited Arbitration Rules. The place of arbitration shall be . . . . The language to be used in the arbitral proceedings shall be . . . . The dispute, controversy or claim shall be decided in accordance with the law of . . . .**

The clause is identical to the recommended clause for the ordinary WIPO Rules, except that it specifically designates the Expedited Rules (and omits the optional provision regarding the number of arbitrators since the Tribunal will always consist of a sole arbitrator). Nevertheless, the Center wisely opted to publish a separate clause for

---

[90] *See* Robert H. Smit, *International Fast-Track Commercial Arbitration in the United States and Canada*, *in* COMPARATIVE LAW YEARBOOK OF INTERNATIONAL BUSINESS 434, 443 (1995); CRAIG, PARK & PAULSSON, *supra* note 35, § 9.08 ("Haste Makes Waste"); REDFERN & HUNTER, *supra* note 2, at 391–93.

[91] On the "pathology" of fast-track arbitration clauses, *see* Davis, Legacé-Glain & Volkovitsch, *supra* note 87, at 73–85.

[92] A non-exhaustive list of institutional expedited arbitration rules includes the Expedited Procedures under the AAA's Commercial Arbitration Rules ("AAA Expedited Procedures"); the Short Arbitration Procedure of the Institution of Engineers of Ireland; the Expedited Commercial Arbitration Rules of the Institute of Arbitrators of Australia; the Short-Form Arbitration Rules of the Hong Kong International Arbitration Centre; the Rules for Expedited Arbitration Procedure of the Arbitration Institute of the Stockholm Chambre of Commerce ("SCC Expedited Procedure"); the Expedited Procedure of the Chamber of Commerce and Industry of Geneva Arbitration Rules ("CCIG Expedited Procedure"). *See also* David C. Downie, Jr., *Fast-Track International Arbitration: Proposed Institutional Rules*, 2 AM. REV. INT'L ARB. 473 (1991).

[93] *See supra* note 7 and accompanying text.

its Expedited Rules to highlight the unique burdens placed upon the parties and the arbitrators in expedited arbitration as well as the many factors the parties should consider before deciding to expedite their arbitration. Among the factors the parties should consider are:[94]

- The importance to the parties of an expedited resolution of their dispute in light of the intellectual property rights at issue, the long-term nature of the parties' relationship, and other relevant circumstances;
- Whether the types of disputes likely to arise under the parties' agreement may require extensive discovery, expert analysis, or lengthy evidentiary hearings, which are generally unavailable in expedited arbitration;
- Whether expedited resolution of their disputes justifies the concentration of time, energy and resources necessary on the part of the parties, their counsel and the arbitrators, to the exclusion of all other projects;
- The potential difficulty in finding suitable arbitrators in a position to make the full time commitment necessary to conduct an expedited arbitration;
- The likelihood that any dispute may involve more than two parties, and therefore be less amenable to expedited resolution;
- The risk that the parties may needlessly have to argue the merits of a dispute over which jurisdiction is ultimately denied since jurisdictional challenges in expedited arbitration will generally have to be consolidated with the merits in the absence of sufficient time to bifurcate the issues and render an interim award;
- The risk that the accelerated pace of expedited arbitration may diminish the parties' opportunity to negotiate a settlement of their dispute;
- The risk that the accelerated pace will adversely affect the quality of decision-making; and
- The risk that an award hastily rendered without due process may be unenforceable.

Of course, at the time of contracting it will frequently be difficult to predict the nature and complexity of disputes likely to arise. Generally speaking, however, prospective claimants are more likely than prospective respondents to favor expedited arbitration with its diminished discovery and promise of speedier relief.

---

[94] The WIPO Center advises that:

Expedited arbitration is a procedure that may be particularly suitable for cases where the value in dispute is insufficiently large to justify recourse either to court litigation or to conventional arbitration. Similarly, it may be considered desirable by small enterprises, which cannot afford to commit the financial resources of management time that would be required by court litigation or conventional arbitration. In addition, where a result is required urgently, expedited arbitration may be the appropriate procedure.

The Services of the WIPO Arbitration Center, supra note 5, at 32 (1994). On the factors to consider in choosing expedited/fast-track arbitration, *see* Tschanz, *supra* note 89, at 56–57; Newman & Burrows, *supra* note 89, at 3; Nickles, *supra* note 88, at 147.

Because not all disputes — particularly complex intellectual property disputes — are suitable for expedited treatment, parties may wish to submit only specific types of disputes to expedited arbitration, and to modify the recommended WIPO clause accordingly.[95] Identifying a subset of disputes for expedited treatment raises other problems, however, including the risk that it will lead to time-consuming interpretation battles as to whether the dispute qualifies for expedited treatment.[96] Hopefully, unsophisticated parties will not unwittingly rely on WIPO's broad expedited arbitration clause to submit all of their potential disputes to expedited arbitration without due consideration of the consequences of doing so.

As far as the additional provisions in WIPO's recommended clause regarding the place of arbitration, the language to be used, and the applicable law are concerned, it is particularly important in expedited arbitration that the parties agree in advance as to those matters, in order to eliminate the need to devote time to them once the dispute arises. Agreement on the place of arbitration is especially important in light of the role the *lex arbitri* may play in an expedited arbitration.[97] Indeed, the parties may wish to consider providing for additional measures — such as simultaneous submissions of statements of claim and defense, limitations on the number of briefs, limitations on discovery, *etc.* — to facilitate the expeditious resolution of the arbitration.

3. *The General Approach and Presentation of WIPO's Expedited Rules*

At first glance, WIPO expedited arbitration appears simply to be ordinary WIPO arbitration conducted by a sole arbitrator in a shortened time-frame. Indeed, WIPO's Expedited Rules consist of the ordinary WIPO Rules modified to provide for a sole arbitrator and tightened deadlines. In that connection, the "Introduction" to the Expedited Rules contains a useful list of the principal modifications introduced to expedite the proceedings:

---

[95] Expedited treatment is often reserved for disputes involving relatively small stakes or for particular issues susceptible of speedy resolution that form part of a larger dispute. The AAA Expedited Procedures, for example, by their terms apply only to disputes involving less than $50,000. *See* Article 54(a), AAA COMMERCIAL ARBITRATION RULES; *see also* Richard Akerman, *Rules for Expedited Arbitration Procedure*, 6 AM. REV. INT'L ARB. 301, 302 (1995) (noting that the SCC Expedited Procedures are intended to give parties alternatives in "minor disputes").

[96] It is therefore important that any disputes as to the definition or scope of the subset of claims be resolved as quickly as possible so as not to frustrate the fast-track nature of the dispute resolution mechanism reserved for it. *See* R. Smit, *supra* note 90, at 439; Davis, Legacé-Glain & Volkovitsch, *supra* note 87, at 74, 83; Downie, *supra* note 92, at 482. Moreover, a recalcitrant party to an arbitration in the United States may seek to delay the arbitral proceedings by seeking a court's intervention to determine the scope of the fast-track clause. *See* R. Smit, *supra* note 90, at 440. Accordingly, parties should provide in their arbitration agreement that the Tribunal has authority to resolve any interpretation questions that may arise and to remand the remaining issues or disputes for arbitration or litigation as appropriate. *See* Downie, *supra* note 92, at 481–82.

[97] *See* R. Smit, *supra* note 90, at 357–455; Davis, Legacé-Glain & Volkovitsch, *supra* note 87, at 72–74.

(i) The Statement of Claim must accompany (and not be filed later and separately from) the Request for Arbitration. Similarly, the Statement of Defense must accompany the Answer to the Request.

(ii) There is always a sole arbitrator.

(iii) Any hearings before the sole arbitrator are condensed and may not, save in exceptional circumstances, exceed three days.

(iv) The time limits applicable to the various stages of the arbitral proceedings have been shortened. In particular, the proceedings should, whenever reasonably possible, be declared closed within three months (as opposed to nine months under the WIPO Arbitration Rules) of either the delivery of the Statement of Defense or the establishment of the Tribunal, whichever event occurs later, and the final award should, whenever reasonably possible, be made within one month (as opposed to three months under the WIPO Arbitration Rules) thereafter.

Relatively few modifications to the ordinary WIPO Rules were required to expedite proceedings because, unlike other institutional arbitration rules, the conduct of the proceedings under the WIPO Rules are largely left to the Tribunal's discretion without extensive intervention by the Center or time-consuming procedural formalities.[98]

In practice, however, expedited arbitration may become a very different animal from ordinary arbitration. Parties will have to prepare their cases up front, develop their positions without extensive discovery and expert assistance, and perhaps also expect a somewhat rougher justice.[99] Nevertheless, expedited arbitration is designed to produce an award that is as final, binding and enforceable as any other award; it simply does so more quickly.

A word on the presentation of WIPO's Expedited Rules is warranted. The pamphlet of WIPO Mediation Rules, Arbitration Rules and Expedited Rules circulated

---

[98] Other institutional arbitration rules, such as the ICC Rules, might require more extensive modifications to accommodate expedited arbitration. *See* Davis, Legacé-Glain & Volkovitsch, *supra* note 87, at 87–88 (discussing the need to address the ICC's Terms of Reference and scrutiny of award procedures in order to accommodate fast-track arbitration). Other arbitral institutions have adopted approaches similar to that of the WIPO Center in promulgating expedited arbitration rules. The CCIG Expedited Procedure does not require a sole arbitrator, but similarly shortens or authorizes the administrator to shorten various deadlines and limits the parties' written statement of position and evidentiary hearings. *See* CCIG Expedited Procedure, Rule 31. The AAA Expedited Procedures call for notices by phone, a sole arbitrator, a one-day hearing and an award within 14 days from the hearing. *See* AAA Expedited Procedures, Rules 53–57. Like the WIPO Expedited Rules, the SCC Expedited Rules provide for a sole arbitrator, limit the number of statements of position, grant the Tribunal discretion as to the need for evidentiary hearings, and impose a three-month deadline (subject to extension by the Tribunal with the administrator's approval) for the final award. *See* Akerman, *supra* note 95, at 302–03.

[99] One of the members on the drafting committee for the Expedited Rules aptly noted that ''WIPO is offering the international community the choice between two systems of arbitration. The standard approach gives priority to what might be called legal security. . . . The alternative approach, expedited arbitration, is designed for parties who consider time to be of the essence, and who are willing to accept the marginal reduction in legal security for greater speed and lower costs.'' Jan Paulsson, *Fast-Track Arbitration in Europe (with special Reference to the WIPO Expedited Arbitration Rules)*, 18 HASTINGS INT'L & COMP. L. REV. 713, 715 (1995).

by the Center includes only an introduction to the Expedited Rules and a list of the modifications made in the Expedited Rules to the ordinary WIPO Rules. As helpful as that introduction and list of modifications are, it would have been useful also to include the complete text of the Expedited Rules (rather than make them available upon request from the Center). In fact, the text of the Expedited Rules contains some modifications (relating to the fact that expedited arbitration will always be conducted by a sole arbitrator) that are omitted from the list of modifications contained in WIPO's pamphlet of rules. On the other hand, not all of the ordinary WIPO Rules have been modified in the text of the Expedited Rules to reflect the fact that a sole arbitrator will preside over the proceedings.[100]

C. *The Salient Features of WIPO's Expedited Rules*

It is worth examining in detail several of the modifications that were, and were not, made in the Expedited Rules relating to permissible modifications of the time limits prescribed in the Rules, the Request for Arbitration and Answer, the constitution of the Tribunal, and specific time limits imposed on hearings, expert reports and the final award.

1. *Article 4(f)-(h): Permissible Modification of Time Limits in the Expedited Rules*

Article 4(f) and (g), which governs the parties' right to reduce or extend certain time periods, has been modified only to delete reference to time periods relevant to the constitution of a three-person Tribunal because a sole arbitrator will always be appointed. Thus, the parties retain authority to reduce or extend the time periods for the Answer under Article 11 and for the parties' joint nomination of the sole arbitrator under Article 14(b). The continued reference in Article 4(f) of the Expedited Rules to the parties' right to reduce or extend the time periods in Articles 41(a) and 42(a) are confusing because they correspond to provisions which have been deleted from the Expedited Rules. Since the Statement of Claim governed by Article 41(a) in the ordinary WIPO Rules must accompany the Request for Arbitration under Article 10 of the Expedited Rules, time limits no longer apply to the Statement of Claim. Moreover, the parties' authority to reduce or extend the time limit for the Answer, which under the Expedited Rules must be accompanied by the Statement of Defense, necessarily includes the power to modify the time limits for the Statement of Defense governed under the ordinary WIPO Rules by Article 42(a). As under the ordinary Rules, Article 4(f) of the Expedited Rules should not be construed to preclude the parties from modifying the time periods prescribed for challenges to arbitrators (Articles 25 and

---

[100] The Expedited Rules, for example, continue to include Article 35 dealing with the "Truncated Tribunals" as well as the provision of Article 38(c) authorizing the "presiding arbitrator alone" to grant extensions of time limits fixed by the Rules. EDITOR'S NOTE: The WIPO Expedited Arbitration Rules are reproduced in their entirety in the Appendix *infra*.

26), hearings (Article 53), expert reports (Article 55), the closure of the proceedings or the final award (Article 63), or the correction of the award (Article 66).

Article 4(g), which governs the Center's right to extend certain time periods, has similarly been modified to exclude reference to those time periods which only apply to the constitution of a three-member Tribunal. Thus, the Center retains its authority to extend the time periods for the Answer (Article 11), the parties' joint nomination of the sole arbitrator (Article 14(b)), the parties' payment of administrative fees (Articles 67(d) and 68(e)), and the parties' payment of deposits (Article 70(e)). Subsection (h) was added to Article 4 of the Expedited Rules to authorize the Center, in consultation with the parties, to reduce the time period prescribed in Article 11 for the Answer to the Request. That authority is appropriate (and would be appropriate under the ordinary WIPO Rules as well) prior to the constitution of the Tribunal. However, once the Tribunal has been established, which may occur prior to Article 11's 20-day deadline for the Answer, and necessarily will occur prior to its alternative 10-day deadline, the Center should at least consult, and probably defer to, the Tribunal before reducing the deadline for the Answer.

Article 4 of the Expedited Rules remains silent on the Tribunal's authority to reduce or extend time limits prescribed in the Expedited Rules.[101] While the Tribunal retains its general authority under Article 38(c) to extend periods of time fixed by the Rules "in exceptional cases" — and expedited arbitrations presumably qualify as "exceptional cases" — the Tribunal should also expressly be allowed to reduce the deadlines fixed in the Rules in order to expedite the proceedings. For example, it may be appropriate to allow the Tribunal to reduce the time periods fixed for the Answer under Article 11, challenges of arbitrators under Articles 25 and 26, and expert reports under Article 55.[102] In short, the Tribunal should be afforded sufficient flexibility to tailor the relevant time limits as speed and justice require.

2. *The Request for Arbitration and Answer to the Request*

The pleadings stage of an international arbitration presents a number of opportunities for a recalcitrant party to delay the arbitration.[103] The WIPO Expedited Rules introduce several procedural innovations designed to reduce those delays and expedite the arbitration as a whole.

Specifically, Articles 10 through 12 are modified to require that the Request for Arbitration and Answer to the Request be accompanied by the Statement of Claim and

---

[101] *See supra* notes 74–81 and accompanying text.

[102] Participants in the Fast-Track Arbitration recommended granting this power to shorten time limits to the Tribunal. *See* H. Smit, *supra* note 88, at 141; Ballem, *supra* note 89, at 153.

[103] *See, e.g.*, James M. Rhodes & Lisa Sloan, *The Pitfalls of International Commercial Arbitration*, 17 VAND. J. TRANSNAT'L L. 19, 36 (1984). Pleadings stage delays were analyzed at the 1990 Stockholm Congress of the ICCA. ICCA, PREVENTING DELAY AND DISRUPTION OF ARBITRATION, XᵀᴴH INTERNATIONAL ARBITRATION CONGRESS, STOCKHOLM (Albert Jan van den Berg, gen. ed., 1991), at 103–30.

Statement of Defense prescribed in Articles 41 and 42, respectively; Article 11 also shortens the deadline for the Answer from 30 days to 20 days after receipt of the Request, or ten days after the Tribunal is appointed, whichever is later. Articles 41 and 42 require that the Statements of Claim and Defense contain comprehensive statements of the facts, legal arguments and documentary evidence supporting the parties' respective positions, and that the Statement of Defense further include any counter-claim or set-off alleged by the Respondent together with the facts, legal arguments and evidence supporting that counterclaim or set-off.

The modifications to Articles 10–12 and 41–42, while simple, reorder in a fundamental way the presentation of the parties' cases. Rather than being permitted to submit skeletal, notice-type pleadings at the outset of the arbitration to be followed by disclosure or discovery and more fully developed pre-hearing memorials later, the parties are required to marshall their evidence and legal arguments and present their entire cases at the outset, subject to supplementation in the post-hearing briefs contemplated by Article 53(e).

This restructuring of the pleadings may have significant strategic consequences. The requirement that the Request for Arbitration contain the Statement of Claim may disadvantage the claimant who, at that early stage of the dispute, lacks sufficient information to substantiate its claim or seek the appropriate remedy. A claimant may also prefer not to disclose all of its arguments and evidence prior to the respondent's formulation of a defense. The requirement that the claimant include its documentary evidence, including evidence concerning confidential intellectual property, in its Request for Arbitration may also render problematic application of Article 52 of the Expedited Rules, which authorizes a party to apply to the Tribunal for special confidential treatment of trade secrets it wishes to submit in the arbitration. Obviously, the Tribunal will not yet have been constituted and in a position to rule on any such application at the time the Request for Arbitration is submitted. The general confidentiality provision of Article 74, however, should alleviate most concerns about the confidential nature of the information disclosed in the Request; as to any information requiring special measures of protection, the claimant might simply include its application for such measures with its Request without disclosing the substance of that information.

The consequences of the requirement that the Answer include the Statement of Defense, and of the modified deadlines for the Answer, may be even more disadvantageous for the respondent. While the claimant can take as much time as it needs to compose its Statement of Claim, the respondent will have to formulate and present its case within the tight deadlines prescribed for the Answer. Moreover, rather than the 30 days the respondent is allotted to submit its Answer (which need not include its Statement of Defense) in an ordinary WIPO arbitration, the respondent may have as few as 20 days to submit its Answer accompanied by its Statement of Defense in an expedited arbitration.[104] Finally, as the party more likely to want and/or need discovery to develop its case, the respondent may be particularly disadvantaged by having to submit its Statement of Defense prior to any discovery in the arbitration.

Another consequence of requiring the parties to present their cases in the Request and Answer prior to discovery, rather than in post-discovery pre-hearing memorials, is that the parties' fully developed positions may not be memorialized for the benefit of the Tribunal prior to the hearing. This risks leaving the Tribunal insufficiently prepared to assume the active role necessary for it to conduct the hearing fairly and expeditiously and may also result in surprise and delay at the hearing caused by arguments and evidence presented for the first time.[105] The Tribunal may avoid this result by exercising its authority under Article 43(b), entitled "Further Witness Statements," to require the parties to deliver to the Tribunal and to each other all documents and other evidence that each party intends to present at the hearing in support of its claim or defense.[106]

Not all institutional expedited arbitration rules effect such a restructuring of the pleadings. The Stockholm Chamber of Commerce ("SCC") Expedited Procedure, for example, simply limits the parties' written submissions to one each, other than the original Statement of Claim and Defense.[107] The Chamber of Commerce and Industry of Geneva ("CCIG") Expedited Procedure, on the other hand, like the WIPO

---

[104] On the other hand, under some circumstances the Respondent may be allotted *more* time to submit its Answer in an expedited arbitration than in an ordinary arbitration. If, for example, the parties fail to choose a sole arbitrator within the 15 days afforded them under Article 14(b), and the Center thereafter takes more than 5 days to appoint the arbitrator, the respondent will effectively have more than the 30 days allowed it under the ordinary WIPO Rules to submit its Answer. That result is appropriate in light of Article 12's requirement that the Answer contain the respondent's Statement of Defense. The respondent could request a further extension from the Center pursuant to the Center's authority under Article 4(g) to extend the deadline for the Answers, or from the Tribunal pursuant to the Tribunal's general power under Article 38(c) to extend periods of time fixed by the Rules.

[105] Article 44 of the WIPO Expedited Rules, which governs amendments to claims and defenses, does not preclude the risk of amended or supplemented claims and defenses being asserted for the first time at the hearing because it allows such amendments or supplementation as a matter of course unless the Tribunal rules otherwise. That approach is consistent with the liberal amendment regime of most major institutional arbitration rules (*see* AAA INTERNATIONAL RULES, art. 4; UNCITRAL RULES, art. 20), but is not immune from criticism. *See* Downie, *supra* note 92, at 480–81 (recommending that amendments in fast-track arbitration be disallowed, unless the tribunal affirmatively determines that justice requires otherwise, in order to discourage frivolous and dilatory amendments).

[106] This was the procedure adopted during the Fast-Track Arbitration. *See* H. Smit, *supra* note 88, at 139–41 (noting how the requirement promoted voluntary disclosure by the parties as well as the efficiency of the hearings); Nickles, *supra* note 88, at 146 (stating that this requirement "allowed the parties to spend their time at the . . . hearing more effectively, by concentrating on the key issues in the arbitration rather than using their limited time to make routine evidentiary submissions").

[107] *See* SCC EXPEDITED RULES, sec. 12(1).

Expedited Rules, appears to contemplate a single exchange of written submissions prior to the hearing.[108]

3. *Article 14: Appointment of a Sole Arbitrator*

Under Article 14(a) of the Expedited Rules, the Tribunal will always consist of a sole arbitrator. Use of a sole arbitrator will avoid at least three types of delay inherent in arbitrations conducted by three-member Tribunals: (i) delays in the constitution of a three-member Tribunal, in which each party is allocated time to designate an arbitrator and the two party-appointed arbitrators then have additional time to designate the chair; (ii) delays entailed by the need to coordinate the schedules of three arbitrators often located in different parts of the world; and (iii) delays entailed by debate among the members of the Tribunal as to procedural and substantive issues.[109] For these reasons, several other arbitral institutions have also opted to go with a sole arbitrator in expedited proceedings.[110]

Use of a sole arbitrator is not absolutely necessary to expedite arbitration, however, and not all institutional expedited arbitration rules eliminate the possibility of a three-member Tribunal.[111] Indeed, a three-member Tribunal may help to assuage some of the uncertainties associated with the perceived diminished "legal security" of expedited arbitration.[112] Parties derive a degree of comfort from having their dispute decided by three arbitrators rather than one, particularly when the Tribunal includes arbitrators selected by the parties.[113] Moreover, if expedited treatment is reserved for certain issues only, the requirement that a sole arbitrator be used may force the parties to proceed with two different arbitrations if a three-member Tribunal is preferred for the remaining claims. If a three-member Tribunal is used, however, it is important to keep any delays in constituting the Tribunal to a minimum. This might be achieved by

---

[108] CCIG Article 31(b) provides: "upon deposit of the request for arbitration, each party may state its position only once in writing on the claims asserted against it." *See* Tschanz, *supra* note 89, at 52–53 (explaining that, under the CCIG Expedited Procedure, "the request for arbitration must include all the available evidence, must attach all the exhibits and also the witness statements, if any, and of course the same applies to the answer and any counterclaim; and a reply to any counterclaim will also have to be complete").

[109] The use of a sole arbitrator may also lower costs because two fewer arbitrators will have to be paid for their time. As one commentator has noted, however, "the fees payable to the sole arbitrator in expedited arbitration will be no less than those payable in ordinary arbitration. Indeed, it may be that accelerated proceedings may be so disruptive that they justify fixing the sole arbitrator's fee at a higher level within the *ad valorem* range." Paulsson, *supra* note 99, at 716 n.6.

[110] *See, e.g.*, AAA EXPEDITED RULES, art. 54; SCC EXPEDITED RULES, sec. 1.

[111] The CCIG Expedited Procedure, for example, does not require a sole arbitrator. *See also* Downie, *supra* note 92, at 482–84 (recommending the use of three arbitrators, unless the parties agree otherwise, to conduct fast-track arbitration). Indeed, the Fast-Track Arbitration was conducted by a tribunal of three arbitrators. *See* H. Smit, *supra* note 88, at 138.

[112] *See* Paulsson, *supra* note 99, at 715–16 (noting the "marginal reduction in legal security for greater speed at lower costs" associated with expedited arbitration by a sole arbitrator).

[113] *See* REDFERN & HUNTER, *supra* note 2, at 204, 218; R. Smit, *supra* note 90, at 423; Steven R. Bond, *How to Draft an Arbitration Clause*, 6(2) J. INT'L ARB. 65, 75 (1989).

maintaining the 15-day deadline for the parties to agree on the number of arbitrators and, if a three-member Tribunal is desired, to select their party-appointed arbitrators and, if possible, the chair. If the parties are unable to agree on the number or identity of the arbitrators by that deadline, the decision as to the number of arbitrators and the appointment of all of the arbitrators may be left to the arbitral institution. The presiding arbitrator could then be authorized to make any procedural rulings on her own in order to expedite the proceedings.[114]

The WIPO Expedited Rules appropriately shorten various time limits applicable to the constitution of the Tribunal. Under Article 14(b), the parties are allowed 15 days rather than the 30 days provided for in Article 16 of the ordinary WIPO Rules to agree on an arbitrator. It is unclear whether a party may ask the Center to appoint the arbitrator before those 15 days have elapsed if it becomes obvious that the parties will be unable to agree on a sole arbitrator. It would appear preferable, particularly in an expedited arbitration context, not to require that the 15-day time period expire before the Center will appoint an arbitrator. Article 25 also shortens the deadline for challenging an arbitrator's appointment from 15 days to 7 days from notification of the arbitrator's appointment.[115] Curiously, the time limit under Article 26 for the other party's response to any challenge has not similarly been shortened from 15 days to 7 days, although it would appear to be appropriate to do so. Neither the parties, the Center, nor the Tribunal is expressly authorized to further reduce those deadlines regarding challenges to arbitrators.[116]

4. *Article 53: Hearings*

Several of the most important modifications in the WIPO Expedited Rules are found in Article 53(b) and (e) concerning hearings. Those subsections provide:

> **(b) If a hearing is held, it shall be convened within 30 days after the receipt by the Claimant of the Answer to the Request and the Statement of Defense. The Tribunal shall give the parties adequate advance notice of the date, time and place of the hearing. Except in exceptional circumstances, hearings may not exceed three days. Each party shall be expected to bring to the hearing such persons as necessary to adequately inform the Tribunal of the dispute.**
> ...
> **(e) Within such short period of time after the hearing as is agreed by the parties or, in the absence of such agreement, determined by the Tribunal, each party may communicate to the Tribunal and to the other party a post-hearing brief.**

---

[114] *See* WIPO RULES, art. 61 (authorizing the presiding arbitrator to make any decisions on his own absent a majority) and art. 38(c) (authorizing the presiding arbitrator to grant time extensions on his own).

[115] Article 53(c) of the AAA Expedited Procedures also provides for a 7-day time period for challenges to arbitrators. Article 31(a) of the CCIG Expedited Procedure authorizes the CCIG to shorten the time limits for the appointment of arbitrators, which presumably includes the time limits for challenging arbitrators.

[116] The need to shorten the deadline for challenges was raised in the Fast-Track Arbitration. *See* H. Smit, *supra* note 88, at 141.

Unlike other expedited arbitration rules, the WIPO Expedited Rules do not authorize the Tribunal to dispense with an evidentiary hearing altogether if either of the parties requests such a hearing.[117] Instead, Article 53(b) seeks to expedite the proceedings by requiring that the hearing be convened within 30 days after claimant's receipt of the Answer to the Request and Statement of Defense. While Statements of Claim and Defense will already have been submitted, thirty days nevertheless is precious little time to prepare for the hearing. Some or all of the following may have to occur prior to the hearing: a preparatory conference held under Article 47 to formulate the issues and schedule the arbitral proceedings;[118] discovery completed under Article 48(b); applications for special confidential treatment made under Article 52; expert reports submitted under Article 55; site visits performed under Article 50; notices of experiments submitted under Article 49; further written statements, including any pre-hearing memoranda, submitted under Article 43; applications for interim relief made under Article 46; and witness statements submitted under Article 54(c). Indeed, it appears likely that, in many if not most cases, the Tribunal will be called upon to exercise its authority under Article 38(c) to extend the 30-day deadline for the hearing.[119]

The actual hearing also provides a recalcitrant party with an opportunity to delay arbitral proceedings.[120] The WIPO Expedited Rules seek to curb that delay by imposing a three-day limit on hearings "except in exceptional circumstances."[121] The theory underlying that limit on the duration of hearings is that it requires the parties to

---

[117] *Compare* SCC EXPEDITED RULES, sec. 16 ("[a]n oral hearing will be arranged only if a party so requests and if the arbitrator deems it necessary"). The CCIG Expedited Procedure, like the WIPO Expedited Rules, requires the Tribunal to hold a hearing unless the parties authorize it to dispense with the hearing, but also imposes limits on that hearing. *See* CCIG EXPEDITED PROCEDURE, art. 31(c) ("unless the parties authorize the arbitral tribunal to decide on the basis of the documentary evidence only, the arbitral tribunal shall hold a single hearing for the examination of the parties, witnesses and expert witnesses as well as for oral argument"). The availability of procedures akin to summary judgment in the United States would therefore appear to be limited under either the WIPO Expedited Rules or the CCIG Expedited Procedure. For a recent U.S. decision rejecting due process challenges to awards rendered without evidentiary hearings, *see* Intercarbon Bermuda, Ltd. v. Caltrex Trading & Transp. Corp., 146 F.R.D. 64 (S.D.N.Y. 1993).

[118] Use of a preliminary conference reflects the modern trend in international arbitration, and defining the issues and establishing a schedule is especially important in expedited arbitration. *See* Michael Hoellering, *Is a New Practice Emerging from the Experience of the American Arbitration Association?*," 4 INT'L TAX & BUS. L. 230, 233–34 (1986); Silverman, *supra* note 88, at 156–157; Downie, *supra* note 92, at 484–85.

[119] *See* Davis, Legacé-Glain & Volkovitsch, *supra* note 87, at 80 (suggesting that time limits imposed on specific stages of the arbitral proceedings may became a "straightjacket with many arms").

[120] *See* Rhodes & Sloan, *supra* note 103, at 37; ICCA, *supra* note 103, at 197–331 (discussing delays encountered at the hearing stage of international arbitrations).

[121] Similarly, Article 56 of the AAA Expedited Procedures imposes a one-day limit on hearings. In the Fast-Track Arbitration, a one-day hearing was held in which each side was allowed three hours for argument, examination or cross-examination of witnesses or for any other purpose. *See* H. Smit, *supra* note 88, at 139.

prepare their cases in advance and focus their arguments and evidentiary presentations on the key issues.[122]

While a three-day hearing may suffice for most disputes subject to expedited arbitration, it may not suffice for all, and the Tribunal retains authority to extend the hearing or call additional hearings in exceptional circumstances. In that connection, it bears noting that the reference in Article 53(b) both to the "hearing" in the singular and to "hearings" in the plural is somewhat confusing as to how the thirty-day and three-day time periods in the Article are to be applied. If more than one hearing is held, must each hearing be convened within thirty days? Does the three-day limit apply to each hearing or is it an aggregate total limit for all of the hearings?[123] In any event, the Tribunal should always endeavor to schedule hearings consecutively, a practice-tested means of expediting the hearing stage of international arbitrations.[124]

Article 53(b)'s final requirement, although not worded quite as a requirement, is that the parties "bring to the hearing such persons as necessary to adequately inform the Tribunal of the dispute."[125] That requirement is designed to facilitate completion of the hearing as expeditiously as possible and to avoid the need to schedule additional hearings to hear particular witnesses. Disagreements may arise, however, as to which persons are necessary to adequately inform the Tribunal of the dispute. Clearly, each side should make available any witnesses on which it intends to rely in support of its case as well as any other witnesses the Tribunal directs be made available. The identity of the party representatives and witnesses to be heard at the hearing should generally

---

[122] At the hearing in the Fast-Track Arbitration, although the parties were free to use their allotted time for examination of witnesses or any other purposes, they largely forewent that opportunity in favor of arguing the key issues in the case. *See* H. Smit, *supra* note 88, at 140; *see also* Allen Poppleton, *The Arbitrator's Role in Expediting the Large and Complex Commercial Case*, 36(4) ARB. J. 6, 7 (1981) (noting that the parties will concentrate the presentations of their cases in accordance with the limited time afforded them); Nickles, *supra* note 88, at 146–47.

[123] The CCIG Expedited Procedure limits hearings to "a single hearing for the examination of the parties, witnesses and expert witnesses as well as for oral argument." CCIG EXPEDITED PROCEDURE, art. 31(c). One of the principal drafters of those Rules has explained, with respect to the limitation to a single hearing, that "a single hearing does not mean a single day of hearing. It can be a hearing lasting several consecutive days. A single hearing does not rule out a pre-hearing conference. . . ." Tschanz, *supra* note 89, at 52–53.

[124] Consecutive hearings not only minimize the difficulties associated with assembling parties and arbitrators of various nationalities at the hearing but also frequently result in the hearings being heard in fewer days than would be the case with multiple non-consecutive hearings. *See* Poppleton, *supra* note 122, at 9; Downie, *supra* note 92, at 486. Only the AAA's Supplementary Procedures for International Commercial Arbitration contain a specific provision concerning the scheduling of multiple hearings. *See* AAA SUPPLEMENTARY PROCEDURES, art. 5 ("The AAA will attempt to schedule consecutive hearings to reduce the need for unnecessary travel").

[125] A similar direction was issued by the Tribunal in the Fast-Track Arbitration, namely that all witnesses be made available at the hearing. *See* H. Smit, *supra* note 88, at 140. The requirement that each party "bring" such persons to the hearing does not mean that such persons must also actually be present during the hearing, as the Tribunal retains authority under Article 54 to direct that "any witness shall retire during any part of the proceedings, particularly during the testimony of other witnesses."

be agreed on with the Tribunal in advance of the hearing. In most cases, the Tribunal should ensure that all testimonial evidence is submitted in the form of witness statements in advance of the hearing to eliminate the need for direct testimony at the hearing.[126]

Article 53(e) accords each party a right to submit a post-hearing brief within a period of time agreed on by the parties or, in the absence of such agreement, determined by the Tribunal. Unlike Articles 41 and 42, which dictate what the Statements of Claim and Defense must contain, Article 53(e) allows the parties and the Tribunal to tailor the contents of the post-hearing briefs to the needs of the case. If, for example, the hearing is devoted exclusively to examination of witnesses, post-hearing briefs may set forth the parties' arguments based on that evidence and applicable law.[127] In fact, whether post-hearing briefs are necessary at all will depend on the parties' prior opportunities to present their cases in writing, such as in their Statements of Claim and Defense and any further written submissions. As noted above, the post-hearing briefs contemplated by Article 53(e) appear to have been conceived as an alternative to pre-hearing memorials of the type frequently submitted in international arbitration. If such pre-hearing memorials are submitted in WIPO expedited arbitrations, it may no longer also be necessary to submit post-hearing briefs.[128]

5. *Article 55(a): Deadline for Expert Reports*

At the end of Article 55(a), which authorizes a Tribunal to appoint one or more independent experts and to establish the expert's terms of reference, the WIPO Expedited Rules add the following sentence: "The terms of reference shall include a requirement that the expert report to the Tribunal within 30 days of receipt of the terms of reference." That deadline is designed to expedite the proceedings, but could raise problems unless flexibly construed. The thirty-day deadline, for instance, could be *too short* if, as frequently is the case in intellectual property disputes, the issues submitted to the expert are of a complex technical nature. In such "exceptional" cases, the Tribunal could extend the deadline pursuant to its general authority under Article 38(c). On the other hand, the 30-day time period may be *too long* in certain cases, particularly in light of the requirement in Article 53(b) that the hearing be convened within 30 days of receipt of the Answer. Because the expert's terms of reference will not be established until well after the respondent's Answer is submitted, the expert's report will ordinarily not be due until *after* the hearing has been held. That, of course, is an untenable result and inconsistent with the requirement in Article 55(c) that the

---

[126] *See* WIPO Expedited Rules, art. 54(d) (authorizing the Tribunal to direct that the testimony of witnesses be submitted in written form by way of signed statements, sworn affidavits or otherwise).

[127] In that connection, it has been suggested that, at the hearing, "[a]rguments of any kind should be cut off and the parties directed to argue the point in their post-hearing briefs." Poppleton, *supra* note 122, at 10.

[128] As noted above, it is generally preferable that all argument and evidence, including testimonial evidence, be submitted to the Tribunal in advance of the hearing rather than during or after the hearing. *See* Nickles, *supra*, note 87, at 146; H. Smit, *supra* note 88, at 139–40.

parties be afforded the opportunity to question the expert, presumably on the basis of his report, at a hearing. While the Tribunal is authorized to extend the 30-day time limit for the hearing until after the expert report is submitted, it is not also expressly authorized by the Expedited Rules to shorten the 30-day time limit for the expert's report. Unless the Rules are construed to allow the Tribunal to shorten the 30-day time period for the expert's report, the timing of the report will therefore dictate the timing of the hearing, rather than vice versa — the cart before the horse.

6. *Article 63: The Time Limit for the Final Award*

Article 63 of the WIPO Expedited Rules sets "target" time limits for the closure of proceedings and the final award as a means of expediting the proceedings:

> **(a) The arbitration should, wherever reasonably possible, be heard and the proceedings declared closed within not more than *three months* after either the delivery of the Statement of Defense or the establishment of the Tribunal, whichever event occurs later. The final award should, wherever reasonably possible, be made within *one month* thereafter.**
>
> **(b) If the proceedings are not declared closed within the period of time specified in paragraph (a), the Tribunal shall send the Center a status report on the arbitration, with a copy to each party. It shall send a further status report to the Center, and a copy to each party, at the end of each ensuing period of *one month* during which the proceedings have not been declared closed.**
>
> **(c) If the final award is not made within *one month* after the closure of the proceedings, the Tribunal shall send the Center a written explanation for the delay, with a copy to each party. It shall send a further explanation, and a copy to each party, at the end of each ensuing period of *one month* until the final award is made. (emphasis added)**

This differs from the ordinary WIPO Rules only insofar as the time limit for the closure of proceedings is reduced from nine months to three months and the subsequent time limit for the final award is reduced from three months to one month.[129] It nevertheless raises several issues concerning (i) the appropriateness of the time periods prescribed; (ii) the "soft" nature of those time periods; and (iii) permissible modifications of those time periods.

Three months from the receipt of the Answer or appointment of the Tribunal is not a lot of time to complete the arbitral proceedings, which may include each of the steps described above prior to the hearing in addition to the hearing and post-hearing briefs. Parties, therefore, should be particularly careful about the scope of the disputes they submit to expedited arbitration. The one-month time period following the closure of

---

[129] Other arbitral institutions also impose deadlines for the closure of hearings and/or the final award in their expedited arbitration rules. *See* CCIG EXPEDITED PROCEDURE, art. 31(d) ("the awards shall be rendered within six months from the date when the CCIG hands the file over to the arbitrators"); SCC EXPEDITED RULES, sec. 21 ("[a]n award shall be made not later than three months after the case has been submitted to the arbitrator"); AAA EXPEDITED PROCEDURES, art. 57 ("Unless otherwise agreed by the parties, the award shall be rendered not later than fourteen days from the date of the closing of the hearing").

proceedings for the final award, on the other hand, should generally be sufficient for the Tribunal to prepare a reasoned award provided it has set aside a block of time to do so. In that connection, the Center wisely opted not to dispense with the requirement in its Expedited Rules that the award be reasoned.[130] Particularly in expedited arbitration, with the heightened uncertainties concerning "legal security" it may entail, requiring the arbitrator to articulate a rational basis for his decision helps to ensure the integrity of the process, avoid unprincipled compromises and maximize the enforceability of the award.[131]

It is important to note that the deadlines imposed on the closure of proceedings and the final award in Article 63 are not hard and fast deadlines. Rather, they serve as guidelines to follow "wherever reasonably possible." On the one hand, the use of such "soft" deadlines will ensure that the Tribunal's mandate will not expire before it is able to render an award and that the time limit can be extended where necessary to afford the parties a sufficient opportunity to present their cases.[132] This directory rather than mandatory approach enhances the enforceability of the award and is generally the approach recommended by commentators.[133] On the other hand, the use of merely directory time limits raises the risk that extensions of those time limits will be routinely granted. That, in fact, was precisely why the CCIG, in its Expedited Procedure, chose to impose a mandatory rather than directory time limit for the final

---

[130] Other institutional expedited arbitration rules do not require a fully reasoned award. *See* CCIG EXPEDITED PROCEDURE, art. 31(e) ("the award shall summarily state reasons, unless the parties waive the requirement of reasons"); SCC EXPEDITED RULES, sec. 23 (requiring the award only briefly to recount the parties' position and include an order or declaration unless a party timely requests a reasoned award); AAA COMMERCIAL ARBITRATION RULES, art. 42 (requiring only that the award be in writing and signed by a majority of the arbitrators).

[131] Many national laws require arbitral awards to be reasoned in order to be enforced. *See* ALBERT JAN VAN DEN BERG, THE NEW YORK CONVENTION OF 1958, 380–81 (1981).

[132] Untimely awards or awards rendered without affording the parties due process are subject to attack in subsequent enforcement proceedings. *See* R. Smit, *supra* note 90, at 443–47 (describing challenges to awards in the United States based on grounds of untimeliness and due process). In the United States, untimely awards are all the more likely to be denied enforcement in expedited arbitration, in which the importance placed by the parties on speed is implicit. *See* Gov't of India v. Cargill, Inc., 867 F.2d 130, 134 (2d Cir. 1989) (untimely award will be invalid if parties' agreement itself makes a deadline for the award jurisdictional); Anderson v. Nichols, 359 S.E.2d 117, 121 (W. Va. 1987) (award might have been vacated had "arbitration clause provided that time was of the essence").

[133] *See e.g.*, CRAIG, PARK & PAULSSON, *supra* note 35, at 165–66 ("parties wishing to insist on the need for speedy resolution of their disputes are doubtless best served by an exhortatory statement of intent coupled with some stipulations of a practical nature"); REDFERN & HUNTER, *supra* note 2, at 391–93. That approach is also consistent with the approach adopted by some U.S. courts which have held that contractual time limits for the award should be construed as merely directory, and therefore represent "a goal, set to encourage prompt determination of the issues submitted to arbitration," rather than a temporal limit on the arbitrator's authority to render an award. *See* Brandon v. Hines, 439 A.2d 496, 511 (D.C. Cir. 1981); Gov't of India v. Cargill, Inc., 867 F.2d at 134; Tomczak v. Erie Ins. Exch., 268 F. Supp. 185, 189 (W.D. Pa. 1967).

award.[134] Indeed, the only consequence of failing to adhere to the deadlines established in Article 63 of the WIPO Expedited Rules is that the Tribunal will have to provide the Center and the parties with status reports and/or explanations for the delay.[135]

The last question raised by Article 63, is who, if anyone, can extend the prescribed time limits for the closure of proceedings and the final award? Presumably, the parties can extend those time limits by agreement, although Article 63 is not listed in Article 4(f) among those Articles whose time limits the parties can agree to extend. Moreover, experience suggests that parties are unlikely to reach agreement on anything once a dispute has arisen. The Center also is not authorized, by Article 4(g) or otherwise, to extend the Article 63 time limits. While the Tribunal has the general authority under Article 38(c) to extend time limits fixed by the Rules, it is unclear whether that authority extends to the time limits in Article 63 which are imposed on the Tribunal itself. After all, the only effect of extending those time limits will be to relieve the Tribunal of its reporting obligations. Perhaps the best approach is to allow the Tribunal to extend the time limits for the closure of proceedings and the final award whenever the interests of justice require, subject to approval by the Center to avoid abuses.[136]

D. *Conclusions: Expedited Arbitration — A Step Back to the Future?*

With its Expedited Rules, the WIPO Center has answered the call for a more expeditious form of arbitration. The salient features of its Expedited Rules — the use of a sole arbitrator, shortened time limits for the appointment and challenge of arbitrators, the requirement that the parties present their cases at the outset of the arbitration, and target deadlines for the closure of proceedings and the final award —

---

[134] One of the principal drafters of the CCIG Expedited Procedure has explained with respect to the use of extendable time limits, "this was not the solution favored by the CCIG. The reason is that if the arbitration institution is specifically given the power to extend the time limit of an expedited arbitration, then there is a high likelihood that it will give extensions as a matter of routine and it will even do so in cases where the extension could have been avoided had the parties been under a clearly nonextendable deadline from the start." Tschanz, *supra* note 89, at 56; *see also* R. Smit, *supra* note 25, at 73 n.60 (noting that the ICC court routinely extends the six-month time limit for awards under Article 18 of the ICC Rules).

[135] The status report requirements are likely to serve more as an incentive to proceed expeditiously with the proceedings than as a sanction with any real "teeth" for failing to do so. If the reports generated to satisfy those reporting obligations are anything but short and sweet, it might be argued that the Tribunal would be better off spending its time taking affirmative steps to accelerate the proceedings or drafting its award rather than preparing status reports.

[136] This is similar to the approach adopted in the SCC Expedited Procedure which provides with respect to the three-month time limit for the award that, "at the request of the arbitrator, the institute may . . . extend this period if there are special reasons therefor." SCC EXPEDITED RULES, sec. 21. This is also the approach recommended by participants in the Fast-Track Arbitration. *See* H. Smit, *supra* note 88, at 141 (suggesting that the Tribunal should have authority to extend the deadline for the final award subject to approval by the institution); *but see* Tschanz, supra note 89, at 55–57 (explaining that the CCIG Expedited Procedure provides that the six-month time limit for the award is nonextendable in order to avoid routine extensions).

are all reasonable means of expediting the arbitration while preserving due process and the enforceability of the award. While some may prefer expedited procedures which allow for the possibility of a three-member Tribunal, avoid reorganizing the conventional order of pleadings, or impose non-extendible time limits for the final award, the WIPO Expedited Rules certainly deserve serious consideration by parties seeking expeditious resolution of their intellectual property disputes. Moreover, in most cases any perceived shortcomings in the Expedited Rules can be remedied by careful drafting of the parties' arbitration agreement, by subsequent agreement of the parties, or by rulings of the Tribunal.[137]

The demand for and ultimate success of the WIPO Expedited Rules, however, remain to be seen.[138] Some advocates, in the wake of the Fast-Track Arbitration, have heralded expedited arbitration as the wave of the future.[139] Others see in it something of a return to arbitrations past, with their less formal procedures and faster results.[140] From either perspective, expedited arbitration "raises a question about where we have been, where we are now, and where we may be headed."[141] Will expedited arbitration lead us back to the faster and rougher justice of arbitrations past? Or, as perhaps seems more likely, does the increasing number and larger stakes of the disputes we submit to international arbitration commit us to the slower, more proceduralized form of adjudication that arbitration has become? Only time will tell.

---

[137] *See* WIPO EXPEDITED RULES, art. 2 (authorizing the parties to modify the Expedited Rules), 4(f)-(h) (authorizing the parties and the Center to modify periods of time prescribed in the Expedited Rules), art. 38(c) (authorizing the Tribunal to extend time periods prescribed in the Rules) and art. 58 (providing that the parties may waive any provision of the Rules).

[138] The WIPO Expedited Rules have yet to be tested in practice. Similarly, the CCIG Expedited Procedure, which was first offered to the public in January 1992, also has yet to be used. As one commentator has noted, "WIPO Expedited Arbitration may well turn out to be heralded by critics only to 'fail at the box office'." Paulsson, *supra* note 99, at 715.

[139] *See* H. Smit, *supra* note 88, at 142 (speculating that international arbitral institutions will promulgate institutional rules for accelerated forms of arbitration and that "there is no doubt that many lawyers, and especially their clients, will be most interested in this novel form of expedited dispute settlement"); Tschanz, *supra* note 89, at 57 ("expedited arbitration involves a trend in international arbitration," "a potential new practice of international arbitration, one that is more work intensive and resource intensive," "a new kind of international arbitration [that] is quicker . . . more high risk and high stake").

[140] *See* Mustill, *supra* note 83, at 122–25 (noting the similarities between the fast, flexible procedures of arbitration past and the objectives of expedited arbitration proposed); Remarks of Arthur W. Rovine, transcript of proceedings at Fast-Track Arbitration Seminar of Baker & McKenzie, at 15 (Apr. 7, 1994) (fast-track arbitration "will be what arbitration was originally intended to be when it started out many, many years ago. Before it became the highly judicialized process that it so often is, particularly in big international cases."); *see also* Remarks of George A. Bermann, *id.* at 31 (noting the similarities between fast-track arbitration and the Stuttgart Model experiment of civil litigation in 19th Century Germany, both of which involve "a single pretrial conference, a single hearing, a single exchange of documents, a single opportunity for oral advocacy and a judgment within a very short period of time").

[141] Tschanz, *supra* note 89, at 57.

COMPOSITION AND ESTABLISHMENT OF THE TRIBUNAL

Articles 14 to 36

Toby Landau*

I. GENERAL OBSERVATIONS

The effective constitution of an arbitral tribunal may appear, at first sight, as a straightforward and uncontroversial part of the overall arbitral process. Any practitioner with experience in this field, however, will vouch for the contrary: composing and establishing a tribunal is a task that is often fraught with difficulty, and in some cases, a cause for the entire arbitral process to break down. It is self-evident that no arbitration can proceed without a tribunal. It follows that any party that considers an arbitration as contrary to its interests will capitalize on every opportunity to obstruct the appointment process, or to challenge a tribunal once appointed. Once constituted, there are many factors that may result in a dysfunctional tribunal thereafter, or indeed a need to make substitute appointments. Even if a tribunal has been appointed, its very constitution may still provide a ground for defeating the enforcement of a subsequent award.[1]

In analyzing any arbitration rules or provisions for the composition and establishment of the arbitral tribunal, five main factors may be particularly relevant: the extent to which party autonomy is protected; controls on quality and qualifications of those appointed; the efficiency and speed of appointment; the extent to which problems in the constitution of a tribunal will be solved, and support provided; and the question of costs.

Party Autonomy

It is often said that one of the central advantages of arbitration over litigation is the ability to choose one's judge. An arbitral tribunal may reflect any blend of legal and technical expertise as the parties desire. Indeed, the parties' choice may be guided by any consideration — from a candidate's actual qualifications, experience or standing, to a tactical or speculative analysis of a candidate's likely response to a particular issue, or his or her potential influence on other members of the tribunal. In the field of intellectual property, the ability of an arbitrator to handle highly technical disputes may be of particular importance — and a very significant reason for resorting to

---

* MA, BCL (Oxford University); LL.M. (Harvard Law School); ACIArb; Barrister-at-Law, Essex Court Chambers, London; Member of the New York Bar.

[1] Under Art. V.1.(d) of the New York Convention, an arbitration award may not be enforced if the constitution of the tribunal was not in accordance with the agreement of the parties, or the law of the country where the arbitration took place.

arbitration in the first place. The choice of arbitrator may be the single most determinative step that a party may take in an arbitration. However much care is taken in drafting an arbitration agreement, or in selecting an institution and rules, the success or failure of an international arbitration will often depend in large measure upon the quality of the arbitrators. Party autonomy and flexibility in the selection process is, therefore, of utmost importance, and must be reflected in any institutional rules.

Quality Control

Whilst party autonomy is of vital importance, it cannot be without limits. There must be some check on the impartiality and neutrality of the arbitrators chosen by the parties, as a safeguard for other parties, to ensure that an award is enforceable, and for the sake of the integrity of the process overall. Minimum requirements as to independence, impartiality, and sometimes nationality are laid down by most arbitration rules, and some institutions (such as the the LCIA[2]) accept nominations of candidates, but make the actual appointments themselves. Similarly, effective mechanisms for challenge must also be available, and procedures for the replacement of any arbitrators who have been disqualified. However, any mechanisms for such "quality control" must be very carefully drawn. It is a fact of life that recalcitrant parties, or parties with weak cases, will search out opportunities to derail the arbitral process. Obstruction is often seen as an attractive alternative to facing the substance of a claim, and challenge procedures (and unclear criteria for challenge) often appear as fruitful avenues for obstruction.

The Efficiency and Speed of Appointment

Once an arbitration has been commenced, it is almost always in the interests of at least one party to establish the tribunal very quickly. This is for a number of different reasons. Most importantly (especially in the field of intellectual property) there may well be a need to obtain urgent interim measures of protection, for example, to secure relevant evidence, to safeguard assets against dispersal, to maintain the status quo, or to prevent a party from carrying out a threatened breach of contract. No such interim measure can be obtained from a tribunal until it has been fully constituted,[3] and in the meantime, a party can only seek whatever support may be available from a national court. Given the difficulties and uncertainties of this, the time between the commencement of the arbitration and the constitution of the tribunal is often a period in which one or more parties will be entirely exposed.

Under the old LCIA Rules,[4] it was said that the average period of time between the initial request for arbitration and the constitution of a tribunal was 16 weeks. Most

---

[2] Art. 5.5: "The LCIA Court alone is empowered to appoint arbitrators . . . ."

[3] Unless some other provision has been made in the parties' agreement or the applicable arbitration rules.

[4] The LCIA Rules effective from January 1, 1985. These have now been replaced by new rules, effective as from January 1, 1998.

arbitration practitioners have experience of ad hoc and institutional arbitration cases in which much more than 16 weeks have elapsed before all arbitrators have been appointed. Indeed, the very flexibility and autonomy in the choice of arbitrator that is guaranteed to parties in most systems is often turned into a powerful tool for delay and obstruction by recalcitrant parties.

Speed in constituting the tribunal is also relevant in several other respects. No procedural orders or directions for the conduct of the arbitration can be given until the tribunal has been established. Time limits (contractual or statutory) may apply to the bringing of any claims, and some time limits depend upon the appointment of an arbitrator.[5] Further, the costs expended on pursuing the arbitration may only be recoverable, under some regimes, from the time when the tribunal was constituted.

Therefore, a further vital element in the constitution of a tribunal, after the party autonomy referred to above, is the prevention of delay and uncertainties in the appointment procedure.[6] It will be apparent that there may be something of a tension between these two factors.

Problem Solving and Support

Some parties fail or refuse to appoint an arbitrator, or to agree to any candidate proposed by others. Some arbitrators resign, after an arbitration has commenced. Some arbitrators become disqualified, some become obstructive, and some pass away. Some arbitration clauses contemplate two parties, when in fact there are three, or more. Arbitrations can become unworkable or cease to operate properly for a very wide variety of reasons. Insofar as any of these concern the composition, establishment and continued existence of the tribunal, it is extremely important that institutional rules provide appropriate mechanisms to solve them — to allow, for example, for default appointments, for replacement arbitrators, and for truncated tribunals. If a tribunal ceases to operate properly, a party may become as exposed as if no tribunal had been constituted.

Costs

It has become something of an incantation in favor of arbitration to recite that arbitration is cheaper than litigation. Arbitration is not always cheaper than litigation, and one of several reasons for this is that there is one expense that is not imposed in most national judicial systems: the cost of the judge. A further factor in assessing institutional rules will almost always be the costs that may be incurred. This subject is addressed elsewhere in connection with Articles 67 to 72 of the WIPO Rules.

---

[5] See the discussion of different types of time limits in ALAN REDFERN & MARTIN HUNTER, THE LAW AND PRACTICE OF INTERNATIONAL COMMERCIAL ARBITRATION 192 *et seq.* (2d ed. 1991) [hereinafter REDFERN & HUNTER].

[6] *See, e.g.,* Article 9 of the new LCIA Rules, which now provides for ''Expedited Formation'' of the tribunal, to deal with cases of ''exceptional urgency.''

II.   THE WIPO RULES

The following analysis considers Articles 14 to 36 of the WIPO Rules from a comparative stance, in the light of other institutional rules,[7] and using the criteria outlined above as a guide.[8]

Number of Arbitrators

Article 14
(a)   **The Tribunal shall consist of such number of arbitrators as has been agreed by the parties.**
(b)   **Where the parties have not agreed on the number of arbitrators, the Tribunal shall consist of a sole arbitrator, except where the Center in its discretion determines that, in view of all the circumstances of the case, a Tribunal composed of three members is appropriate.**

Commentary

Summary

1.   Article 14 provides, in the first instance, for unrestricted party autonomy: the parties are free to agree on the number of arbitrators that will make up the arbitral tribunal.

2.   By Article 14(b), if the parties do not, or cannot, agree on the number of arbitrators, a sole arbitrator will be appointed (in accordance with the appointment procedure in Article 16). The Center retains a discretion, however, to rule that three arbitrators be appointed, where it determines, in view of all the circumstances of the case, that this is "appropriate." Where this discretion is exercised, the procedure for appointing the three arbitrators is set out in Article 17(c).

The Time of Agreeing

3.   An agreement as to the number of arbitrators will usually be enshrined in the arbitration agreement itself, and to this end the contract clauses recommended by WIPO for referring both future and existing disputes to arbitration encourage the parties to make a choice between a sole arbitrator or three arbitrators:

The arbitral tribunal shall consist of [three arbitrators][a sole arbitrator].

4.   Although it is common to find any such agreement in the arbitration clause itself, and although not expressly so stated, this Rule would, of course, allow the

---

[7] Since this paper was presented, in March 1997, new rules have been brought into effect (as from January 1, 1998) by both the LCIA and the ICC. Account has been taken of these new rules, and unless otherwise stated in the text, it is the new rules to which reference is made below.

[8] The analysis in this paper concentrates on the ICC, LCIA and AAA rules for comparisons. For a very thorough analysis and comparison of the rules of appointment of 20 arbitration institutions, *see* Guillermo Aguilar Alvarez, *Selecting Arbitrators for Construction Disputes, in* ICCA CONGRESS SERIES NO. 5, PREVENTING DELAY AND DISRUPTION OF ARBITRATION, XTH INTERNATIONAL ARBITRATION CONGRESS, STOCKHOLM 427 (Albert Jan van den Berg ed., 1991).

parties to make such an agreement at any later stage, after the arbitration agreement has been concluded, and, indeed, to vary the terms of any prior agreement. This is made clear, for example, in Article 5 of the UNCITRAL Arbitration Rules, which provides that: "If the parties have not previously agreed on the number of arbitrators . . . and if within fifteen days after the receipt by the respondent of the notice of arbitration the parties have not agreed that there shall be only one arbitrator . . . ." Similarly, in the context of the recent revision of the ICC Rules, it had been suggested that the old ICC Article 2(3) (now Article 8(3)) be amended in order to emphasize to inexperienced users that they may reach a consensus at any time.[9] This suggestion was not, however, adopted.

Presumably, a stage will be reached in WIPO proceedings when it is too late for the parties to make such an agreement. Unlike the UNCITRAL Arbitration Rules, this is not made clear in the Rule (although may ultimately be a matter of common sense).[10]

5. The advantage of agreeing to the number of arbitrators at a later stage is obvious: it may only be after a dispute has arisen that the parties will be in a position to assess the nature and complexity of the dispute, and consequently the appropriate number of arbitrators. The disadvantage, however, of avoiding a choice in the arbitration agreement in the hope of agreeing the number of arbitrators at a later stage is also obvious: as a general rule, after a dispute has arisen, parties may well find it extremely difficult to agree on anything.

The Default Presumption of a Sole Arbitrator

6. Article 14(b) is in line with the rules of many other arbitral institutions. The ICC Rules provide that where the parties have not agreed upon the number of arbitrators a sole arbitrator will be appointed unless "the dispute is such as to warrant the appointment of three arbitrators."[11] Likewise, the LCIA Rules state that: "A sole arbitrator shall be appointed unless the parties have agreed in writing otherwise, or unless the LCIA Court determines that in view of all the circumstances of the case a three-member tribunal is appropriate."[12] See also Article 5 of the AAA International Arbitration Rules.

When is it "Appropriate" to Appoint Three Arbitrators?

7. The factors that the WIPO Center will consider in the exercise of its discretion will presumably be exactly the same factors that normally inform parties'

---

[9] See Richard H. Kreindler, *Impending Revision of the ICC Arbitration Rules — Opportunities and Hazards for Experienced and Inexperienced Users Alike*, 13(2) J. INT'L ARB. 45, 57 (1996), where it was suggested that the following words be added to Article 2(3) of the previous ICC Rules:

> Where the parties have agreed, whether in an initial agreement or in a subsequent modification thereof . . . .

[10] Even after the appointment of an arbitrator, the parties may make a subsequent agreement to release the arbitrator: see Article 31.

[11] Art. 8(2).

[12] Art. 5.4.

agreements and the drafting of arbitration clauses in this regard. An arbitration will be less expensive, and will involve less delay, if a sole arbitrator is provided for: appointments for meetings or hearings can more easily be arranged, and, according to one source, an arbitration conducted by a sole arbitrator is likely, in general, to cost about half as much, overall, as an arbitration when there are three arbitrators.[13] This appears to be borne out by the Schedule of Fees referred to in Article 69(b).[14] The appointment of a sole arbitrator also avoids the delays that are sometimes inherent in the deliberations of a three-member panel.

The Case Against Sole Arbitrators

8.   Sole arbitrators are, however, comparatively rare in international disputes, except in small cases, or where the dispute is between nationals of states with broadly similar cultural backgrounds. On the one hand, parties may well have cause for concern if the outcome of their dispute lies in the hands of only one individual, who may well have his or her own idiosyncrasies or particular perspectives that will not be moderated by any other arbitrator, and who is unlikely to reflect the tradition or legal cultures of all the parties. On the other hand, the sole arbitrator himself may regret the absence of any deliberations with fellow tribunal members. As Redfern & Hunter state:

> . . . it must be borne in mind that a sole arbitrator carries out a lonely task. Unlike the situation of a single judge sitting in court there is usually no appeal against the substance of his decision. Many arbitrators who are active in this international field prefer to sit with two others so that there can be a discussion of the case. This may be a factor in the prevailing trend towards the appointment of three arbitrators.[15]

The importance of the tribunal reflecting what may be the several different legal cultures of all the parties cannot be overstated, especially if arbitration is seen as a dispute resolution system that entails the parties foregoing the procedural protections that are usually built into national judicial systems.

9.   Hence, Article 5 of the UNCITRAL Arbitration Rules, for example, provides that if the parties have not agreed upon the number of arbitrators, three shall be appointed. Similarly, the UNCITRAL Model Law, by Article 10(2) provides that "Failing [a determination by the parties], the number of arbitrators shall be three."[16]

10.   During the drafting of the new English Arbitration Act 1996, a debate took place as to whether the Act should follow the Model Law, or provide for a sole

---

[13] REDFERN & HUNTER, *supra* note 5 at 161.

[14] Kreindler, *supra* note 9 at 63, suggests:

Experienced practitioners are familiar with the unofficial rule of thumb that an amount in dispute exceeding one million U.S. dollars is likely to result in a three-person tribunal.

[15] REDFERN & HUNTER, *supra* note 5 at 203.

[16] The Center for Public Resources Rules for Non-Administered Arbitration of International Disputes (the "CPR Rules") follow the UNCITRAL Rules in this respect (Rule 5.1), as do the Stockholm Chamber of Commerce Rules (Art. 5), and the Rules of CIETAC (Art. 14).

arbitrator as the default provision, if parties failed to agree themselves. In the end, it was decided that the default should be a sole arbitrator:

> 15(3): If there is no agreement as to the number of arbitrators, the tribunal shall consist of a sole arbitrator.[17]

This was explained at paragraph 79 of the official DAC Report on the Act[18] in the following terms:[19]

> Article 10(2) of the Model Law stipulates that failing such determination, the number of arbitrators shall be three. This we have not adopted, preferring the existing English rule that in the absence of agreement the default number shall be one. The employment of three arbitrators is likely to be three times the cost of employing one, and it seems right that this extra burden should be available if the parties so choose, but not imposed on them. The provision for a sole arbitrator also accords both with common practice in this country, and the balance of responses the DAC received . . . .

11. It is to be noted that this decision has been criticized by some. Whilst delays in the arbitral process may well be more likely if the tribunal consists of three arbitrators rather than one, this is normally moderated by empowering the chairman to act alone with respect to certain parts of the procedure. Further, and importantly, it may well be easier and quicker to constitute a tribunal consisting of three arbitrators than a sole arbitrator, given the likelihood that the parties will fail to agree on one candidate.[20] If one party fails to agree, the other party may have to wait (in the case of the English Act) for 28 days before applying to the Court for assistance.[21] Indeed, for such an application to be made, more time may elapse whilst leave to serve a summons out of the jurisdiction is obtained — and for service of the same. In contrast, where three arbitrators are to be appointed, a default mechanism exists whereby a party-appointed arbitrator may be appointed as sole arbitrator, if the other party has failed or refused to make an appointment.[22] Under the WIPO rules, a period of 30 days may have to elapse before a default appointment is made, whether or not the tribunal is to

---

[17] For a recent case where this provision was the subject of some discussion, *see* The Villa, [1998] 1 Lloyd's Rep. 195.

[18] Departmental Advisory Committee on Arbitration Law ("DAC") Report on the Arbitration Bill, February 1996.

[19] The DAC Report, together with the DAC Supplementary Report on the Arbitration Act (January 1997), constitutes an authoritative explanation of the provisions of the new English Act, endorsed throughout the Parliamentary debates on the Act. Both Reports are obtainable from the Business Law Unit of the UK Department of Trade and Industry, in London.

[20] Every "fast-track" arbitration handled by the ICC has apparently involved a panel of three arbitrators. *See* comment by Benjamin Davis in *Conference on Rules for Institutional Arbitration and Mediation*, Geneva, January 20, 1995, published by WIPO, at p.138.

[21] English Arbitration Act 1996, sec. 16(3). This period may be abridged by application to the Court.

[22] Sec. 17. This mechanism, whilst peculiarly English, has been upheld in other countries in the context of challenges under Art. (1)(d) of the New York Convention. *See, e.g.,* S.A. Pando Compania Naviera v. S.a.S. Filmo, *Corte di Appello* of Venice, May 21, 1976 (on an earlier version of the same provision).

consist of a sole or three arbitrators.[23] Under Article 4(g), the Center has no power to abridge (as opposed to extending) this time limit. This is now in direct contrast to Article 9 of the LCIA Rules, which provides for "Expedited Formation" of a tribunal, in cases of "exceptional urgency." This article contains a power for the LCIA Court to abridge or curtail time limits. This provision was a response to the need for urgent measures in arbitration, and the difficulty of setting up a specific system for the grant of interim measures before the constitution of the tribunal.

More Than Three Arbitrators?

12.   Whilst Article 14 allows the parties a free choice as to the number of arbitrators, it provides that, in default of agreement, the tribunal may only consist of one or three arbitrators. Similarly, the WIPO recommended arbitration clauses suggest a choice between a sole arbitrator and three arbitrators. Will any other number ever be desirable? Whilst it is true that the greater the number of arbitrators appointed, the greater the delay and expense incurred in the proceedings, it has recently been suggested that in the field of Intellectual Property and, specifically, disputes involving advanced technologies (so-called "High-Tech" disputes), the old formula of one or three arbitrators may well be inappropriate.[24] Where a dispute involves complex and technical issues, lawyers may well be entirely inappropriate as arbitrators — able to understand the applicable law, but quite unable to make sense of the facts as presented by the parties. The problem of complex and difficult factual issues has traditionally been addressed by the use of party-appointed experts, and/or experts appointed by the tribunal. As Hill has pointed out, each of these solutions has its own problems:[25]

   i.   Party-appointed experts often (perhaps usually) disagree. Different analyses will be presented, and may well be equally well-reasoned, equally technical, and consequently difficult for a non-technical tribunal to evaluate. Preferring one such expert over another may well, in the end, be a product of some non-technical criteria (*e.g.*, which report is better written).

   ii.   Tribunal-appointed experts (as are provided for in Article 55 of the WIPO Rules) may not solve this difficulty, given that under virtually all systems, each party will have the opportunity of commenting on such an expert's evidence — usually with the assistance of its own expert. This is expressly provided for in Article 55 of the WIPO Rules:

   55(a):   The Tribunal may, after consultation with the parties, appoint one or more independent experts to report to it on specific issues designated by the Tribunal . . . .

---

[23] Arts. 16(b) and 17.

[24] *See, e.g.,* Richard Hill, *Constituting Arbitral Tribunals in Hi-Tech Cases,* available on the Internet: http://www.batnet.com/oikoumene/tacr.html. The following paragraphs are largely drawn from this article.

[25] *See also* Robert Goldscheider, *The Employment of Experts in Mediating and Arbitrating Intellectual Property Disputes,* 6 AM. REV. INT'L ARB. 399 (1995).

55(b): . . . upon receipt of the expert's report, the Tribunal shall communicate a copy of the report to the parties, which shall be given the opportunity to express, in writing, their opinion on the report . . . .

55(c): At the request of a party, the parties shall be given the opportunity to question the expert at a hearing. At this hearing, the parties may present expert witnesses to testify on the points at issue.

The tribunal will therefore be met by the same divergence of analyses — and, as is made express again in Article 55 — it will still be for the tribunal to attempt to formulate its own view, rather than simply follow its own expert (and thereby effectively delegate its decision-making responsibility).[26]

13. If the solution to this difficulty lies in the appointment of expert arbitrators, rather than lawyers (which, after all, is often declared an advantage of arbitration over litigation), there are further difficulties:

i. A sole arbitrator who is an expert but not a lawyer, and is faced with complex legal argument, may well be in the same position as the lawyer faced with complex technical facts. Indeed, a sole arbitrator who is not a lawyer may well be at risk of some error in the procedure such as to endanger any final award. A sole arbitrator qualified in law and the relevant facts may well not be agreed upon — especially by that party who has a weak legal or factual case.

ii. In a three-member tribunal, similar difficulties arise if the chairman is an expert but not a lawyer. However, if the chairman is to be a lawyer, it is extremely unlikely that any other expert will be appointed — each party will want its own appointed arbitrator to be in a position of strength within the tribunal, and each may assume that the other will, accordingly, appoint a lawyer. The dynamics of constituting a three-member panel are such that most consist of three lawyers.

14. Richard Hill has suggested two possible answers to this difficulty:

i. The use of technical assessors to assist a tribunal — a technical expert that would participate in the deliberations of the tribunal, but have no right to vote. The parties would have to agree on this type of composition of the tribunal — and the WIPO Rules do not appear to cater for this in terms.[27]

ii The use of five-member tribunals — this would allow for a lawyer to preside, each party to appoint a lawyer as arbitrator, and each party to appoint an expert as arbitrator. This could negate the need for party-appointed expert witnesses, and allow the tribunal to properly address the technical as well as legal issues.

---

[26] Article 55(d) of the WIPO RULES:

The opinion of any expert on the issue or issues submitted to the expert shall be subject to the Tribunal's power of assessment of those issues in the context of all the circumstances of the case, unless the parties have agreed that the expert's determination shall be conclusive in respect of any specific issue.

[27] Alternatively (as is common in some forms of arbitration) a tribunal made up of three experts could be assisted by a legal assessor, again as a non-voting member of the panel.

15.   Article 14 would allow for a five-member tribunal, but only if this were agreed upon by the parties. If not agreed, the tribunal may only consist of a sole arbitrator, or three arbitrators. It is submitted that this is an appropriate restriction — it would be quite wrong to impose a five-member tribunal on parties, with its potential for increased costs and delay.

16.   However, it is worth pointing out that if the parties did agree on a five-member tribunal, this is not catered for in the remaining Rules, and may well cause difficulties. Some of the Rules that would not apply include:
—   Articles 16 and 17: Default Appointment Procedures;
—   Article 18: Multiple parties;
—   Article 35: Truncated Tribunals.

17.   Notwithstanding the difficulties inherent in the use of party-appointed or tribunal-appointed experts, it is likely that an agreement that a five-member panel be appointed would only be reached in the rarest of cases, given the risks as to additional delay, expense and overall inconvenience.

An Even Number?

18.   Finally, while the parties may be free, under Article 14(a), to appoint however many arbitrators they desire, it is to be noted that many national systems of law contain a mandatory requirement to the effect that the number of members of an arbitral tribunal must be uneven.[28] The arbitration laws of Belgium, France and the Netherlands require an uneven number of arbitrators, but "save" other arbitration agreements by requiring the appointment of a further arbitrator.[29] In contrast, the position under the new English Arbitration Act 1996, is that the parties may agree on an even number of arbitrators if they wish (s.15(1)), but unless otherwise agreed by them, such an agreement "shall be understood as requiring the appointment of an additional arbitrator as chairman of the tribunal." (s.15(2)) It is therefore incumbent upon the parties to specify that they intend an even number of arbitrators, and do not intend the appointment of a further chairman.

Appointment Pursuant to Procedure Agreed Upon by the Parties

Article 15
(a)   If the parties have agreed on a procedure of appointing the arbitrator or arbitrators other than as envisaged in Articles 16 to 20, that procedure shall be followed.
(b)   If the Tribunal has not been established pursuant to such procedure within the period of time agreed upon by the parties or, in the absence

---

[28] Some such countries referred to by REDFERN & HUNTER, *supra* note 5 (as of 1991) are: Belgium, Brazil, Colombia, Costa Rica, Ecuador, Germany, Iraq, Italy (*arbitrato irrituale*), The Netherlands, Spain, Syria, Taiwan, Venezuela. *See also* PIETER SANDERS, INTERNATIONAL ENCYCLOPEDIA OF COMPARATIVE LAW, Vol. VXI, Chap.12 (*Arbitration*) [hereinafter SANDERS], at § 12-142.

[29] Belgium: JudC art. 1684 par. 2; France: CCProc. art. 1454; The Netherlands: CCProc. art. 1026 par. 3.

of such an agreed period of time, within 45 days after the commencement of the arbitration, the Tribunal shall be established or completed, as the case may be, in accordance with Article 19.

Commentary

Summary

19.   Article 15(a) extends the primacy of party autonomy to the procedure for appointing the arbitrators — the parties are free to agree not only on the number of arbitrators, but also on the mechanism by which the arbitrators are to be appointed.[30] Only if no such procedure has been agreed will the default mechanisms apply as set out in Articles 16 to 20.

20.   Once again, there is nothing in the rules to prevent an agreement on the procedure for appointment after the dispute has arisen (although this is not made express) — and once again, where a specific procedure is desired, it may be prudent for parties to specify a procedure in their arbitration agreement, given the difficulties of so agreeing thereafter. The model clause recommended by WIPO contains no options pursuant to this Article.

21.   Article 15(b) provides for the failure of any agreed upon procedure:

   i.   if the parties have agreed upon a time period for the appointment of the arbitrators, and the appointments have not been made within that period or

   ii.   if no time period has been agreed, and the tribunal has not been constituted within 45 days after the commencement of the arbitration (as defined in Article 7 — the date on which the Request for Arbitration is received by the Center),

the Tribunal is then appointed (or completed) in accordance with Article 19.

Effect of Default

22.   If a sole arbitrator or presiding arbitrator has not been appointed, the list procedure set out in Article 19(b) will be used. If, on the other hand, one party has appointed its arbitrator, but the other has not, the latter party will simply have an arbitrator imposed on it by the Center, pursuant to Article 19(a). There is therefore something of an incentive for recalcitrant parties to follow their agreed upon procedures for appointment.

Extensions of Time

23.   By Article 4(f), the parties may agree to reduce or extend the period of time referred to in Article 15(b).

By Article 4(g), the Center has, at the request of a party or on its own motion, a discretion to extend (but not abridge) the periods of time referred to in Article 15(b).

---

[30] Most other arbitration rules do not contain an equivalent provision. See, however, sec. 16(1) of the English Arbitration Act 1996: "The parties are free to agree on the procedure for appointing the arbitrator or arbitrators, including the procedure for appointing any chairman or umpire."

Given the way in which Article 4(g) is drafted, it appears that this discretion extends to time periods agreed by the parties.

Procedures That May be Agreed

24.   A key procedure for appointment that may be agreed by the parties, which otherwise is not expressly provided for in the WIPO Rules, is the appointment of three arbitrators by all parties jointly, thereby avoiding the pitfalls of party-appointed arbitrators. Such a procedure, however, has its own dangers, such as delays in agreeing, that may render the constitution of the tribunal a troublesome and lengthy task. This is considered in the context of Article 17 below.

Appointment of a Sole Arbitrator

Article 16

(a) Where a sole arbitrator is to be appointed and the parties have not agreed on a procedure of appointment, the sole arbitrator shall be appointed jointly by the parties.

(b) If the appointment of the sole arbitrator is not made within the period of time agreed upon by the parties or, in the absence of such an agreed period of time, within 30 days after the commencement of the arbitration, the sole arbitrator shall be appointed in accordance with Article 19.

Commentary

Summary

25.   Where:

   i.   the parties have agreed (pursuant to Article 14(a)) that a sole arbitrator will be appointed, but have not agreed how this appointment will be effected (pursuant to Article 15(a)) or

   ii.   the parties have reached no agreement as to the number of arbitrators (pursuant to Article 14(a)), and the Center has not exercised its discretion to order a three-member tribunal (pursuant to Article 14(b)),

a sole arbitrator will be appointed jointly by the parties.

26.   Once again, Article 16(b) provides for the failure of any agreed upon or applicable procedure:

   i.   if the parties have agreed upon a time period for the appointment of a sole arbitrator, but have failed to reach any agreement within that period or

   ii.   if no time period has been agreed, and a sole arbitrator has not been agreed upon within 30 days after the commencement of the arbitration (as defined in Article 7 — the date on which the Request for Arbitration is received by the Center),

the sole arbitrator is then appointed in accordance with the list procedure in Article 19(b).

27.   As noted above, the 30-day time limit can be abridged by agreement (which is somewhat unlikely to occur) but can only be extended — not abridged — by the Center.[31] A period of delay is therefore inherent in this part of the procedure.[32]

Refusal by the Nominated Arbitrator and Extensions of Time

28.   Clearly, there are two requirements for the appointment of an arbitrator by agreement: the parties must agree upon their choice, and the person chosen must accept the appointment.[33] If the agreed upon candidate declines the appointment, and any of the time limits in Article 16(b) are exceeded, it would appear that the list procedure set out in Article 19(b) would then apply, unless the time limits are extended.

29.   By Article 4(f), the parties may agree to reduce or extend the period of time referred to in Article 16(b).

30.   By Article 4(g), the Center has, at the request of a party or on its own motion, a discretion to extend the periods of time referred to in Article 16(b). Given the way in which Article 4(g) is drafted, it appears that this discretion extends to time periods agreed by the parties.

Other Rules

31.   The period of 30 days from the date on which the Request for Arbitration was received by the Center is in line with most other institutional rules, such as, for example, the ICC Rules,[34] and the LCIA Rules.[35] For good reason, longer periods tend to be provided for in rules for ad hoc arbitration.[36]

Appointment of Three Arbitrators

Article 17

(a)   Where three arbitrators are to be appointed and the parties have not agreed upon a procedure of appointment, the arbitrators shall be appointed in accordance with this Article.

(b)   The Claimant shall appoint an arbitrator in its Request for Arbitration. The Respondent shall appoint an arbitrator within 30 days from the date on which it receives the Request for Arbitration. The two arbitrators thus appointed shall, within 20 days after the appointment

---

[31] Art. 4(g).

[32] *Compare* Article 9 of the LCIA Rules, which now provides for "Expedited Formation" of a tribunal.

[33] Per Art. 23.

[34] Art. 8(3).

[35] Art. 5.4.

[36] For example, the UNCITRAL Rules, Art. 6, provide that the arbitrator must be selected by the parties within thirty days of a party's proposal for a sole arbitrator, but that proposal need not be made within any defined period of time after the initial pleadings. Under CPR Rule 5.3, the parties must initiate discussions on the potential arbitrator within 20 days after delivery of the notice of defense (which, by Rule 3.4, is to be delivered to the Claimant 30 days after receipt of the notice of arbitration), and select the arbitrator within 20 days thereafter.

of the second arbitrator, appoint a third arbitrator, who shall be the presiding arbitrator.

(c)   Notwithstanding paragraph (b), where three arbitrators are to be appointed as a result of the exercise of the discretion of the Center under Article 14(b), the Claimant shall, by notice to the Center and to the Respondent, appoint an arbitrator within 15 days after the receipt by it of notification by the Center that the Tribunal is to be composed of three arbitrators. The Respondent shall appoint an arbitrator within 30 days after the receipt by it of the said notification. The two arbitrators thus appointed shall, within 20 days after the appointment of the second arbitrator, appoint a third arbitrator, who shall be the presiding arbitrator.

(d)   If the appointment of any arbitrator is not made within the applicable period of time referred to in the preceding paragraphs, that arbitrator shall be appointed in accordance with Article 19.

Commentary

Summary

32.   Where:

i.   the parties have agreed (pursuant to Article 14(a)) upon a three-member tribunal, but have not specified any particular procedure for the appointment of the three arbitrators, (pursuant to Article 15(a)) or

ii.   the parties have made no agreement as to the number of arbitrators, and the Center has exercised its discretion (pursuant to Article 14(b)) to appoint a three-member tribunal,

the tribunal will be constituted in accordance with this Article. In the case of situation i. above, the regime in Article 17(b) applies, and in the case of situation ii. above, the regime in Article 17(c) applies.

33.   The regime in Article 17(b) follows a usual format: the Claimant appoints its arbitrator, the Respondent then appoints its arbitrator, and the two arbitrators thereafter appoint a third arbitrator to act as chairman. In line with the LCIA Rules,[37] and the ICC Rules,[38] but unlike the UNCITRAL Rules,[39] the appointments are made in the initial pleadings. The Respondent has 30 days to appoint its arbitrator from the date of the Claimant's Request for Arbitration, and the two arbitrators have a further 20 days to appoint a chairman.

34.   The regime in Article 17(c) follows the same format, with the same time periods, save that the Claimant is given just 15 days in which to appoint its arbitrator, from the receipt by it of notification by the Center of the exercise of the latter's discretion.

---

[37] Arts. 1.1(e) and 2.1(d).

[38] Art. 8(4).

[39] Arts. 3 and 7.

Extensions, of Time

35. By Article 4(f), the parties may agree to reduce or extend the period of time referred to in Article 17(b) and (c).

By Article 4(g), the Center has, at the request of a party or on its own motion, a discretion to extend (but not abridge) the periods of time referred to in Article 17(b) and (c).

The Problem with Party-Appointed Arbitrators

36. The system of party-appointed arbitrators provided for here is, of course, well known in international commercial arbitration. Compare, in addition to the ICC and LCIA Rules mentioned above, Article 7 of the UNCITRAL Arbitration Rules, Article 11(3)(a) of the UNCITRAL Model Law; and Section 16(5) of the English Arbitration Act 1996.

37. There is a body of opinion, however, that the system of party-appointed arbitrators is flawed, and that appointments by institutional bodies is to be preferred.

38. It is often said that parties prefer to appoint their own arbitrators, in that this provides some means for influencing the appointment of the chairman, or because it ensures that the appointing parties' particular backgrounds and possibly perspectives are represented on the tribunal. As Sanders states[40]:

> ... in an international commercial arbitration a party-appointed arbitrator, having the same nationality as the party who appointed him may have within the arbitral tribunal some advantage. He may help to make understandable and explain the position of "his" party who entered into the international contract against the background of the law and usages prevailing in the country to which both that party and the arbitrator belong. In a domestic arbitration this argument in support of party arbitration cannot be advanced.

39. The appointment of a party-nominated arbitrator in an international arbitration is, of course, a theoretically distinct exercise from the non-neutral party appointments that are common in certain trade arbitrations, and in some domestic systems (notably in America). Whatever a party's reasons for selecting an arbitrator, under virtually all international rules, a party-appointed arbitrator must be non-partisan.[41] However, as stated by Robert Smit:

> In practice ... the party-appointed arbitrator system of international arbitration shares many features with its American stepsister of dubious integrity, the institution of partisan arbitrators. Under both systems, rather than selecting each arbitrator solely on the basis of his qualifications and integrity, parties tend to choose their party-appointed arbitrators on the basis of advocacy skills and perceived willingness to toe the party line, and to nominate a chairman based on the potential for symbiosis between the nominee and the party's party-appointed arbitrator. Ironically, even if the party-appointed arbitrator chosen in fact is completely neutral, he will frequently be viewed by his co-arbitrators as expounding to some extent the party line, thereby

---

[40] *Supra* note 28 at § 12-143.
[41] *See* Art. 22 below.

diminishing his influence within the panel and, most notably, with the chairman. Finally, the incentive to compromise inherent in the party-appointed arbitrator system also lends itself to the "splitting-the-baby" phenomenon with which arbitration is widely associated in the United States.[42]

Nomination or Appointment? A Possible Solution

40.   Under the WIPO Rules, party-appointment occurs where the parties have so agreed, or where the Center determines that a three-member panel is appropriate. Unlike most other arbitral institutions, the actual appointments of arbitrators are not made by the Center, unless a default has occurred (Article 19) or there is a multi-party situation within Article 18.

41.   It would appear that the objections to party-appointed arbitrators could be met by allowing for party nomination, but not appointment. In this way, the WIPO Center would retain the last say, and a (albeit perhaps theoretical) power to veto any nomination that appears to be inappropriate.

42.   Indeed, most of the major institutional rules contain provisions that supplement or in some circumstances militate against simple party appointments. For example, Article 8(4) of the ICC Rules provides:

> Where the dispute is to be referred to three arbitrators, each party shall *nominate* in the Request for Arbitration and the Answer thereto respectively one arbitrator for *confirmation* by the Court.
> The third arbitrator, who will act as chairman of the arbitral tribunal, shall be *appointed by the Court*, unless the parties have agreed upon another procedure for such appointment, in which case the nomination will be subject to *confirmation* pursuant to Article 9. . . . (Emphasis added)

Article 9 of the ICC Rules then sets out detailed provisions with respect to the appointment and confirmation of arbitrators. Article 9(1) provides as follows:

> In confirming or appointing arbitrators, the Court shall consider the prospective arbitrator's nationality, residence and other relationships with the countries of which the parties or the other arbitrators are nationals and the prospective arbitrator's availability and ability to conduct the arbitration in accordance with these Rules. . . .

---

[42] Robert Smit, *The CPR Rules For Non-Administered Arbitration of International Disputes: A Critical and Comparative Commentary*, 2 AM. REV. INT'L ARB. 411, 423 (1991), citing the large amount of material on this topic, which includes: Richard Mosk, *The Role of Party-Appointed Arbitrators in International Arbitration: The Experience of the Iran-United States Claims Tribunal*, 1 TRANSNAT'L LAW. 253 (1988); Murray L. Smith, *Impartiality of the Party-Appointed Arbitrator*, 6 ARB. INT'L 320 (1990); M. Scott Donahey, *The Independence and Neutrality of Arbitrators*, 9(4) J. INT'L ARB. 31 (1992); Hans Smit, *The New International Rules of the A.A.A.*, 2 AM. REV. INT'L ARB. 1 (1991); George W. Coombe, Jr., *The Selection and Conduct of the Party-Appointed Arbitrator: International and Domestic U.S. Ethical Considerations*, 1 A.B.A. INT'L COMMERCIAL ARB. COMMITTEE NEWSL. 1 (Jan. 1993). *See also* Andreas Lowenfeld, *The Party-Appointed Arbitrator in International Controversies: Some Reflections*, 30 TEXAS INT'L L.J. 59 (1995); Martin Hunter, *Ethics of the International Arbitrator*, 53 ARBITRATION 219 (1987).

43. Similarly, Article 5.5 of the LCIA Rules provides:

> The Court alone is empowered to appoint arbitrators.

Article 5.6 provides:

> In the case of a three-member Arbitral Tribunal, the chairman (who will not be a party-nominated arbitrator) shall be appointed by the LCIA Court.[43]

44. However cosmetic confirmation by an administering institution may in fact be, it is submitted that the removal of the final appointing power from the parties (as long as this does not entail any potential for additional delay in the constitution of a tribunal), serves a useful purpose in protecting the integrity of the given system.

The Missing Option: Appointment of All Arbitrators by the Parties

45. Article 5.3 of the CPR Rules expressly provides for a procedure to apply where the parties have agreed on a tribunal consisting of a sole arbitrator or three arbitrators, none of whom is to be appointed by either party alone. In other words, provision is made for a panel of three arbitrators, none of whom is a party-appointed arbitrator. This is a novel provision which meets the criticisms set out above. Such a provision, however, is missing in the WIPO Rules, as it is from nearly all other institutional rules, as well as the UNCITRAL Arbitration Rules.[44] Just such a provision was suggested in the course of the revision of the ICC Rules, by way of amendment to the old ICC Article 2(4). As noted by Kreindler:[45]

> . . . just as, in the case of a one-person tribunal, the parties may select the arbitrator, so, in the case of a three-person tribunal, the parties may select all three arbitrators.

This suggestion did not find its way into the final draft of the new ICC Rules.

Appointment of Three Arbitrators in Case of Multiple Claimants or Respondents

Article 18

(a) Where

(i) three arbitrators are to be appointed,

(ii) the parties have not agreed on a procedure of appointment, and

(iii) the Request for Arbitration names more than one Claimant, the Claimants shall make a joint appointment of an arbitrator in their Request for Arbitration. The appointment of the second arbitrator and the presiding arbitrator shall, subject to paragraph (b) of this Article,

---

[43] *See* Jan Paulsson, *Vicarious Hypochondria and Institutional Arbitration*, 6 ARB. INT'L 226, 242 (1990):

> The operant principle is that even if they agree *inter se*, parties do not have the unfettered right to transform anyone they like into an ICC or an LCIA arbitrator.

[44] Such a provision is "missing" from the WIPO Rules, in that it is not made express. Appointment of all three members by the parties would, of course, be permitted pursuant to Article 15(a), if so agreed by the parties.

[45] Kreindler, *supra* note 9 at 58.

take place in accordance with Article 17(b), (c) or (d), as the case may be.

(b)   Where
    (i)   three arbitrators are to be appointed,
    (ii)   the parties have not agreed on a procedure of appointment, and
    (iii)   the Request for Arbitration names more than one Respondent,
the Respondents shall jointly appoint an arbitrator. If, for whatever reason, the Respondents do not make a joint appointment of an arbitrator within 30 days after receiving the Request for Arbitration, any appointment of the arbitrator previously made by the Claimant or Claimants shall be considered void and two arbitrators shall be appointed by the Center. The two arbitrators thus appointed shall, within 30 days after the appointment of the second arbitrator, appoint a third arbitrator, who shall be the presiding arbitrator.

(c)   Where
    (i)   three arbitrators are to be appointed,
    (ii)   the parties have agreed upon a procedure of appointment, and
    (iii)   the Request for Arbitration names more than one Claimant or more than one Respondent,
paragraphs (a) and (b) of this Article shall, notwithstanding Article 15(a), apply irrespective of any contractual provisions in the Arbitration Agreement with respect to the procedure of appointment, unless those provisions have expressly excluded the application of this Article.

Commentary

Summary

46.   Article 18 addresses the very common situation in which the number of parties to an arbitration exceeds that contemplated by the arbitration agreement. The problem with multi-party cases is often that there are more parties than possible arbitrator appointments.[46]

---

[46] This topic has generated a very substantial body of literature. *See*, for example, Gerald Aksen, *Les arbitrages multiparties aux Etats-Unis*, 1981 REV. ARB. 98; Andreas Austmann, *Commercial Multi-Party Arbitration: A Case-by-Case Approach*, 1 AM. REV. INT'L ARB. 341 (1990); MULTI-PARTY ARBITRATION, VIEWS FROM INTERNATIONAL ARBITRATION SPECIALISTS (Institute of International Business Law and Practice / ICC 1991); Anthony Diamond, *Multi-Party Arbitrations: A Plea for a Pragmatic Piecemeal Solution*, 7 ARB. INT'L 403 (1991); ISAAK I. DORE, THEORY AND PRACTICE OF MULTIPARTY COMMERCIAL ARBITRATION (1990); Marc F. Guarin, *International Approaches to Court-Ordered Consolidation of Arbitral Proceedings*, 4 AM. REV. INT'L ARB. 519 (1993); ICC — FINAL REPORT ON MULTI-PARTY ARBITRATIONS BY THE WORKING GROUP CHAIRED BY JEAN-LOUIS DEVOLVÉ 1996 (ICC Int'l Court of Arb. Bull. 26-No. 1 of 1995); Philippe Leboulanger, *Multi-Contract Arbitration*, 13(4) J. INT'L ARB. 43 (1996); Sir Michael Mustill, *Multipartite Arbitrations: An Agenda for Law-Makers*, 7 ARB. INT'L 393 (1991); Albert Jan van den Berg, *ICC Arbitration Rules and Appointment of Arbitrators in Cases involving Multiple Defendants*, *in* FESTSCHRIFT FÜR OTTOARNDT GLOSSNER ZUM 70. GEBURTSTAG (1994);

47.   Article 18 deals with the situation where three arbitrators are to be appointed (either by virtue of an agreement by the parties pursuant to Article 14(a) or by virtue of the Center's discretion pursuant to Article 14(b)). Two cases may arise: firstly where no procedure for the appointment of arbitrators has been agreed upon (pursuant to Article 15(a)), and secondly, where some such procedure has been agreed upon:

 i. Where the parties have not agreed on any procedure for appointing the arbitrators (pursuant to Article 15):

- If the Request for Arbitration names more than one Claimant, all Claimants must jointly appoint one arbitrator (Article 18(a)).
- If the Request for Arbitration names more than one Respondent, all Respondents must jointly appoint one arbitrator (Article 18(b)).
- If the Respondents fail to jointly appoint an arbitrator within 30 days after receiving the Request for Arbitration, arbitrators for both the Claimant(s) and the Respondent(s) are appointed by the Center (entailing the nullification of any appointment made to date by the Claimant(s) (Article 18(b)). The two arbitrators so appointed must then appoint a chairman, within 30 days (Article 18(b)).

 ii. Where the parties have agreed upon a procedure of appointment (pursuant to Article 15):

- if more than one Claimant or Respondent is named, the agreed upon procedures for appointment are to be ignored, and replaced by the mechanisms in this Article — unless the parties have expressly excluded Article 18 in their agreement.

Exclusion of the Center's Powers

48.   If parties have agreed upon a mechanism for the appointment of arbitrators, this will not prevent the Center from imposing appointments in a multiparty situation, however detailed the parties' agreement may have been. In order to avoid this, the parties must have expressly excluded Article 18 — which they are not reminded about by the WIPO recommended arbitration clause. As stated in the context of earlier articles, it must be borne in mind that the parties may make such an agreement at any stage — even after a dispute has arisen, and by way of varying an earlier arbitration agreement.[47] Ultimately, of course, the powers vested in the Center by Article 18(c) are extremely important in order to prevent a breakdown in the arbitral process as a result of the joining of multiple parties.

J. Gillis Wetter, *A Multi-party Arbitration Scheme for International Joint-Ventures*, 3 ARB. INT'L 2 (1989).

[47] Article 18(c) refers to provisions in the "Arbitration Agreement." This is defined in Article 1 as: an arbitration clause in a contract or in the form of a separate contract.

The Problem — Dutco

49.   Arbitration clauses that provide for three arbitrators, as a general rule,[48] contemplate two parties: each party will appoint (or nominate) one arbitrator, and the two arbitrators will then appoint (or nominate) a third, or an institution will appoint the third. It has been seen that under the WIPO Rules, if no agreement as to the procedure for appointment has been reached (under Article 15), each party appoints one arbitrator pursuant to Article 17.

50.   However, multi-party situations frequently arise — and arise in many different forms. For example, different entities may be parties to different but related or even incorporated contracts, all providing for arbitration; many different parties may have entered into one contract; related parties to the original contracting parties may assert claims or have claims asserted against them as a result of, for example, assignment, novation, succession, agency or even the so-called "groups of companies" theory that has developed in a long line of ICC awards,[49] whereby non-signatories have been brought into the ambit of an arbitration clause.

51.   The problems that can arise in such cases were brought to the fore as a result of the French *Cour de Cassation*'s ruling in the case of *Siemens AG and BKMI Industrienlagen GmbH v. Dutco Construction Co.* ("*Dutco*"), of January 7, 1992.[50] That case concerned a contract between an employer and a construction consortium acting as the main contractor. A dispute arose between one of the members of the consortium and the two others. The arbitration clause in the consortium agreement provided for three arbitrators (to be appointed in accordance with the ICC Rules). The one member requested arbitration against the two others, and the ICC Court of Arbitration called upon the two defendants to jointly nominate an arbitrator. To avoid the nomination of a substitute, the two defendants complied, whilst at the same time reserving their rights. After the tribunal had been constituted, and had rendered an interim award, the defendants (unsuccessfully) challenged the award before the Paris *Cour d'Appel*. On appeal, the Paris *Cour de Cassation* (overruling the lower court) held that:

---

[48] Such clauses do not always contemplate that there will be two parties, as provision may be made for appointment in a multi-party situation. For example, it may be agreed that all three arbitrators will be jointly appointed by all parties (whether there are two or more parties).

[49] This line began with the well-known award, and subsequent judgment of the Paris Court of Appeal, in *Dow Chemical v. Isover Saint-Gobain. See* 9 Y.B. COM. ARB. 1342 (1984).

[50] Cass.Civ. 7 Jan. 1992, 119 J. DROIT INT'L (CLUNET) 712 (1992); 1992 REV. ARB. 479, *commented by* Pierre Bellet at 473–82; 18 Y.B. COM. ARB. 140 (1993). This case has been the subject of a considerable number of commentaries and, largely, criticism. *See, e.g.,* Eric A. Schwartz, *Multi-Party Arbitration and the ICC — In the Wake of Dutco*, 10(3) J. INT'L ARB. 5 (1993), for an interesting analysis from the ICC's perspective, and a large number of citations to other commentaries. *See also* Fritz Nicklisch, *Multi-Party Arbitration and Dispute Resolution in Major Industrial Projects*, 11(4) J. INT'L ARB. 57 (1994). The case has resulted in significant amendments to the LCIA and ICC Rules.

Whereas, the principle of equality of the parties in the designation of arbitrators is a matter of public policy; it can be waived only after the dispute has arisen.[51]

To this end, two or more defendant parties cannot be required to jointly nominate an arbitrator if the claimant has had an opportunity to exercise its own choice.

A Solution?

52.   The *Dutco* decision has been roundly criticized, and remains of uncertain scope.[52] Hitherto, most institutional rules had made no specific provision for multi-party cases.[53] The new LCIA and ICC Rules now deal with this problem in terms. Article 10 of the ICC Rules provides as follows:

1.   Where there are multiple parties, whether as Claimant or as Respondent, and where the dispute is to be referred to three arbitrators, the multiple Claimants, jointly, and the multiple Respondents, jointly, shall nominate an arbitrator for confirmation pursuant to Article 9.

2.   In the absence of such a joint nomination and where all parties are unable to agree to a method for the constitution of the Arbitral Tribunal, the Court may appoint each member of the Arbitral Tribunal and shall designate one of them to act as chairman. In such case, the Court shall be at liberty to choose any person it regards as suitable to act as arbitrator, applying Article 9 when it considers this appropriate.

Similarly, Article 8 of the LCIA Rules now provides as follows:

8.1   Where the Arbitration Agreement entitles each party howsoever to nominate an arbitrator, the parties to the dispute number more than two and such parties have not all agreed in writing that the disputant parties represent two separate sides for the formation of the Arbitral Tribunal as Claimant and Respondent respectively, the LCIA Court shall appoint the Arbitral Tribunal without regard to any party's nomination.

8.2   In such circumstances, the Arbitration Agreement shall be treated for all purposes as a written agreement by the parties for the appointment of the Arbitral Tribunal by the LCIA Court.

53.   Article 18 of the WIPO Rules, whilst far more complicated in terms of drafting than the simple solutions of the new ICC and LCIA Rules, does go a long way in solving multi-party complications, with respect to appointment. It also addresses part of the *Dutco* reasoning in terms: Article 18(b) makes it clear that if multiple

---

[51] As translated by Eric Schwartz, *supra* note 50, at 11.

[52] See *id.* at 14–16.

[53] The English Arbitration Act 1996, in the light of *Dutco*, makes provision for multi-party situations in Section 18 ("Failure of appointment procedure"). The Court is given a power to make appointments where necessary and appropriate, and also to revoke any appointments already made, in order to maintain equality as between the various parties (Sec. 18(3)).

For an analysis of the different amendments that were considered in the course of the recent revision of the ICC Rules, *see* Kreindler, *supra* note 9, at 59–62, and Albert Jan van den Berg, *The ICC Arbitration Rules and Appointment of Arbitrators in Cases Involving Multiple Defendants*, in FESTSCHRIFT FÜR OTTOARNDT GLOSSNER 19 *et seq.* (1994).

respondents fail to make a joint appointment of an arbitrator, equality is maintained by the imposition of appointments on all parties — including a claimant who has already made an appointment.

54.   However, on one view, the rest of Articles 18(a) and (b) fall foul of the decision in *Dutco*: in adopting the WIPO rules in an arbitration clause (before a dispute has arisen), the parties will have agreed to unequal treatment, as Article 18(a) forces multiple Claimants to jointly appoint one arbitrator, whilst affording a single Respondent its own choice,[54] and similarly Article 18(b) (in the first instance) denies each of several Respondents its own choice of arbitrator, in circumstances where a single Claimant would have had a free choice.[55] To be safely within *Dutco*, Article 18 would have to provide for the appointment of all arbitrators by the Center (or at least two arbitrators) if multiple Claimants cannot agree on a joint appointment.

55.   It may be, on one reading of *Dutco*, that the safest solution in every multi-party case is for the Center simply to revoke all appointments already made, and impose appointments on all parties, equally. Hence the solutions that have now been adopted by the LCIA and ICC.

Different Seats

56.   For all the fall-out from *Dutco*, it is to be borne in mind that that decision colors France as a potential arbitral seat — but has not, to date, been followed in other jurisdictions. Indeed, on the contrary, there are concrete indications that it will not be followed in certain other countries.[56] The importance, therefore, of Article 18 is that it presents a flexible solution, that solves the problems of multiparties, and may do so without any further complications in many other countries where a WIPO arbitration may have its seat.

57.   It seems clear that it will still be possible, if the seat of an arbitration is not in France, for the Center (and, for that matter, any other arbitral institution) to appoint only one arbitrator on behalf of the multiple parties, rather than appointing all three arbitrators, in order not to deprive one party of its freedom to appoint its own arbitrator.

Other Scenarios Not Catered For?

58.   Article 18 only applies where three arbitrators are to be appointed. It therefore appears to have no application where (if this were ever to happen) the parties have agreed that any other number of arbitrators are to be appointed, but where the

---

[54] This will rarely be a problem, however, as a matter of practice: multiple Claimants will invariably be sufficiently allied as to be able to jointly appoint one arbitrator.

[55] The (possibly theoretical) danger with Article 18(b) is that multiple Respondents will do their best to jointly appoint an arbitrator within the 30-day time limit, in order to avoid appointments being imposed upon them by the Center, and may later seek to raise a *Dutco* defense at some future stage.

[56] *See, e.g.,* Arab Republic of Egypt v. Westland Helicopters Ltd. (*Cour de justice,* Geneva, November 26, 1982, *aff'd by* the *Tribunal fédéral suisse,* May 16, 1983), involving an ICC arbitration against six defendants. The ICC appointed one arbitrator for all six defendants, as part of a three-member tribunal. The Swiss Supreme Court upheld the ICC process.

agreed upon mechanism fails to operate by reason of the number of parties to the arbitration. This is a potential lacuna in the Rules, although most situations are likely to be solved by the Center making appointments pursuant to its powers under Article 19.

Extensions of Time

59. By Article 4(f), the parties may agree to reduce or extend the period of time referred to in Article 18(b).

60. By Article 4(g), the Center has, at the request of a party or on its own motion, a discretion to extend — but not abridge — the periods of time referred to in Article 18(b).

Default Appointment

Article 19

(a) **If a party has failed to appoint an arbitrator as required under Articles 15, 17 or 18, the Center shall, in lieu of that party, forthwith make the appointment.**

(b) **If the sole or presiding arbitrator has not been appointed as required under Articles 15, 16, 17 or 18, the appointment shall take place in accordance with the following procedure:**

   (i) **The Center shall send to each party an identical list of candidates. The list shall comprise the names of at least three candidates in alphabetical order. The list shall include or be accompanied by a brief statement of each candidate's qualifications. If the parties have agreed on any particular qualifications, the list shall contain only the names of candidates that satisfy those qualifications.**

   (ii) **Each party shall have the right to delete the name of any candidate or candidates to whose appointment it objects and shall number any remaining candidates in order of preference.**

   (iii) **Each party shall return the marked list to the Center within 20 days after the date on which the list is received by it. Any party failing to return a marked list within that period of time shall be deemed to have assented to all candidates appearing on the list.**

   (iv) **As soon as possible after receipt by it of the lists from the parties, or failing this, after the expiration of the period of time specified in the previous sub-paragraph, the Center shall, taking into account the preferences and objections expressed by the parties, invite a person from the list to be the sole or presiding arbitrator.**

   (v) **If the lists which have been returned do not show a person who is acceptable as arbitrator to both parties, the Center shall be authorized to appoint the sole or presiding arbitrator. The Center shall similarly be authorized to do so if a person is not able or does not wish to accept the Center's invitation to be the sole or**

presiding arbitrator, or if there appear to be other reasons precluding that person from being the sole or presiding arbitrator, and there does not remain on the lists a person who is acceptable as arbitrator to both parties.

(c)   **Notwithstanding the provisions of paragraph (b), the Center shall be authorized to appoint the sole or presiding arbitrator if it determines in its discretion that the procedure described in that paragraph is not appropriate for the case.**

Commentary

Summary

61.   Article 19 constitutes an essential safeguard against both recalcitrance and breakdowns in the machinery of the appointment process. It falls into two parts:

  i.   a simple authority on the part of the Center to make appointments itself where none have been made pursuant to Articles 15, 17 or 18 (Article 19(a));

  ii.   a list procedure for the appointment of a sole or presiding arbitrator, where the same has not been appointed pursuant to Articles 15, 16, 17 or 18 (Article 19(b)), with an additional discretion to make such appointments without the use of the list procedure, where "appropriate" (Article 19(c)).

62.   This Article therefore treats the appointment of a sole or presiding arbitrator differently from the appointment of a party-appointed arbitrator: if one party defaults in appointing its own arbitrator, there would be little justification in giving the non-defaulting party a say in the appointment of his adversary's arbitrator (although this does appear to be the position under the CPR Rules, which make no such distinction[57]).

Default Appointment and Agreed Qualifications

63.   Article 19(a) states, simply, that the Center shall make an appointment (of a party-appointed arbitrator), where a party has failed to do so. No mention is made as to the criteria the Center will adopt in selecting such an arbitrator. Where the parties have agreed on any qualifications that the arbitrators are to have, it must be implicit that the Center will take this into account. It may also take into account the qualities of any other arbitrators that have already been appointed by the other parties, with a view to producing a balanced, even tribunal. For example, if the other party-appointed arbitrator is an expert, rather than a lawyer, this may indicate that an expert should be appointed on behalf of the defaulting party. Equally, if the arbitrator already appointed

---

[57] CPR RULE 6.4.

Compare the rule in English law (now Sec. 17 of the Arbitration Act 1996) that if a party fails to appoint his arbitrator, the non-defaulting party may (after a specified time period and upon due notification) appoint his arbitrator as sole arbitrator. Although constituting something of a powerful deterrent to recalcitrant parties, and although such appointments may be set aside, this provision has been criticized by many, and doubts have been expressed in some courts as to the enforceability of any award rendered by such a sole arbitrator.

is the same nationality as the appointing party, it may appear fairer if the default appointment reflects the nationality of the defaulting party.[58] There appear to be many criteria that might have relevance in this regard.[59] See, for example, the factors that are now referred to in Article 9 of the ICC Rules. Article 5.5 of the LCIA Rules spells out the factors that should be relevant for any default appointment:

> ... The LCIA Court will appoint arbitrators with due regard for any particular method or criteria of selection agreed in writing by the parties. In selecting arbitrators consideration will be given to the nature of the transaction, the nature and circumstances of the dispute, the nationality, location and languages of the parties and (if more than two) the number of the parties.

The List Procedure

64. The list procedure set out in Article 19 is relatively straightforward: names are suggested in the first instance by the Center, taking into account any particular qualifications that the parties may have agreed upon. Each party may (within 20 days) delete and express a preference for any of the names on the list.[60] If any party fails to do so within 20 days, it will lose the right to object to any candidate on the list. As soon as possible thereafter (and, in any event, within 20 days), the Center will make an appointment, based on the preferences and objections that have been expressed.

65. The Center retains a necessary flexibility in finally appointing a sole or presiding arbitrator under this Article. Article 19(b)(iv) states that in making an appointment, the Center shall "tak[e] into account" the parties' preferences or objections, rather than be strictly bound by them, and Article 19(b)(v) allows the Center a free hand, where the lists do not result in an acceptable candidate, or the chosen candidate does not accept the invitation to be appointed (or is disqualified, or for any other reason cannot act). Further, Article 19(c) allows the Center to make any such appointment without using the list procedure at all.

66. Clearly, there will be many cases where there is simply no consensus between the parties, or for some other reason the chosen candidate is unavailable. Equally, there will be cases where an appointment must be made as a matter of urgency, such that there is no time to indulge each party with a list of possible candidates. It would be extremely impracticable for the Center to have to operate the list procedure for every appointment. Indeed, such a requirement, whilst reflecting the principle of party autonomy, would simply provide any recalcitrant party with an easy mechanism to veto any appointment, and to delay.

---

[58] The restriction as to nationality in Article 20 does not apply to party-appointed arbitrators, arguably for this reason.

[59] *Compare* Art. 11(5) of the UNCITRAL Model Law:

> The court or other authority, in appointing an arbitrator, shall have due regard to any qualifications required of the arbitrator by the agreement of the parties and to such considerations as are likely to secure the appointment of an independent and impartial arbitrator . . . .

[60] Unlike CPR Rule 6.4, names on the list are to be ordered by preference *after* names that are objected to have been deleted. In this way, if candidates are disqualified, they will not remain on the list.

67. Most other arbitral institutions provide for the direct appointment of arbitrators without the use of a list procedure. These include, for example, ICC Rules, Articles 8 and 9; AAA Rules, Article 6; LCIA Rules, Article 5. The UNCITRAL Rules, Article 6 and the CPR Rules, Rule 6.4 both do provide for a list procedure.

68. Undoubtedly, the list procedure is slower than direct appointment by an institution, but it does have the merit of providing for at least an element of choice by the parties (which may be significant, from a psychological point of view, in encouraging a party to participate fully in an arbitration, and to reduce the risk of subsequent challenges). Moreover, Articles 19(b) and (c) have been designed in such a way as to avoid the possible pitfalls with such a system:

i. As pointed out above, the procedure may be by-passed if there is insufficient time available for it.

ii. The option given to the Center in Article 19(c) to make a direct appointment without using the list procedure avoids the risk that a party will effectively disqualify the more suitable candidates by repeatedly deleting their names from the list. The experience of the Iran-US Claims Tribunal with the UNCITRAL Rules (which do not contain such an option) is a testament to the wisdom of Article 19(c).[61]

iii. Unlike the list procedure in the CPR Rules, the parties are required by Article 19(b) to return the lists to the Center, rather than to each other. In this way, there is little risk that the arbitrator who is ultimately selected might learn from one of the parties as to any party's order of preference, or whether any party had objected to him/her (which could conceivably result in a degree of bias or predisposition on the part of the arbitrator).

iv. The Center, rather than the parties, proposes the candidates, and compiles the list.

69. Under certain systems, the list procedure has been very successful. For example, with respect to the rules of the Netherlands Arbitration Institute, Albert Jan van den Berg has noted as follows:

> . . . [I]n 80% of the cases, the preferences expressed by the parties are the same. The high success rate seems to be explained simply by reason of the fact that each side does not know what the other is doing. A certain objectivity thus enters into the parties' consideration.[62]

Dutco?

70. A literal reading of the *Dutco* decision, which has been mentioned above, might lead one to query the validity of any appointment by the Center, pursuant to Article 19(a) or 19(b) where a party has failed to comment on the names on the list

---

[61] *See* STEWART A. BAKER & MARK D. DAVIS, THE UNCITRAL ARBITRATION RULES IN PRACTICE: THE EXPERIENCE OF THE IRAN-UNITED STATES CLAIMS TRIBUNAL 28 (1992), where this "burning of candidates" phenomenon is described.

[62] *Conference on Rules for Institutional Arbitration and Mediation*, WIPO, Geneva, January 20, 1995, at p.21.

within the required 20 days. The result in each case would appear to offend the rule of public policy emphasized in that case, in that a defaulting party would have an arbitrator imposed on it, in circumstances where the other party retains a choice (and this would be pursuant to an agreement entered into before the dispute had arisen). One can only assume that the *Dutco* reasoning would not extend to a case where one party is guilty of a willful default.

Extensions of Time

71.   By Article 4(f), the parties may agree to reduce or extend the period of time referred to in Article 19(b)(iii).

72.   By Article 4(g), the Center has, at the request of a party or on its own motion, a discretion to extend — but not abridge — the periods of time referred to in Article 19(b)(iii).

Nationality of Arbitrators

Article 20

(a)   **An agreement of the parties concerning the nationality of arbitrators shall be respected.**

(b)   **If the parties have not agreed on the nationality of the sole or presiding arbitrator, such arbitrator shall, in the absence of special circumstances such as the need to appoint a person having particular qualifications, be a national of a country other than the countries of the parties.**

Commentary

Summary

73.   Article 20 allows the parties to make any agreement they wish with respect to the nationality of arbitrators, but provides, in the absence of such an agreement, for a presumption that a sole or presiding arbitrator is to be of a neutral nationality.

74.   This presumption is displaced where there are ''special circumstances,'' which are stated as including ''the need to appoint a person having particular qualifications.''

75.   Article 20(b) only applies to sole or presiding arbitrators. This enables an appointment to be made on behalf of a party which reflects that party's nationality, and therefore provides for a balanced tribunal where the other party has appointed an arbitrator of its nationality.

Other Rules

76.   Most rules contain a similar provision to Article 20. The UNCITRAL Rules provide, at Article 6(4) as follows:

> In making the appointment, the appointing authority shall have regard to such considerations as are likely to secure the appointment of an independent and impartial arbitrator and shall take into account as well the advisability of appointing an arbitrator of a nationality other than the nationalities of the parties.

77. Article 6(4) of the AAA International Arbitration Rules provides:

> At the request of any party or on its own initiative, the administrator may appoint nationals of a country other than that of any of the parties.

78. The ICC Rules place some control on the nationality of all arbitrators, whether or not they are sole arbitrators or chairmen. Article 9(1) of the ICC Rules provides:

> In confirming or appointing arbitrators, the Court shall consider the prospective arbitrator's nationality, residence and other relationships with the countries of which the parties or the other arbitrators are nationals . . . .

Article 9(5) provides as follows:

> The sole arbitrator or the chairman of the Arbitral Tribunal shall be of a nationality other than those of the parties. However, in suitable circumstances and provided that neither of the parties objects within the time limit fixed by the Court, the sole arbitrator or the chairman of the Arbitral Tribunal may be chosen from a country of which any of the parties is a national.

Where the ICC Court is to appoint an arbitrator on behalf of a party which has failed to nominate one, the National Committee of the country of which that party is a national is called upon for a proposal.[63]

79. Article 6 of the LCIA Rules provides as follows:

> 6.1 Where the parties are of different nationalities, a sole arbitrator or chairman of the Arbitral Tribunal shall not have the same nationality as any party unless the parties who are not of the same nationality as the proposed appointee all agree in writing otherwise.
>
> 6.2 The nationality of parties shall be understood to include that of controlling shareholders or interests.
>
> 6.3 For the purpose of this Article, a person who is a citizen of two or more states shall be treated as a national of each state; and citizens of the European Union shall be treated as nationals of its different Member States and shall not be treated as having the same nationality.

80. In contrast, Article 11(1) of the Model Law provides:

> No person shall be precluded by reason of his nationality from acting as an arbitrator, unless otherwise agreed by the parties.[64]

Article 11(5) of the Model Law, however, provides as follows (and similar to the UNCITRAL Rules):

---

[63] ICC RULES Art. 9(6).

[64] REDFERN & HUNTER, *supra* note 5 at 225, note that Section 11 of the International Commercial Arbitration Act of British Columbia has been amended in order to provide for national neutrality, in the wake of *Nippon Steel Corp. v. Quinette Coal Ltd.*, an arbitration between Japanese and Canadian parties, in which a Canadian was chosen by the Chief Justice as third arbitrator, with consequent disquiet. *See* comment by Smith in [1989/90] 4 OIL & GAS L. & TAX'N REV. 105.

The court or other authority . . . in the case of a sole or third arbitrator, shall take into account . . . the advisability of appointing an arbitrator of a nationality other than those of the parties.

The Need for National Neutrality

81.   Redfern & Hunter state:

In an ideal world, the nationality of a sole arbitrator, or of the presiding arbitrator, should be irrelevant. The qualifications, experience and integrity of the arbitrator are the factors which should count. The country in which he was born or the passport which he carries should be irrelevant.[65]

However, it is now an extremely widespread practice in international arbitration that sole or presiding arbitrators are drawn from different nationalities from that of the parties to the dispute. Indeed, most parties and practitioners in the field would consider such a requirement as fundamental.[66] This is explicable by reference to the old adage that justice must not only be done, but must be seen to be done: it may not be the case that people of the same nationality automatically favor each other over other nationalities, but as long as this could be a risk, or an appearance is given that there is such a risk, it is to be avoided. A greater degree of confidence may be inspired on all sides if there is no chance that one party will get a better hearing because of some cultural or national identification between that party and the arbitrator. Indeed, the kinds of identification that may exist as between the nationals of one country may be difficult to pin down. They may range from an easy linguistic understanding, to shared legal cultures, perspectives, or even loyalties. At worst, of course, national identification could even manifest itself in some shared interest in the outcome of the dispute.[67]

82.   There is always the risk, however, that the best candidate will be disqualified by such a requirement, when in fact there is no risk whatsoever of such bias or partiality. Further, an insistence on neutral nationality may well produce other oddities, such as an arbitration where the law applicable to the merits of the dispute is that of one or other of the parties, but with which the sole or presiding arbitrator is entirely unfamiliar. The difficulties of such a scenario may be recognized by Article 20, which contemplates that the presumption in favor of national neutrality may be overridden in certain circumstances, where, for example, particular qualifications of an arbitrator will take precedence over his nationality.

83.   Further, unlike some of the other rules referred to above, Article 20 makes no mention of domicile, or native language, when these may be just as significant as nationality. There are many other relevant factors that might also be taken into account, such as, for example, the nationality of the parties' representatives, or the nationality of the party-appointed arbitrators.

---

[65] REDFERN & HUNTER, *supra* note 5, at 223.

[66] *See, e.g.,* Pierre Lalive, *On the Neutrality of the Arbitrator and of the Place of Arbitration, in* SWISS ESSAYS ON INTERNATIONAL ARBITRATION 23 (1984); William W. Park, *Neutrality, Predictability and Economic Co-Operation,* 12(4) J. INT'L ARB. 99 (1995).

[67] *See,* however, the discussion as to impartiality and independence in the context of Article 22, below.

84.   Nationality, in the end, is simply one of several objective criteria to test impartiality. It is submitted, as will be seen below in the context of Article 22, that impartiality is the overall objective, and that a neutral nationality should not be allowed to become an end in itself — it is only relevant insofar as it provides some guide to, indication of or justifiable doubts as to impartiality. This is to be borne in mind in the operation of Article 20, if the risk is to be avoided that the most appropriate and qualified candidate is disqualified on, ultimately, wholly irrelevant grounds. In the context of intellectual property, this may be all the more important, in that the pool of qualified candidates may well be small in any given case.

Communication Between Parties and Candidates for Appointment as Arbitrator

Article 21
No party or anyone acting on its behalf shall have any *ex parte* communication with any candidate for appointment as arbitrator except to discuss the candidate's qualifications, availability or independence in relation to the parties.

Commentary

Summary

85.   Article 21 addresses the level of permissible contact between a party and a candidate for appointment. Article 45 regulates the position once arbitrators have been appointed.

The "Beauty Parade" Issue

86.   This is something of a novel provision, which is not reflected in other arbitration rules, although some rules do regulate the routing of party-arbitrator communications.[68]

87.   It is a basic proposition that *ex parte* communications between parties and arbitrators should be avoided, and there is no reason why different rules should apply before a candidate has been appointed. The problem has become more acute in recent years, as more and more attention is placed on the selection process.

88.   Whereas it has always been common for parties to research the background and experience of potential arbitrators, and to seek advice and views from others, it has become more common for parties to make direct contact with the candidates concerned. Where administrative arrangements or appointments are not made by an arbitral institution, this will be necessary in order to establish availability, fees and to clarify any potential conflicts. There is a fine line, however, between administrative enquiries such as these, and enquiries that touch upon the merits of the dispute. There is something of a temptation for appointing parties to test out a candidate's position on a particular issue, or his or her reaction to a line of argument. Indeed, the mechanism of the "beauty parade" — whereby different candidates are asked the same set of

---

[68] *See, e.g.,* Article 13 of the LCIA Rules, which requires all communications between a party and a candidate to be made through the Registrar, until the tribunal is formed.

questions, and directly compared in order for a choice to be made — appears to be increasing in popularity.

89. The ''beauty parade'' method of choosing may be appropriate in the selection of a party's representatives. In that context, each candidate can, in effect, ''bid'' for the appointment by making presentations and providing examples of the ways in which the case might be handled. However, it is submitted that great care must be taken in using this method of selection for arbitrators. No candidate for an arbitral appointment should allow himself or herself to enter into any discussion of the merits of the case, or indeed a hypothetical case that might raise similar issues. Indeed, if such a discussion were to take place, there may well be grounds for challenging the arbitrator, once appointed — even in the absence of Article 21.

90. It might be noted in this regard that the new LCIA Rules are very clear on this issue. Article 5.2 provides (in part) as follows:

> 5.2 . . . No arbitrator, whether before or after appointment, shall advise any party on the merits or outcome of the dispute.

91. Ultimately, where the line is to be drawn between administrative matters and merits will depend upon each candidate's own view. Undoubtedly it will be good practice in each case for the candidate to make a full note of any such interview (and, of course, to indicate that this will be done), and to disclose the same to all other parties on being appointed.

Impartiality and Independence

Article 22

(a) Each arbitrator shall be impartial and independent.

(b) Each prospective arbitrator shall, before accepting appointment, disclose to the parties, the Center and any other arbitrator who has already been appointed any circumstances that might give rise to justifiable doubt as to the arbitrator's impartiality or independence, or confirm in writing that no such circumstances exist.

(c) If, at any stage during the arbitration, new circumstances arise that might give rise to justifiable doubt as to any arbitrator's impartiality or independence, the arbitrator shall promptly disclose such circumstances to the parties, the Center and the other arbitrators.

Commentary

Summary

92. Article 22 imposes two familiar criteria for every arbitrator: ''impartiality'' and ''independence.'' Every candidate for appointment has a duty to disclose any matter that might give the appearance of partiality or dependence, and this is a duty owed not only to all parties, but also to the Center and to any other arbitrator who has already been appointed. The duty arises before the acceptance of an appointment, and (by Article 22(c)) continues throughout the course of the arbitration.

93.   If any arbitrator is not impartial or independent, or does not appear to be impartial or independent (this being a significantly different test[69]), he or she may be challenged by a party under Article 24. Further, any eventual award may be challenged at the enforcement stage. A failure to disclose a matter, of itself, does not appear to be a ground for challenge under Article 24, unless it can be shown that either the failure itself, or the matter that was not disclosed, gives rise to justifiable doubts as to the arbitrator's impartiality or independence.[70]

94.   In the light of the discussion above[71] of the different conceptions of the party-appointed arbitrator, it will be seen that the standards of "impartiality" and "independence" operate as a central control on the integrity of international arbitral tribunals — which may well be different from some domestic systems. The criteria in Article 22 limit the extent to which any party may appoint an arbitrator who will have some predisposition towards that party's case. It is to be noted in this regard that Article 22 makes no distinction between party-appointed arbitrators and other arbitrators for the purposes of impartiality and independence.

95.   Further, it is to be remembered that "neutrality" is one of the key advantages of international arbitration, and that one of the key aspects of this (other than the place of the arbitration and the laws and procedures to be applied) is the nature of the arbitral tribunal itself. There is widespread consensus that neutrality is a basic qualification for any international arbitral tribunal, given the adjudicative (as opposed to conciliatory) nature of the process. As one commentator recently put the position:

> According to the fundamental principle that regarding every judgment the deciding authority must enjoy a position *super partes,* the predominant scholarship and jurisprudence both at national and international levels agree that the adjudicating authority in arbitration must assume the position of an outside party, fully independent and separate from the disputants.[72]

---

[69] The U.S. Supreme Court as well as English courts have held that the mere appearance of bias is sufficient to challenge an arbitrator. *See* W. Michael Tupman, *Challenge and Disqualification of Arbitrators in International Commercial Arbitration*, 38 ICLQ 26, 50 (1989), *citing* Commonwealth Coatings Corp v. Continental Casualty Co., 393 U.S. 145, 149–50 (1968), and Metropolitan Properties Co. v. Lannon, [1969] Q.B. 577, 599 (*per* Lord Denning). In contrast (and confusingly) other U.S. federal courts have held that the mere appearance of bias is not sufficient to disqualify an arbitrator. See, amongst many others, Sheet Metal Workers Int'l Ass'n v. Kinney Air Conditioning Co., 756 F.2d 742, 746 (9th Cir. 1985); Morelite Construction Corp. v. New York City District Council Carpenters Ben. Funds, 748 F.2d 79, 83 (2d Cir. 1984).

[70] Interestingly, the IBA Rules of Ethics for International Arbitrators, *reprinted in* THE ROSTER OF INTERNATIONAL ARBITRATORS 3 (Hans Smit & Vratislav Pechota eds. 1997), state in Art. 4.1 that a failure to disclose "creates an appearance of bias, and may of itself be a ground for disqualification."

[71] *See* discussion under Article 17, *supra.*

[72] Aldo Berlinguer, *Impartiality and Independence of Arbitrators in International Practice*, 6 AM. REV. INT'L ARB. 339, 340 (1995), which refers to the wealth of material on this topic.

Of the many other articles, *see, e.g.*, William W. Park, *Neutrality, Predictability and Economic Co-operation*, 12(4) J. INT'L ARB. 99 (1995); J. Lani Bader, *Arbitrator Disclosure — Probing the Issues,*

96. It will be seen that different rules use different combinations of the three main adjectives "independence," "impartiality" and "neutrality." Ultimately, it is submitted that the most important criterion is one of impartiality, and that the other two tests are only relevant insofar as they relate to this criterion. "Independence" is not an end in itself, unless it necessarily reflects a lack of partiality — which may not be so in all cases. As explained below, it is suggested that there are situations in which "dependent" arbitrators may well be perfectly impartial — and may well be the only available candidates for appointment.

Other Rules

97. The LCIA Rules, in Articles 5.2 and 5.3, provide for the same criteria as Article 22: both "independence" and "impartiality":

> 5.2 All arbitrators conducting an arbitration under these Rules shall be and remain at all times impartial and independent of the parties; and none shall act in the arbitration as advocates for any party. No arbitrator, whether before or after appointment, shall advise any party on the merits or outcome of the dispute.
>
> 5.3 Before appointment by the LCIA Court, each arbitrator shall . . . sign a declaration to the effect that there are no circumstances known to him likely to give rise to any justified doubts as to his impartiality or independence, other than any circumstances disclosed by him in the declaration. Each arbitrator shall thereby also assume a continuing duty forthwith to disclose any such circumstances to the LCIA Court, to any other members of the Arbitral Tribunal and to all the parties if such circumstances should arise after the date of such declaration and before the arbitration is concluded.

98. As explained above, all appointments in LCIA arbitration are made by the LCIA.[73] In this way, the integrity of the process is maintained, whatever the individual desires of the parties in making their nominations. It would appear, therefore, that parties could not agree to appoint a particular tribunal, if the LCIA itself considered that the candidates were not impartial or independent. The same is of course true with the ICC.[74]

99. In contrast, Article 7 of the AAA International Arbitration Rules provides for the same criteria of "impartiality" and "independence," but also allows for party autonomy:

> Unless the parties agree otherwise, arbitrators acting under these rules shall be impartial and independent.

12(3) J. INT'L ARB. 39 (1995); Donald E. Zubrod, *Evident Partiality and Misconduct of Arbitrators*, 11(2) J. INT'L ARB. 115 (1994); M. Scott Donahey, *The Independence and Neutrality of Arbitrators*, 9(4) J. INT'L ARB. 31 (1992); Guillermo Aguilar Alvarez, *The Challenge of Arbitrators*, 6 ARB. INT'L 203 (1990).

[73] Art. 5.5 of the LCIA Rules, as described above.

[74] For a discussion of this issue, *see* Jan Paulsson, *Vicarious Hypochondria and Institutional Arbitration*, 6 ARB. INT'L 226, 242–43 (1990).

It is to be noted that unlike the LCIA and ICC, the WIPO Center has no power to review the qualifications of the arbitrators appointed by the parties.

Article 7 goes on to provide for a very similar duty of disclosure as in Article 22 above, and the LCIA Rules.

100.   Similarly, the UNCITRAL Rules impose tests of both "impartiality" and "independence."[75]

101.   Unlike the WIPO, LCIA, AAA and UNCITRAL Rules, the ICC Rules only provide for "independence," with no mention of "impartiality." Article 7(1) provides that:

> Every arbitrator must be and remain independent of the parties involved in the arbitration.

Similarly, Article 7(2) imposes a duty of disclosure with respect to "independence" only, as follows:

> Before appointment or confirmation, a prospective arbitrator shall sign a statement of independence and disclose in writing to the Secretariat any facts or circumstances which might be of such a nature as to call into question the arbitrator's independence in the eyes of the parties.

Article 11(1), however, allows for challenges to arbitrators for "an alleged lack of independence *or otherwise*" (emphasis added), which may well include "impartiality."[76]

102.   Just as arbitration rules emphasize the criteria of impartiality and independence, so do most modern national arbitration laws. The UNCITRAL Model Law provides in Article 12(2) for both "impartiality" and "independence," and this formula is reflected in statutes as well as codes of ethics throughout the world.[77]

Definitions

103.   None of the rules referred to above includes a definition of the criteria used. In contrast, Rule 7.3 of the CPR Rules lists the following circumstances as (non-exhaustive) examples of matters that "might cause doubt regarding the arbitrator's independence or impartiality":

> bias, interest in the result of the arbitration, and past or present relations with a party.

It appears that a similar non-exhaustive list of factors had been included in preliminary drafts of the UNCITRAL Rules, but were deleted from the final draft.[78]

---

[75] *See* Arts. 6(4), 9 and 10.

[76] *See* Stephen R. Bond, *The Selection of ICC Arbitrators and the Requirements of Independence*, 4 ARB. INT'L 300 (1984).

[77] For a survey of different national laws and codes of ethics in this regard, *see* SANDERS, *supra* note 28, at §§ 147–148.

[78] *See* STEWART A. BAKER & MARK D. DAVIS, THE UNCITRAL ARBITRATION RULES IN PRACTICE: THE EXPERIENCE OF THE IRAN-UNITED STATES CLAIMS TRIBUNAL, 47–49 (1992).

104. According to the IBA Rules of Ethics for International Arbitrators,[79] the following factors may be considered as giving rise to justifiable doubts as to an arbitrator's impartiality or independence:

(a) a material interest in the outcome of the dispute;

(b) a position already taken in relation to the dispute;

(c) current direct or indirect (*i.e.* via a member of family, firm or partner) business relationship with a party or a potentially important witness;

(d) past business relationships of such a magnitude or nature as to be likely to affect an arbitrator's judgment;

(e) continuous and substantial social or professional relationships with a party or a potentially important witness.[80]

105. It is important to realize that "impartiality" and "independence" are two very different concepts, although the latter may be a test of the former. Lists of factors as set out in the previous paragraph often confuse aspects of both concepts.

106. The concept of "partiality" concerns bias: the extent to which an arbitrator may be predisposed towards one party or one view of a case. In contrast, the concept of "dependence" concerns the extent to which an arbitrator is related or connected to a party or an issue. Such a relationship or connection is susceptible of measurement. It could be direct or indirect, professional or personal, or indeed financial. In contrast, impartiality is less concrete. As Redfern and Hunter state:

> Impartiality is thus a much more abstract concept than independence, in that it involves primarily a state of mind which presents special difficulties of measurement.[81]

107. As a matter of practical reality, it may well be difficult to find an arbitrator who has a complete and absolute absence of connections with any party, other arbitrator or relevant issue. This is particularly so the more specialized the particular field in question. For example, in certain specialized commodity trades, and indeed technical areas raising questions of intellectual property, the pool of appropriate candidates for appointment may be very small, if the arbitrator is to have relevant experience or knowledge. Indeed, an absence of any connection to a particular field may be a distinct disadvantage, given that one reason for choosing arbitration over litigation in certain trades is the very fact that the arbitrators (unlike judges) will have some familiarity with the relevant commercial or technical area.

108. Some degree of connection or some relationship may be inevitable. The question is the permitted degree. It is suggested that the control must be impartiality. No arbitrator should have a connection with a party or issue such that he or she can no longer be objective, neutral or without any predisposition. But if partiality is not a real risk or consequence of a particular relationship, there is no obvious reason why an

---

[79] *Supra*, note 70.

[80] *See id.* at Arts. 3.2–3.5.

[81] REDFERN & HUNTER, *supra* note 5, at 220. Matters are often confused still further by the use of the term "neutrality," as to which *see id.* at 221.

arbitrator should be disqualified on the basis such a relationship alone. As Justice White stated in *Commonwealth Coatings Corp. v. Continental Casualty Co.*, 393 U.S. 145 (1968) at 149–50:

> it is often because [arbitrators] are [persons] of affairs, not apart from but of the market-place, that they are effective in their adjudicatory function. . . . I see no reason automatically to disqualify the best informed and most capable potential arbitrators.

Indeed, if any dependence, per se, were sufficient to disqualify an arbitrator, a premium would be placed on extensive and burdensome disclosure (for its own sake), and the scope for disrupting the arbitral process would be enhanced.

109.   Just as an absence of any connections or relationships whatsoever may be unrealistic, the existence of a predisposition, or "partiality" may be elusive. It is often said, therefore, that the only way to measure impartiality, as a practical matter, is to assess the existence and nature of an arbitrator's independence. Thus independence, like nationality, is one objective test of impartiality — but not an end in itself.

110.   It has been suggested that "bright-line" standards are needed for evaluating the independence and impartiality of arbitrators, in order to clarify an arbitrator's duty of disclosure, and to forestall the opportunity for vexatious challenges.[82]

The Debate in England

111.   After much discussion and extensive public consultation on this issue, the English Arbitration Act 1996 included as a ground for the removal of arbitrators:

> that circumstances exist that give rise to justifiable doubts as to his impartiality[83]

No mention was made of a lack of "independence."

---

[82] In an article entitled *Practical Issues in Selecting Party-Appointed Arbitrators in International Arbitration: Clear Applicable Ethics Standards* (to date unpublished), Doak Bishop and Lucy Reed have set out suggested guidelines for this purpose, which highlight the types of issues that have often been raised in the course of challenges. Their analysis follows the following structure:

A.   *Disqualifying Factors for Potential Party-Appointed Arbitrators*

— Significant Financial Interest in Project or Party
— Close Family Relationship with Party
— Decision-making or Controlling Role in Project or Party
— Public Position Taken on Specific Matter in Dispute

B.   *Non-Disqualifying Factors for Potential Party-Appointed Arbitrators*

— Professional Writings and Lectures
— Professional Associations
— Position in Same or Similarly-Situated Industry or Government
— Prior Arbitrations

C.   *Factors Bearing Close Scrutiny for Potential Party-Appointed Arbitrators*

— Past Business Relationship with Party
— Attenuated Family Relationship with Party
— Friendship with Party.

[83] Section 24(1)(a).

112. Indeed, in Section 1(a) of the Act, a general principle is laid down as follows:

> the object of arbitration is to obtain the fair resolution of disputes by an impartial tribunal without unnecessary delay or expense.

Again, a separate quality of ''independence'' is not included.

113. The reasons for what at first sight might appear a striking omission, follow the analysis above, and are set out in the DAC Report of February 1996,[84] the relevant paragraphs of which bear quoting in full:

> 101. The Model Law (Article 12) specifies justifiable doubts as to the independence (as well as impartiality) of an arbitrator as grounds for his removal. We have considered this carefully, but despite efforts to do so, no-one has persuaded us that, in consensual arbitrations, this is either required or desirable. It seems to us that lack of independence, unless it gives rise to justifiable doubts about the impartiality of the arbitrator, is of no significance. The latter is, of course, the first of our grounds for removal. If lack of independence were to be included, then this could only be justified if it covered cases where the lack of independence did *not* give rise to justifiable doubts about impartiality, for otherwise there would be no point including lack of independence as a separate ground.
>
> 102. We can see no good reason for including ''non-partiality'' lack of independence as a ground for removal and good reasons for not doing so. We do not follow what is meant to be covered by a lack of independence which does not lead to the appearance of partiality. Furthermore, the inclusion of independence would give rise to endless arguments, as it has, for example, in Sweden and the United States, where almost any connection (however remote) has been put forward to challenge the 'independence' of an arbitrator. For example, it is often the case that one member of a barristers' Chambers appears as counsel before an arbitrator who comes from the same Chambers. Is that to be regarded, without more, as a lack of independence justifying the removal of the arbitrator? We are quite certain that this would not be the case in English law. Indeed the Chairman[85] has so decided in a case in chambers in the Commercial Court.[86] We would also draw attention to the article ''Barristers' Independence and Disclosure'' by Kendall in (1992) 8 Arb. Int. 287. We would further note in passing that even the oath taken by those appointed to the International Court of Justice; and indeed to our own High Court, refers only to impartiality.
>
> 103. Further, there may well be situations in which parties desire their arbitrators to have familiarity with a specified field, rather than being entirely independent.
>
> 104. We should emphasize that we intend to lose nothing of significance by omitting reference to independence. Lack of this quality may well give rise to justifiable doubts about impartiality, which is covered, but if it does not, then we cannot at present see anything of significance that we have omitted by not using this term.

---

[84] *See supra* note 18.

[85] Lord Saville of Newdigate.

[86] *i.e.* a private, interlocutory court hearing.

Independence Amongst Practitioners

114.   As any newcomer to the field will vouch, the world of international commercial arbitration is small. Research published in 1996 concluded as follows:

> First, the much heralded competition for arbitration business favored a few institutions and settings. The International Chamber of Commerce was clearly the leading, even dominant, institution . . . . Second, the same, relatively few, names of arbitrators were repeated over and over on both sides of the Atlantic. These individuals are not tied to any single institution but rather handle arbitrations under the auspices of multiple institutions or as ad hoc proceedings. We could quite quickly see a senior generation — the ''grand old men'' of arbitration (which included no women) — and a younger generation of lawyers in their forties (which is characterized by slightly more diversity). And it was clear that this international arbitration community was relatively small and linked together pretty closely. Members of the inner circle and outsiders often referred to this group as a ''mafia.''[87]

115.   The degree of familiarity and contact between individual arbitrators and between arbitrators and counsel in the international field continues to grow, and continues to be reinforced by the modern and now widespread phenomenon of the international arbitration conference. With extraordinary frequency, conferences are held all over the world to debate recurring arbitration topics. Locations may change, but the same practitioners tend to appear, whether as delegates or speakers. Whilst many of these conferences provide useful fora for the exchange of information on what otherwise tends to be a confidential process, an undoubted consequence of so much contact between the same people is that many international arbitral panels consist of individuals who know one another very well, and who may well be extremely familiar with one or possibly both counsel.

116.   Insofar as this familiarity exists between an arbitral tribunal and the legal representatives of one side alone, or between a chairman and one arbitrator alone, there is a danger that the situation could be characterized as a lack of independence, and be deployed for the purpose of a challenge. Challenges based on this form of dependence may be unwelcome, but must be anticipated. It is suggested that the most prudent way of addressing (and avoiding) this danger, is by adopting an over-cautious approach to disclosure. As long as every type of relationship is volunteered by practitioners before appointment, no challenges could be made thereafter under most systems.

---

[87] YVES DEZALAY & BRYANT G. GARTH, DEALING IN VIRTUE — INTERNATIONAL COMMERCIAL ARBITRATION AND THE CONSTRUCTION OF A TRANSNATIONAL LEGAL ORDER, 9–10 (1996). These conclusions were based on a detailed study, drawing from a large number of interviews with individuals active in this field. The following excerpts from such interviews are quoted in a footnote to the quotation above:

> The more you see of international arbitration, the more you know the people who are involved, and they tend to be repetitively involved . . . especially in the ICC, it's a club of friends [with the] same names coming up all the time . . . It is a club. They nominate one another. And sometimes you're counsel, and sometimes you're arbitrator . . . It's a mafia because people appoint one another. You always appoint your friends — people you know.

Availability, Acceptance, and Notification

Article 23

(a) Each arbitrator shall, by accepting appointment, be deemed to have undertaken to make available sufficient time to enable the arbitration to be conducted and completed expeditiously.

(b) Each prospective arbitrator shall accept appointment in writing and shall communicate such acceptance to the Center.

(c) The Center shall notify the parties of the establishment of the Tribunal.

Commentary

Summary

117. Article 23 addresses several different, but important, aspects of the appointment process.

(a) Firstly, for an appointment to be made, each arbitrator must accept a nomination in writing, and must forward such acceptance to the Center. Curiously, there appears to be no requirement that a copy of such acceptance be forwarded directly to any of the parties.

(b) Secondly, the Center is under a duty to notify the parties of the establishment of the Tribunal.

(c) Thirdly, and quite distinctly, all arbitrators so appointed are under a duty, in effect, to make sufficient time available to enable the proper conduct of the case.

118. Various time limits in the WIPO Rules run from the date of appointment of an arbitrator. See, for example, Article 17(b) ("The two arbitrators thus appointed shall, within 20 days after the appointment of the second arbitrator"), and similarly Articles 17(c) and 18(b). An important question is therefore the exact point at which, under the Rules, an arbitrator is to be considered "appointed."

119. Has an arbitrator been appointed before he or she has "accepted" the appointment under Article 23(b)? Does the time limit in Articles 17 and 18 run from the date of appointment or the date of acceptance? If the relevant date is the latter, there appears to be a lacuna in the Rules, given that there is no duty under Article 23(b) for an arbitrator to notify his or her acceptance to the parties. Indeed, the duty on the Center in Article 23(c) to notify the parties appears to concern the "establishment of the Tribunal," rather than the acceptance of each individual arbitrator. It might be reasonable to suggest that no arbitrator could be considered "appointed" until that arbitrator has accepted. Certainly under some national laws, written confirmation is a statutory requirement.[88]

120. Article 22(b) imposes a duty to disclose "before accepting appointment." This would appear to delay the time periods in Articles 17 and 18, if an opportunity is to be allowed for such disclosure (and possible comment by the parties, other

---

[88] *See, e.g.*, Netherlands Arbitration Act 1986, Art. 1029(1).

arbitrators or the Center) before the arbitrator accepts the appointment. On any view, the rules are unclear in this respect.

121.   A further difficulty arises where an arbitrator does not accept appointment. The rules do not specify whether an appointment has simply not been made in such circumstances, or whether the appointing party is to be considered in default at that point.[89]

The Duty of Availability

122.   As pointed out above, the pool of candidates for appointment in international arbitration is small, and most arbitrators are extremely busy. The temptation to accept appointments can be compelling, and may override a sensible assessment of the potential demands of appointments already accepted. Indeed, it is common for long periods of time to elapse between hearings, simply because of the various commitments of different members of a tribunal. The duty in Article 23(a) is therefore to be welcomed.

123.   Few other arbitral rules include such a duty on the arbitrators themselves. Article 9(1) of the ICC Rules allows the ICC Court to take availability into account, but this is not imposed as a duty on the arbitrators themselves:

> In confirming or appointing arbitrators, the Court shall consider . . . the prospective arbitrator's availability and ability to conduct the arbitration in accordance with these Rules.

However, on one view, such a duty is implicit in the general duty of arbitrators under Article 7(5) of the ICC Rules:

> By accepting to serve, every arbitrator undertakes to carry out his responsibilities in accordance with these Rules.

124.   One question that arises from Article 23(a) (and, indeed, from Article 7(5) of the ICC Rules) is whether or not the relationship between the parties and the tribunal, or alternatively each arbitrator, is to be characterized as one of contract. The status of an arbitrator is a difficult and well-worn area of debate, with different possible analyses as between simple contract (adapted to cover multiple parties) and notions of "status."[90] Whether or not duties that are imposed on an arbitrator sound in contract will obviously have an impact on the consequences of breach. What is the sanction if an arbitrator's diary is full, in breach of Article 23(a)? Could an arbitrator be removed, or sued for damages? It is likely that an arbitrator could be removed under

---

[89] See Commentary by Eric A. Schwartz in *Conference on Rules for Institutional Arbitration and Mediation* arising out of a WIPO Conference in Geneva in January 1995.

[90] For an interesting analysis of this question from an English law perspective, *see* MUSTILL & BOYD, COMMERCIAL ARBITRATION 223 (2d ed. 1989). In *K/S Norjarl A/S v. Hyundai Heavy Industries Co*, [1991] 1 Lloyd's Rep. 524, Browne-Wilkinson V-C commented that an arbitrator's duties flowed from the conjunction of contract and status. On this analysis, an arbitration agreement is a bilateral contract which becomes trilateral on the arbitrator's appointment. Under the trilateral contract the arbitrator assumes the status of a quasi-judicial adjudicator with the duties and disabilities inherent in that status.

Article 32, a failure to be available being a failure "to fulfill . . . the duties of an arbitrator," as defined in Article 23(a). Any recourse by way of damages may, in turn, depend upon the existence and scope of an arbitrator's immunity from suit (as to which see Article 77).

Challenge of Arbitrators

Article 24

(a) Any arbitrator may be challenged by a party if circumstances exist that give rise to justifiable doubt as to the arbitrator's impartiality or independence.

(b) A party may challenge an arbitrator whom it has appointed or in whose appointment it concurred only for reasons of which it becomes aware after the appointment has been made.

Article 25

A party challenging an arbitrator shall send notice to the Center, the Tribunal and the other party, stating the reasons for the challenge, within 15 days after being notified of that arbitrator's appointment or after becoming aware of the circumstances that it considers give rise to justifiable doubt as to that arbitrator's impartiality or independence.

Article 26

When an arbitrator has been challenged by a party, the other party shall have the right to respond to the challenge and shall, if it exercises this right, send, within 15 days after receipt of the notice referred to in Article 25, a copy of its response to the Center, the party making the challenge and the arbitrators.

Article 27

The Tribunal may, in its discretion, suspend or continue the arbitral proceedings during the pendency of the challenge.

Article 28

The other party may agree to the challenge or the arbitrator may voluntarily withdraw. In either case, the arbitrator shall be replaced without any implication that the grounds for the challenge are valid.

Article 29

If the other party does not agree to the challenge and the challenged arbitrator does not withdraw, the decision on the challenge shall be made by the Center in accordance with its internal procedures. Such a decision is of an administrative nature and shall be final. The Center shall not be required to state reasons for its decision.

Commentary

Summary

125. As challenges to arbitral tribunals become increasingly common (whether motivated by a genuine objection, or a means of derailing the process), so the importance of an effective and efficient challenge procedure cannot be overstated.

126. Articles 24 to 29 of the WIPO rules set out a clear and familiar procedure for the administration and determination of challenges. By Article 24, challenges may be made by a party (not by the Center) on one ground alone: the existence of justifiable doubts as to the arbitrator's impartiality or independence.[91] No challenge can be made on the basis of any matter disclosed prior to appointment, insofar as the party seeking to challenge concurred in the appointment thereafter, unless the relevant matters only came to light subsequently (Article 24(b)). Article 24(b), in this respect, follows Article 10 of the UNCITRAL Rules, as well as most other arbitral rules.

127. It is to be noted that Article 24 is far narrower than certain other corresponding provisions in other arbitration rules. For example, the ICC Rules provide that a challenge of an arbitrator may be made on the grounds of an alleged lack of independence *"or otherwise."*[92] In contrast, Article 24 of the WIPO Rules is limited to challenges based on a lack of impartiality or independence alone. No other ground may be relied upon — even if there are other manifest grounds for objecting to an appointment (*e.g.*, if a party fails to appoint an arbitrator with the qualifications that he may be required to have).[93]

128. Article 25 imposes a time limit on the raising of challenges. Any challenge must be brought within 15 days of an arbitrator's appointment. The exact time at which an arbitrator is to be considered "appointed" is, however, unclear, given the wording of Article 23(b), which provides that each arbitrator is to accept his or her appointment in writing, and communicate the same to the Center.[94] Alternatively, where relevant circumstances only come to light after an arbitrator has been appointed, Article 25 provides that a challenge may be made within 15 days of a party becoming aware of such circumstances. There is therefore no scope for a party to obstruct the proceedings by deploying a challenge whenever it appears tactically advantageous — whatever stage the arbitration may have reached. The fact that Article 25 requires a reasoned notice of challenge to be sent to the tribunal, as well as the other party and the Center, serves several useful purposes: a significant disincentive with respect to spurious challenges that might alienate other members of the tribunal; a means by which other members of the tribunal may be informed of possibly relevant circumstances, and a basis for other members of the tribunal to advise the arbitrator challenged.

---

[91] For an analysis of this test, see the discussion under Article 22 above.

[92] Art. 11(1) (emphasis added).

[93] It is arguable that such an objection could be brought within Article 32. Article 12(2) of the UNCITRAL Model Law, in contrast, allows for a challenge to an arbitrator "if he does not possess qualifications agreed to by the parties."

[94] See the discussion of the difficulties that arise from this under Article 23 above.

129. By Article 26, the other party has the right to respond to the challenge made. No formal provision is made for a response by the arbitrator challenged. Article 27 allows a tribunal to continue, notwithstanding a pending challenge. This is a significant provision, given that it constitutes a powerful disincentive for any party to launch a spurious challenge. In reality, however, few arbitral tribunals will continue during the pendency of a challenge, especially given the short time period in which such a challenge will be resolved in accordance with the rules.

130. Article 28 allows for two possible outcomes short of removal by the Center: agreement between the parties, or withdrawal by the arbitrator. In either of these two cases, Article 28 absolves the arbitrator from any blame — and arguably an action for breach of contract, at least without more. A provision along these lines was first introduced by the UNCITRAL Arbitration Rules.[95] It is designed to facilitate acceptance or withdrawal. As Sanders points out:

> Once a party has shown lack of confidence, an arbitrator may be inclined to withdraw unless the challenge is completely unfounded and may have been raised only for delaying purposes. Both the arbitrator and the party who appointed him may prefer, even when they deem the challenge unjustified, not to have the challenge rejected, whereafter the arbitral proceedings will be conducted by a tribunal in which one of its members was confronted with a challenge by the other party.[96]

131. Article 29 provides for the determination of challenges by the Center, which is empowered to act in accordance with its own internal rules. In this connection, the WIPO Arbitration Consultative Commission, according to its guide,[97] provides:

> opinions and advice to the WIPO Arbitration Center on non-routine issues in respect of which the WIPO Arbitration Rules require a decision to be taken by the Center in the course of the administration of an arbitration — such as the challenge, release or replacement of an arbitrator. . . . For this purpose, the Center constitutes, whenever required, ad hoc committees composed of three members of the Consultative Commission.

132. It is to be remembered that circumstances that give rise to a challenge to an arbitrator, may also give rise to an application to set aside an award, or an application to defeat the recognition and enforcement of an award.

Other Rules

133. Unlike *ad hoc* arbitration, it is a common and unsurprising theme amongst institutional arbitration rules for challenges to be addressed by the institution itself (rather than a national court, or the arbitrators themselves).[98] The procedure for such challenges varies little as between different sets of rules. For example, the ICC Rules

---

[95] Art. 11(3).

[96] SANDERS, *supra* note 28 at § 150.

[97] at 11.

[98] For a detailed survey of different challenge procedures, *see* Aldo Berlinguer, *Impartiality and Independence of Arbitrators in International Practice*, 6 AM. REV. INT'L ARB. 339 (1995).

provide in Article 11 that challenges are to be made by a party to the ICC Secretariat within 30 days "from receipt by that party of the notification of the appointment or confirmation of the arbitrator" or within 30 days "from the date when the party making the challenge was informed of the facts and circumstances on which the challenge is based if such date is subsequent to the receipt of such notification."

134. Article 10 of the LCIA Rules follows similar lines, but differs in one important respect. A 15-day time limit is imposed from "the formation of the Arbitral" or (if later) after a party becomes aware of any relevant circumstances to ground a challenge.[99] Unlike the WIPO and ICC time limits, under the LCIA Rules a challenge must be brought within a specified number of days from the appointment of the entire tribunal — not just the appointment of the particular arbitrator in question.

135. Therefore, in contrast to the LCIA Rule, under WIPO Article 25 an objection must be raised by a respondent before that party has appointed his own arbitrator, and by a claimant, before a chairman has been appointed. It may be that the WIPO (and ICC[100]) approach is preferable, given that it avoids a "wait-and-see" approach to challenges, and thereby minimizes delays and disruption in the constitution of the tribunal.

136. The categories of circumstances that may be potentially relevant to a challenge under the LCIA Rules are set out in Articles 10.1, 10.2 and 10.3. These are far broader than the equivalent WIPO Rule, although the same categories may be contemplated by Article 32.

137. Unlike the WIPO Rules, the new ICC Rules now expressly afford the arbitrator who has been challenged, as well as the other party or parties and any other members of the Arbitral Tribunal, an opportunity "to comment in writing within a suitable period of time," such comments to be "communicated to the parties and to the arbitrators."[101] The old ICC Rules did not provide that the comments of the arbitrator concerned would be disclosed to the parties or other arbitrators. It was thought that this had the significant advantage, as described by Stephen Bond:

> of allowing arbitrators to comment freely, without fear of revealing information relating to the inner workings of the Arbitral Tribunal or the attitude of the arbitrators toward the conduct of the challenging party or their fellow arbitrator.[102]

Whilst this remains the position under the WIPO procedure, the ICC Rule has now been changed, in the light of criticisms that the old procedure was harsh, and had something of a "star chamber" flavor (*i.e.* a denial of due process). Again as Bond comments:[103]

---

[99] Art. 10.4.

[100] *See similarly* Article 8 of the AAA INTERNATIONAL RULES.

[101] Art. 11(3).

[102] Stephen Bond, *The Constitution of the Arbitral Tribunal, in* THE NEW 1998 ICC RULES OF ARBITRATION, ICC INTERNATIONAL COURT OF ARBITRATION BULLETIN, SPECIAL SUPPLEMENT 24 (November 1997).

[103] *Id.*

It will have to be seen whether the advantage of transparency in the challenge procedure outweighs the risks of a lengthier challenge procedure, violation of the "secrets du délibéré" and frank comments giving rise to disharmony within the Arbitral Tribunal.

The WIPO procedure avoids all these risks.

138. According to Craig, Park & Paulsson,[104] in ICC arbitration only 9% of challenge procedures made after the appointment and confirmation of arbitrators succeed, whilst 72% of challenges made before an arbitrator has been confirmed by the ICC Court succeed. Whether or not different criteria may be applied by one institution at different stages of the arbitral process is an area that has given rise to debate.[105] On one view, the absence of a system of "confirmation" of arbitral appointments by the WIPO Center may have the effect of reducing the number of challenges in practice.

"Administrative" and "Final" Determinations by the Center

139. Interestingly, Article 29 of the WIPO Rules emphasizes that any decision taken by the Center with respect to the challenge of an arbitrator is "administrative" in nature, rather than judicial, and is "final," without the requirement that any reasons be given. On one view, it is extremely difficult to see how such a determination, which would be based on submissions by each side in accordance with Articles 25 and 26, could be characterized as anything other than judicial. However, just as the ICC Court of International Arbitration characterizes its determinations as both "administrative" and "final," the WIPO Center seeks to do the same, in order (at least in part) to avoid any form of review.[106]

Does the WIPO Center Have the Last Say?

140. It is to be noted that there may well be mandatory provisions of the law of the seat of an arbitration that permit parties to bypass the WIPO Center's ruling (and, equally, the ICC Court's or LCIA Court's ruling) and to submit the challenge to an ordinary court.[107] In France, it would appear that an arbitral institution such as the WIPO Center or ICC or LCIA Court could, according to its rules, finally decide on a challenge.[108] In the Netherlands, as well as all countries that have adopted the UNCITRAL Model Law, if a challenge is rejected by an arbitral institution such as the WIPO Center or the ICC or LCIA Court, an application may still be made to a local

---

[104] W. LAWRENCE CRAIG, WILLIAM W. PARK, & JAN PAULSSON, INTERNATIONAL CHAMBER OF COMMERCE ARBITRATION 216–17 (2d ed. 1990).

[105] *See, e.g.*, Berlinguer, *supra* note 98, at 359.

[106] For a discussion of the scope for interlocutory judicial review of ICC Court determinations, *see* Jan Paulsson, *Vicarious Hypochondria and Institutional Arbitration*, 6 ARB. INT'L 226, 237–44 (1990). *See also* Berlinguer, *supra* note 98, at 365 (a discussion of judicial review of institutional decisions). The French courts have ruled that the function of the ICC Court in this respect is "administrative" and therefore not within their judicial review procedures: *see* Trib. gr. inst. de Paris, October 22, 1984, and Paris, 1ere. Ch. A., May 15, 1985, 1985 REV.ARB. 141.

[107] *See* CRAIG, PARK & PAULSSON, *supra* note 104, at 218.

[108] *See* ICCA HANDBOOK II, Ch.III 2 (Derains).

court.[109] Section 24(2) of the English Arbitration Act limits the exercise of the powers of the English Court to remove an arbitrator as follows:

> If there is an arbitral or other institution or person vested by the parties with power to remove an arbitrator, the court shall not exercise its power of removal unless satisfied that the applicant has first exhausted any available recourse to that institution or person.

It is therefore implicit that the English Court would have power to determine a challenge notwithstanding the role of the WIPO Center. However, it is extremely unlikely that the Court would reverse any determination of the Center, being an institution empowered in this regard by the agreement of the parties.

141. Perhaps the clearest exception to this principle is ICSID arbitration, which is placed beyond the reach of national arbitration laws by the Washington Convention 1965.

Release from Appointment

Article 30
At the arbitrator's own request, an arbitrator may be released from appointment as arbitrator either with the consent of the parties or by the Center.

Article 31
Irrespective of any request by the arbitrator, the parties may jointly release the arbitrator from appointment as arbitrator. The parties shall promptly notify the Center of such release.

Article 32
At the request of a party or on its own motion, the Center may release an arbitrator from appointment as arbitrator if the arbitrator has become *de jure* or *de facto* unable to fulfill, or fails to fulfill, the duties of an arbitrator. In such a case, the parties shall be offered the opportunity to express their views thereon and the provisions of Articles 26 to 29 shall apply *mutatis mutandis*.

Commentary

Summary

142. Articles 30, 31 and 32 address the removal or withdrawal of arbitrators in circumstances other than a challenge by a party on the grounds of a lack of impartiality or independence (which is dealt with in Articles 24 to 29, as discussed above).

143. Under most modern systems of arbitration, an arbitral appointment once made is irrevocable, unless all parties agree to remove an arbitrator, or an arbitral or other institution has been vested by the parties with such a power (or, of course, a court

---

[109] Dutch CCProc., Art. 1035.

has such a power under a national law).[110] There are obvious reasons for such a rule (*i.e.* in order to make arbitration an effective and final form of dispute resolution). Equally, there may be many circumstances which justify the removal of an arbitrator for reasons other than a lack of impartiality or independence. Articles 30, 31 and 32 contemplate the following three types of case:

    i.   an arbitrator may himself wish to be released from his appointment;

    ii. all parties may wish the arbitrator to be released;

    iii. an arbitrator may become *de jure* or *de facto* unable to fulfill his duties.

Arbitrator's Own Request

144.   The first of these three categories may arise for a variety of reasons. For example, an arbitrator may be faced with an arbitration that has turned out very differently from that which was represented when he accepted his appointment. What may have appeared as a short case could evolve into a lengthy arbitration, such as to be beyond an arbitrator's available time. Alternatively, the parties may have agreed a procedure as between themselves that the arbitrator finds unacceptable, or impossible in the light of other commitments. Whilst the tribunal is to have the last say on the conduct of the arbitration under Article 38 of the WIPO Rules, a deadlock may still develop where all parties have a different view of the position from that of the tribunal. Further, an arbitrator may discover a conflict during the course of the proceedings which compromises him, and renders his continued participation improper or impossible as far as he is concerned.

145.   In the absence of a provision such as Article 30, it would be unclear whether or not an arbitrator could release himself, in the absence of an agreement between the parties or a challenge. As a matter of practical reality, of course, an arbitrator may resign — or in other words, simply refuse to act. The consequences of this, however, could be an action for breach of contract, and it is unlikely that this would be caught by the exclusion of liability in Article 77 of the WIPO Rules.[111] Whether or not an arbitrator can release himself from his appointment may be a question answered differently in different national systems, particularly in light of the debate as to the nature of an arbitral appointment, and whether this is to be characterized as true "contract," or something else.[112]

146.   By way of example of one approach to this issue, the English Arbitration Act 1996 implicitly acknowledges that, as a matter of practice, an arbitrator may resign whether entitled to do so or not. Accordingly, the Act addresses the *consequences* of such a resignation, rather than the entitlement to resign itself, and makes provision for, in effect, an arbitrator to be absolved of such consequences if the circumstances so justify:

---

[110] *See, e.g.*, Sections 23 and 24 of the English Arbitration Act 1996.

[111] Art. 77: "Except in respect of deliberate wrongdoing, the arbitrator or arbitrators, WIPO and the Center shall not be liable to a party for any act or omission in connection with the arbitration."

[112] As to this debate, see the discussion and references, *supra*, under Article 23.

(1)   The parties are free to agree with an arbitrator as to the consequences of his resignation as regards —
    (a)   his entitlement (if any) to fees or expenses, and
    (b)   any liability thereby incurred by him.

(2)   If or to the extent that there is no such agreement the following provisions apply.

(3)   An arbitrator who resigns his appointment may (upon notice to the parties) apply to the court —
    (a)   to grant him relief from any liability thereby incurred by him, and
    (b)   to make such order as it thinks fit with respect to his entitlement (if any) to fees or expenses or the repayment of any fees or expenses already paid.

(4)   If the court is satisfied that in all the circumstances it was reasonable for the arbitrator to resign, it may grant such relief as is mentioned in subsection (3)(a) on such terms as it thinks fit.[113]

147.   Insofar as Article 30 of the WIPO Rules provides a mechanism for an arbitrator to resign in the absence of the agreement of all parties, it remains entirely unclear whether or not that arbitrator will remain exposed in terms of an action for breach of contract, or the loss of any entitlement to fees. One might suppose that the Center would not "release" an arbitrator without substantial cause, and that this alone might suggest that no action for breach of contract will lie, but the prospect of an action by a dissatisfied party cannot be entirely discounted. This is particularly so if costs are thrown away as a consequence of the arbitrator's or the Center's action.

148.   It is to be noted that by imposing a requirement that an arbitrator's resignation be consented to by either all parties or the Center, Article 30 acts as a control on resignations by party-appointed arbitrators procured by recalcitrant parties. It is conceivable that a party might arrange for its appointed arbitrator to resign in order to stall the proceedings, or provide an opportunity to substitute another arbitrator. This may even be a risk from a very early stage, if a party wishes to change his appointee having discovered the identity of the other party's appointee. As long as no such resignation is allowed in the absence of the other party's or the Center's consent, this risk would appear to be minimal. However, as stated above, if an arbitrator does simply resign without complying with Article 30, there may be little that can be done as a matter of practical reality. This scenario appears to fall outside of the safeguards in Article 33 (replacement of arbitrators).

Agreement that Arbitrator Be Released

149.   The second category is addressed in Articles 30 and 31, and is uncontroversial. Arbitration is a consensual mechanism — it is grounded upon and depends upon an agreement between the parties. The parties therefore remain free to amend their agreement, or indeed abandon their agreement and conclude a new one. Accordingly, the parties are free to agree to remove an arbitrator. This would remain the position, even if the WIPO Rules had not expressly acknowledged so.

---

[113] English Arbitration Act 1996, Sec. 25.

Inability to Fulfill Duties as Arbitrator

150. The third category is extremely important, and in effect widens the ambit of the challenge procedure set out in Articles 24 to 29 to catch cases other than a lack of impartiality or independence. If the parties agree that an arbitrator is no longer fit or able to conduct the proceedings, this would be addressed under Article 31. However, in such circumstances the arbitrator in question has no guarantee of a reasoned decision, or indeed an opportunity to voluntarily withdraw.

151. The reference in Article 32 to the provisions of Articles 26 to 29 applying *"mutatis mutandis"* to challenges under this rule excludes the time limit in Article 25. There does not therefore appear to be any specific time limit on objections here, which might allow a party to adopt a "wait-and-see" approach to a possible objection. One control on this, however, is likely to be the waiver provision in Article 58 of the Rules, on the basis that the tribunal's proper conduct of the arbitration constitutes a requirement of the Rules, such that any transgression by any arbitrator must be the subject of a timely objection.[114]

152. In common with most other rules, the references to *de jure* and *de facto* inability to act remain undefined. *De jure* inability is usually taken to refer to a loss of a legal capacity to act as an arbitrator or to fulfill an arbitrator's duties. *De facto* inability, in contrast, normally refers to a physical inability. Any narrow or technical definition, however, is unnecessary. The requirements for the proper conduct of the arbitration and the duties of the arbitrators are either set out in or are implicit in the WIPO Rules themselves. Any inability to comply with these requirements might qualify for the purposes of Article 32. A failure to fulfill agreed upon qualifications is also likely to be a ground for challenge under this Article.

153. On any view, the mechanism provided by Article 32 is likely to be one of last resort. It is unlikely that a party will make an application unless it is confident that an arbitrator is really unable to fulfill his duties — given that an unsuccessful application is bound to have an adverse effect on that party's standing in the arbitration thereafter. Equally, it is unlikely, save in the most extreme of cases, that the Center would release an arbitrator in the absence of a request by a party to do so — although this power is conferred on it by this Article.[115] It is to be noted that, unlike certain other institutional rules, the procedure in Article 32 does not allow for a request to be made by another arbitrator.

---

[114] Art. 58: "A party which knows that any provision of, or requirement under, these Rules, or any direction given by the Tribunal, has not been complied with, and yet proceeds with the arbitration without promptly recording an objection to such non-compliance, shall be deemed to have waived its right to object."

[115] A similar power is conferred on the ICC Court by Article 12(2) of the ICC Rules. Stephen Bond, *supra* note 102, has commented on this provision as follows:

This allows the ICC Court to act on information which the parties themselves may not possess, such as the long-term illness of an arbitrator or a violation of the ICC Rules that the Court alone becomes aware of or, as in one case, where the dissension between two arbitrators becomes so great that they threaten each other with criminal proceedings. It is a procedure rarely used, but constitutes an additional safeguard for the parties and for the integrity of ICC arbitration.

Other Rules

154.   Similar mechanisms exist in most arbitration rules. For example, Article 10 of the LCIA Rules stipulates a series of circumstances that might qualify for the revocation of an arbitrator's authority, including an arbitrator's death, serious illness, refusal to act, inability or unfitness to act,[116] acting in deliberate violation of the arbitration agreement or not acting fairly and impartially as between the parties, or not conducting or participating in the arbitration proceedings with reasonable diligence, avoiding unnecessary delay or expense.[117] Unlike the WIPO Rule, with respect to the first category (Article 10.1) the LCIA Court is empowered to revoke the arbitrator's authority at the request of the remaining arbitrators. This would allow, for example, some members of a tribunal to report obstruction by an arbitrator — something that may only occur during the tribunal's deliberations, at a stage that is no longer apparent to the parties.[118]

Replacement of an Arbitrator

Article 33

(a)   Whenever necessary, a substitute arbitrator shall be appointed pursuant to the procedure provided for in Articles 15 to 19 that was applicable to the appointment of the arbitrator being replaced.

(b)   In the event that an arbitrator appointed by a party has either been successfully challenged on grounds which were known or should have been known to that party at the time of appointment, or has been released from appointment as arbitrator in accordance with Article 32, the Center shall have the discretion not to permit that party to make a new appointment. If it chooses to exercise this discretion, the Center shall make the substitute appointment.

(c)   Pending the replacement, the arbitral proceedings shall be suspended, unless otherwise agreed by the parties.

Article 34

Whenever a substitute arbitrator is appointed, the Tribunal shall, having regard to any observations of the parties, determine in its sole discretion whether all or part of any prior hearings are to be repeated.

Commentary

Summary

155.   Once a tribunal has been appointed, a vacancy may subsequently arise for a variety of reasons. As set out in the introduction to this section, the efficient filling of a

---

[116] Art. 10.1.

[117] Art. 10.2.

[118] *See also* Articles 11(1) and 12(1), 12(2) and 12(3) of the ICC RULES, and Articles 8 to 10 of the AAA INTERNATIONAL RULES.

vacancy is as important as the initial constitution of the tribunal itself. However, rather than simply reproducing the same provisions that were used for the initial appointment of the arbitrators, any mechanism for the replacement of arbitrators must serve a further purpose: insofar as it is possible, it must deter parties and arbitrators from attempting to disrupt the arbitration by creating vacancies in the first place, or appointing non-independent arbitrators.

156. Article 33 serves both purposes. Article 33(a) refers back to the appointment provisions in Articles 15 to 19, on the basis that an arbitrator is to be appointed in the same manner as the arbitrator to be replaced, and further that the justifications behind Articles 15 to 19 apply equally to an initial as well as a substitute appointment.

157. If this were the only provision, it would be open for a party to force or encourage its appointed arbitrator to resign or otherwise be removed, in order to appoint another (perhaps more sympathetic) arbitrator. Accordingly, Article 33(b) empowers the Center to make a substitute appointment instead of a party in the following situations:

i. A party-appointed arbitrator has been successfully challenged on grounds that were known or should have been known to the party that appointed him, at the time of the appointment.

ii. A party-appointed arbitrator has been released from appointment pursuant to Article 32.

158. To this end, a party may not get, in effect, a second appointment if the first appointment itself was tainted, or if the chosen arbitrator proved unable or perhaps unwilling to act. This constitutes something of an incentive for a party to exercise its right of choice with care.

159. The Center's power of appointment here is, however, discretionary. There are bound to be many instances in which it would be appropriate for a party to have a second appointment. An arbitrator may well fall foul of Section 32 with no hint of bad faith on the part of the appointing party, where, for example, he falls ill, or suffers from some other incapacity that could not have been predicted or catered for.

160. Articles 33(c) and 34 are uncontroversial. A tribunal with a vacancy is no longer a fully constituted panel in accordance with the parties' agreement — unless it is saved by Article 35. As such, it may not properly continue until the vacancy has been filled, unless the parties otherwise agree. Equally, once the tribunal has been reconstituted, there will arise a practical matter: the extent to which the prior proceedings must be repeated, or the tribunal must retrace its steps.[119] By Article 34, this latter consideration is one for the sole discretion of the reconstituted tribunal itself — whether the replaced arbitrator is the chairman or not.[120] One can only assume that

---

[119] For a general discussion of this issue, including guidelines, *see* REDFERN & HUNTER, *supra* note 5, at 235–36.

[120] *Compare* Article 14 of the UNCITRAL Arbitration Rules, which imports an inflexible rule for sole and presiding arbitrators:

if a sole arbitrator has been replaced, all prior hearings would be repeated (although, by the terms of Article 34, the matter remains in the discretion of the new arbitrator).

Dutco?

161. As pointed out in relation to Article 19 above, a literal reading of the *Dutco*[121] decision, might lead one to query the validity of any appointment by the Center — even an appointment under Article 33(b). On one view, the exercise of the Center's discretion under this Article to fill a vacancy has the potential to offend the rule of public policy emphasized in that case: one party would have an arbitrator imposed on it, in circumstances in which the other party retains a choice (and this would be pursuant to an agreement entered into before the dispute had arisen). Again as pointed out above, it is likely that the Center would only exercise its discretion in circumstances in which the appointing party was at fault, and further that the *Dutco* reasoning would not extend to such cases. This is yet to be tested.

A Gap in Article 33(b)

162. One scenario is not catered for in Article 33(b). As pointed out above,[122] it remains possible, at least in theory, for a party to procure the resignation of an arbitrator under Article 30. It is conceivable, if unlikely, that an arbitrator's resignation might be engineered in such a way as to stall the proceedings, or even provide an opportunity to substitute another arbitrator (or simply to enable one party to change his appointee having discovered the identity of the other party's appointee). To an extent, this may have been adequately addressed by the requirement in Article 30 that a resignation be consented to by the Center or the other parties. If no such consent is given, an arbitrator will not be treated as having vacated the tribunal, such that no replacement need be made. If the arbitrator in question refuses to participate, the tribunal may still continue as a truncated tribunal under Article 35 of the Rules.

163. The fact that no reference is made to Article 30 in Article 33(b), however, means that the Center will never have a discretion to make an appointment itself, where an arbitrator has resigned. As such, there is no direct disincentive to a party attempting to procure a resignation of his appointed arbitrator.

Other Rules

164. Following from the previous observation on Article 33(b), it is to be noted that the corresponding provision in both the LCIA Rules and the ICC Rules are far wider, giving the LCIA Court and the ICC Court respectively a discretion to fill a vacancy itself in all cases — including a resignation:

> In the event that the LCIA Court determines that any nominee is not suitable or independent or impartial or if an appointed arbitrator is to be replaced for any reason,

---

If under articles 11–13 the sole or presiding arbitrator is replaced, any hearings held previously shall be repeated; if any other arbitrator is replaced, such prior hearings may be repeated at the discretion of the arbitral tribunal.
[121] *Supra* note 50.
[122] *See* discussion under Article 30, above.

the LCIA Court shall have a complete discretion to decide whether or not to follow the original nominating process.[123]

When an arbitrator is to be replaced, the Court has discretion to decide whether or not to follow the original nominating process.[124]

165. In contrast, the AAA International Rules do not provide for appointment by the institution itself:

If an arbitrator withdraws after a challenge, or the administrator sustains the challenge, or the administrator determines that there are sufficient reasons to accept the resignation of an arbitrator, or an arbitrator dies, a substitute arbitrator shall be appointed pursuant to the provisions of Article 6, unless the parties otherwise agree.[125]

Truncated Tribunal

Article 35

(a) **If an arbitrator on a three-person Tribunal, though duly notified and without good cause, fails to participate in the work of the Tribunal, the two other arbitrators shall, unless a party has made an application under Article 32, have the power in their sole discretion to continue the arbitration and to make any award, order or other decision, notwithstanding the failure of the third arbitrator to participate. In determining whether to continue the arbitration or to render any award, order or other decision without the participation of an arbitrator, the two other arbitrators shall take into account the stage of the arbitration, the reason, if any, expressed by the third arbitrator for such non-participation, and such other matters as they consider appropriate in the circumstances of the case.**

(b) **In the event that the two other arbitrators determine not to continue the arbitration without the participation of a third arbitrator, the Center shall, on proof satisfactory to it of the failure of the arbitrator to participate in the work of the Tribunal, declare the office vacant, and a substitute arbitrator shall be appointed by the Center in the exercise of the discretion defined in Article 33, unless the parties agree otherwise.**

Commentary

Summary

166. Once a tribunal has been constituted, there remains a chance that at a subsequent stage it may cease to function properly. In particular, an arbitrator may

---

[123] LCIA RULES, Art. 11.1. *See also* Article 11.2, which imposes a time limit on a party's opportunity to re-nominate.

[124] ICC RULES, Art. 12(4). *See also* Article 12(5), which, in certain circumstances, gives the ICC Court a discretion not to fill a vacancy, if such arises subsequent to the closing of the proceedings.

[125] Art. 10.

become incapacitated, compromised, conflicted or may die. Alternatively an arbitrator may become obstructive, reluctant to conduct the arbitration, or refuse to conduct it properly. In such a case, the parties have recourse against the arbitrator under Articles 30–32. However, the consequences for the parties of removing an arbitrator may be very serious indeed — it may cause delay, and may necessitate the repeat of prior proceedings. Indeed, an arbitrator may become obstructive or refuse to perform his duties at a very late stage in the proceedings. As Redfern & Hunter point out, delay, both in locating and appointing a replacement and in allowing the replacement to familiarize himself or herself with the case, is inevitable — and this situation may be all the more complex if the arbitrator refuses to participate or resigns after the conclusion of all hearings, and at the stage of deliberations.[126]

167.   Article 35 provides an alternative remedy, in the case of three-person tribunals. Where an arbitrator "fails to participate in the work of the Tribunal," in certain circumstances the remaining two arbitrators may continue the functions of the tribunal themselves, including rendering final awards. Article 35 applies to both party-appointed arbitrators and chairmen. The remaining two arbitrators will only be so empowered, however, where:

    i.   an arbitrator "fails to participate in the work of the Tribunal"

    ii.   this failure is "without good cause"

    iii.   the arbitrator in question has been duly notified (presumably by the remaining two arbitrators)

    iv.   no party has made an application under Article 32 to the Center to have an arbitrator released from his appointment.

168.   On the one hand, this is an extremely useful provision, in that it protects the arbitral process from possible disruption by one member of the tribunal, and allows the process to be completed without delay or extra cost. Indeed, in the absence of such a provision (or agreement between the parties), it is unlikely under most legal systems that such a so-called "truncated" tribunal would have any authority to continue the proceedings itself.

169.   On the other hand, it is to be noted that this provision gives arbitrators a very significant power — in effect to exclude one of their number. As a matter of theory, the inclusion of Article 35 in the WIPO Rules, and the choice of these Rules by the parties, means that the parties have contracted into such a possibility. However, the result of this mechanism is that a party could be bound by an award that has been rendered by a tribunal which does not include an arbitrator of its choice. Further, under Article 35, the question whether an arbitrator has "failed to participate in the work of the Tribunal" appears to be in the other two arbitrators' sole discretion. The potential for a split amongst the arbitrators to escalate into the exclusion of one arbitrator cannot, therefore, be wholly excluded. What constitutes a failure to participate remains unclear and open to interpretation.

---

[126] *See* REDFERN & HUNTER, *supra* note 5, at 234–36.

170.   Whether or not the remaining two arbitrators do in fact decide to continue the proceedings themselves rather than to allow for an arbitrator's replacement, is left up to the arbitrators themselves by the Rules, although Article 35 sets out a series of factors upon which this decision is to be based:

i.   the stage of the arbitration;

ii.   the reason, if any, expressed by the third arbitrator for his non-participation;

iii.   "such other matters as they consider appropriate in the circumstances of the case."

Given that the power granted by Article 35 to continue the proceedings lies in the remaining two arbitrators' "sole discretion," these factors present nothing more than a general guide. The only way to challenge the decision by the remaining two arbitrators to exclude the third arbitrator would appear to be for a party (or the Center) to challenge the remaining arbitrators under Articles 24 to 32.

171.   Under Article 35(2), the Center may declare an arbitral office "vacant," where:

i.   the other two arbitrators have not decided to continue alone, under Article 35(1), and

ii.   the Center is furnished with proof of the third arbitrator's failure to participate.

It is to be noted that this, in effect, gives the other two arbitrators absolute control: in the event that they do exercise their discretion to act alone under Article 35(1), the question of the Center being convinced of the third arbitrator's refusal or failure to participate does not arise at all.

172.   Once an arbitral office has been declared "vacant" under Article 35(2), a replacement will be appointed in accordance with Article 33 (unless the parties otherwise agree) — *i.e.* the Center will decide whether a replacement arbitrator is to be appointed by a party, or by the Center itself, depending on the circumstances and nature of the original arbitrator's delinqueny.

Signing the Award

173.   It has been noted that obstruction by one arbitrator may take place at a very late stage. It is not unknown, in particular, for one arbitrator to refuse to sign a final award. Under some systems, the signature of all arbitrators is a prerequisite to a valid and enforceable award, thereby strengthening the position of an obstructive arbitrator. Article 62(d) of the WIPO Rules avoids this position (in accordance with the possibility of a truncated tribunal):

> The award shall be signed by the arbitrator or arbitrators. The signature of the award by a majority of the arbitrators, or, in the case of Article 61, second sentence, by the presiding arbitrator, shall be sufficient. Where an arbitrator fails to sign, the award shall state the reason for the absence of the signature.

The Problem of Truncated Tribunals and Other Rules

174.   There have been many documented cases in which arbitral tribunals have continued proceedings and rendered awards without the participation of one of their members. Dr. M.A. Solhchi, in an article in 1993,[127] notes examples going back as far as 1799 (the *Jay Treaty Cases*). Many other, more recent examples have been analyzed in a wealth of sources.[128]

175.   Whilst the issue has been alive for many years, it is only recently that national legislatures and arbitral institutions have begun to make specific provision for it. Article 35 of the WIPO Rules is virtually identical to Article 11 of the AAA International Arbitration Rules, and also Section 30 of the Bermuda International Conciliation and Arbitration Act 1993.[129] Similar provisions have now been included

---

[127] Dr. M.A. Solhchi, *The Validity of Truncated Tribunal Proceedings and Awards*, 9 ARB. INT'L 303 (1993).

[128] *See, e.g.*, Reports of Schwebel and Böckstiegel, *in* PREVENTING DELAY OR DISRUPTION OF ARBITRATION, ICCA Congress Series No. 5 (Albert Jan van den Berg, gen. ed., 1991), pp. 241–47, 270–274; French-Mexican Claims Commission Cases, *discussed in* A. H. FELLER, THE MEXICAN CLAIMS COMMISSION 70–77 (1935); *Advisory Opinion of the International Court of Justice* of 1950 (in the Interpretation of the Peace Treaties with Bulgaria, Hungary and Romania) I.C.J.Reports 65 (1950); STEPHEN M. SCHWEBEL, INTERNATIONAL ARBITRATION: THREE SALIENT PROBLEMS 144–296 (1987); Order of May 17, 1985, in Sedco, Inc. v. National Iranian Oil Co. Case No. 129, 8 Iran-US C.T.R. 34; Uiterwiyk Corp. v. Islamic Republic of Iran, Award No. 375-381-1 (July 6, 1988), 19 Iran-US C.T.R. 107, 116; the many other citations in Dr. Solhchi's article, *supra. See also*, on a related theme, Stephen M. Schwebel, *The Majority Vote of an International Arbitral Tribunal*, 2 AM. REV. INT'L ARB. 402 (1991).

[129] Section 30 of the Bermuda International Conciliation and Arbitration Act 1993:

Failure of an arbitrator to participate in proceedings

30. (1)   Any resignation by an arbitrator shall be addressed to the arbitral tribunal and shall not be effective unless the arbitral tribunal determines that there are sufficient reasons to accept the resignation, and if the arbitral tribunal so determines the resignation becomes effective on the date designated by the arbitral tribunal.

(2)   If an arbitrator on a three-person or five-person arbitral tribunal fails to participate in the arbitration, the other arbitrators have, unless the parties otherwise agree, the power in their sole discretion, to continue the arbitration and to make any decision, ruling or award, notwithstanding the non-participation of that arbitrator.

(3)   In determining whether to continue the arbitration or to render any decision, ruling, or award without the participation of an arbitrator, the other arbitrators shall take into account the stage of the arbitration, the reason, if any, expressed by the arbitrator for his non-participation and such other matters as they consider appropriate in the circumstances of the case.

(4)   In the event of the other arbitrators determining not to continue the arbitration without the non-participating arbitrator, the arbitral tribunal shall declare the office vacant and a substitute arbitrator shall be appointed pursuant to Article 15 of the Model Law, unless the parties agree on a different method of appointment.

See also, Art. 660 of the Iranian Civil Procedure Code:

Where one of the arbiters after he has been informed, does not appear in the session held for proceeding or consultations, or he appears but refuses to give an award, the award given by the majority of votes shall be valid even if unanimity of votes has been a condition in the agreement for arbitration.

in the new ICC and LCIA Rules, although the way in which the problem has been addressed is different.

176. In the course of the revision of the ICC Rules, it was recognized that the ICC has had its own experience with truncated tribunals. The lesson of this experience was clear: insofar as institutional rules do not provide for the non-participation of an arbitrator, any award rendered by a truncated tribunal will be open to challenge. As one example, in one ICC case (under the old rules) involving a Yugoslav Claimant against a German Defendant, the Yugoslav party-nominated arbitrator refused, at the last minute, to continue to participate on the panel. The Swiss Chairman and the German party-nominated arbitrator decided to proceed on their own, and rendered an award. That award was then challenged before the Swiss Federal Supreme Court, the challenge being successful because the prior ICC Rules did not provide for the authority of a truncated tribunal. In such a situation, there is no option for the parties but to commence a new arbitration — which may well entail a repetition of all proceedings to date. Had a provision for truncated tribunals been included in the parties' agreement in that case, there would have been no objection to the final award.

177. Two important policy questions arise in connection with this issue:

i. Should it be left to the remaining arbitrators to decide whether they should function as a truncated tribunal or should this decision be with the parties, or the Center or equivalent arbitral institution? One can imagine (albeit extreme) circumstances in which it might be quite wrong for the remaining arbitrators to be given this exclusive discretion. For example, in a situation where the defaulting arbitrator's non-participation is a direct result of the other two arbitrators, or the presiding arbitrator alone — whether as a result of some conspiracy, friction, or a simple failure to take all views and availability properly into account.

ii. Should a truncated tribunal be allowed at any stage of the proceedings, or should it be restricted to a stage subsequent to the closing of the proceedings, when replacing an arbitrator might be that much more impractical?

178. Article 35 of the WIPO Rules is wide-ranging on both issues — the remaining two arbitrators have an absolute discretion as to whether or not to proceed alone, and they may exercise this discretion at any stage of the proceedings — from (in theory) the very start.

179. In contrast, both the new ICC and LCIA rules are far narrower. The equivalent ICC rule provides as follows:

> Subsequent to the closing of the proceedings, instead of replacing an arbitrator who has died or been removed by the Court pursuant to Articles 12(1) and 12(2), the Court may decide, when it considers it appropriate, that the remaining arbitrators shall continue the arbitration. In making such determination, the Court shall take into account the views of the remaining arbitrators and of the parties and such other matters that it considers appropriate in the circumstances.[130]

---

[130] ICC RULES, Art. 12(5).

Unlike the WIPO Rule, this provision only allows for a truncated tribunal if the ICC Court — not the remaining arbitrators — so decides, and only at a stage "subsequent to the closing of the proceedings." This reflects the view that an arbitral tribunal must at all costs reflect all parties' choice, such that any failure on the part of an arbitrator to participate during the course of an arbitration, must be corrected by that arbitrator's replacement wherever possible and practical. Equally, the ICC provision avoids any risk that the remaining two arbitrators might act in concert against the third.

180.   The equivalent provision in the LCIA Rules[131] is as follows:

> 12.1   If any arbitrator on a three-member Arbitral Tribunal refuses or persistently fails to participate in its deliberations, the two other arbitrators shall have the power, upon their written notice of such refusal or failure to the LCIA Court, the parties and the third arbitrator, to continue the arbitration (including the making of any decision, ruling or award), notwithstanding the absence of the third arbitrator.
>
> 12.2   In determining whether to continue the arbitration, the two other arbitrators shall take into account the stage of the arbitration, any explanation made by the third arbitrator for his non-participation and such other matters as they consider appropriate in the circumstances of the case. The reasons for such determination shall be stated in any award, order or other decision made by the two arbitrators without the participation of the third arbitrator.
>
> 12.3   In the event that the two other arbitrators determine at any time not to continue the arbitration without the participation of the third arbitrator missing from their deliberations, the two arbitrators shall notify in writing the parties and the LCIA Court of such determination; and in the event, the two arbitrators or any party may refer the matter to the LCIA Court for the revocation of that third arbitrator's appointment and his replacement under Article 10.

181.   Unlike the WIPO Rule, this provision also has built-in safeguards. It is broader than the equivalent ICC Rule in that (on one reading[132]) it is not restricted to a stage after the closing of proceedings. It is narrower than the WIPO Rule, however, in that it requires notice to be given to the LCIA Court, as well as the other parties and the third arbitrator.

Should a Vacancy be Filled?

182.   If a vacancy is to be filled, a key issue will be the extent to which the arbitral tribunal must, as put by Redfern & Hunter, "retrace its steps."[133] Little difficulty arises if the oral hearings have not yet begun, given that a replacement arbitrator need only catch up on reading, and review all procedural directions to date. If, on the other hand, a vacancy arises and is filled during the course of the hearing, or even after the completion of a hearing, serious difficulties arise. Redfern & Hunter suggest that if a transcript is available, it may be sufficient for the replacement

---

[131] LCIA RULES, Art. 12 "Majority Power to Continue Proceedings."

[132] The Article is somewhat unclear, in that it refers to a refusal or failure to participate in "deliberations."

[133] REDFERN & HUNTER, *supra* note 5, at 235–36.

arbitrator to read the transcript and thereby bring himself or herself up to date (and, if as a result of such reading, it appears appropriate to recall a witness, this may be done). This is not an easy situation to resolve, and, ultimately, no clear guidelines can be laid down. It would certainly not be unreasonable for a replacement arbitrator, or indeed a party, to insist upon a re-run of all proceedings to date. Indeed, the UNCITRAL Arbitration Rules provide that where a sole arbitrator or the presiding arbitrator is replaced:

> any hearings held previously shall be repeated.[134]

In contrast, the UNCITRAL Arbitration Rules provide that if any other arbitrator is replaced, any hearing held previously:

> may be repeated at the discretion of the arbitral tribunal.[135]

183. Whatever their scope, it may well be that truncated tribunal clauses are to be welcomed in that they constitute a powerful disincentive to any arbitrator or party to attempt any obstructive tactics.

Pleas as to the Jurisdiction of the Tribunal

Article 36

(a) **The Tribunal shall have the power to hear and determine objections to its own jurisdiction, including any objections with respect to form, existence, validity or scope of the Arbitration Agreement examined pursuant to Article 59(b).**

(b) **The Tribunal shall have the power to determine the existence or validity of any contract of which the Arbitration Agreement forms part or to which it relates.**

(c) **A plea that the Tribunal does not have jurisdiction shall be raised not later than in the Statement of Defense or, with respect to a counterclaim or a set-off, the Statement of Defense thereto, failing which any such plea shall be barred in the subsequent arbitral proceedings or before any court. A plea that the Tribunal is exceeding the scope of its authority shall be raised as soon as the matter alleged to be beyond the scope of its authority is raised during the arbitral proceedings. The Tribunal may, in either case, admit a later plea if it considers the delay justified.**

(d) **The Tribunal may rule on a plea referred to in paragraph (c) as a preliminary question or, in its sole discretion, decide on such a plea in the final award.**

(e) **A plea that the Tribunal lacks jurisdiction shall not preclude the Center from administering the arbitration.**

---

[134] Art. 14.

[135] *Id.*

Commentary

Summary

184.   A very significant feature of modern practice in international arbitration is the challenge to jurisdiction. Most respondents to an arbitral claim will consider the viability of challenging the tribunal's jurisdiction, as a further weapon alongside a defense to the merits of the claim. Indeed, there is often something of a correlation between the strength of a party's defense, and the likelihood of challenge to jurisdiction. The need for an effective mechanism to flush out challenges, to determine such challenges quickly, and to deter recalcitrant parties from using jurisdiction as a vehicle of delay is now universally recognized, and most systems cater specifically for this.

185.   There are many different types of jurisdictional challenge. Redfern & Hunter[136] distinguish between "Partial" and "Total" challenges. On this analysis, a partial challenge exists where it is asserted, for example, that certain claims which have been brought before a tribunal do not properly come within its jurisdiction, where for example preconditions to arbitration have yet to be satisfied, or a claim lies beyond the scope of an arbitration clause. In contrast, a total challenge exists where a party attacks the validity or existence of the arbitration agreement itself. It might be argued, for example, that no arbitration agreement was ever concluded; that the agreement is invalid; that consent to arbitration has been vitiated; that the arbitration agreement is unenforceable; that the tribunal has not been properly constituted; or that the subject matter of the reference is not arbitrable. The variety of challenge is a function of lawyers' creativity.

186.   It has long been recognized that in order to prevent a recalcitrant party deploying a jurisdictional challenge in such a way as to derail an arbitration, there should be a mechanism for such challenges to be addressed within the arbitral regime (in order to prevent speculative or tactical trips to local courts), and that parties should be forced to voice any such challenges as soon as they arise, in order that they are not held back for tactical reasons, only to be raised once costs have been incurred, or prospects in the arbitration have changed.

187.   Article 36 of the WIPO Rules follows a familiar format, and provides a regime for the efficient resolution of jurisdiction challenges. Articles 36(a) and (b) embody two distinct but related concepts:

    i.   *"Kompetenz-kompetenz"* (or *"Compétence de la compétence"*):
        This doctrine refers to a tribunal's ability to rule on its own competence, including objections raised as to the existence, validity or scope of the arbitration agreement pursuant to which the tribunal was appointed.[137]

    ii. Separability, or the autonomy of the arbitration clause:
        Under this principle, an arbitration clause contained in a contract is treated as a separate and autonomous contract, the validity of which is

---

[136] REDFERN & HUNTER, *supra* note 5, at 272–74.

[137] For a general discussion of this doctrine, *see* id. at 276–80.

not necessarily tied to that of the main contract. This legal fiction has been developed in order to allow arbitrators to continue to act in cases in which the main contract is impugned (where otherwise the same attack might render ineffective the arbitration clause itself).[138] As Sanders has put it, under this doctrine: "arbitrators who hold the main contract null and void, do not thereby saw off the branch on which they are sitting."[139]

188. Article 36(c) contains time limits within which any objections as to jurisdiction must be raised (subject to an overriding discretion of the tribunal):

i. a "total" challenge must be raised not later than in the Statement of Defense;

ii. a "partial" challenge or a plea that the tribunal is about to exceed the scope of its authority must be raised as soon as the issue arises.

189. Article 36(d), again in line with most modern arbitral rules, and international practice, allows for jurisdiction challenges to be addressed either in a separate award on jurisdiction, or in a final award along with the merits. It is generally recognized that if at all possible, it is preferable for jurisdiction challenges to be determined as separate preliminary issues, given that money spent on fighting the merits of a claim will be money entirely lost if in fact the tribunal lacks jurisdiction.[140] There are those cases, however, where the issues raised by a jurisdiction challenge are closely related or overlap with issues raised by the merits, such that a preferable course is to address the two together at the same time in one award.

190. Article 36(e) isolates the Center from any jurisdiction challenge, thereby allowing it to continue to administer the arbitration, notwithstanding an assertion that the arbitration agreement is invalid or unenforceable, or indeed any other jurisdiction challenge.

191. As noted, these provisions follow a familiar format, and are relatively uncontroversial.[141]

The Form of a Jurisdictional Ruling

192. Article 36(d) does not impose any particular form on the tribunal's jurisdictional ruling.[142] Under the terms of the rule, it would appear that a tribunal could rule on a jurisdiction issue in an order or direction, or some other form short of

---

[138] *See generally* Carl Svernlov, *What Isn't, Ain't: The Current Status of the Doctrine of Separability,* 8(4) J. INT'L ARB. 37 (1991); REDFERN & HUNTER *supra* note 5 at 275; Pieter Sanders, *L'autonomie de la clause compromissoire, in* HOMMAGE À FRÉDÉRIC EISEMANN, (ICC Publ. No. 321) (Paris 1978) 31–43; STEPHEN M. SCHWEBEL, THREE SALIENT PROBLEMS, *supra* note 128, at 1–60; CRAIG, PARK & PAULSSON, *supra* note 104, at 65–72.

[139] SANDERS, INTERNATIONAL ENCYCLOPAEDIA OF COMPARATIVE LAW, *supra* note 28, at 58.

[140] Hence Article 21(4) of the UNCITRAL Rules: "In general, the arbitral tribunal should rule on a plea concerning its jurisdiction as a preliminary question. However, the arbitral tribunal may proceed with the arbitration and rule on such a plea in their final award."

[141] *Compare, e.g.,* LCIA RULES Art. 23; ICC RULES Art. 6(4).

[142] *Compare* ICSID RULE 41(5), which requires that a ruling on jurisdiction be in the form of an award.

an award. Under many systems, this would have the effect of denying a party the right to both challenge and enforce the determination. Whether or not this is in fact the intended result must be considered by each tribunal, bearing in mind the generally accepted principle that an arbitral tribunal may be able to rule on its own jurisdiction in the first instance — but not finally, the final say being with a national court.[143]

The Limits of Separability

193.   Separability as a doctrine has developed over time into what may appear as an all-encompassing principle, applying in all cases in which the validity of the main contract is questioned, whether it is argued that a contract is voidable or void *ab initio*.[144] It would be wrong, however, to assume that an arbitration clause will necessarily survive any attack on the contract. Certain kinds of attack may infect the arbitration clause itself, although the outer limits of separability are still to be precisely defined. For example, Sanders has argued that the doctrine cannot be invoked:

> when the question is raised whether the parties ever concluded a contract (with arbitral clause) at all. When the main contract is non-existent, this applies as well to the arbitral clause embedded in the disputable contract. Unless arbitrators are especially authorized to decide on the existence of the main contract, a distinction has to be made between invalidity and existence.[145]

194.   Similarly, there is authority to suggest that certain types of illegality may render a contract — including an arbitration clause — void or unenforceable.[146] Further, it is to be noted that not all jurisdictions accept the doctrine at all.[147] Whilst the WIPO Rules set out a very broad ambit for this doctrine in Article 35, the potential impact of applicable national law must, as always, be borne in mind.

---

[143] *See generally, Final Report on Interim and Partial Awards*, ICC INT'L CT. ARB. BULL. (Dec. 1990).

[144] *See, e.g.*, the English Court of Appeal decision in Harbour Assurance Co (UK) v. Kansa General International Insurance Co, [1993] 1 Lloyd's Rep 455, in which, for the first time, the doctrine was held to extend to *ab initio* illegality.

[145] SANDERS, INTERNATIONAL ENCYCLOPAEDIA OF COMPARATIVE LAW, *supra* note 28, at 63.

[146] *See, e.g.*, Soleimany v. Soleimany, [1998] 3 W.L.R. 811, a recent decision of the English Court of Appeal in which it was stated that certain types of illegal arrangement may not be arbitrable, as, for a colorful example, a contract between highwaymen relating to their illegal activity. In such cases, the doctrine of separability will not save an arbitration clause.

[147] As one of several examples, on several occasions the Supreme Court of Turkey has denied the principle of separability, holding that only the courts and not arbitrators have the power to adjudge the validity of the main contract, the arbitral clause being regarded as an integral component of the main contract — ICCA HANDBOOK: TURKEY NATIONAL REPORT (KORAL), ch.II.4. For a useful analysis, including a survey of several jurisdictions, see the decision of the Bermuda Court of Appeal in *Sojuznefteexport v. JOC Oil, reported in* 15 Y.B. COM. ARB. 354, 373–85 (1990).

COMMENCEMENT OF THE ARBITRATION AND CONDUCT OF THE ARBITRATION

Articles 6 to 13
Articles 37 and 38
Articles 41 to 45
Articles 47 to 51
Articles 53 to 58

Kathleen Paisley*

I. GENERAL

In choosing between competing arbitral fora for deciding an actual or potential dispute, an important issue to be considered, and one which greatly impacts the parties during the course of the arbitration (for better or worse), is the procedure that will be applied to actually decide the dispute under the relevant rules. Although there are increasing similarities among the various arbitration rules used for international disputes, especially since the recent amendments to many of these rules, differences remain.

In comparing procedures, it is useful to consider the following basic issues: (i) How involved is the arbitral institution in the procedure? (ii) How detailed are the procedures established by the rules? (iii) How flexible is the arbitrator in applying the procedure? (iv) How predictable is the procedure for the parties and the arbitrator? (v) How much control do the parties have over the procedure?

One way of thinking about international arbitration procedures is to consider the role of the arbitral institution during the process. On the one hand are *ad hoc* procedures (such as those under the UNCITRAL Rules) where there is no institution involved, on the other are the more hands-on procedures where the arbitral institution retains a certain degree of control over the arbitral process throughout the proceedings (of the rules most commonly considered for international arbitrations, the ICC Rules could be seen to fall in this category).

* Kathleen Paisley is a partner in the Brussels office of Morrison & Foerster LLP, where her practice focuses on international dispute resolution, particularly in the intellectual property field, including litigation, arbitration and mediation; formerly legal assistant to the arbitrators appointed by the United States at the Iran-United States Claims Tribunal; law clerk to the Honorable Gilbert S. Merritt, United States Court of Appeals for the Sixth Circuit; J.D., Yale Law School (1986); M.B.A., Florida Atlantic University (1984); B.S., Florida Sate University (1981). Ms. Paisley is a member of the bars of the State of New York and the District of Columbia and has successfully completed the C.P.A. examination in the State of Florida. The author thanks Claire Smith Yamauchi, legal assistant in the Brussels office of Morrison & Foerster LLP, for her invaluable assistance in preparing this article.

The procedures established by the WIPO Rules exemplify a philosophy that is grounded in principles of party and arbitrator control over the process. As the WIPO Arbitration Center (the "Center") is a relatively recent creation, its rules reflect the teaching of the rules established by successful modern arbitration institutions, and hence in many respects can be seen to reflect the best of those rules.

The WIPO Rules establish a detailed procedural framework to guide the process, while at the same time allowing significant flexibility to the Tribunal and the parties. Under the WIPO Rules, both the Center and the parties grant the Tribunal primary responsibility over the case at an early stage in the process. Under the WIPO Rules, the Rules govern in the first instance, unless they conflict with a mandatory provision of the law applicable to the arbitration.

Subject to this limitation, the Tribunal may conduct the arbitration in such manner as it considers appropriate provided the parties are treated equally and are given a fair opportunity to present their cases. Thus, in determining the procedure that applies to a WIPO arbitration one must look first to any mandatory provisions of the law applicable to the arbitration, second to the procedure put forth in the WIPO Rules themselves, and third, to the extent it does not conflict with either the applicable law or the Rules, to any requirements imposed by the Tribunal.

Analyzing arbitral procedures solely in terms of their similarities and/or differences with the common or civil-law systems of justice or in terms of their adversarial or inquisitorial nature has correctly been criticized as being overly simplistic.[1] However, there is increasingly a "standard" procedure for conducting an international arbitration,[2] which combines aspects from the common-law tradition, like the right to a hearing, with those that are more typical in the civil-law tradition, like the exchange of extensive written memorials prior to any hearing.[3]

The core of the procedure generally followed in international arbitrations, which is exemplified by the WIPO Rules, can be broadly outlined as follows:
1. The sequential exchange and submission of statements of claim and defense, accompanied to a greater or lesser degree by supporting documentation and/or proffers of same.

---

[1] See Pierre Mayer, *Comparative Analysis of Power of Arbitrators to Determine Procedures in Civil and Common Law Systems, in* ICCA CONGRESS SERIES NO. 7, PLANNING EFFICIENT ARBITRATION PROCEEDINGS; THE LAW APPLICABLE IN INTERNATIONAL ARBITRATION [hereinafter ICCA CONGRESS SERIES NO. 7] 25 (Albert Jan van den Berg ed., 1996) [hereinafter Mayer].

[2] See Paul D. Friedland, *Combining Civil Law and Common Law Elements in the Presentation of Evidence in International Commercial Arbitration*, 12(9) INT'L ARB. REP. 25 (September, 1997) [hereinafter Friedland].

[3] See Mayer, *supra* note 1, at 34 ("The confrontation in the international area of varying types of procedures has encouraged the adoption of hybrid procedures, which borrow the best aspects of each system and combine them, often quite harmoniously."); *see also* Christian Borris, *Common Law and Civil Law: Fundamental Differences and their Impact on Arbitration*, 60(2) THE JOURNAL OF THE CHARTERED INSTITUTE OF ARBITRATORS 78–85 (1994).

2. The holding of some form of preparatory conference either in person or by teleconference to organize the procedure going forward.

3. Further exchange of memorials and witness statements, the extent of which varies according to the complexity of the case.

4. Hearings at which witnesses and/or experts are presented for questioning by the arbitrators, opposing counsel and counsel for the party presenting them, and where counsel for each side presents its case.[4]

The remainder of this article will discuss the rules establishing the procedure to be followed in an arbitration under the WIPO Rules in detail and will compare that procedure to those adopted by some of the other major arbitration centers considered for international disputes, namely the ICC, LCIA, and AAA (international rules), and the principal rules used for *ad hoc* arbitrations, the UNCITRAL rules.[5]

II. COMMENCEMENT OF THE ARBITRATION

Request for Arbitration

Article 6
The Claimant shall transmit the Request for Arbitration to the Center and to the Respondent.

Article 7
The date of commencement of the arbitration shall be the date on which the Request for Arbitration is received by the Center.

Article 8
The Center shall inform the Claimant and the Respondent of the receipt by it of the Request for Arbitration and of the date of the commencement of the arbitration.

Article 9
The Request for Arbitration shall contain:
(i)   a demand that the dispute be referred to arbitration under the WIPO Arbitration Rules;
(ii) the names, addresses, and telephone, telex, telefax or other communication references of the parties and of the representative of the Claimant;
(iii) a copy of the Arbitration Agreement and, if applicable, any separate choice-of-law clause;

---

[4] *See* Friedland, *supra* note 2, at 25 (substituting document production for the holding of a preparatory conference as the second step in the process); *see also* Gind Lörcher, *Improving Procedures for Oral and Written Testimony*, in ICCA CONFERENCE SERIES NO. 7, *supra* note 1 at 145, 146–47 (formulating similar basic procedures) [hereinafter Lörcher].

[5] A comprehensive discussion of the procedural issues addressed herein is found in JACK COE, INTERNATIONAL COMMERCIAL ARBITRATION: AMERICAN PRINCIPLES AND PRACTICE IN A GLOBAL CONTEXT, Chapters 9–10 (1997) [hereinafter COE].

(iv) **a brief description of the nature and circumstances of the dispute, including an indication of the rights and property involved and the nature of any technology involved;**

(v) **a statement of the relief sought and an indication, to the extent possible, of any amount claimed;**

(vi) **any appointment that is required by, or observations that the Claimant considers useful in connection with, Articles 14 to 20.**

Article 10
The Request for Arbitration may also be accompanied by the Statement of Claim referred to in Article 41.

Answer to the Request

Article 11
Within 30 days from the date on which the Respondent receives the Request for Arbitration from the Claimant, the Respondent shall address to the Center and to the Claimant an Answer to the Request which shall contain comments on any of the elements in the Request for Arbitration and may include indications of any counterclaim or setoff.

Article 12
If the Claimant has filed a Statement of Claim with the Request for Arbitration pursuant to Article 10, the Answer to the Request may also be accompanied by the Statement of Defense referred to in Article 42.

Commentary on Articles 6–12

The section of the rules dealing with the commencement of the arbitration establishes the process for the initiation of the arbitration by the Claimant and the initial response by the Respondent.

The arbitration is commenced by the Claimant transmitting a Request for Arbitration (the "Request") to the Center and to the Respondent. Unlike the ICC and LCIA Rules, for example, where the Request is sent first only to the ICC Secretariat and the LCIA Court, respectively, the WIPO Rules, like the AAA Rules, provide that the Request should be sent simultaneously to the Center and the Respondent. (ICC, Art. 4; LCIA, Art. 1; AAA, Art. 2.)

To avoid the possibility of disputes as to the date the arbitration was officially commenced, the WIPO Rules provide expressly that the arbitration shall be deemed to commence on the date the Request is received by the Center, rather than the date it is received by the Respondent. The Center informs the parties that it has received the Request and of the date of the official commencement of the arbitration.

Notwithstanding that the arbitration is officially deemed to commence on the date the Request is received by the Center, the deadline for the Respondent to submit its

Answer to the Request is geared to the Respondent's actual receipt of the Request, not the date of commencement of the arbitration. The rules do not explain the reason for this, but it is presumably out of fairness to the Respondent as this is the date the Respondent is actually placed in a position to respond. However, the date of the commencement of the arbitration remains important as it can trigger the Center's involvement in the appointment process. (WIPO, Art. 15, 16.)

The Request is required to contain the following information:

1. Demand for arbitration under the WIPO Rules;
2. Contact information for both parties;
3. Contact information for the Claimant's representative;
4. A copy of the arbitration agreement and any separate choice-of-law clause;
5. A brief description of the dispute;
6. A statement of the relief sought and, if possible, the amount claimed; and
7. Name of arbitrator appointed by Claimant and any other observations by the Claimant about the appointment of the arbitral panel that it considers useful.

With respect to the merits of the dispute, at a minimum the Request must contain a brief description of the dispute, which should include a description of the rights and property, as well as any technology, involved in the dispute. Moreover, the Request must also contain a statement of the relief sought and, if possible, the amount claimed. Among other things, these provisions are intended to assist the Center to the extent it is involved in the appointment of the members of the Tribunal, as at the time the arbitrators are selected it is most likely that the Statement of Claim describing the dispute in detail will not yet have been filed.

Concerning the date of filing of the Statement of Claim, the rules foresee two possible times for the Claimant to file its detailed Statement of Claim and supporting evidence. Under Article 10 of the WIPO Rules, the Claimant has the option of filing its Statement of Claim together with the Request, in which case the Respondent may, but need not, file its Statement of Defense together with its Answer to the Request (the "Answer"). The only other rules surveyed that provide the Claimant with the option, but do not require it, to present its Statement of Claim together with the Request are the UNCITRAL Rules, which in turn do not provide for the Respondent to present an Answer in addition to its Statement of Defense. (UNCITRAL, Art. 3.) Thus the procedure foreseen by the WIPO Rules is in this respect unique among the rules surveyed.

Most commonly, at the outset of the dispute the Claimant would be expected to file only its Request, including the requisite brief description of the nature of the dispute, and thereafter to file its detailed Statement of Claim under the rule established by Article 41, which provides that the Statement of Claim shall be submitted within 30 days of the Claimant's receipt from the Center of notification of the establishment of the Tribunal.

Given the time it would be expected to take to establish the Tribunal, this would generally give the Claimant a number of additional months to complete its Statement of Claim, without otherwise slowing down the process. Moreover, as discussed below, regardless of when the Statement of Claim is filed the Respondent is not required to respond to the Statement of Claim until later in the process, which would normally create a disincentive for the Claimant to file its Statement of Claim with the Request.

With respect to the timing of input from the parties about the appointment of arbitrators, Article 9 of the WIPO Rules requires the Claimant to include in its Request any arbitral appointment that it is obligated to make under the Rules and to provide any comments on issues related to the appointment of the Tribunal. The Respondent then has 30 days after the receipt of the Request for Arbitration to make any arbitral appointment it is required to make and may include in its Answer any comments related to the appointment of the panel, including responses to the comments made by the Claimant in its Request.

It is noteworthy that the Rules do not provide simply that the Respondent's appointment of its arbitrator shall be included in the Answer, although the timing for the filing of the arbitrator appointment and the Answer is the same. Article 17 requires the Respondent to appoint its arbitrator within *30 days* from receipt of the Request, and Article 11 provides that the Respondent shall file its Answer to the Request, including any comments on the issues raised by the Claimant in its Request, also *within 30 days* from receipt of the Request for Arbitration. Therefore, it would have seemed simpler to require the Respondent to include its arbitral appointment in the Answer. The decision to leave the Respondent the option of filing its appointment separately from its Answer presumably was in the hope that the Respondent might in certain cases file its arbitrator appointment before its Answer (or visa versa), which could speed up the process.

As already mentioned, the Respondent has 30 days from the date of receipt of the Request to submit its Answer to the Center and to the Claimant. The Rules state generally that the Answer shall include the Respondent's views on the issues raised in the Request. Although the Respondent may elect to raise any counterclaims or setoff in the Answer, these issues are more typically left to the Statement of Defense. Moreover, as mentioned above, if the Claimant has filed its Statement of Claim together with its Request, the Respondent may elect to, but is not required to, file its Statement of Defense together with its Answer. It would be surprising were many Respondents to take this option due to the time constraints that typically drive the process.

Representation

Article 13

(a) The parties may be represented by persons of their choice, irrespective of, in particular, nationality or professional qualification. The names, addresses and telephone, telex, telefax or other communication references of representatives shall be communicated to the Center, the other party and, after its establishment, the Tribunal.

(b) Each party shall ensure that its representatives have sufficient time available to enable the arbitration to proceed expeditiously.

(c) The parties may also be assisted by persons of their choice.

Commentary on Article 13

Article 13 of the WIPO Rules deals in detail with representation of the parties. Article 13(a) confirms the principle, which has long been accepted in international arbitration, that the parties may be represented by anyone of their choosing. The WIPO Rules state expressly that neither nationality nor professional qualification shall act to limit whom the parties may choose to represent them.

An important benefit of international arbitration is that it allows the parties to use representatives of their choice, regardless where the case is heard.[6] This approach allows parties to select counsel based upon criteria unrelated to local bar requirements and the like. It thus puts parties in a better position to coordinate their selection of counsel on an international basis, without having to use different lawyers for each jurisdiction where a dispute may arise. This can result in important economies of scale, eliminating the need for a party to re-educate counsel each time a dispute arises in a new country.

Neither the ICC, LCIA or AAA Rules have provisions addressing this issue with the same degree of specificity as the WIPO Rules. The closest provision to Article 13(a) of the WIPO Rules is Article 18 of the LCIA Rules, which provides that a party may be represented by "legal practitioners *or any other* representatives" (emphasis added). This makes clear that the representative need not be a lawyer, but makes no specific mention of nationality or other issues.

As is the case with the other rules discussed, Article 13(a) is limited by the mandatory principles of the law applicable to the arbitration. Most countries that have addressed this issue in their arbitration acts have indicated expressly that a party may be represented by anyone of his or her choice.[7] However, it remains important to be attuned to this issue as it is not clear in some countries how far this freedom extends.[8]

Article 13(b) places the responsibility affirmatively on the parties to ensure that their representatives are able to devote the necessary time to the arbitration. This obligation may be implied in other arbitral rules, but the inclusion of an express provision to this effect is unique to the WIPO Rules. It is intended to discourage the parties (usually the Respondent) from later relying unduly on the schedules of their lawyers as an excuse for delay and to provide the Tribunal and the Center with an express basis in the rules to address such delays.

---

[6] *See, e.g.,* ALAN REDFERN & MARTIN HUNTER, LAW AND PRACTICE OF INTERNATIONAL COMMERCIAL ARBITRATION 282 (2d ed. 1991) [hereinafter REDFERN & HUNTER]; W. LAWRENCE CRAIG, ET AL, INTERNATIONAL CHAMBER OF COMMERCE ARBITRATION, Section 16.05 (1989) [hereinafter CRAIG].

[7] *See, e.g.,* CRAIG, supra note 6, at Section 16.05 (citing the Australian International Arbitration Amendment Act (1989) and other laws).

[8] *See id.*

The ICC Rules deal with party representation only in the context of the hearing. Article 21 provides that parties may appear at hearings in person or through duly authorized representatives and that they may also be assisted by advisors. Outside of the hearing context, the ICC Rules do not address party representation, presumably because it is assumed that parties may be represented as they see fit.

The AAA Rules discuss representation in Article 12. Article 12 states only that any party may be represented in the arbitration, and that if a party chooses to be represented the other parties and the administrator must be informed of the representative's communication details. Once the Tribunal has been established, Article 12 allows direct written communication between parties or their representatives and the Tribunal, without going through or providing copies to the administrator.

The UNCITRAL Rules provide that the parties may be represented by "persons of their choice." Like the WIPO and AAA Rules, the UNCITRAL Rules contain an express provision requiring the parties to communicate the contact details for their representatives to the other party. The UNCITRAL Rules are unique, however, in requiring the notice further to indicate whether the representative is acting as a representative or for assistance purposes only.

Article 18 of the LCIA Rules is the only set of rules surveyed to maintain an express provision granting the Tribunal the authority to request from any party proof of authority granted to its representative(s), although this is not required. In crafting the UNICTRAL Rules, the drafters rejected a provision that would have required the submission of a power of attorney and this issue has been hotly debated in the context of the Iran-United States Claims Tribunal.[9]

III. CONDUCT OF THE ARBITRATION; TRANSMISSION OF THE FILE TO THE TRIBUNAL

Article 37
The Center shall transmit the file to each arbitrator as soon as the arbitrator is appointed.

Commentary on Article 37

Article 37 provides that the Center shall send the file to each arbitrator upon his or her appointment, rather than waiting to send the file until after the "Tribunal" has been appointed. This means that in a three-arbitrator panel the arbitrator appointed by the Claimant typically receives the file first, followed by the arbitrator appointed by the Respondent, and finally the chairperson.

---

[9] *See, e.g.,* Dissenting Opinion of Howard M. Holtzmann in Flexi-van Leasing, Inc. and the Government of the Islamic Republic of Iran, Award No. 259-36-1 (Nov. 5, 1986) (contesting the Tribunal's decision to order the claimant to present a power of attorney); *see also* JACOMIJN VAN HOF, COMMENTARY ON THE UNCITRAL ARBITRATION RULES: THE APPLICATION BY THE IRAN-UNITED STATES CLAIMS TRIBUNAL 31–35 (1991) [hereinafter VAN HOF].

At the stage of transfer to the party-appointed arbitrators, depending on the timing of the appointment, the file generally will consist only of the Request for Arbitration, which in certain cases may be accompanied by the Claimant's Statement of Claim, and perhaps the Respondent's Answer, which in turn may be accompanied by the Respondent's Statement of Defense.

This means that in a three-panel arbitration the arbitrators will receive the file, limited as it may be at this stage, at different times in the process. As previously discussed, Article 14(a) of the rules creates a presumption in favor of a sole arbitrator, unless the parties have expressly agreed otherwise in their arbitration agreement. However, under Article 14(b), the Center is granted the discretion, unless the arbitration agreement provides otherwise, to decide that the circumstances warrant a panel of three arbitrators.[10]

As discussed in another section, in cases where the Center decides that a panel of three arbitrators should be appointed or the parties have agreed on a panel of three arbitrators, and the parties have not agreed upon a procedure for their appointment, the Claimant is given fifteen days after receiving notice from the Center of a three-person panel to appoint its arbitrator, the Respondent has thirty days from receiving the notice to appoint its arbitrator, and the two arbitrators appointed by the parties then have 20 days to appoint the presiding arbitrator and, failing agreement, the Center shall appoint the presiding arbitrator pursuant to the list system put forth in Article 19, which generally would take another 30–45 days.

Under this procedure, assuming all goes well, the arbitrator appointed by the Claimant would receive the file a few weeks in advance of the arbitrator appointed by the Respondent, and it may take another two months and perhaps longer before the presiding arbitrator is appointed and hence receives the file.

Of the rules surveyed, the only other rules expressly to mention the transmission of the file are the ICC Rules.[11] Article 13 of the ICC Rules provides that the Secretariat shall transmit the file to the Arbitral Tribunal as soon as it has been constituted, provided the advance on costs has been paid. The AAA and LCIA Rules make no mention of transmission of the file.

Comparing the ICC and WIPO approaches, in the context of a three-arbitrator panel the ICC Secretariat would seem to wait until the entire Tribunal has been appointed before transmitting the file to any member, whereas under the WIPO system, as discussed above, the file goes to each arbitrator as soon as appointed. However, in cases with a sole arbitrator, which is the default choice under both the ICC and WIPO Rules, this difference in approach has no impact, as in these cases the "Tribunal" and the arbitrator are appointed at the same time (as there is only one).

---

[10] If the parties have opted for expedited arbitration, the appointment of a sole arbitrator is dictated by the rules, unless the parties have expressly agreed otherwise.

[11] The Dutch NAI Rules of the Netherlands Arbitration Institute, which also are often used in international arbitration and were one of the building blocks of the WIPO Rules, provide for the transmission of the file to the arbitrator as soon as s/he is appointed.

In the context of three-arbitrator panels, there are those who would favor waiting until the entire panel is appointed to transmit the file simultaneously to all arbitrators out of a sense of equality among the panel (as is provided for in the ICC Rules). However, the approach selected by the WIPO Rules, which transfers the file at the first possible moment to each individual arbitrator, is in keeping with the basic principle of Tribunal control that forms one of the bases of the WIPO procedure.

General Powers of the Tribunal

Article 38

(a)   **Subject to Article 3, the Tribunal may conduct the arbitration in such manner as it considers appropriate.**

(b)   **In all cases, the Tribunal shall ensure that the parties are treated with equality and that each party is given a fair opportunity to present its case.**

(c)   **The Tribunal shall ensure that the arbitral procedure takes place with due expedition. It may, at the request of a party or on its own motion, extend in exceptional cases a period of time fixed by these Rules, by itself or agreed to by the parties. In urgent cases, such an extension may be granted by the presiding arbitrator alone.**

Commentary on Article 38

Article 38 deals with the general powers with which the Tribunal is endowed. Article 38(a), which is based on Article 15(1) of the UNCITRAL Rules and similar provisions found in the other rules surveyed, lies at the center of the WIPO procedure.[12]

Article 38(a) gives broad powers to the Tribunal, allowing it to use its discretion as to how the arbitration is conducted, unless otherwise dictated by Article 3. As described previously, Article 3 provides that the WIPO Rules shall govern the arbitration, unless the law applicable to the arbitration provides otherwise and the parties are not permitted to derogate from such provision.

The Tribunal's discretion is further tempered by Articles 38(b) and 38(c). Article 38(b) states that in all cases the parties shall be treated with equality and that each party must have a fair opportunity to present its case. Article 38(c) furthermore charges the Tribunal with ensuring that the arbitration takes place with due expedition.

The question that is regularly raised, however, is how these various provisions of the WIPO Rules should be read together. In practice, Article 38 can be seen as establishing a hierarchy for the conduct of the arbitration, as follows:

---

[12] Article 15(1) of the UNCITRAL Rules has been referred to as the "backbone of the Rules" and the "fundamental principle governing the proceedings." *See, respectively,* VAN HOF, supra note 9, at 102; Jamison M. Selby & David P. Stewart, *Practical Aspects of Arbitrating Claims before the Iran-United States Claims Tribunal,* 18 INT'L LAW. 211, 219 (1984).

First, the Tribunal shall apply the WIPO Rules to the extent they contain a provision on a point. The rules form part of the parties' agreement to arbitrate, and the parties' free will to determine the procedure applicable to the decision of their case has repeatedly been described as lying at "the very heart of arbitration."[13]

Second, and as an exception to the basic principle that the WIPO Rules govern, in the case where the law applicable to the arbitration contradicts a WIPO Rule *and* the provision of the arbitration law is of mandatory application and cannot be deviated from by the agreement of the parties, the Tribunal shall apply that mandatory provision of the applicable law to ensure the enforceability of the award.

This provision clarifies the oft-debated issue of when the Tribunal is required to look to the procedural rules of the law applicable to the arbitration to guide its choice of procedure.[14] The WIPO Rules expressly adopt the minimalist view that the only time the Tribunal is required to look to national procedural law is when to do otherwise would conflict with a mandatory provision of that law.[15] This is based on the assumption that the parties desire the award to be enforceable and would have derogated from the WIPO Rules they selected to ensure that enforceability, but otherwise they have opted out of national procedural regimes. If the relevant arbitration law permits derogation from the law, then the WIPO Rules apply by agreement of the parties.[16]

Third, the Tribunal is granted the discretion to conduct the arbitration as it deems appropriate, provided, however, that the parties must at all times be treated with equality and be given an opportunity to present their case. Therefore, the Tribunal has full discretion to interpret or supplement the WIPO Rules, subject only to the provision that this discretion does not extend to treating the parties unequally or to depriving them of the right to be heard.

Fourth, the Tribunal is charged generally with ensuring the arbitration proceeds expeditiously. This responsibility tempers the Tribunal's discretion where the exercise of that discretion would lead unnecessarily to delay. However, the rules provide expressly that the Tribunal may extend any time period fixed by the rules, whether requested by a party or desired by the Tribunal, with or without the agreement of the parties. If pressure of time so requires, the presiding arbitrator alone may grant a time extension.

An important issue that is not specifically addressed by the WIPO Rules nor by the other rules surveyed with the exception of the LCIA Rules, is the extent to which the parties may agree to derogate from the WIPO Rules. The WIPO Rules leave open the extent to which the parties may agree to derogate from the procedure put forth in

---

[13] *See, e.g.,* Mayer, *supra* note 1, at 27.

[14] *See, e.g.,* CRAIG, *supra* note 6, at Chapter 16 (addressing this issue under the ICC Rules).

[15] *See* Mayer, *supra* note 1, at 27.

[16] The WIPO Rules follow standard practice with respect to the law applicable to the arbitration. Article 59(b) provides that the law applicable to the arbitration shall be the law of the place of arbitration, unless the parties have agreed otherwise and such agreement is permitted by the law of the place of arbitration.

the rules. The WIPO Rules specifically refer to certain instances where if the parties agree to a certain procedure the Tribunal and the Center *must* follow their wishes — for example, the parties may agree that no amendments to the claims and/or counterclaims are allowed and the Tribunal is obligated by the Rules to respect the parties' wishes.[17]

But what about where the Rules are silent — may the parties dictate procedure to the Tribunal? For example, Article 43(b) provides that the Tribunal may, in its discretion, allow or require written statements in addition to the Statement of Claim and Statement of Defense. However, the WIPO Rules do not expressly address whether, if the parties jointly agree to a schedule of memorials, the Tribunal is obligated to respect those wishes.

Whether one believes that arbitration is primarily a matter of contract or rather whether arbitration has its own status above the contractual nature of the relationship, the notion of party autonomy jointly to frame the procedure under which their dispute is arbitrated is a fundamental principle of arbitration.[18] The UNCITRAL Model Law provides that an award may be set aside if "the arbitral procedure was not in accordance with the agreement of the parties" and the New York Convention provides a similar ground as a basis for refusal of recognition or enforcement of an award.[19] In what circumstances would it be consistent with these principles for a Tribunal to refuse to comply with a procedure agreed upon by the parties?

The LCIA Rules are the only of the rules surveyed to expressly address this issue. They adopt the view that not only are the parties allowed jointly to agree as to the conduct of the arbitral proceedings, they are encouraged to do so, provided the procedure selected by the parties at all times is consistent with the Tribunal's general duties. Similar to the other rules surveyed, the general duties of the Tribunal are defined in Article 14 to include the duty to act fairly and impartially to all parties, giving each a reasonable opportunity of putting its case and dealing with that of its opponent, and to "adopt procedures suitable to the circumstances of the arbitration, *avoiding unnecessary delay or expense,* so as to provide a fair and efficient means for the final resolution of the parties' dispute." (emphasis added) Subject to an agreement

---

[17] Some have taken the view under the equivalent provision of the UNICITRAL Rules that the Tribunal is only required to apply those provisions of the rules that expressly state that they are of mandatory application, and that with respect to other provisions of the rules the Tribunal has the discretion whether to apply the rules. However, given that the parties have agreed to have their dispute governed by the particular set of rules and that Article 3 of the WIPO Rules states expressly that "these Rules shall be deemed to form part of [the] Arbitration Agreement" and "these Rules shall govern the arbitration," the better interpretation is that, unless the parties have expressly agreed to change a provision of the rules, the Tribunal is bound by the rules. This is provided for more expressly in Article 15 of the ICC Rules, which states that "the proceedings . . . shall be governed by these Rules, and, where these rules are silent, by any rules which the parties may agree, or failing them, the Article Tribunal may agree upon." Thus, the Tribunal's discretion to agree on procedures under the ICC Rules is limited to those cases where the rules are silent.

[18] *See* REDFERN & HUNTER, *supra* note 6.

[19] Model Law, Arts. 34(2)(a)(iv), 36(1)(a)(iv); New York Convention, Art. V.1(d).

between the parties otherwise, the Tribunal is granted the "widest discretion to discharge its duties" allowed under the law applicable to the arbitration, as in WIPO Article 38(a).

Of these, the most difficult to apply in practice against the wishes of the parties is the duty to ensure the arbitral proceedings take place without "unnecessary delay and expense." Assume, for example, that the parties to a reasonably straightforward dispute over a license agreement agree to exchange three rounds of sequential memorials and to extend the time limits to 180 days for each memorial. Most would view this schedule of memorials as creating "undue delay and expense" and hence to agree to the schedule arguably would conflict with one of the Tribunal's basic duties, yet it has been mutually agreed to by the parties.

In practice, what would generally happen is that the Tribunal would endeavor to convince the parties to shorten the schedule of memorials to something more reasonable. If that fails, the Tribunal may ask the relevant administering authority for assistance in convincing the parties to shorten the schedule. However, if the parties both remained steadfast, many Tribunals would tend to obey the parties' wishes so as not to call into question the validity of the award. One experienced arbitrator has suggested that to avoid any limitations on the Tribunal's powers to establish the procedures as it sees fit, one solution is for the Tribunal to ask the parties as one of its first orders of business to agree to the Tribunal's broad authority to set procedure.[20]

Another provision of the LCIA Rules that is unique in comparison with the other rules surveyed is Article 22, which lists a number of "additional powers" that the Tribunal may exercise unless the parties have decided otherwise in writing, which as described above they are encouraged to do by Article 14 of the LCIA Rules. These additional powers may be exercised by the Tribunal on its own motion or on the motion of one of the parties, after giving everyone an opportunity to be heard. They are as follows:

(a) to allow any party, upon such terms (as to costs and otherwise) as it shall determine, to amend any claim, counterclaim, defense and reply;

(b) to extend or abbreviate any time-limit provided by the Arbitration Agreement or these Rules for the conduct of the arbitration or by the Arbitral Tribunal's own orders;

(c) to conduct such enquiries as may appear to the Arbitral Tribunal to be necessary or expedient, including whether and to what extent the Arbitral Tribunal should itself take the initiative in identifying the issues and ascertaining the relevant facts and the law(s) or rules of law applicable to the arbitration, the merits of the parties' dispute and the Arbitration Agreement;

(d) to order any party to make any property, site or thing under its control and relating to the subject matter of the arbitration available for inspection by the

---

[20] *See* Hans Smit, *Roles of the Arbitral Tribunal in Civil-Law and Common-Law Systems with Respect to Presentation of Evidence, in* ICCA SERIES No. 7, *supra* note 1 at 161, 167 [hereinafter Smit].

Arbitral Tribunal, any other party, its expert or any expert to the Arbitral Tribunal;

(e) to order any party to produce to the Arbitral Tribunal, and to the other parties for inspection, and to supply copies of, any documents or classes of documents in their possession, custody or power which the Arbitral Tribunal determines to be relevant;

(f) to decide whether or not to apply any strict rules of evidence (or any other rules) as to the admissibility, relevance or weight of any material tendered by a party on any matter of fact or expert opinion; and to determine the time, manner and form in which such material should be exchanged between the parties and presented to the Arbitral Tribunal;

(g) to order the correction of any contract between the parties or the Arbitration Agreement, but only to the extent required to rectify any mistake which the Arbitral Tribunal determines to be common to the parties and then only if and to the extent to which the law(s) or rules of law applicable to the contract or Arbitration Agreement permit such correction; and

(h) to allow, only upon the application of a party, one or more third persons to be joined in the arbitration as a party provided any such third person and the applicant party have consented thereto in writing, and thereafter to make a single final award, or separate awards, in respect of all parties so implicated in the arbitration.

Many of these powers, such as the power to take evidence, to extend time limits and to permit the amendment of claims, are typically dealt with in the WIPO Rules and other arbitration rules. However, others of the powers listed in Article 22 of the LCIA Rules may in certain arbitration rules be subsumed within the Tribunal's general powers provided for by provisions such as Article 38 of the WIPO Rules. For example, the WIPO Rules do not deal expressly with the additional powers listed under items (c), (g) and (h).

Each approach has its benefits. By encouraging the parties to mold their own procedure and by providing a list of additional powers that the parties can decide whether to grant the arbitrators, the LCIA Rules are perhaps more likely to result in party-driven procedure. The list provided in Article 22 gives the parties a practical basis, not provided expressly in the other rules, on which to consider whether they desire the Tribunal to have certain powers and if not, to restrict them. Moreover, by providing such a list in the rules themselves and expressly giving the parties the power to restrict these additional powers if they so desire, the arbitrators may feel more comfortable exercising these powers in that the parties may be considered more expressly to have agreed to them.

The benefit of the WIPO system that does not contain such a list of additional powers is that it does not risk omitting a power that the Tribunal may later find important to its function. Although the list of additional powers provided for in the LCIA Rules is not exhaustive and Article 14 of the LCIA Rules expressly provides that the arbitrators have the "widest possible discretion" to conduct the arbitration, under a list system the Tribunal may in practice be more hesitant to imply a power that is not listed, than they would be under a system with no list.

All the rules surveyed contain provisions like Article 38 of the WIPO Rules dealing with the powers of the Tribunal. Of the rules surveyed, the AAA Rules most closely resemble the WIPO Rules with respect to the powers of the Tribunal. Article 16(1) of the AAA Rules gives the Tribunal the power to "conduct the arbitration in whatever manner it considers appropriate." It also provides for equal treatment of the parties, and gives each party the right to be heard and a "fair opportunity to present its case." The AAA Rules furthermore require the Tribunal to "conduct the proceedings with a view to expediting the resolution of the dispute," as in WIPO Rule Article 38(c).

Article 15(1) of the UNCITRAL Rules is also very similar to the WIPO Rule, with two exceptions. First, the UNCITRAL Rule does not explicitly make the Tribunal's discretion to conduct the arbitration subject to mandatory principles of the applicable law. However, the Tribunal's obligation to comply with mandatory provisions of law can be implied from its general duty to issue an enforceable award. Furthermore, the UNCITRAL Rules contain no provision placing the Tribunal under the affirmative duty to ensure the arbitration occurs expeditiously. Although this too can be assumed from the Tribunal's general duties, this omission may be of more practical consequence.

Although the ICC Rules are the only of the rules surveyed that do not speak of the Tribunal's general power to conduct the arbitration as it considers appropriate, this should be inferred from the reference in Article 20 to establishing the facts "by all appropriate means." Article 15(2) of the ICC Rules, moreover, requires the Tribunal to "act fairly and impartially and ensure that each party has a reasonable opportunity to present its case." In comparison to the WIPO and AAA Rules on this subject, the ICC Rule is a bit more flexible as it does not require the parties to be treated "equally," but rather places the burden on the Tribunal to act fairly and impartially.[21] Timely conduct of the arbitration is referred to in ICC Article 20, "Establishing the Facts of the Case," which requires the Tribunal to "proceed within as short a time as possible to establish the facts of the case."

IV. PRESENTATION OF WRITTEN SUBMISSIONS

Statement of Claim

Article 41

(a) Unless the Statement of Claim accompanied the Request for Arbitration, the Claimant shall, within 30 days after receipt of notification from

---

[21] The initial drafts of the UNCITRAL Rules required the parties to be treated with "absolute equality," but this was changed in favor of the present text out of concern that what might be equal is not always fair. *See* VAN HOF, *supra* note 9, at 102.

the Center of the establishment of the Tribunal, communicate its Statement of Claim to the Respondent and to the Tribunal.

(b)   The Statement of Claim shall contain a comprehensive statement of the facts and legal arguments supporting the claim, including a statement of the relief sought.

(c)   The Statement of Claim shall, to as large an extent as possible, be accompanied by the documentary evidence upon which the Claimant relies, together with a schedule of such documents. Where the documentary evidence is especially voluminous, the Claimant may add a reference to further documents it is prepared to submit.

Statement of Defense

Article 42

(a)   The Respondent shall, within 30 days after receipt of the Statement of Claim or within 30 days after receipt of notification from the Center of the establishment of the Tribunal, whichever occurs later, communicate its Statement of Defense to the Claimant and to the Tribunal.

(b)   The Statement of Defense shall reply to the particulars of the Statement of Claim required pursuant to Article 41(b). The Statement of Defense shall be accompanied by the corresponding documentary evidence described in Article 41(c).

(c)   Any counterclaim or setoff by the Respondent shall be made or asserted in the Statement of Defense or, in exceptional circumstances, at a later stage in the arbitral proceedings if so determined by the Tribunal. Any such counterclaim or setoff shall contain the same particulars as those specified in Article 41(b) and (c).

Further Written Statements

Article 43

(a)   In the event that a counterclaim or setoff has been made or asserted, the Claimant shall reply to the particulars thereof. Article 42(a) and (b) shall apply *mutatis mutandis* to such reply.

(b)   The Tribunal may, in its discretion, allow or require further written statements.

Commentary on Articles 41–43

Articles 41 to 43 of the WIPO Rules establish the procedure for the submission of written memorials and evidence in a WIPO arbitration. The procedure for the submission of written memorials and evidence adopted under the WIPO Rules is similar to that established by the other major arbitral institutions surveyed, but in each case there are slight variations that can have important implications.

The procedure for the presentation of written memorials under the WIPO Rules is straightforward. As mentioned earlier, the first step is for the Claimant to present its Request, which may, but need not, be accompanied by its Statement of Claim. The Respondent then has 30 days to submit its reply to the Request.

In the more common case that the Statement of Claim has not been presented together with the Request for Arbitration, the Claimant is given 30 days from the date the Claimant receives notification from the Center of the Tribunal's establishment to submit its Statement of Claim to the Center and the Respondent. Thus, the Claimant may take advantage of the period that the Respondent and the Center are going through the appointment process to draft its Statement of Claim and accumulate the evidence to support it.

The Statement of Claim must give a complete explanation of the claim, both the facts surrounding it and legal arguments supporting it, and must also state the relief desired by the Claimant. Moreover, Article 41(c) requires submission of documents to be used in evidence by the Claimant, and a list of said documents. The rules furthermore provide expressly that where evidence is particularly voluminous, the Claimant can make a proffer of proof, rather than submitting the documents themselves.

The next step in the process is for the Respondent to present its Statement of Defense. The rules provide that the Statement of Defense must be presented at the later of two dates: either 30 days after the Respondent receives the Statement of Claim, or 30 days after notification by the Center that the Tribunal has been established. This means that in cases where the Claimant voluntarily submits its Statement of Claim with the Request, the Respondent can then choose either to submit its Statement of Defense 30 days later or wait until 30 days after receiving the notice that the Tribunal has been established. In most cases, the Respondent would be expected to wait, which means the Respondent will be able to use the time the parties and the Center are going through the appointment process (often a number of months) to prepare its Statement of Defense.

By submitting the Statement of Claim together with the Request, the Claimant should shorten the total time of the arbitration by roughly 30 days. If the Claimant waits to file the Statement of Claim until after being notified of the Tribunal's establishment, the Claimant then has 30 days do so and the Respondent has 30 days thereafter to submit its Statement of Defense. Under this scenario, the initial round of memorials is complete 60 days after the establishment of the Tribunal. In the case where the Statement of Claim is submitted together with the Request and the Respondent waits until the latest date possible to submit its Statement of Defense (as it would be expected to do), the initial memorials would be complete 30 days after the establishment of the Tribunal. Thus, the difference would be 30 days.

This means that the only guaranteed timesaving to the Claimant from filing the Statement of Claim together with the Request is 30 days. However, the Tribunal may be less lenient in granting extensions of time to file the Statement of Defense in cases where the Statement of Claim had been filed early, but this is difficult to predict and is likely to vary significantly among different Tribunals.

The Statement of Defense must reply to the facts and arguments laid out in the Statement of Claim, and evidence in the form of documents also must be submitted. Counterclaims or setoffs must be included in the Statement of Defense, unless the Tribunal makes a special exception for this to be done later in the proceedings.

The content of the counterclaim or setoff must conform to Article 41(b) and (c) by including a comprehensive statement of the facts and legal arguments supporting the counterclaim or request for setoff, including a statement of the relief sought, and shall to the extent possible be accompanied by supporting documentation.

The Claimant has 30 days from the date of receipt of the Statement of Defense (or 30 days from the date of the establishment of the Tribunal if this is later) to reply to the counterclaim or setoff. The Claimant's reply must conform with Article 42(b) by including a response to the particulars of the counterclaim or request for setoff and again must be accompanied by any documentary evidence.

Written statements in addition to the above (other than amendments) are referred to in Article 43 of the WIPO Rules. Article 43(b) allows for additional written statements to be accepted or required by the Tribunal at its discretion, without further guidance. As discussed above, the parties may agree to additional memorials, in which case the Tribunal would be expected to follow the parties' wishes, with the possible exception where doing so would contravene the Tribunal's duty to ensure the arbitration proceeds expeditiously.

In cases where the parties do not mutually agree, it would be typical in important cases for the Tribunal at the request of either party or on its own initiative to permit a second round of memorials. The rules leave to the Tribunal's discretion whether this round of memorials shall be made simultaneously or sequentially. Depending on the case, each approach has its benefits, but the strong trend is toward sequential filings.[22] For example, it would not be uncommon for the Tribunal to grant the Claimant 30 days to reply to the Statement of Defense and the Respondent then to be given 30 days to reply to that filing.

As is the case more generally in international arbitration, it is important for a Tribunal acting under the WIPO Rules to anticipate potential procedural issues, including for example the exchange of further memorials, and to issue an early scheduling order addressing such issues. In this way the parties, who are often from different procedural backgrounds, can predict the future course of the proceedings, and the possibility of abuse is limited.[23]

Comparing the procedure for the submission of written memorials established by the WIPO Rules to the other rules surveyed one can make the following general observations. The procedures established by the AAA, LCIA, and UNCITRAL Rules

---

[22] *See* CRAIG, *supra* note 6, at section 24.01 (stating that sequential filings are the norm in ICC arbitration).

[23] *See id.* at section 16.04 (making a similar point under the ICC Rules).

are all quite similar to the WIPO procedure with certain variations. Even after the most recent amendments to the ICC Rules, the ICC Rules remain the most divergent from the other procedures surveyed because of the Terms of Reference procedure, which remains the hallmark of an ICC arbitration.

AAA Rules: Unlike the other rules surveyed, the AAA Rules require the Claimant to submit its Statement of Claim together with the Request for Arbitration. Although the AAA Rules require the Statement of Claim to be submitted up-front, the rules are more general about what it must include. The AAA Rules require a "description" of the claims, as opposed to the "comprehensive statement of the facts and legal arguments" required by the WIPO Rules.

In practice, however, the Claimant in an AAA arbitration will want to be as complete as possible in presenting its claims, as the AAA Rules do not guarantee the Claimant another opportunity to present its case. In certain cases, this approach may prove difficult for the Claimant, who may not have a sufficient basis at this early stage of the process to fully lay out its case and seek the appropriate relief.[24] Similar considerations kept the drafters of the UNICITRAL Rules, on which the WIPO Rules provisions are crafted with respect to this issue, from *requiring* the Statement of Claim to be submitted together with the Notice of Arbitration, but instead this was kept as an option (as it is the WIPO Rules).[25]

Like the WIPO Rules, the AAA Rules then give the Respondent 30 days to submit its Statement of Defense responding to the issues raised in the Notice of Arbitration and raising any counterclaims or setoffs to the Claimant and other parties, if any, and to the administrator. The Respondent is given the same 30-day time period to reply regarding the number of arbitrators or place or language of the arbitration. The Claimant then has 30 days to file a written Statement of Defense to any counterclaim or setoff raised by the Respondent in its statement of defense.

Like the WIPO Rules, the AAA Rules do not provide for another round of memorials, but give the Tribunal the authority to allow further written statements and to set the time limits for their submission. The rules state that in principal that the time limit should not be longer than 45 days, but the Tribunal is allowed to extend the time if necessary.

The AAA procedure, by requiring the Statement of Claim to be submitted up-front, should generally result in a somewhat speedier process after the filing of the Request for Arbitration than the WIPO procedure and other procedures surveyed. However, it is important to keep in mind that the disadvantage of this approach is that the Claimant must wait to file its Request for Arbitration until it is ready with its

---

[24] *See* Robert H. Smit, *The Center for Public Resources Rules for Non-Administered Arbitration of International Disputes: A Critical and Comparative Commentary*, 2 AM. REV. INT'L ARB. 411, 418 (1991) (making a similar point about Article 3.3 of the Center for Public Resources Rules and furthermore noting that the Claimant may not wish to disclose the details of its case before reviewing the initial defense by the Respondent).

[25] *See* VAN HOF, *supra* note 9, at 29.

Statement of Claim, which means that the total time elapsed from the time the Claimant decides to bring the claim until it is decided may be longer. The WIPO and other procedures surveyed have the benefit of allowing the Claimant to opt to use the downtime while the Tribunal is being established to draft its Statement of Claim, which may in fact result in a shorter total process time.

LCIA Rules: The LCIA Rules follow the WIPO approach with the exception that the LCIA Rules are the only one of the rules surveyed to expressly provide for the parties to file a second round of memorials in all cases. Moreover, all pleadings under the LCIA Rules are exchanged through the Registrar, rather than directly between the parties.

Like the WIPO Rules, the LCIA Rules provide for the Claimant to submit with its Request for Arbitration only "a brief statement describing the nature and circumstances of the dispute, and specifying the claims advanced by the Claimant against another party to the arbitration." (LCIA, Art. 1.) This is then followed by a detailed statement of claim, in this case called a Statement of Case, setting out "in sufficient detail the facts and any contentions of law on which it relies, together with the relief claimed." (LCIA, Art. 15.)

As is one of the possibilities under the WIPO Rules, the Statement of Case shall be submitted within 30 days of receiving notification of the formation of the Tribunal. The LCIA Rules do not give the Claimant the option of submitting the Statement of Case together with the Request for Arbitration. However, the Claimant may notify the Tribunal that it will treat the Request for Arbitration as a Statement of Case, which is effectively the same.

The Respondent is given 30 days from receiving the Statement of Case or written notice that the Claimant intends to treat its Request as a Statement of Case to submit its Statement of Defense, together with its counterclaims. By tying the Respondent's deadline to submit its Statement of Defense to the Claimant's presentation of its Statement of Claim, rather than making it the later of that date or the establishment of the Tribunal (as the WIPO Rules do), the LCIA Rules create a greater incentive for the Claimant to present its Statement of Case as early as possible, to put pressure on the Respondent to do the same with its Statement of Defense. (LCIA, Art. 15.) The WIPO Rules are again the only ones to require documentary evidence to be submitted with the Statement of Defense, the same as for the Statement of Claim.

As mentioned above, the LCIA Rules are the only of the rules surveyed to give the parties an express right to a second round of memorials. Article 15.4 gives the Claimant 30 days from receipt of the Statement of Defense to file with the Registrar a Statement of Reply that shall include its defense to any counterclaims that were raised in the Statement of Defense. The LCIA Rules go on to give a deadline of 30 days from receipt of the above Statement of Reply for the Respondent to send a Statement of Reply to Counterclaim to the Registrar.

The express inclusion in the rules of a right to reply has the benefit of expressly combining the Claimant's reply to the Statement of Defense with any reply to the counterclaims. This approach eliminates some possibility for delay while the parties debate the form and content of any second round of memorials. However, in a well-managed arbitration, this issue should have been decided well in advance and should not result in any delay. Moreover, the more flexible approach adopted by the WIPO Rules has the benefit that in simple cases the second round of memorials may be eliminated altogether, whereas under the LCIA Rules there is always a second round unless the parties have expressly agreed otherwise.

UNCITRAL Rules: The UNCITRAL Rules also provide for a procedure very similar to the other rules surveyed with the predominant difference being that the rules themselves do not provide any time deadlines for the submission of the Statement of Claim or the Statement of Defense. The UNCITRAL arbitration rules are also the only other of the rules surveyed to provide the option for, but not requiring (as the AAA Rules do), the Claimant to submit the Statement of Claim with the Request. In cases where the Claimant does not take this option, which is often the case, the deadline for the submission of the Statement of Claim is not set until the Tribunal is formed. Although this inevitably must lead to some delay, in a well-managed arbitration this will be among the first orders of business and the delay should not be great.

ICC Rules: The procedure that varies the most from the basic model adopted by the WIPO and other rules surveyed and described above is the ICC procedure. Under the procedure established by the ICC Rules, after receipt of the Request for Arbitration and the Answer, it is for the arbitrators, together with the parties, to draw up an agreed set of Terms of Reference. After their adoption, the Terms of Reference guide the course of the arbitration.

Under the ICC Rules, the Claimant submits a Request for Arbitration containing, among other things, "a description of the nature and circumstances of the dispute giving rise to the claims" and "a statement of the relief sought" corresponding to Article 41(b) of the WIPO Rules.

The Request is forwarded to the Respondent from the Secretariat (instead of simultaneously from the Claimant to the Tribunal and the Respondent as in the WIPO Rules), and the Respondent has 30 days from receipt of the Request to file its Answer thereto, unless granted an extension by the Secretariat. In addition to commenting on the claims and the relief sought, the Answer must include the Respondent's appointment of any arbitrator it is entitled to appoint, the Respondent's comments concerning the number of arbitrators and their choice, as well as its comments on the place of arbitration, applicable law and language. The Respondent may request an extension of time with respect to the other aspects of the Answer, but must nominate its arbitrator and file its comments concerning the number of arbitrators and their choice in a timely manner or the Court proceeds without the Respondent's input. (ICC, Art. 5.)

Counterclaims must be filed with the Answer, and once again are described briefly as "a description of the nature and circumstances of the dispute giving rise to the counterclaim(s)" and "a statement of the relief sought, including, to the extent possible, an indication of any amount(s) counterclaimed.'' (ICC, Art. 5.) The Claimant then has 30 days from the date of receiving the counterclaim(s) from the Secretariat to file its reply to any request for setoff or counterclaims, although the Secretariat may extend the time for filing.

Under the ICC procedure, the Secretariat waits until the Tribunal has been appointed to forward the file to the arbitrators. (ICC, Art. 17.) As discussed above, after receipt of the file, the Tribunal draws up a document defining its Terms of Reference. Of the rules surveyed, the ICC Rules are the only ones to provide for the Tribunal to draw up formal Terms of Reference for the arbitrators (the ICC, UNCITRAL and WIPO Rules all provide for Terms of Reference for experts).

The Terms of Reference are drawn up based on the memorials as they stand at the time. The Tribunal may at its option decide whether to prepare the Terms of Reference based solely on the papers or in the presence of the parties. However, if either of the parties desires to comment in person on the Terms of Reference, the Tribunal usually will acquiesce to this request (which typically means both parties will be present). The Terms of Reference are required to include:

a) the full names and descriptions of the parties;

b) the addresses of the parties to which notifications and communications arising in the course of the arbitration may be made;

c) a summary of the parties' respective claims and of the relief sought by each party, with an indication to the extent possible of the amounts claimed or counterclaimed;

d) unless the Arbitral Tribunal considers it inappropriate, a list of issues to be determined;

e) the full names, descriptions and addresses of the arbitrators;

f) the place of the arbitration; and

g) particulars of the applicable procedural rules and, if such is the case, reference to the power conferred upon the Arbitral Tribunal to act as *amiable compositeur* or to decide *ex aequo et bono*.

The recent amendments to the ICC Rules eliminated the requirement that the Terms of Reference contain a definition of the issues to be decided, although they continue to require that the parties' respective claims and defenses be described. The definition of the list of issues has often created disagreement between the parties as to their content and hence to cause delay. Moreover, parties have complained that it is difficult to define the issues at this early stage in the process. For these reasons, the decision was taken to remove the list of issues from the Terms of Reference, in the hope of streamlining the process.

After they are completed, the Terms of Reference must be signed by the parties and the Tribunal. The Tribunal is given two months from the date it receives the file from the Secretariat to submit the signed Terms of Reference to the parties, unless it requests an extension from the ICC Court or one is granted by the Court on its own initiative. If any party refuses to take part in the preparation of the Terms of Reference or to sign them, the Tribunal submits them to the Court for approval. After the Terms of Reference are either signed by the parties and the Tribunal or approved by the Court, the arbitration proceeds.

After the Terms of Reference have been signed, as discussed below the parties are precluded from making any "new claims or counterclaims" outside of the timetable established by the Terms of Reference, unless expressly authorized by the Tribunal, taking into account the nature of the new claim or counterclaim, the stage of the arbitration and other relevant circumstances. (ICC, Art. 19.)

Either when drawing up the Terms of Reference or as shortly as possible thereafter, the Tribunal, after consulting with the parties, prepares a provisional timetable it intends to follow in the case and submits it to the ICC Court and the parties. The provisional scheduling order will provide, among other things, whether any further memorials are to be filed and if so whether they will be simultaneous or sequential. Subsequent modifications to the timetable shall be notified by the Tribunal to the Court and the parties. The requirement of a provisional time table was added in the recent amendments of the ICC Rules, with the goal of speeding up proceedings.

The ICC Rules do not contain detailed provisions dealing with the further procedures, and instead opt for a provision granting the Tribunal the authority to ascertain the facts through "all appropriate means."[26]

Amendments to Claims or Defense

Article 44
Subject to any contrary agreement by the parties, a party may amend or supplement its claim, counterclaim, defense or setoff during the course of the arbitral proceedings, unless the Tribunal considers it inappropriate to allow such amendment having regard to its nature or the delay in making it and to the provisions of Article 38(b) and (c).

Commentary on Article 44

Article 44 of the WIPO Rules covers any amendments to claims, counterclaims or defenses. Unless the parties have agreed otherwise, the WIPO Rules favor allowing amendment.

Article 44 provides that unless the parties agree otherwise, a party may (a) amend or (b) supplement its (i) claim; (ii) counterclaim; (iii) defense or (iv) setoff, any time during the proceedings unless the Tribunal considers it inappropriate to permit the amendment having regard to its nature or the delay in making the amendment, and provided that permitting the amendment would not contravene the Tribunal's obligations under Article 38(b) and (c) of the rules to ensure the parties are treated with equality and that the arbitration proceeds expeditiously.

---

[26] *See* CRAIG, *supra* note 6, at section 23.01.

The lenient approach to amendment adopted by the WIPO Rules is very similar to that taken by the AAA and UNCITRAL Rules with the exception that those rules provide expressly that the amendment is not allowed if it would take the claims outside the scope of the arbitration agreement. Such a limitation should be implied in the WIPO Rules, but is not stated expressly.

Article 4 of the AAA Rules provides that any party may "amend or supplement its claim, counterclaim or defense, unless the Tribunal considers it inappropriate to allow such amendment or supplement because of the party's delay in making it, prejudice to the other parties or any other circumstances." The amendment or supplement may not be made if it "would fall outside the scope of the agreement to arbitrate." Article 20 of the UNCITRAL Rules is virtually identical.

Article 22 of the LCIA Rules addresses amendment within the context of granting the Tribunal so-called "additional powers." As with the other additional powers listed in Article 22 of the LCIA Rules, unless the parties have agreed otherwise, the Tribunal has the power "to allow any party, upon such terms (as to costs and otherwise) as it shall determine, to amend any claim, counterclaim, defence and reply."

The LCIA language is more limited than the equivalent WIPO, UNCITRAL and AAA Rules because it mentions only "amendment" of claims, whereas the other rules also expressly permit "supplementing the claims." Excluding any reference to the supplementing of claims seems to indicate a somewhat stricter approach under the LCIA Rules than under the equivalent WIPO, UNCITRAL and AAA Rules. By allowing the claims to be supplemented, the other rules would seem more likely to permit claims that are arguably new, but related, than would be the case under the LCIA Rules. Moreover, unlike the other rules, the LCIA Rules do not spell out the standard under which the amendment would be judged.

Before granting a party leave to amend, the LCIA Rules also expressly require the Tribunal to give the parties a reasonable opportunity to be heard. Although the LCIA Rules are the only rules surveyed that deal expressly with the right of the parties to comment on the proposed amendment, in practice it would be typical for a Tribunal to give the parties the right to comment before permitting the amendment.

The ICC Rules do not expressly address the amendment of claims or counter-claims, but they do state expressly that new claims or counterclaims may not be brought that fall outside of the Terms of Reference after the Terms of Reference have been signed, unless the Tribunal expressly authorizes the new claim or counterclaim. The recent amendments to the ICC Rules added the clause granting the Tribunal the discretion to allow new claims; under the old rules new claims were *per se* precluded. However, the parties have always been allowed to offer new arguments or evidence in support of claims and counterclaims within the scope of the Terms of Reference.[27] As would be expected, this has at times led to debates over whether a claim is really new (as only new claims are expressly disallowed) or within the scope of the Terms of Reference.

---

[27] *See* COE, *supra* note 5, at Section 9.6.

Communication Between Parties and Tribunal

Article 45

Except as otherwise provided in these Rules or permitted by the Tribunal, no party or anyone acting on its behalf may have any *ex parte* communication with any arbitrator with respect to any matter of substance relating to the arbitration, it being understood that nothing in this paragraph shall prohibit *ex parte* communications which concern matters of a purely organizational nature, such as the physical facilities, place, date or time of the hearings.

Commentary on Article 45

Article 45 of the WIPO Rules deals with communication between the parties and the arbitrators. This article incorporates the basic principle applied in international arbitration generally that the parties and their representatives refrain from any *ex parte* communication with any arbitrator with regard to the substance of the arbitration. Communication of a purely organizational nature is expressly permitted by the WIPO Rules, and Article 45 expressly lists examples of permissible communication, including physical space and the place, date and time of hearings. The WIPO Rules deal only with communications with "arbitrators" and fail expressly to address the often more difficult issue of communication with potential arbitrators.

The general principle adopted in international arbitration is that *ex parte* contact is not allowed and may call into question the validity of the award. The United States Court of Appeals for the Ninth Circuit has stated the principle succinctly as follows:

> Ex parte evidence to an arbitration panel that disadvantages any of the parties in their right to be heard violates the parties' rights and is ground for vacation of the arbitration award.[28]

Communication with the arbitrators is not addressed at all by the ICC Rules, but is covered more extensively by the AAA and LCIA Rules than the WIPO Rules. Turning first to the AAA Rules, the AAA Rules in principle forbid *ex parte* communication between parties or their representatives and the arbitrators or candidates for appointment as party-appointed arbitrator or presiding arbitrator. The only exception is that parties are allowed to "advise the candidate [for party-appointed arbitrator] of the general nature of the controversy and of the anticipated proceedings and to discuss the candidate's qualifications, availability or independence in relation to the parties, or to discuss the suitability of candidates for selection as third arbitrator where the parties or the party-designated arbitrators are to participate in that selection."[29] The last sentence

---

[28] Pacific Reinsurance Management Corporation v. Ohio Reinsurance Management Corp., 935 F.2d 1019, 1025 (1991) (court refused to overturn award because *ex parte* communication found not to prejudice the opposing party); *see* detailed discussion of this issue in Coe, supra note 5, at Section 10.6.

[29] *See* Hans Smit, *Managing an International Arbitration: An Arbitrator's View*, 5 AM. REV. INT'L ARB. 129, 131 (1994) (taking the view that communications between a party-appointed arbitrator and the parties concerning the appointment of the presiding arbitrator are generally accepted where the party-appointed arbitrator takes part in the selection process, even where the rules are silent).

of Article 7(2) then goes on to state that no party or anyone acting on its behalf shall have *any ex parte* communication relating to the case with *any* candidate for presiding arbitrator.

Article 13 of the LCIA Rules deals with this communication between parties and the arbitral tribunal in a different manner than the WIPO and AAA Rules. *Ex parte* communications are not mentioned, but are understood to be forbidden by the first part of Article 13, which requires that all communications between parties and arbitrators be made through the Registrar before the Tribunal is formed. Subsequent communications also must be made through the Registrar unless the Tribunal specifies that they can be made directly between itself and the parties, according to Article 13.2. In this case, the Registrar must be sent copies simultaneously. Like the WIPO Rules, the LCIA Rules fail to specifically address communications with potential arbitrators.

Both the ICC and the UNCITRAL Rules are silent on the subject of communication between the parties and the arbitrators. Article 15(3) of the UNCITRAL Rules provides that all documents or information supplied to the arbitral Tribunal by one party shall at the same time be communicated to the other party. This could be seen implicitly to prohibit *ex parte* contact, but in rather an indirect way.

V. PREPARATORY CONFERENCE

Article 47

The Tribunal may, in general following the submission of the Statement of Defense, conduct a preparatory conference with the parties for the purpose of organizing and scheduling the subsequent proceedings.

Commentary on Article 47

Article 47 deals with preparatory conferences.[30] Article 47 grants the Tribunal the discretion to hold a preparatory conference, but does not require it to do so. If a preparatory conference is to be held, the rules suggest that it would generally best be held after the submission of the Statement of Defense, but again leaves this to the discretion of the Tribunal.

The WIPO Rules state that the purpose of the preparatory conference is to organize and schedule the subsequent proceedings. The WIPO Rules give no further guidance on the subject matter of the preparatory conference, which is left wholly to the discretion of the Tribunal.

The basic role of the preparatory conference is for the Tribunal to hear the parties with respect to future procedures in the case and then to issue rulings addressing these issues — that is, to provide what has been aptly described as a "blueprint" for the

---

[30] An excellent discussion of preparatory conferences and other pertinent issues related to the procedural issues addressed herein is found in Howard M. Holtzmann, *Balancing the Need for Certainty and Flexibility in International Arbitration Procedures, in* INTERNATIONAL ARBITRATION IN THE 21ST CENTURY: TOWARDS "JUDICIALIZATION" AND UNIFORMITY? (TWELFTH SOKOL COLLOQUIUM) 3 (Richard B. Lillich and Charles N. Brower eds., 1993) and in COE, *supra* note 5 at Section 9.7.

further proceedings.[31] This can have significant benefits for both the Tribunal and the parties going forward.

From the Tribunal's perspective, a preparatory conference permits the arbitrators to hear the parties' views about procedural issues before issuing its scheduling orders and on this basis to anticipate certain potential pitfalls that might arise going forward. From the parties' perspective, it allows them a chance to express their views about further proceedings in the case, and hence can act to increase predictability. Moreover, there can be a great benefit to both the parties and the arbitrators from having seen and interacted with each other. Properly handled, these benefits can include increased trust and simply having a better feel for what to expect.

The only other of the rules surveyed to mention expressly a preparatory conference are the AAA Rules. Article 16(2) provides that the Tribunal may hold a preparatory conference for the purpose of "organizing, scheduling and agreeing to procedures to expedite the subsequent proceedings." Like the WIPO Rules, no further detail is given about the subject matter of the preparatory conference.

Under the ICC Rules the information exchanged by the parties during the course of the drawing up by the Tribunal of the Terms of Reference and the related scheduling order may perform the same function as a preparatory conference. By requiring the parties and the Tribunal to focus early on the issues to be decided and the procedure by which they will be decided, the Terms of Reference procedure brings to light issues similar to those that would be addressed during a typical preparatory conference. Moreover, as discussed above, in many cases the Terms of Reference will be drafted in the presence of the parties, in which case it will come even closer to a typical preparatory conference. However, a "preparatory conference" as such is not provided for in the ICC Rules.

The LCIA and UNCITRAL Rules make no mention of a preparatory conference. This does not mean, however, that the holding of a preparatory conference is in any way precluded or discouraged in arbitrations held under those rules, as it is always in the discretion of the Tribunal to hold a preparatory conference. Indeed, UNCITRAL has prepared a Note addressing in detail some possible issues that might be considered in organizing arbitral proceedings, which can be useful for the parties and the arbitrators in planning for such a preparatory conference.

The UNCITRAL Notes propose the following issues for consideration when organizing arbitral proceedings, and then provide useful commentary with respect to each issue listed:[32]

1.   Set of arbitration rules
     If the parties have not agreed on a set of arbitration rules, would they wish to do so?

---

[31] *See* COE, *supra* note 5, at Section 9.7.

[32] UNCITRAL Draft Notes on Organizing Arbitral Proceedings, A/CN.9/423, April 10, 1996 [hereinafter UNCITRAL Notes].

2. Language of proceedings
    (a) Possible need for translation of documents, in full or in part
    (b) Possible need for interpretation of oral presentations
    (c) Cost of translation and interpretation
3. Place of arbitration
    (a) Determination of the place of arbitration, if not already agreed upon by the parties
    (b) Possibility of meetings outside the place of arbitration
4. Administrative services that may be needed for the arbitral tribunal to carry out its functions
5. Deposits in respect of costs
    (a) Amount to be deposited
    (b) Management of deposits
    (c) Supplementary deposits
6. Confidentiality of information relating to the arbitration; possible agreement thereon
7. Routing of written communications among the parties and the arbitrators
8. Telefax and other electronic means of sending documents
    (a) Telefax
    (b) Other electronic means (e.g. electronic mail and magnetic or optical disk)
9. Arrangements for the exchange of written submissions
    (a) Scheduling of written submissions
    (b) Consecutive or simultaneous submissions
10. Practical details concerning written submissions and evidence (e.g. method of submission, copies, numbering, references)
11. Defining points at issue; order of deciding issues; defining relief or remedy sought
    (a) Should a list of points at issue be prepared?
    (b) In which order should the points at issue be decided?
    (c) Is there a need to define more precisely the relief or remedy sought?
12. Possible settlement negotiations and their effect on scheduling proceedings
13. Documentary evidence
    (a) Time limits for submission of documentary evidence intended to be submitted by the parties; consequences of late submission
    (b) Whether the arbitral Tribunal intends to require a party to produce documentary evidence
    (c) Should assertions about the origin and receipt of documents and about the correctness of photocopies be assumed as accurate?
    (d) Are the parties willing to submit jointly a single set of documentary evidence?
    (e) Should voluminous and complicated documentary evidence be presented through summaries, tabulations, charts, extracts or samples?

14. Physical evidence other than documents
    (a) What arrangements should be made if physical evidence will be submitted?
    (b) What arrangements should be made if an on-site inspection is necessary?
15. Witnesses
    (a) Advance notice about a witness whom a party intends to present; written witnesses' statements
    (b) Manner of taking oral evidence of witnesses
        (i) Order in which questions will be asked and the manner in which the hearing of witnesses will be conducted
        (ii) Whether oral testimony will be given under oath or affirmation and, if so, in what form an oath or affirmation should be made
        (iii) May witnesses be in the hearing room when they are not testifying
    (c) The order in which the witnesses will be called
    (d) Interviewing witnesses prior to their appearance at a hearing
    (e) Hearing representatives of a party
16. Experts and expert witnesses
    (a) Expert appointed by the arbitral Tribunal
        (i) The expert's terms of reference
        (ii) The opportunity of the parties to comment on the expert's report, including by presenting expert testimony
    (b) Expert opinion presented by a party (expert witness)
17. Hearings
    (a) Decision whether to hold hearings
    (b) Whether one period of hearings should be held or separate periods of hearings
    (c) Setting dates for hearings
    (d) Whether there should be a limit on the aggregate amount of time each party will have for oral arguments and questioning witnesses
    (e) The order in which the parties will present their arguments and evidence
    (f) Length of hearings
    (g) Arrangements for a record of the hearings
    (h) Whether and when the parties are permitted to submit notes summarizing their oral arguments
18. Multi-party arbitration
19. Possible requirements concerning filing or delivering the award
    Who should take steps to fulfill any requirement

Depending on the circumstances, it can be useful in preparing for a preparatory conference, or otherwise for further scheduling of an arbitration, for the Tribunal to forward the UNCITRAL Notes or a subset thereof to the parties in advance, to assist them in thinking of issues they may want to discuss at the conference or address in the scheduling order. Every issue addressed in the UNCITRAL Notes is not relevant in every case, and indeed many issues addressed in the Notes are covered by the WIPO and other arbitration rules, but the Notes provide a useful tool in planning both the conference itself and the further proceedings, and hence can prove an important vehicle for demystifying the arbitral process.

VI. EVIDENCE

Article 48

(a) The Tribunal shall determine the admissibility, relevance, materiality and weight of evidence.

(b) At any time during the arbitration, the Tribunal may, at the request of a party or on its own motion, order a party to produce such documents or other evidence as it considers necessary or appropriate and may order a party to make available to the Tribunal or to an expert appointed by it or to the other party any property in its possession or control for inspection or testing.

Commentary on Article 48

Article 48 deals with the Tribunal's power to judge the admissibility, relevance, materiality and weight of the evidence, and its authority to order the production of documents and evidence.[33]

Article 48(a) provides that the Tribunal shall determine the admissibility, relevance, materiality and weight of evidence. However, it does not provide guidance as to whether the Tribunal should make such a determination by applying rules of evidence from a national legal system or based on some other standard. The prevailing view, which should be inferred in the WIPO Rules, is that the Tribunal is at liberty to decide what standard to apply to this issue.[34]

The LCIA Rules are the only rules surveyed that deal expressly with the question of what principles should be applied to determine the admissibility and weight of evidence, and leave it completely to the discretion of the Tribunal. Under Article 22 dealing with additional powers of the Tribunal, the LCIA Rules state that unless the parties agree otherwise, the Tribunal shall have the power ''to decide whether or not to apply any strict rules of evidence (or any other rules) as to the admissibility, relevance or weight of any material tendered by a party on any matter of fact or expert opinion.''

---

[33] An insightful explication of the issues addressed in this section of the rules in the context of the Iran-United States Claims Tribunal is found in CHARLES BROWER & JASON BRUESCHKE, THE IRAN-UNITED STATES CLAIMS TRIBUNAL, Chapter 6 (1998) [hereinafter BROWER & BRUESCHKE].

[34] *See* Andrew Rogers, *Improving Procedures for Discovery and Documentary Evidence*, ICCA SERIES No. 7, *supra* note 1 at 131, 140 (1994) [hereinafter Rogers]; *see also* Smit, *supra* note 20, at 167–69 (taking the view that in deciding this question arbitrators should consider the social policy underlying the evidentiary rule at issue). The need for the development of some uniform principles to guide evidentiary issues before international arbitrations is discussed in BROWER & BRUESCHKE, *supra* note 33, at 197–98 and has led the International Bar Association to adopt the Supplementary Rules Governing the Presentation and Reception of Evidence in International Commercial Arbitration, *reprinted in* 10 Y.B. COM. ARB. 152–56 (1985).

Recognizing that parties might be concerned about lack of predictability with respect to the treatment of the evidence submitted by them, one distinguished arbitrator has summarized the "common sense principles" applied by the Iran-United States Claims Tribunal in judging these issues as follows:

1. Contemporaneous written exchanges of the parties antedating the dispute are the most reliable source of evidence;

2. The actual course of conduct between the parties to the dispute . . . constitutes the best evidence of the proper interpretation of their contract;

3. The failure of a party to object in writing to a writing (e.g., an invoice) it has received at or shortly after the time of receipt is strong evidence of its acceptance;

4. Statements of a party contradicting the position it has taken in the proceedings are strong evidence against that position; and

5. When it reasonably should be expected that certain evidence exists and that it is in the control of a party, the failure of that party to produce such evidence gives rise to a justifiable inference that such evidence, if produced, would be adverse to that party.[35]

The AAA Rules contain language identical to Article 48(a) of the WIPO Rules, except that they go on to say that in making this determination the Tribunal shall take into "account applicable principles of legal privilege, such as those involving the confidentiality of communications between a lawyer and client." (AAA, Art. 20.)

Although most would agree that a limitation on the admission of documents covered by legal privilege should be presumed in the other rules surveyed, instances have been cited where international tribunals have point blank refused to apply the privilege.[36] This is relatively uncommon, however. It is more usual for arbitrators to have to decide what rules they should apply to this issue, taking into account different legal traditions. For example, in continental Europe, privilege does not typically extend to in-house counsel, which is contrary to the expectation of in-house counsel from many other places in the world, who presume their documents are privileged. One commentator has suggested that parties should consider agreeing on this issue between themselves to avoid unexpected surprises.[37]

Article 48(b) of the WIPO Rules gives the Tribunal the authority to order the production of any evidence it considers necessary or appropriate, either documentary or otherwise. The Tribunal may order a party to make evidentiary property available as requested by a party or on its own motion. Such evidence may be required to be made available to the Tribunal or to an appointed expert for inspection or testing. The reference to the "testing" of evidence is unique among the rules surveyed and, like the

---

[35] Charles Brower, *Evidence Before International Arbitration Tribunals: The Need for Some Standard Rules*, 28 INT'L LAW. 47, 54 (1994).

[36] *See* COE, *supra* note 5, at section 9.10 (citing a major arbitration in the United States where the arbitrators reportedly held that the privilege did not apply).

[37] *See id.*

rules discussed in the next section of this article, was included in the WIPO Rules to better tailor the rules for deciding intellectual property cases.

Like Article 48(b) of the WIPO Rules, all of the rules surveyed contain provisions expressly granting the Tribunal the power to order the submission of evidence. (See ICC, Art. 20; AAA, Art. 19; LCIA, Art. 22; UNCITRAL, Art. 24.) Under all the rules surveyed, including Article 48(b), the Tribunal is given full discretion when and how to order the production of evidence with no input on this issue from the rules themselves. Even without a specific rule granting the Tribunal the power to order document submission, the prevailing view is that this is part of the Tribunal's inherent powers.[38]

Although reference is not made to the word "discovery," Article 48 of the WIPO Rules is the closest the rules come to permitting what is known in common-law countries as discovery.[39] Under the WIPO Rules, as well as the other rules surveyed, the Tribunal may specifically order the production of specific documents or categories of documents, and an order from the Tribunal is required before production is mandatory. Moreover, such an order may be made either at the request of a party or on the Tribunal's own motion. Allowing the Tribunal to order discovery on its own motion differs from common-law discovery — it would be unheard of in a typical litigation in the United States, for example, for a court to order production of a document that had not been requested by one of the parties.[40]

Unless the parties have expressly agreed to it, rarely will a tribunal in an international arbitration allow comprehensive discovery as is practiced in the United States.[41] More commonly, if any discovery is allowed at all, it is targeted discovery geared to the production of certain specified documents or evidence or categories of documents or evidence.

Typically, the procedure for requesting discovery in international arbitration operates as follows:[42] After the submission of the initial round of memorials, one or both of the parties will ask the other to produce certain specific documents or categories of documents. If the other party refuses, the demanding party may apply to

---

[38] See GARY B. BORN, INTERNATIONAL COMMERCIAL ARBITRATION IN THE UNITED STATES 81, 825 (1994); Arthur L. Marriott, *Evidence in International Arbitration*, 5 ARB. INT'L 280, 284 (1989).

[39] For a comprehensive discussion of discovery in international arbitration, *see* W. G. O. Morgan, *Discovery in Arbitration*, 3(3) J. INT'L ARB. 9 (1986) and more recently Marc Blessing, Document Discovery in International Arbitration, presented at the Ninth Annual Arbitration Conference of the Institute for Transnational Arbitration (June 1998) [hereinafter Blessing].

[40] Although systematic distinctions between the inquisitorial versus adversarial nature of the process are not always helpful in comparing arbitral procedures, the Tribunal's power to order a document on its own motion is properly seen to reflect a more inquisitorial role for the Tribunal. *See* Jan Paulsson, *Overview of Methods of Presenting Evidence in Different Legal Traditions*, ICCA SERIES NO. 7 *supra* note 1 at 113, 121 (1994) [hereinafter Paulsson].

[41] There are exceptions, however. CRAIG, *supra* note 6, at Section 26.01 cites an example of a Swiss arbitration involving substantial sums in which the Tribunal ordered the discovery of thousands of pages of documents.

[42] *See, e.g.*, Blessing, *supra* note 39, at 3, which description is in keeping with the author's experience.

the Tribunal for an order that the document(s) be produced. It is typical for the Tribunal to require that the request be detailed with respect to the description of the document(s) and its relevance to the proceeding. It is then for the Tribunal to decide whether it would be appropriate to admit the document, taking into account the importance of the document and the respective rights of the parties. If the request is granted, the Tribunal will issue an order for the party holding the document to produce it, which may form the basis for an application by the demanding party for court assistance in enforcing the request.

As an alternative to ordering the production of documents, if a party fails to provide important evidence at the request of the other party, the Tribunal may decide to draw an adverse inference from the failure to produce the evidence, unless the party failing to produce the evidence provides the Tribunal with a convincing reason for its failure.[43] It may be more typical in international arbitration for the Tribunal to draw an adverse inference from a party's failure to produce evidence than to actually order document production, and some would argue this is more suited to the nature of the arbitral process.[44] A Tribunal is also obviously likely to draw an adverse inference in cases where the Tribunal has ordered the production of evidence and a party fails to produce it, again unless the party failing to produce provides a convincing reason for its failure.

VII. EXPERIMENTS, SITE VISITS, AGREED PRIMERS AND MODELS

Experiments

Article 49

(a) A party may give notice to the Tribunal and to the other party at any reasonable time before a hearing that specified experiments have been conducted on which it intends to rely. The notice shall specify the purpose of the experiment, a summary of the experiment, the method employed, the results and the conclusion. The other party may by notice to the Tribunal request that any or all such experiments be repeated in its presence. If the Tribunal considers such request justified, it shall determine the timetable for the repetition of the experiments.

(b) For the purposes of this Article, "experiments" shall include tests or other processes of verification.

---

[43] *See, e.g.*, Rogers, *supra* note 34, at 140.

[44] In the context of the Iran-U.S. Claims Tribunal, the Tribunal drew adverse inferences from a party's unexplained failure to submit documents in its possession or control. *See* GEORGE ALDRICH, THE JURISPRUDENCE OF THE IRAN-U.S. CLAIMS TRIBUNAL 339 (1996). The Iran-United States Claims Tribunal's practice with respect to the drawing of adverse inferences also is discussed in BROWER & BRUESCHKE, *supra* note 33, at 194–96 (taking the view that the Tribunal was overly reluctant to draw adverse inferences).

Site Visits

Article 50
The Tribunal may, at the request of a party or on its own motion, inspect or require the inspection of any site, property, machinery, facility, production line, model, film, material, product or process as it deems appropriate. A party may request such an inspection at any reasonable time prior to any hearing, and the Tribunal, if it grants such a request, shall determine the timing and arrangements for the inspection.

Agreed Primers and Models

Article 51
The Tribunal may, where the parties so agree, determine that they shall jointly provide:
(i)   a technical primer setting out the background of the scientific, technical or other specialized information necessary to fully understand the matters in issue; and
(ii)   models, drawings or other materials that the Tribunal or the parties require for reference purposes at any hearing.

Commentary on Articles 49–51

Articles 49–51 refer to experiments, site visits and agreed primers and models. With the exception of the provisions of the LCIA Rules dealing with site inspections, none of the rules surveyed have provisions similar to these provisions. These provisions were expressly included in the WIPO Rules to better tailor them for intellectual property disputes.

Experiments

Article 49 sets forth the procedure for a party to submit evidence in an arbitral proceeding under the WIPO Rules that has been gained through experiments. Experiments are defined broadly to include "tests or other processes of verification." To give just one example, in a semiconductor patent infringement case, reverse engineering analysis to show infringement would likely come under the definition of an "experiment" and be subject to the rules described below.

Article 49 provides that if either party intends to rely on evidence gained through experiments at the hearing, it must place the Tribunal and the other party on notice at a reasonable time in advance of the hearing that it intends to do so. The notice must specify the following information:
Purpose of the experiment;
Summary of the experiment;
Method employed;

Results; and

Conclusion.

The other party then has the opportunity to provide notice to the Tribunal that any or all such experiments be repeated in its presence. If the Tribunal considers such request justified, it shall determine the timetable for the repetition of the experiments.

Site Visits

Article 50 deals with site visits. "Site visits" is defined broadly to include a wide range of inspections covering "any site, property, machinery, facility, production line, model, film, material, product or process." Thus, many things may be inspected under this provision that go far beyond the typical "site" visit, for example in large construction cases, and the list is geared to include inspections typically of assistance in intellectual property cases.

Under Article 50, the Tribunal may carry out an inspection if requested to do so by a party or at its own initiative if it considers it appropriate. If a party wants to request a site visit, it must do so well in advance of the hearing. If the Tribunal agrees to the request, the Tribunal schedules the inspection.

As mentioned above, the LCIA Rules are the only other of the rules surveyed to contain a provision on site inspections. Like the WIPO rule, the LCIA rule on site inspections is broadly worded. Article 22.1(d) of the LCIA Rules gives the Tribunal the power to "order any party to make any property, site or thing under its control and relating to the subject matter of the arbitration available for inspection by the Arbitral Tribunal." However, the LCIA Rules do not deal with the procedure for requesting such a site inspection, as the WIPO Rules do in some detail.

Agreed Primers and Models

Article 51 deals with agreed technical primers and models. In cases involving sophisticated technology, the provision to the Tribunal of agreed primers and models can be extremely helpful in assisting the Tribunal in understanding the technical underpinnings of the case and where the parties' differences lie.[45] Sometimes preparing the agreed primer or model can have the collateral benefit that the parties may be able to limit the issues in dispute for the Tribunal.

Article 51 provides that, if the parties agree, the Tribunal may require them jointly to provide the Tribunal with a technical primer setting out the background of the scientific, technical or other specialized information necessary to fully understand the matters in issue. For the most part, the parties should agree on the information contained in the primer, although in some cases areas of disagreement will be noted in the primer. In addition to the technical primer, Article 51 furthermore allows the Tribunal with the permission of the parties to require the parties jointly to provide

---

[45] See CRAIG, *supra* note 6, at Section 25.04 (discussing the importance of demonstrative evidence in international arbitration and using as examples licensing disputes).

reference materials in the form of ''models, drawings or other materials'' for use at the hearing.

VIII.   HEARINGS AND WITNESSES

Hearings

Article 53

(a)   **If either party so requests, the Tribunal shall hold a hearing for the presentation of evidence by witnesses, including expert witnesses, or for oral argument or for both. In the absence of a request, the Tribunal shall decide whether to hold such a hearing or hearings. If no hearings are held, the proceedings shall be conducted on the basis of documents and other materials alone.**

(b)   **In the event of a hearing, the Tribunal shall give the parties adequate advance notice of the date, time and place thereof.**

(c)   **Unless the parties agree otherwise, all hearings shall be in private.**

(d)   **The Tribunal shall determine whether and, if so, in what form a record shall be made of any hearing.**

Witnesses

Article 54

(a)   **Before any hearing, the Tribunal may require either party to give notice of the identity of witnesses it wishes to call, as well as of the subject matter of their testimony and its relevance to the issues.**

(b)   **The Tribunal has discretion, on the grounds of redundance and irrelevance, to limit or refuse the appearance of any witness, whether witness of fact or expert witness.**

(c)   **Any witness who gives oral evidence may be questioned, under the control of the Tribunal, by each of the parties. The Tribunal may put questions at any stage of the examination of the witnesses.**

(d)   **The testimony of witnesses may, either at the choice of a party or as directed by the Tribunal, be submitted in written form, whether by way of signed statements, sworn affidavits or otherwise, in which case the Tribunal may make the admissibility of the testimony conditional upon the witnesses being made available for oral testimony.**

(e)   **A party shall be responsible for the practical arrangements, cost and availability of any witness it calls.**

(f)   **The Tribunal shall determine whether any witness shall retire during any part of the proceedings, particularly during the testimony of other witnesses.**

Commentary on Articles 53–54

Article 53 of the WIPO Rules deals in detail with hearings and Article 54 with witnesses. Due to the relationship between these issues, leading to the fact that in many of the rules surveyed they are treated together in one rule, this section will consider these rules together.

Under the WIPO Rules, if requested to do so by either party, the Tribunal *must* hold a hearing the purpose of which may be to present evidence through witnesses, including expert witnesses, or for oral argument or for both. Imbedded in this provision, which is found in many arbitration rules and indeed in many national arbitration acts, is the notion that due process requires a fair hearing in person, if a party requests it.[46] The LCIA and ICC Rules are explicit that a hearing must be held if requested by either party, and the practice under the UNCITRAL and AAA Rules would also be to hold a hearing if requested to do so, although this is not expressly provided for in the rules. (LCIA, Art. 19; ICC, Art. 20.)

In cases where the parties have not requested a hearing, under the WIPO Rules the Tribunal is given the discretion whether to hold a hearing on its own accord or to decide the case on the documents. The same is expressly provided for under Article 20 of the ICC Rules and can be implied in the other rules surveyed.

The WIPO Rules state that unless the parties agree otherwise, all hearings will be held in private. One of the many important benefits of arbitration in deciding disputes, as opposed to litigation, is that it is confidential. Maintaining this confidentiality requires hearings to be held in private, and the private nature of hearings is provided for in the other rules surveyed. (AAA, Art. 20; LCIA, Art. 19; UNCITRAL, Art. 25; ICC, Art. 21.) As discussed in the section dealing with confidentiality generally, maintaining confidentiality is particularly important in intellectual property cases and is one of the many reasons parties choose to arbitrate intellectual property cases.

Under the WIPO Rules, the Tribunal has the discretion to decide whether to keep a record of the hearing and, if it decides to do so, the form the record should take. Generally speaking, if one or both of the parties request a transcript of the hearing and are willing to pay for it, the Tribunal will agree to it, unless there are valid objections from the other side.[47] Neither the ICC nor the LCIA Rules contain provisions dealing with the recording of hearings, whereas the AAA and UNICTRAL Rules require a transcript if the parties mutually request it or at the will of the Tribunal. (AAA, Art. 20; UNCITRAL, Art. 25.)

With respect to the procedure for cases where hearings will be held, the WIPO Rules require the Tribunal to give the parties ''adequate'' advance notice of the date,

---

[46] *See* Mayer, *supra* note 1, for a discussion of various laws that require the holding of a hearing if either side so requests.

[47] *See* CRAIG, *supra* note 6, at Section 25.02 (observing that under the ICC Rules arbitrators are reluctant to refuse the creation of a transcript where the requesting party has good reasons, even over the objection of the other side. Good reasons for the creation of a transcript may include the size of the dispute, the controversial nature of expected testimony, and the likelihood of judicial review).

time, and place of the hearing. Similar provisions are found in all the rules surveyed, with the AAA Rules establishing the precise date at which the notice shall be given. (AAA, Art. 20.) The ICC and LCIA Rules provide for "reasonable notice," whereas the WIPO Rules follow the UNCITRAL language by opting instead for "adequate" notice. (ICC, Art. 21; LCIA, Art. 19; UNCITRAL, Art. 25.)

Article 54 of the WIPO Rules provides the procedure for the giving of testimony by witnesses.[48] Before any hearing, the Tribunal has the discretion to require either party to give notice of the witnesses it intends to call, as well as the subject matter of their testimony and its relevance to the issues. The WIPO Rules, like the LCIA Rules, do not mandate the exchange of witness lists and leave the time for any exchange of lists to the discretion of the Tribunal. (LCIA, Art. 20.) In comparison, the UNCITRAL and AAA Rules mandate witness lists and dictate that they must be exchanged at least 15 days in advance of the hearing. (AAA, Art. 20; UNCITRAL, Art. 25.)

The WIPO Rules provide that the testimony of witnesses may, either at the choice of a party or as directed by the Tribunal, be submitted in written form. Witness statements are increasingly the norm in international arbitration. The issue that often arises with respect to witness statements is the extent to which they are seen to replace, rather than supplement, oral testimony. Some have expressed the view that in a case where extensive witness statements have been presented in advance of the oral hearing, the hearing should generally be limited to cross-examination by opposing counsel and questions from the Tribunal, whereas others have taken the view that direct testimony remains appropriate at least to address issues that have arisen since the statements were presented.[49]

A provision similar to the WIPO Rules is found in the LCIA Rules, which allow written witness statements unless the Tribunal has ordered otherwise. (LCIA, Art. 20.) Both the AAA and UNICTRAL Rules *per se* allow written witness statements (as opposed to leaving this issue to the discretion of the Tribunal). (AAA, Art. 5; UNICTRAL, Art. 25.) The submission of witness statements is not expressly addressed in the ICC Rules, but can be presumed from the Tribunal's general powers.

The WIPO Rules state expressly that the witness statement may be made by way of a signed statement, sworn affidavit or otherwise. Moreover, the Tribunal may, but need not, require as a condition of admitting the witness statement that the witness be made available to testify orally. Of the rules surveyed, the LCIA Rules are the only ones to address these issues expressly, and do so in a manner similar to the WIPO Rules. (LCIA, Art. 20.)

Witness statements and witness lists are one way to limit the time for the hearing. The WIPO Rules, like the LCIA Rules, expressly provide the Tribunal with the discretion to limit or refuse to limit or refuse the appearance of any witness, whether witness of fact or expert witness. The WIPO Rules state that the refusal should be

---

[48] For an interesting proposal for the taking of testimony by witnesses in international arbitration, *see* Lörcher, *supra* note 4, at 150–52.

[49] *Cf.* Smit, *supra* note 20, at 167 with Friedland, *supra* note 2, at 4.

based on the grounds of redundancy or irrelevance, whereas the LCIA Rules make no such limitation. (LCIA, Art. 20.) Arbitrators remain hesitant, however, *per se* to exclude specific witnesses out of fear of the award being challenged. One approach that was followed with good results at the Iran-United States Claims Tribunal was to set a time limit for each side to present its arguments at the hearing and then to allow the parties the discretion to use the time as they saw fit.

One sometimes controversial issue in international arbitration is the use of cross-examination. The presentation of testimony by witnesses, and in particular the cross-examination of such witnesses by the opposing party, is one of the areas where the common and civil-law traditions vary widely. Under the common-law approach, witnesses are relied on heavily by parties to prove their case, and cross-examination by the opposing party is an inherent and important part of the process. Under the civil-law system, where the case is typically more strongly guided from the bench, the presentation of witnesses is less typical and cross-examination is not common practice.

The presentation of witness testimony is a good example of the blending of the common and civil-law traditions.[50] The WIPO Rules provide expressly that any witness who gives oral testimony may be questioned, under the control of the Tribunal, by each of the parties. The Tribunal is furthermore allowed to put questions to the witnesses at any time during the examination.

The approach taken by the WIPO Rules is to combine the practices of the civil and common law by expressly allowing *both* each of the parties (which is the common-law approach) and the Tribunal (which is the civil-law approach) to question the witnesses. The approach followed by the LCIA Rules is identical to that of the WIPO Rules. This is the increasing trend in international arbitration generally, but the WIPO and LCIA Rules are unique in dealing with this issue expressly in the rules — most rules simply leave the form of the testimony to the Tribunal's discretion. (LCIA, Art. 20; ICC, Arts. 20–21; AAA, Art. 20; UNCITRAL, Art. 25.)

Under the WIPO Rules, the right of the Tribunal to question the witnesses is unlimited, whereas the questioning by the parties is expressly placed "under the control of the Tribunal." This limitation allows the Tribunal to intervene to exclude testimony that it considers to be repetitive or irrelevant, which it is expressly given the right to do under Article 54(2), or to control questioning that it considers otherwise inappropriate.

The extent to which the Tribunal will actually act to intervene to control cross-examination is one of the areas where even those skeptical of making broad distinctions based on the common or civil background of the arbitrator observe that the

---

[50] As previously mentioned herein, others have pointed out the dangers in making analogies to the "civil" and the "common" law approaches to adjudication, as there is wide diversity within each tradition, and in many respects the differences between the German and French procedures may be as significant as between the French and the English. *See, e.g.,* Mayer, *supra* note 1, at 25; Paulsson, *supra* note 40, at 116–17.

background of the arbitrator does matter.[51] Arbitrators from a civil-law background are observed to be more willing to intervene to limit cross-examination.

Another issue that may arise is whether witnesses will be allowed to be present during the testimony of other witnesses. Like the LCIA and UNCITRAL Rules, the WIPO Rules leave this to the discretion of the Tribunal. The WIPO Rules furthermore provide expressly that a party presenting a witness is responsible for the practical arrangements, costs, and availability of any witness it calls — this issue is not dealt with in the other rules surveyed but can be presumed.

The model followed by the WIPO Rules for hearings and witnesses is similar to that adopted by the other rules surveyed. With the exception of the LCIA Rules, the WIPO Rules on hearings and witnesses are the most detailed of the rules surveyed to be applied to these issues. However, the LCIA Rules pick up on a number of important issues that are not expressly addressed in the WIPO Rules.

With respect to hearings, the LCIA Rules provide that in advance of the hearings the Tribunal may submit a list of questions to the parties to which it wishes them to pay special attention. This can be useful to the parties by focusing them on the issues that the Tribunal considers in advance of the hearing to be the most important. Although not precluded by the WIPO Rules, having a specific provision foreseeing the provision of such a list may make the Tribunal more inclined to provide one.

Another issue that is dealt with expressly in the LCIA Rules is the setting of time limits for hearings. The LCIA Rules provide in Article 19 that the Tribunal "shall have the fullest authority to establish time-limits for meetings and hearings, or for any parts thereof." The setting of time limits for hearings can often be the source of contention between the parties. Because notions of due process argue in favor of allowing parties a full opportunity to be heard, Tribunals can at times be reluctant to limit the time for the hearing significantly in comparison with the request of one of the parties, yet this is often necessary for the arbitration to proceed "expeditiously" and is a practical necessity given the logistical limitations of the average international arbitration.[52] The inclusion of a provision expressly giving the Tribunal the "fullest authority" to set time limits is helpful in clarifying this issue.

The LCIA Rules also address two important issues with respect to witnesses that are not covered by the WIPO Rules — witness preparation and party witnesses. (LCIA, Art. 20.) Like with cross-examination, these are issues on which approaches adopted in different national legal systems may differ, and it is helpful that the rules take a specific position so as to allow predictability.

With respect to witness preparation, the LCIA Rules expressly provide that, subject to mandatory provisions of applicable law, it shall not be improper for any party or its legal representative to interview any witness or potential witness for the

---

[51] *See* Friedland, *supra* note 2, at 4.

[52] *See* Craig, *supra* note 6, at Section 24.01 (discussing the practical problems created by extensive hearings in international arbitrations). As discussed above, if the parties jointly agree on a hearing longer than the Tribunal deems necessary, the Tribunal is likely to acquiesce.

purpose of presenting his testimony in written or oral form. (LCIA, Art. 20.) Although some preparation of witnesses is standard practice in international arbitration, it is useful for the rules to take an express position on this issue.

Another issue that can cause contention in international arbitration is the treatment of party witnesses. Under the civil-law system, parties to the case typically cannot be treated as witnesses, whereas under the common law anyone can be treated as a witness and the fact that the witness is also a party to the case is a factor to be considered in weighing his or her testimony.

The LCIA Rules provide expressly that anyone can be heard as a witness on any issue of fact or expertise "notwithstanding that the individual is a party to the arbitration or was or is an officer, employee or shareholder of any party." The Iran-United States Claims Tribunal settled this issue by compromising on an approach that allowed parties to provide information to the Tribunal, but not officially swearing them as witnesses.[53]

Experts Appointed by the Tribunal

Article 55

(a) The Tribunal may, after consultation with the parties, appoint one or more independent experts to report to it on specific issues designated by the Tribunal. A copy of the expert's terms of reference, established by the Tribunal, having regard to any observations of the parties, shall be communicated to the parties. Any such expert shall be required to sign an appropriate confidentiality undertaking.

(b) Subject to Article 52, upon receipt of the expert's report, the Tribunal shall communicate a copy of the report to the parties, which shall be given the opportunity to express, in writing, their opinion on the report. A party may, subject to Article 52, examine any document on which the expert has relied in such a report.

(c) At the request of a party, the parties shall be given the opportunity to question the expert at a hearing. At this hearing, the parties may present expert witnesses to testify on the points at issue.

(d) The opinion of any expert on the issue or issues submitted to the expert shall be subject to the Tribunal's power of assessment of those issues in the context of all the circumstances of the case, unless the parties have agreed that the expert's determination shall be conclusive in respect of any specific issue.

---

[53] *See* Howard M. Holtzmann, *Some Lessons of the Iran-United States Claims Tribunal*, PRIVATE INVESTORS ABROAD — PROBLEMS AND SOLUTIONS IN INTERNATIONAL BUSINESS, Section 16.04(4) (parties and party representatives may not be considered witnesses, but they may be heard and questioned and an award can take into account the information provided by an interested person).

Commentary on Article 55

Article 55 addresses the appointment of experts by the Tribunal.[54] Tribunal-appointed experts are more common in cases involving highly technical subject matter where specific expertise is deemed to be necessary to have a full understanding of the factual issues at stake.

Given the nature of intellectual property disputes, which often involve highly technical subjects such as biotechnology, computer science, pharmaceuticals, semiconductors and the like, one can expect that Tribunal-appointed experts are more likely to be appointed in intellectual property cases than in the average case. Moreover, this is more true in pure intellectual property disputes, such as patent or software copyright infringement, than in licensing disputes. But licensing disputes often can in themselves require the Tribunal to decide highly technical issues relating to, for example, the validity of the underlying patent, which also may lead the Tribunal to opt for the appointment of an expert.

Given the potential importance of Tribunal-appointed experts in the type of cases being arbitrated under the WIPO Rules, the provisions of the WIPO Rules addressing this subject are the most detailed of those surveyed. Although based in large part on Article 27 of the UNCITRAL Rules, Article 52 of the WIPO Rules addresses subjects not considered by the UNCITRAL Rules, such as the signature of confidentiality undertakings by the expert, which can be of great import in intellectual property cases.

The procedure established by the WIPO Rules for the appointment of the expert is as follows:

1. The Tribunal consults with both the parties about the appointment of one or more independent experts. The expert's task shall be limited to reporting to the Tribunal "on one or more specific issues designated to it by the Tribunal."
2. If it decides that an expert(s) is warranted taking into account the comments of the parties, the Tribunal shall appoint an expert(s). The expert(s) shall be required to sign "an appropriate confidentiality undertaking."
3. The Tribunal shall prepare terms of reference for the expert(s) and shall give the parties the opportunity to provide observations about the terms of reference.[55]
4. The Tribunal shall "establish" the terms of reference and communicate them to the parties.
5. The expert(s) shall prepare the report and communicate it to the Tribunal.
6. Unless the report contains confidential information, the Tribunal shall send the report to the parties, who shall be given the opportunity to "express, in writing,

---

[54] A comprehensive study of the use of tribunal and party-appointed experts in international arbitration is found in ARBITRATION AND EXPERTISE, Institute of International Business Law and Practice (1994), *see also* BROWER & BRUESCHKE, *supra* note 33, at 198–204 (containing a useful discussion of this issue under the practice of the Iran-United States Claims Tribunal) and COE, *supra* note 5, at Section 9.11 (comparing the treatment of experts under various procedures).

[55] There is no requirement with respect to the order of steps 2, 3 and 4.

their opinion on the report.'' The parties are also given the opportunity to examine any document on which the expert(s) has relied in preparing the report.

7. If either party requests, a hearing will be held about the expert report. The parties are given the chance to question the expert and to present their own experts to testify on the points at issue.

One procedural issue of some importance that is addressed in the AAA, LCIA, and UNCITRAL Rules, but not in the WIPO Rules, is the obligation of the parties to provide the Tribunal-appointed expert with information it requests. (ICC, Art. 20; AAA, Art. 22; LCIA, Art. 21; UNCITRAL, Art. 27.) These other rules all contain an express provision requiring the parties to provide the expert with relevant information s/he may require to complete the report, and the AAA and UNCITRAL Rules provide further that if there is a dispute between the expert and a party about the relevance of any requested information, it shall be decided by the Tribunal. It is not apparent why the drafters of the WIPO Rules decided not to include this element of the UNCITRAL Rules in Article 55 of the WIPO Rules.

Article 55 of the WIPO Rules provides further that, unless the parties have expressly agreed that the expert's opinion shall be conclusive with respect to any specific issue, the expert's opinion remains subject to the ''the Tribunal's assessment of those issues in the context of all the circumstances of the case.'' Therefore, although it would be more common for the Tribunal to follow the expert's report, the Tribunal is not required to do so and experience indicates that there are times when the Tribunal may reject the expert report either in whole or in part.

IX. MISCELLANEOUS ISSUES

Default

Article 56

(a) **If the Claimant, without showing good cause, fails to submit its Statement of Claim in accordance with Article 41, the Tribunal shall terminate the proceedings.**

(b) **If the Respondent, without showing good cause, fails to submit its Statement of Defense in accordance with Article 42, the Tribunal may nevertheless proceed with the arbitration and make the award.**

(c) **The Tribunal may also proceed with the arbitration and make the award if a party, without showing good cause, fails to avail itself of the opportunity to present its case within the period of time determined by the Tribunal.**

(d) **If a party, without showing good cause, fails to comply with any provision of, or requirement under, these Rules or any direction given by the Tribunal, the Tribunal may draw the inferences therefrom that it considers appropriate.**

Commentary on Article 56

Article 56 discusses the various types of default that may occur during the course of proceedings and the impact such default has on the Tribunal's treatment of the case.

Generally speaking, two related issues decide how default is treated under the WIPO Rules — first, who is the defaulting party, and second, when does the default occur. Rarely, if ever, will default by a party responding to a claim be sufficient to end proceedings, unless the party bringing the claim agrees that it should have this effect. This is true whether the defaulting party is the Respondent in answering the initial claims or the Claimant in responding to any counterclaims.

Keeping in mind these basic principles, Article 57(a) of the WIPO Rules provides that if the Claimant, without showing good cause, fails to submit its Statement of Claim, the Tribunal "shall terminate the proceedings." The Tribunal is not given discretion to continue the case, as it would have were the Claimant's default to occur later in the proceedings. This is presumably because, at this point in the proceeding, prior to the Respondent's filing of its Statement of Defense and possible counterclaims, the Respondent is not yet deemed to have a sufficient interest in the proceeding to mitigate against outright termination. Were the Respondent to desire to continue the case — for example, to raise counterclaims — it could bring its own arbitration under the relevant agreement.

In the more common case where the Respondent without good cause fails to submit its Statement of Defense, Article 56(b) authorizes the Tribunal to proceed with the arbitration and issue the award, but this is not mandatory.

Article 56(c) deals with the situation where any party without good cause fails to "avail itself of the opportunity to present its case within the time period determined by the tribunal." This is geared to parties who, after the submission of the initial Statements of Claim and Defense, either stop participating in the proceedings altogether or fail to present their memorials in the time allotted. In such case the Tribunal may, but need not, proceed with the arbitration and make the award.

If the party failing to participate is the Respondent, the Claimant generally will wish the case to proceed. Unless there are strong reasons not to do so, the Tribunal generally will agree to continue the case. However, were the Claimant for some reason to ask the Tribunal to terminate the action because of the Respondent's default (for example, to avoid counterclaims) the Tribunal should agree to do so, unless there are other parties involved that might be adversely affected.

If the Claimant is the defaulting party, the Tribunal would follow the Respondent's wishes with respect to continuation of the case. Generally, the Respondent will wish the case to terminate, and the Tribunal will agree to this request. It is conceivable that the Tribunal would allow the case to proceed if there were other parties involved that might be adversely affected by the dismissal, but it is difficult to imagine when this would arise. If the Respondent wishes the case to continue (for example, because of counterclaims), the Tribunal would be expected to agree to this request.

Article 56(d) addresses adverse inferences created by default. It provides that if a party without good cause fails to comply with the WIPO Rules or any direction given by the Tribunal, the Tribunal is free to draw any inference it deems appropriate from this failure. For example, as discussed above, were the Tribunal to order one of the parties to produce documents under Article 48 and the party were to fail to do so without good cause, the Tribunal would likely infer from this that the documents would have provided information against that party's interest.

All of the rules surveyed have provisions addressing default. (ICC, Art. 6; AAA, Art. 23; LCIA, Art. 15; UNCITRAL, Art. 28.) Although the WIPO Rules would appear most closely modelled on the UNCITRAL Rules, the principles underlying all the default provisions are similar. However, the WIPO Rules are unique in containing an express provision in Article 56(d) permitting the Tribunal to draw adverse inferences from the failure to comply with the WIPO Rules or Tribunal directions. Although the Tribunal's authority to draw adverse inferences would be implied in the other rules surveyed, having an express provision in the rules increases predictability and is an improvement over the other rules surveyed.

Closure of Proceedings

Article 57

(a) **The Tribunal shall declare the proceedings closed when it is satisfied that the parties have had adequate opportunity to present submissions and evidence.**

(b) **The Tribunal may, if it considers it necessary owing to exceptional circumstances, decide, on its own motion or upon application of a party, to reopen the proceedings it declared to be closed at any time before the award is made.**

Commentary on Article 57

Article 57 addresses the closure of the proceedings. Article 57(a) gives the Tribunal full discretion to close the proceedings when it is satisfied that each party has had "adequate" opportunity to present its case. In cases where one of the parties has requested a hearing, closure could only occur after that hearing was held, but otherwise the rules give the Tribunal complete freedom to decide when the parties have had adequate opportunity to be heard, taking into account the Tribunal's obligations under Article 38(b).

After the proceedings have been declared closed by the Tribunal but before the award is made, Article 57(b) gives the Tribunal the right to reopen the proceedings. The rules provide that such a decision may be made at the request of a party or on the Tribunal's own motion if "exceptional circumstances" warrant the reopening. This places the burden on the moving party to show that there is a good reason to reopen the proceeding and that substantial prejudice would not result from doing so.

The ICC Rules are the only other of the rules surveyed to refer to the closure of the "proceedings," and provide that the Tribunal can declare the proceedings closed when it is satisfied that each party has had "reasonable" opportunity to present its case. (ICC, Art. 22.) Moreover, in a recent amendment to the ICC Rules, after closing the proceedings the Tribunal is required to inform the ICC Court when it expects to submit a draft award. Here again, as with many of the recent changes to the ICC Rules, the goal is to increase the speed with which the award is issued.

Both the AAA and UNCITRAL Rules have provisions that are similar to Article 57, but each of these rules refers to closure of hearings rather than the closure of proceedings. (AAA, Art. 24; UNCITRAL, Art. 29.) The use of the term "proceedings" extends more broadly than simply the hearings and would seem to be an improvement over the AAA and UNCITRAL approaches. Thus, for example, in a case where post-hearing briefs had been ordered, the "proceedings" would be ordered closed only after those briefs were submitted.[56] The LCIA rules do not refer at all to closure of the proceedings.

The inclusion in arbitral rules of a provision dealing with the closure of proceedings is a good example of the rules anticipating a potential problem before it arises. It would not be unheard of for a party to submit a document long after the hearing and request the Tribunal to take it into account in rendering its award. Although the Tribunal would be fully justified in excluding the document under its general powers, officially closing the proceedings has the benefit of increasing predictability and would reduce any concern the Tribunal may have over challenge to the enforcement of the award based on the refusal to admit the late-filed document.

Waiver

Article 58

A party which knows that any provision of, or requirement under, these Rules, or any direction given by the Tribunal, has not been complied with, and yet proceeds with the arbitration without promptly recording an objection to such non-compliance, shall be deemed to have waived its right to object.

Commentary on Article 58

Article 58 addresses waiver. It provides that a party who (1) knows that a provision or requirement of the WIPO Rules or any direction has not been complied with *and* (2) proceeds with the arbitration *without* (3) promptly raising an objection to the noncompliance, shall waive its right to object thereto.

Article 58 is based closely on Article 30 of the UNCITRAL Rules and Article 25 of the AAA Rules, with the AAA Rules adding a requirement that the objection must

---

[56] *See* CRAIG, *supra* note 6, at Section 25.06 (discussing the distinction between the closure of "hearings" and "proceedings").

be made in writing. A written objection is not required by the UNCITRAL or WIPO Rules.

The LCIA provision on waiver is also very similar to the WIPO Rule, but applies the waiver concept more broadly to any provision of the Arbitration Agreement (including the LCIA Rules) and clarifies that the waiver is irrevocable, which can be assumed from the WIPO, UNCITRAL and AAA Rules.

Article 33 of the ICC Rules applies the waiver concept even more broadly than the LCIA Rules to cover non-compliance with, in addition to "any provision of, or requirement under, these Rules, or any direction given by the Tribunal" as in the WIPO Rules, "any other rules applicable to the proceedings, . . . any requirement under the arbitration agreement relating to the constitution of the Arbitral Tribunal, or to the conduct of the proceedings." Also, although the WIPO and other rules discussed herein all require that a party "promptly" raise an objection to non-compliance, the ICC rules do not mention a time frame. Moreover, the ICC rules refer to "raising" an objection, but here, too, the form of the objection is not prescribed.

The inclusion of an express provision in the rules on waiver is another example of the rules anticipating a potential problem before it arises. The purpose of the waiver provisions is to avoid the situation where a party tries to rely on the Tribunal's or the other party's alleged failure to abide by the Rules or the arbitration agreement long after those acts have been committed, typically in the context of trying to avoid enforcement of the award. By expressly including waiver provisions in the rules themselves, any risk in this respect is diminished.

INTERIM MEASURES OF PROTECTION; SECURITY FOR CLAIMS AND COSTS; AND COMMENTARY ON THE WIPO EMERGENCY RELIEF RULES (*IN TOTO*)

Article 46

*Richard Allan Horning**

INTRODUCTION

The ability of an injured party to have recourse to a decision maker for orders for relief of an interim nature is an important element in the protection of intellectual property. The "first mover advantage," and the "law of increasing returns," place a high premium on the ability of the owners of intellectual property rights to quickly fence out infringing rivals. This is particularly true where the enterprise exceeding licensed rights to technology and thereby infringing patents, copyrights, trademarks, trade secrets or other forms of licensed intellectual property is new and marginally capitalized, in that its assets are likely to be difficult to reach in execution on a monetary award or judgment, or where the continuing effect of the infringement will be hard to detect and thus difficult or impossible to quantify in monetary terms. In intellectual property disputes there is also always a concern that the infringing party might place important evidence beyond reach, by alteration, spoliation, transfer or subterfuge, or that the infringer will retransfer the technology to third parties. The Silicon Valley shibboleth, "Speed is God, and time is the instrument of the devil," sums up the entrepreneur's perspective rather nicely: quickly obtained injunctions and other relief orders are often the only real remedy.

The national courts typically have a defined and developed procedure for hearing and determining pleas for interim relief.[1] The clerk's office maintains customary business hours for the filing of papers in initiation of the proceedings, and in emergencies the court can be approached directly after hours. The enabling statutes

---

* Partner, Tomlinson Zisko Morosoli & Maser LLP, Palo Alto, California. B.A. University of California, 1966; J.D. Duke University School of Law, 1969. The views expressed are those of the author. The author wishes to acknowledge, with appreciation, the assistance of Benjamin Gluck, a student at Stanford Law School, Stanford, California, in the research and preparation of this paper.

[1] *See, e.g.*, Richard Allan Horning, *Provisional Relief in Technology Litigation*, in INTELLECTUAL PROPERTY LITIGATION IN TECHNOLOGY CASES 95 (1992).

and procedural rules often permit the presentation of *ex parte* applications for relief, and usually provide for a hearing on the application for interim relief on an accelerated time schedule, often joined with the accelerated gathering of proof.[2] A preliminary assessment of the likelihood of the applicant prevailing after a full trial is usually part of the judicial or statutory formula governing the granting or denial of a request for interim relief. The party securing an interim order is usually required to post monetary security against a decision, taken later after a full trial on the merits, that the granting of interim relief, in light of the fully developed facts or applicable law, was improvident. The national court system sometimes, but not always, permits expedited appeals to be taken from decisions to grant or withhold interim relief.

Resort to the national courts for interim relief offers another important advantage to the owner of intellectual property: the full coercive powers of the courts are available to secure compliance with judicial orders for interim relief. Property can be seized, and individuals incarcerated, in exercise of the ultimate weapons for securing compliance with judicial orders.[3]

Parties contracting for the creation, exploitation and use of intellectual property often find it advantageous to anticipate the possibility of disputes and to consider the alternatives to the national courts for dispute resolution. Intellectual property contracts, like other contracts, may provide for the exclusive use of arbitration as the dispute resolution mechanism. Among the reasons often thought felicitous to the adoption of an arbitration clause are: (1) the supposed simplicity of arbitration compared to civil litigation in the national courts; (2) the supposed lower cost of arbitration as contrasted to civil litigation (particularly of the American style); (3) the confidentiality of arbitration as compared to the "public" nature of the records and proceedings in civil litigation; (4) the supposed greater speed and efficiency of the arbitration process compared to the delays often experienced in the civil courts; (5) the ability to command the attention of decision makers skilled in the relevant legal or technical areas as opposed to the sometimes one-off education of judges of national courts of general jurisdiction whose main qualification for the judiciary often seems to have been "friends in high places" or political patronage; (6) the avoidance of what owners of intellectual property often feel is the arbitrary and unpredictable nature of trials by jury, where verdicts are sometimes perceived to turn on the sympathy vote of under-educated jurors swayed by the emotional arguments of counsel; (7) the supposed final and binding character of arbitration as contrasted to the potential for seemingly endless appeals and remands in the civil courts; and (8) the ability to determine in advance the rules of law applicable to the proceedings as contrasted with the possible exposure to

---

[2] In the United States, a party can apply for and secure emergency orders permitting the commencement of "discovery" efforts immediately upon the initiation of the litigation. In the absence of such orders, initiation of discovery is deferred until a fixed time has passed; in some cases the deferral is indefinite subject to the power of the court, at the first pre-trial conference, to allow "discovery" to proceed.

[3] *See, e.g.,* Blue Sympathy Shipping Company Ltd. v. Serviocean International, S.A., 1994 WL 597144 (S.D.N.Y. July 6, 1994).

local parochial interests and choice-of-law rules that often appear to favor the legal regime of the country first acquiring jurisdiction. Contract provisions mandating dispute resolution by exclusive recourse to arbitration are thought to be particularly well adapted to the requirements of international transactions, where neither party is particularly comfortable with the thought that the other contracting party might be able to have recourse to a national court system and local jury not particularly well-versed in either international transactions, intellectual property law or the technical subject matter of the license.[4]

The proper relationship between the arbitral tribunal and the national courts on the subject of interim relief has long occupied the attention of scholars and the courts.[5]

---

[4] *See* Charles N. Brower, *Introduction, in* INTERNATIONAL ARBITRATION IN THE 21ST CENTURY: TOWARDS "JUDICIALIZATION" AND UNIFORMITY? — TWELFTH SOKOL COLLOQUIUM at ix (Richard B. Lillich and Charles N. Brower eds., 1995).

[5] *See generally*, Stewart A. Baker & Mark D. Davis, *Arbitral Proceedings Under the UNCITRAL Rules: The Experience of the Iran-United States Claims Tribunal*, 23 GEO. WASH. J. INT'L L. & ECON. 267 (1989); STEWART A. BAKER & MARK D. DAVIS, THE UNCITRAL ARBITRATION RULES IN PRACTICE: THE EXPERIENCE OF THE IRAN-UNITED STATES CLAIMS TRIBUNAL (1992); Marc Blessing, *International Arbitration Procedures*, 17 INT'L BUS. LAW. 408, 451 (1989); Karl-Heinz Böckstiegel, *Applying the UNCITRAL Rules: The Experience of the Iran-United States Claims Tribunal*, 4 INT'L TAX & BUS. LAW. 266 (1986); Kevin J. Brody, *An Argument for Pre-Award Attachment in International Arbitration under the New York Convention*, 18 CORNELL INT'L L.J. 99 (1985); Charles N. Brower & Ronald E.M. Goodman, *Provisional Measures and the Protection of ICSID Jurisdictional Exclusivity against Municipal Proceedings*, 6 ICSID REV.-FOREIGN INVESTMENT L.J. 431 (1991); Charles N. Brower & W. Michael Tupman, *Court-Ordered Provisional Measures under the New York Convention*, 80 AM. J. INT'L L. 24 (1986); Bernardo M. Cremades, *Is Exclusion of Concurrent Courts' Jurisdiction over Conservatory Measures to be Introduced through a Revision of the Convention?*, 6(3) J. INT'L ARB. 105 (1989); Georges R. Delaume, *ICSID Tribunals and Provisional Measures — A Review of the Cases*, 1 ICSID REV.-FOREIGN INVESTMENT L.J. 237 (1986); Paul D. Friedland, *Provisional Measures in ICSID Arbitration*, 2 ARB. INT'L 335 (1986); Michael F. Hoellering, *Interim Measures and Arbitration: The Situation in the United States*, 46 ARB. J. 22 (1991); Michael F. Hoellering, *Interim Relief in International Arbitration, in* ARBITRATION AND THE LICENSING PROCESS 3–55 (Robert Goldscheider & Michael de Haas eds. 1984); Michael F. Hollering, *Interim Relief in Aid of International Commercial Arbitration,* 1984 WIS. INT'L L.J. 1; Michael F. Hoellering, *Conservatory and Provisional Measures in International Arbitration: The AAA's Experience*, 47 ARB. J. 40 (1992); Andrew S. Holmes, *Pre-Award Attachment under the UN Convention on the Recognition and Enforcement of Foreign Arbitral Awards*, 21 VA. J. INT'L L. 785 (1981); Wolfgang Kühn, *Preliminary Remedies in Arbitration Matters*, 12 INT'L BUS. LAW. 111 (1984); Edward R. Leahy & Kenneth J. Pierce, *Sanctions to Control Party Misbehavior in International Arbitration*, 26 VA. J. INT'L L. 291 (1986); Eric H.K. Lee, *Security for Costs in International Arbitrations*, 5 BUS. L. REV. 286 (1984); Neil E. McDonnell, *The Availability of Provisional Relief in International Commercial Arbitration*, 22 COLUM. J. TRANSNAT'L L. 273 (1984); William E. Keitel, Note, *Pre-Arbitration Attachment: Is it Available in International Disputes?*, 1 REV. LITIGATION 211 (1981); Jan Paulsson, *Fast-Track Arbitration in Europe (with Special Reference to the WIPO Expedited Arbitration Rules)*, 18 HASTINGS INT'L COMP. L. REV. 713 (1995); Alan Redfern, *Arbitration and the Courts: Interim Measures of Protection — Is the Tide About to Turn*, 30 TEX. INT'L L. J. 71 (1995); Douglas Reichert, *Provisional Remedies in the Context of International Commercial Arbitration,* 3 INT'L TAX & BUS. LAW. 368 (1986); Hans Smit, *Provisional Relief in International Arbitration: The*

The principle of party autonomy permits entities to attempt contractually to specify the effect of an arbitration clause on the respective powers of national courts and arbitrators to grant interim relief.[6] All too often, however, the applicable contract is silent on the role of the courts and the arbitrators in entertaining and determining applications for various forms of interim relief.[7]

The power of arbitrators to render interim awards and make interim orders, including interim relief, is said to be "inherent."[8] Premising the exercise of authority to grant interim relief or make other provisional orders on the "inherent power" of arbitrators is probably viewed by sober business men and women as unsatisfactory. This view has some experiential basis, given the reluctance of some national courts to approve of the exercise of a power to grant provisional remedies not specifically contemplated by the rules governing the arbitration.[9]

The specific interim relief rules of the international arbitral institutions have thus assumed an important role in the debate on the power of arbitrators, and the relationship of the exercise of that power to the exercise of power by the national courts in international arbitration. In this paper I remark upon some of the issues in this debate in the context of WIPO Article 46 and the WIPO Emergency Relief Rules (which are reproduced in their entirety in the Appendix *infra*.)

ICC and Other Proposed Rules, 1 AM. REV. INT'L ARB. 388 (1990); David E. Wagoner, *Interim Relief in International Arbitration*, 51 DISPUTE RESOLUTION JOURNAL 68 (October 1996).

[6] A contract might, for example, provide for the settlement of "any and all disputes arising under or related to the agreement between the parties," while at the same time providing that "either party shall be free, not withstanding the initiation of a demand for arbitration in accordance with this agreement, to seek interim equitable relief from any court of competent jurisdiction." Another variation on this theme is an arbitration clause providing for arbitration but stating that "neither party shall be precluded hereby from seeking provisional remedies in the courts of any jurisdiction, including but not limited to temporary restraining orders and preliminary injunctions to protect its rights and interest, but such shall not be sought as a means to avoid or stay arbitration."

[7] In the drafting of Article 9 of the UNCITRAL Model Law, the United States in particular noted the wide range of interim relief measures available from the national courts, and their particular importance to the protection of trade secrets and proprietary information. Sixth Secretariat Note, Analytical Compilation of Government Comments, A/CN.9/263 (19 March 1985), *reproduced in* HOWARD M. HOLTZMANN & JOSEPH E. NEUHAUS, A GUIDE TO THE UNCITRAL MODEL LAW ON INTERNATIONAL COMMERCIAL ARBITRATION 342 (1989) [hereinafter GUIDE TO UNCITRAL MODEL LAW].

[8] Michael Hoellering, *Interim Measures and Arbitration: The Situation in the U.S.*, unpublished paper delivered at ICCA CONFERENCE ON INTERIM MEASURES AND ARBITRATION, Bologna, Italy, April 19, 1991. *See also*, Ramos Mendez, *Arbitrage International et Mesures Conservatoires*, 1985 REV. ARB. 56; Eric A. Schwartz, *The Practices and Experiences of the ICC Court*, in CONSERVATORY AND PROVISIONAL MEASURES IN INTERNATIONAL ARBITRATION 57–58 (1993) [hereinafter CONSERVATORY AND PROVISIONAL MEASURES].

[9] Piero Bernardini, *The Powers of the Arbitrator*, in CONSERVATORY AND PROVISIONAL MEASURES *supra* note 8 at 29.

Interim Measures of Protection; Security for Claims and Costs

Article 46

(a)   At the request of a party, the Tribunal may issue any provisional orders or take other interim measures it deems necessary, including injunctions and measures for the conservation of goods which form part of the subject-matter in dispute, such as an order for their deposit with a third person or for the sale of perishable goods. The Tribunal may make the granting of such measures subject to appropriate security being furnished by the requesting party.

(b)   At the request of a party, the Tribunal may, if it considers it to be required by exceptional circumstances, order the other party to provide security, in a form to be determined by the Tribunal, for the claim or counter-claim, as well as for costs referred to in Article 72.

(c)   Measures and orders contemplated under this Article may take the form of an interim award.

(d)   A request addressed by a party to a judicial authority for interim measures or for security for the claim or counter-claim, or for the implementation of any such measures or orders granted by the Tribunal, shall not be deemed incompatible with the Arbitration Agreement, or deemed to be a waiver of that Agreement.

I. THE POWERS CONFERRED ON THE ARBITRATORS

Arbitration rules should be viewed as a source of arbitral power and authority. As a creature of contract, arbitration ultimately derives its power not from notions of inherent authority, but rather from the positive expressions and agreements of the parties. That expression can be either positive — the parties by contract specifically empower the arbitrators to grant certain forms of interim relief — or it can be implied through the adhesion of the parties to a particular set of rules providing for the possibility of interim relief and provisional remedies.

The issue of positive power vs. implied power was mooted in the context of the interim relief issue during the drafting of what became Article 17 of the UNCITRAL Model Law. The UNCITRAL Model Law Working Group ultimately opted to use the implied power approach — the parties are deemed to have given the arbitral tribunal power to make interim awards by adopting in their agreement a set of rules conferring this power on the arbitrators.[10]

The implied agreement of the parties conferring power to grant interim relief upon the arbitrators was left in an ambiguous state in the 1988 ICC Rules. Article 8(5) of the 1988 ICC Rules neither mandated nor excluded the possibility of provisional measures

---

[10] *See* Guide to UNCITRAL Model Law *supra* note 7 at 530.

by the arbitrators,[11] and thus did not reserve or create any specific power in the arbitrators to entertain applications for interim relief. The leading treatise on ICC arbitration took the view that under the 1988 ICC Rules, "ICC arbitrators ha[d] the inherent power to make interlocutory orders relevant to the arbitration and addressed to the parties."[12] In Article 23 of the new 1998 ICC Rules of Arbitration the ambiguity was eliminated: the ICC Rules now specifically confer upon the arbitrators the power to order "any interim or conservatory measure [the arbitration tribunal] deems appropriate."[13]

The 1985 LCIA Rules addressed the subject of arbitral power by specifically conferring upon the arbitration tribunal power to entertain and grant certain forms of interim relief. Some powers to render interim relief in LCIA arbitrations governed by the 1985 LCIA Rules were exclusive to the arbitration tribunal, while the power to afford other forms of interim relief was specifically shared with the national courts. In the 1985 LCIA Rules the arbitration tribunal had the exclusive power to order the posting of security for costs,[14] order disproportionate interim payments for the costs of arbitration,[15] require the preservation, storage or sale of property,[16] and compel the inspection and production of property and documents.[17] The power to make a pre-award order requiring the posting of security for the payment of the award was shared between the courts and the arbitrator in the 1985 LCIA Rules.[18] The 1985 LCIA Rules contemplated that the parties could have resort to a competent court for other non-specified pre-award conservatory measures.[19]

---

[11] Eric A. Schwartz, *The Practices and Experience of the ICC Court*, CONSERVATORY AND PROVISIONAL MEASURES, *supra* note 8 at 46.

[12] W. LAURENCE CRAIG, WILLIAM W. PARK & JAN PAULSSON, INTERNATIONAL CHAMBER OF COMMERCE ARBITRATION (2d ed. 1991) [hereinafter ICC ARBITRATION], § 26.05, at 416. Article 21 of the 1988 ICC Rules was the only then-extant ICC Rule specifically contemplating the possibility of an interim ruling. This Article mandated that all awards, "whether partial or definitive," were subject to scrutiny by the ICC Court of Arbitration.

The 1998 ICC Rules draw an appropriate distinction between orders and awards, permitting the tribunal to fashion interim measures as either. ICC RULES, Article 23 (1998). Only "awards" are subject to scrutiny by the ICC Court. ICC RULES, Article 27 (1998).

[13] ICC RULES, Article 23(1) (1998). The new ICC provision begins with the proviso "unless the parties have otherwise agreed," thus giving recognition to the freedom of the parties to contractually alter the power of the arbitrators in respect of orders for conservatory or interim measures. The 1998 LCIA Rules give similar recognition to this specific example of party autonomy. *See* LCIA RULES, Article 25.1 (1998). There is no similar limitation in the 1997 AAA International Rules, although other provisions of the 1997 AAA International Rules do recognize party autonomy. *See* AAA INTERNATIONAL RULES, Article 28.5 and Introduction (1997).

[14] LCIA RULES, Article 15.2 (1985).

[15] LCIA RULES, Article 15.1 (1985).

[16] LCIA RULES, Article 13.1(h) (1985).

[17] LCIA RULES, Articles 13.1(g),(i) (1985).

[18] LCIA RULES, Article 15.4 (1985).

[19] LCIA RULES, Article 15.4 (1985).

Under the new 1998 LCIA Rules the power to make interim relief orders is no longer shared with the national courts, except in those situations where relief is required before the arbitration tribunal has been formed "and in exceptional cases thereafter."[20] LCIA arbitrators are now empowered to order the preservation, storage, sale or other disposal of *any* property or thing under the control of any party[21] and, on a provisional basis, may order *any* relief which the arbitrators could grant in the final award, including the payment of money.[22] The power to require a party to post security for payment of the award is no longer shared with the national courts under the 1998 LCIA Rules.[23]

The UNCITRAL Rules grant to the arbitration tribunal virtually unlimited authority to order interim measures. Under the UNCITRAL Rules the tribunal has the power to

> take any interim measures it deems necessary in respect of the subject matter of the dispute, including measures for the conservation of the goods forming the subject matter in dispute, such as ordering their deposit with a third person or sale of perishable goods.[24]

The AAA International Arbitration Rules adopted in 1991 followed the example of the UNCITRAL Rules. AAA International Rule 22 provided that

> [a]t the request of any party, the tribunal may take any interim measures it deems necessary in respect of the subject-matter of the dispute, including measures for the conservation of goods which are the subject matter in dispute, such as ordering their deposit with a third party or the sale of perishable goods.[25]

Under the new 1997 AAA International Rules "the tribunal may take whatever interim measures it deems necessary, including injunctive relief and measures for the protection or conservation of property."[26]

Not surprisingly given the nature of the consultation process which led to the adoption of the WIPO Rules,[27] WIPO Article 46(a) grants broad powers to the arbitrators.

---

[20] LCIA RULES, Article 25.3 (1998).

[21] LCIA Article 25.1(b) (1998). Note, however, that the conservatory measures, including sale, available under this Article must concern "property or thing[s] . . . relating to the subject matter of the arbitration."

[22] LCIA RULES, Article 25.1(c) (1998).

[23] LCIA RULES, Article 25.1(a) (1998).

[24] UNCITRAL RULES, Article 26. *See also*, CALIFORNIA CODE OF CIVIL PROCEDURE § 1297.171. ("Unless otherwise agreed by the parties, the arbitral tribunal may, at the request of a party [to an international commercial contract providing for arbitration], order a party to take any interim measure of protection as the arbitral tribunal may consider necessary in respect to the subject matter of the dispute"). Article 9 of the UNCITRAL MODEL LAW contains a similar broadly worded grant of power.

[25] AAA INTERNATIONAL ARBITRATION RULES, Article 22.1 (1991).

[26] AAA INTERNATIONAL ARBITRATION RULES, Article 21.1 (1997).

[27] *See* Hans Smit, *Managing an International Arbitration: An Arbitrator's View*, WORLDWIDE FORUM ON THE ARBITRATION OF INTELLECTUAL PROPERTY DISPUTES 216 (1994) [hereinafter WORLDWIDE FORUM].

> At the request of a party, the Tribunal may issue any provisional orders or take other interim measures it deems necessary, including injunctions and measures for the conservation of goods which form part of the subject matter in dispute, such as an order for the deposit with a third person or for the sale of perishable goods. The Tribunal may make the granting of such measures subject to appropriate security being furnished by the requesting party.[28]

In keeping with the modern trend in arbitration rules, the WIPO Rules have thus conferred broad powers on the arbitration tribunal to fashion appropriate interim relief — "any provisional orders . . . or other interim measures it deems necessary."[29] The WIPO Rules, in contrast to some of their predecessors, specifically refer to the existence of injunctive powers as being possessed by the arbitrators.[30] This reference might be viewed as further broadening the tribunal's powers, although it could also be viewed as merely referencing the phraseology favored by American and English courts in describing certain forms of interim relief.[31] It would seem to be an important reference, however, since the concept of an injunction, and the possibilities of its extended reach, are well known.

II.   THE LACK OF COERCIVE POWER

Whatever the arbitration rules may state about the possibilities of interim relief from an arbitral tribunal, arbitrators lack one often important element in the calculus of interim relief considerations that is exclusively reserved to the national courts — coercive power. In his 1996 Keating Lecture, Sir Michael Kerr commented on this power in noting the critical role of national courts in international arbitration:

> [I]t has to be accepted as a fact of life that international arbitration cannot function without the assistance of national courts. Only they possess the coercive powers to enforce agreements to arbitrate, as well as the resulting awards. Without the intervention and assistance of the national courts, international arbitration would be wholly ineffective.[32]

---

[28] WIPO Arbitration Rules, Article 46(a).

[29] "At the request of a party, the Tribunal may, if it considers it to be required by exceptional circumstances, order the other party to provide security, in a form to be determined by the Tribunal, for the claim or counter-claim, as well as for costs referred to in Article 72 [concerning the award of the legal costs and others incurred by a party during the arbitration]." WIPO Arbitration Rules, Article 46(b).

[30] The 1997 AAA International Rules use the phrase "injunctive relief" in providing the arbitrators with the power to take interim measures. See AAA International Rules, Article 21.1 (1997).

[31] The UNCITRAL Model Law could be viewed in some sense as giving an even broader grant of power: unlike the UNCITRAL Model Rules, AAA International Rules, and WIPO Rules, the Model Law omits the reference to the examples. The commentary on the Model Law makes it clear, however, that the absence of the examples was not intended to necessarily broaden the arbitrators powers, but rather viewed the deleted examples as too geared to a particular type of transaction. See Guide to UNCITRAL Model Law, *supra* note 7 at 530–31.

[32] Sir Michael Kerr, *Concord & Conflict in International Arbitration*, The Keating Lecture, October 29, 1996, London.

The lack of coercive power, however, does not mean that arbitrators are totally powerless to secure compliance with interim orders and awards. According to the Craig-Park-Paulsson dictum, interim orders and awards of arbitrators are almost always accepted.[33] The failure of a party to obey an interim order for preservation of evidence will almost certainly cause the arbitrator to draw adverse inferences.[34] Although controversial, it has been suggested that the failure of a party to carry out an interim order might be taken into account in other respects, particularly concerning damages.[35] As Stephen Bond aptly sums up, "legally binding force does not seem to be an inherent characteristic of interim measures."[36]

III. THE EFFECT OF AN APPLICATION TO SECURE RELIEF FROM A COURT

There are a myriad of circumstances in which a party bound by an arbitration clause might require an interim remedy affecting a third party beyond the jurisdictional reach of the arbitration tribunal. Issues concerning interim relief may arise before the arbitration tribunal is summoned, when there may be no available alternative but the courts. Even as to a party properly brought before an arbitration tribunal the coercive power of the national courts might be required for effective interim relief.

English decisional law recognizes that the power of the national court to grant interim relief is compatible with arbitration;[37] the American courts, however, have struggled with their proper role in relation to the granting of interim relief in international arbitrations.[38] The *McCreary Tire* line of decisions suggests that the courts are powerless to act in the face of an arbitration clause not specifically providing for the jurisdiction of the national courts to act on applications for interim

---

[33] The Craig-Park-Paulsson dictum observes that

[a]s with other orders by the tribunal, disobedience of an interlocutory order carries with it no immediate legal sanction for the recalcitrant party. . . . Nevertheless, parties do comply almost always with interlocutory orders of the arbitral tribunal since failure to do so is likely to be interpreted as an act of bad faith and influence the decision on the merits.

ICC ARBITRATION *supra* note 12 § 26.05, at 416.

See also, Piero Bernardini, *supra* note 9, at 79 n. 40.

[34] Robert von Mehren, *Rules of Arbitral Bodies Considered from a Practical Point of View*, 9 INTERNATIONAL ARBITRATION 105, 111 (1992).

[35] *See* Seventh Secretariat Note, A/CN.9/264, on Article 18.5 of the UNCITRAL Model Law, GUIDE TO UNCITRAL MODEL LAW, *supra* note 7 at 543.

[36] Stephen R. Bond, *The Nature of Conservatory and Provisional Measures*, in CONSERVATORY AND PROVISIONAL MEASURES, *supra* note 8 at 16.

[37] *See, e.g.*, Mareva Compania Naviera, S.A. v. International Bulk Carriers, S.A., [1980] 1 All E.R. 213 (C.A. 1975); The Rena K, 1979 Q.B. 377 (1978); Channel Tunnel Group Ltd. v. Balfour Beatty Constr. Ltd., 1993 App. Cas. 334 (1993); Coppée-Lavalin SA/NV v. Ken-Ren Chem. & Fertilizers Ltd., [1994] 2 W. L. R. 631 (court order requiring the posting of security for costs is available in exceptional cases).

[38] *See generally*, George Bermann, *Provisional Relief in Transnational Litigation*, 35 COLUM. J. TRANSNAT'L L. 553, 597 (1997); William W. Park, *Text and Context in International Arbitration*, 15 B. U. INT'L L. J. 191, 205 (1997).

relief, given the lack of a specific reservation of such jurisdiction in the New York Convention.[39] The *McCreary Tire* line of decisions suggests that arbitration rules providing for the possibility of interim relief from arbitral tribunals may be the only mechanism for securing relief. By contrast, the line of decisions starting with *Carolina Power & Light Co. v. Uranex* suggests that coercive remedies and other interventions available only through the machinery of the state may often facilitate the arbitration process rather than denigrate it, and thus resort to the courts for interim measures is not necessarily inconsistent with the reference of the merits of the dispute to arbitration.[40] A recent analysis of these conflicting decisions suggests that

> the [New York] Convention's drafters intended to enhance the viability of private dispute resolution in order to reduce the overall costs of international business transactions. Judges who wish to preserve the integrity of this aim should examine the Convention's travaux préparatoires and accept the fact that article II(3) does not strip courts of the authority to grant pre-award interim measures. This would put an end to the expensive controversy that has surrounded the issue for twenty years. As a result, interim measures will secure their position in the framework of judicial power that gives force to privately chosen methods of dispute resolution.[41]

IV. THE RESERVATION OF POWER TO SEEK INTERIM RELIEF FROM THE COURTS

In assessing the power of an arbitration tribunal to grant interim relief and any restrictions on that power, and the role of the courts, one must look to the contract of the parties. To the extent that that contract does not alter the powers of the arbitrators, one must look to the specific rules of the institution adopted by the parties to govern the resolution of the dispute. In the 1988 ICC Rules, for example, the ICC specifically recognized the need for resort to the national courts for certain forms of interim relief prior to the appointment of the arbitrator.

> Before the file is transmitted to the arbitrator, and in exceptional circumstances even thereafter, the parties shall be at liberty to apply to any competent judicial authority for interim or conservatory measures, and they shall not by so doing be held to infringe the agreement to arbitrate or to affect the relevant power reserved to the arbitrator.

---

[39] McCreary Tire & Rubber Co. v. CEAT S.p.A., 501 F.2d 1032 (3rd Cir. 1974); Merrill, Lynch, Pearce, Fenner & Smith, Inc. v. McCollum, 666 S.W.2d 604 (1984), *cert. den.* 469 U.S. 1127 (1985); Cooper v. Ateliers de la Motobecane S.A., 57 N.Y.2d 408 (1982) (apparently superceded by enactment of New York CPLR § 7502(c); *see* Alvenus Shipping, Ltd. v. Delta Petroleum (U.S.A.) Ltd., 876 F. Supp. 482 (S.D.N.Y. 1994)).

[40] *See, e.g.*, Carolina Power & Light Co. v Uranex, 451 F.Supp. 1044, 1051 (N.D.Cal. 1977); Compania de Navegacion y Financiera Bosnia S.A. v. National Unity Maritime Salvage Co., 457 F.Supp. 1013 (S.D.N.Y. 1978); Teradyne, Inc. v. Mostek Corp., 797 F.2d 43 (1st Cir. 1986). *See generally*, Richard W. Hulbert, *The American Law Perspective, in* CONSERVATORY AND PROVISIONAL MEASURES, *supra* note 8 at 96.

[41] Charles H. Brower II, *What I Tell You Three Times is True: U.S. Courts and Pre-Award Interim Measures Under the New York Convention*, 35 VA. J. INT'L L. 971, 1022 (1995).

> Any such application and any measures taken by judicial authority must be notified without delay to the Secretariat of the International Court of Arbitration. The Secretariat shall inform the arbitrator thereof.[42]

The 1988 ICC Rule thus contemplated resort to the courts in situations where the arbitration has not been effective initiated, but only "in exceptional circumstances thereafter."[43]

In disputes governed by the new 1998 ICC Rules the parties may have resort to the courts for interim or conservatory measures "in appropriate circumstances" — as contrasted with the 1988 "exceptional circumstances" — after the arbitration has been initiated. This broadening of the circumstances where the ICC Rules specifically contemplate that recourse to the national courts may be appropriate would seem to place the ICC Rules more in alignment with other institutional rules.

The UNCITRAL Rules,[44] the 1991 and 1997 AAA International Arbitration Rules,[45] and WIPO Article 46(d) all broadly recognize that parties may need to seek recourse to the coercive power of the courts in some instances. Each of these sets of rules provide that the act of seeking such recourse is not antithetical to the continuation of the arbitration process. Thus WIPO Article 46(d) provides that:

> [a] request addressed by a party to a judicial authority for interim measures or for security for the claim or counter-claim, or for the implementation of any such measures or orders granted by the Tribunal, shall not be deemed incompatible with the Arbitration Agreement, or deemed to be a waiver of that Agreement.[46]

The WIPO Rules, in keeping with all major arbitration rules, thus recognize that the initiation of court proceedings to secure interim relief, or for the implementation of interim measures ordered by the tribunal, is not fatal to the arbitration clause or the arbitration process. By the same token, the creation of a power in the arbitration tribunal to grant interim relief does not, in and of itself, seem to bar making such applications to the national courts, although in the United States the *McCreary Tire* line of cases suggests that the granting of such relief by a national court could be problematical. Parties who wish to make it clear that they may have recourse to the

---

[42] ICC RULES, Article 8(5) (1988).

[43] The 1998 LCIA Rules contain a similar formulation. "The power of the Arbitral Tribunal under Article 25.1 shall not prejudice howsoever any party's right to apply to any state court or other judicial authority for interim or conservatory measures before the formation of the Arbitration Tribunal and, in exceptional cases, thereafter." LCIA RULES, Article 25.3 (1998).

[44] "A request for interim measures addressed by any party to a judicial authority shall not be deemed incompatible with the agreement to arbitrate, or as a waiver thereof." UNCITRAL RULES, Article 26(3).

[45] AAA INTERNATIONAL ARBITRATION RULES, Article 22.3 (1991); AAA INTERNATIONAL ARBITRATION RULES, Article 21.3 (1997).

[46] WIPO ARBITRATION RULES, Article 46(d). The Working Group on the UNCITRAL Model Law also took the view that interim measures by a national court are compatible with arbitration. *See* GUIDE TO UNCITRAL MODEL LAW, *supra* note 7 at 332.

national courts for interim relief would be well advised to specify these rights in their contract.[47]

V. THE GROUNDS FOR INTERIM RELIEF IN ARBITRATION

A number of reasons have been given why arbitrators might wish to exercise the power to award interim relief. In appropriate cases the tribunal may wish to:

(1) preserve the status quo during the pendency of the proceedings;[48]

(2) give the parties an equal opportunity to present their case;[49]

(3) create reasonable and practical measures relating to the performance of the contract pending the final award;[50]

(4) provisionally restructure the situation so as to remedy an imbalance detrimental to one party which could cause the party interim irreparable harm.[51]

As stated above modern arbitration rules theoretically give the arbitrators unlimited possibilities, in the absence of a specific contractual prohibition, to fashion creative interim remedies. WIPO Article 46(a) gives some guidance as to the mode and manner in which that power can be exercised.

First, the WIPO Rules empower the arbitrator to act only upon a request from a party. As contrasted to an arbitrator operating under the now superseded 1985 LCIA Rules,[52] the exercise of power by a WIPO arbitrator upon the arbitrator's own initiative is prohibited.[53]

Second, there is no requirement in the WIPO Rules compelling the arbitrator to act only after a hearing or other proceeding at which all parties are permitted to be heard. A WIPO tribunal may act *ex parte* upon a proper request.[54] This power to act *ex parte* was given to the tribunal by the specific design and intent of the drafters of the WIPO Rules.[55]

---

[47] *See* Brower & Tupman, *supra* note 5; Colleen Higgins, *Interim Measures in Transnational Maritime Arbitration*, 65 TUL. L. REV. 1519 (1991).

[48] ICC ARBITRATION *supra* note 12 at § 26.05.

[49] *Id.*

[50] *Id.*

[51] Piero G. Parodi, *Interim Measures in Respect to Arbitration in the Construction Business*, in ICCA CONGRESS SERIES NO. 5, PROCEEDINGS OF XTH INTERNATIONAL ARBITRATION CONGRESS 485 (Albert Jan van den Berg ed., 1990).

[52] LCIA RULES, Article 13.1 (1985). The 1998 LCIA Rules now prohibit *sua sponte* interim relief orders. *See* LCIA RULES, Article 25.1 (1998). ("On the application of any party . . .").

[53] WIPO ARBITRATION RULES, Article 46(a).

[54] The 1998 LCIA Rules eliminated the requirement contained in the 1985 LCIA Rules that the parties be afforded a "proper opportunity to state their views" before a interim remedy could be fashioned by the arbitration tribunal. *Compare* LCIA RULES, Article 13.1 (1985) with LCIA RULES, Article 25.1 (1998). LCIA Article 19.1 (1998), however, gives a party expressing the desire therefore the right to be heard orally before the tribunal, thus apparently continuing in place the 1985 requirement that the parties be heard before any interim relief may be afforded.

[55] Marc Blessing, *The Conduct of Arbitral Proceedings Under the Rules of Arbitration Institutions: The WIPO Arbitration Rules in a Comparative Perspective*, in CONFERENCE ON RULES FOR INSTITUTIONAL ARBITRATION AND MEDIATION ¶ 46.2 at 54 (WIPO 1995).

Third, the interim relief powers of the tribunal are constrained by pertinent restrictions contained in the contract itself. The tribunal cannot afford relief that is specifically prohibited by the contract to which it owes the very existence of its ultimate authority and power. It should be observed, however, that it may be difficult to compel a tribunal to adhere to what is viewed by one of the parties as the spirit of the contract in the absence of specific language of restriction.[56]

Fourth, the interim relief to be granted must be "necessary." This same language is used in the UNCITRAL Rules, Article 26(1). The insightful study of Article 26(1) by Matti Pellonpaa and David Caron[57] suggests that "necessity is to be assessed against the basic function of interim measures, which is to preserve the rights of the arbitrating parties."[58] "Necessity" is to be contrasted with merely "desirable" or "recommendable."[59] The Pellonpaa and Caron study also indicates that the "necessity" requirement is linked to the notion of "irreparable" prejudice or harm to one of the parties. "Irreparable" prejudice or harm is thought to mean something broader than the "irreparable injury" requirement set out in the American equity jurisprudence; Pellonpaa and Caron suggest that "grave" or "substantive" might have been a better choice of words when actual practice is taken into account.[60]

Fifth, if "required by exceptional circumstances," a WIPO tribunal may order a party to post security against the costs of the arbitration, including the legal costs of the party, or even against the award itself.[61] While the LCIA Rules grant arbitrators similar powers, albeit without the "exceptional circumstances" limitation contained in the WIPO Rules,[62] there is nothing comparable in either the ICC or AAA International Rules. The language of the WIPO Rule, and the fact that it is stated separately from the provision of the general power to afford interim relief, suggests that the power to order the posting of security against either the costs or the award is to be exercised sparingly, rather than routinely.[63]

Finally, the examples of particular forms of interim relief set forth in Article 46(a) are just that, examples. This seems apparent from the contrast between the specific grant of power — "any provisional orders or . . . other interim measures" — and the word "including." "Including" does not, in this context, appear to be a word of limitation. The examples in WIPO Article 46(a) have been derived from the traditional formula, rather than a formulation particularly adapted to the requirements of intellectual property disputes. The power to order the sale of perishable goods invokes

---

[56] *See, e.g.*, Advanced Micro Devices, Inc. v. Intel Corporation, 9 C. 4th 362, 36 Cal.Rptr.2d 581 (1994).

[57] MATTI PELLONPAA & DAVID CARON, THE UNCITRAL ARBITRATION RULES AS INTERPRETED AND APPLIED (1994).

[58] *Id.* at 441.

[59] *Id.*

[60] *Id.* at 442.

[61] WIPO RULES, Article 46(b).

[62] *See* LCIA RULES, Articles 15.2 and 15.4 (1985) and LCIA RULES, Article 25.1(a) and 25.2 (1998).

[63] Marc Blessing, *in* CONFERENCE ON RULES, *supra* note 54 at 59.

the image of a maritime arbitrator ordering the sale of bananas seized in Rotterdam harbor, as contrasted to an order enjoining the production of DRAMs in Singapore.

VI. SECURITY AS A CONDITION OF INTERIM RELIEF

The WIPO Rules contemplate that the arbitration tribunal may condition the granting of interim relief upon the posting of "appropriate security." A similar provision is found in the UNCITRAL Model Law.[64] The AAA International Rules and UNCITRAL Rules, in contrast, provide for security for "the costs of the measures,"[65] and for security against the potential damages sustained as a result of an interim order later overturned.[66] The broader WIPO language should be viewed as a helpful improvement, focusing on the full impact of an interim relief order on the distrained party.[67]

VII. FORMALITIES OF INTERIM RELIEF

The interim relief to be obtained from the arbitration tribunal is phrased in Article 46(a) in terms of "provisional orders and other interim measures." Article 46(c) provides that the tribunal may put the order or measure in the form of an interim award.[68] This option is in keeping with the similar UNCITRAL[69] and AAA International Arbitration Rules.[70]

This language was adopted to give the arbitrators the necessary flexibility to adapt their interim decisions to the exigencies of local national court system restrictions on the enforcement of interim measures. The form of the interim measure — order or award — may make a dramatic difference to a party endeavoring to secure assistance from the national courts in enforcing the interim directive of the tribunal, as it has been questioned whether the New York Convention admits of the enforcement of interim awards.[71] This issue, and the whole question of the difference in national laws and the attitudes of national courts toward the enforcement of interim orders and awards of arbitrators, is beyond the scope of this paper.[72]

It is worth noting, however, that in *Island Creek Coal Sales Company v. City of Gainesville, Florida*,[73] the Sixth Circuit held that AAA Commercial Arbitration Rule

---

[64] UNCITRAL MODEL LAW, Article 17.

[65] AAA INTERNATIONAL ARBITRATION RULES, Article 21.2 (1997).

[66] UNCITRAL RULES, Article 26(2).

[67] Marc Blessing, *in* CONFERENCE ON RULES, *supra* note 56 at 55.

[68] WIPO ARBITRATION RULES, Article 46(c).

[69] UNCITRAL RULES, Article 26(2).

[70] AAA INTERNATIONAL ARBITRATION RULES, Article 21.2 (1997).

[71] *See, e.g.*, Wagoner, *supra* note 5; Redfern, *supra* note 5.

[72] *See generally*, PROVISIONAL REMEDIES IN INTERNATIONAL COMMERCIAL ARBITRATION: A PRACTITIONER HANDBOOK (Axel Bosch and Joanna Farnsworth eds. 1994).

[73] 729 F.2d 1046 (6th Cir. 1984).

43[74] conferred authority on the arbitrator to grant interim relief, and affirmed the interim award commanding Gainesville to continue to perform the contract pending further order of the tribunal. In the *Sperry International Trade* litigation,[75] arising out of an international arbitration having its seat in the United States, the Second Circuit held that a District Court could recognize and enforce an interim award of the arbitrator that was final as to the collateral matter of the drawing upon a letter of credit. There was no discussion of the New York Convention in either the *Island Creek Coal* or *Sperry* decisions, and the results in both cases seem to turn on the collateral nature of the interim award or the characterization of the issue as an independent claim.

VIII. EXPLICIT RECOGNITION OF THE PREARBITRATION PROBLEM

The power of an arbitrator to offer interim relief under the WIPO Rules does not eliminate the possibility of judicially-granted interim relief, as discussed above. It may, however, affect the extent of such relief. When the arbitrator is not yet capable of granting interim relief but the factual questions which need to be determined seem particularly suited to determination by the arbitrators ultimately responsible for factual determinations, the interim relief fashioned by the court might be extended only for the period of time needed to allow the arbitrator to become involved and to rule on the underlying factual issue.

This possibility was recognized in *Merrill Lynch, Pierce, Fenner & Smith, Inc. v. Salvano*.[76] In *Salvano* the trial court issued a temporary restraining order barring a former Merrill Lynch employee from soliciting Merrill Lynch clients or disclosing client information. After the arbitration panel began considering the case, Merrill Lynch requested that the court extend the temporary restraining order. An appeal was then taken from the order extending the restraining order. The United States Court of Appeals for the Seventh Circuit held that the trial court abused its discretion in extending the judicial restraining order once the arbitration tribunal was in place. The Seventh Circuit took the view that the restraining order should have been imposed only "until the arbitration panel is able to address the issue,"[77] explaining that though a court may be authorized to grant injunctive relief pending arbitration "we do not go so far as to determine that that authority extends ad infinitum."[78] This approach has been used in other American cases.[79]

---

[74] "[A]rbitrator may grant any remedy or relief that the arbitrator deems just and equitable and within the scope of the agreement of the parties, including, but not limited to, specific performance of a contract." *Id.* at 1049.

[75] Sperry International Trade, Inc. v. Government of Israel, 689 F.2d 301 (2nd Cir. 1982).

[76] 999 F.2d 211 (7th Cir. 1993).

[77] *Id.* at 215.

[78] *Id.*

[79] *See, e.g.*, Performance Unlimited, Inc. v. Questar Publishers, Inc., 52 F.3d 1373 (6th Cir. 1995) (court should grant relief only until panel is available to grant relief); Merrill Lynch, Pierce, Fenner & Smith, Inc. v. Grall, 836 F. Supp. 428, 431, 434 (W.D. Mich. 1993) (quoting *Salvano* and issuing injunction "until the arbitration panel is able to address whether the preliminary injunction should remain in

All of the major international arbitration rules give parties the possibility of delaying the composition of the arbitration tribunal. The exercise of this possibility is likely when, as is often the situation, one party has a substantial incentive to or perceives a substantial advantage in delaying the proceedings. To afford the parties the possibility of an interim relief remedy prior to the constitution of the arbitration tribunal WIPO has proposed a "radical"[80] innovation labeled WIPO Emergency Relief Rules. These rules provide for accelerated appointment of an interim decision maker, both *ex parte* and *inter partes* proceedings, and the quick rendition of an order or award determined to be "urgently necessary to preserve the rights of the parties."[81]

A. *Specific Agreement is Required to Have Resort to the WIPO Emergency Rules*

The WIPO Emergency Relief Rules ("the Procedure") require that the parties, in their contract, positively affirm their intent to avail themselves of the Procedure. This approach, rather than the automatic inclusion of the Procedure in existing contracts and future contracts which would arise had the Procedure been incorporated in the regular WIPO Rules, was thought appropriate because of the "radical nature" of the Procedure.[82]

To encourage the use of the Procedure, the recommended WIPO arbitration clause would be amended. As amended the recommended clause acknowledges the agreement of the parties to have disputes determined in accordance with the WIPO Arbitration Rules "in conjunction with the WIPO Emergency Relief Rules." The explanatory note directs parties not wishing to adopt the Procedure to strike out the language of inclusion. It is obviously the hope of WIPO that by specifying the inclusive language in the recommended arbitration clause, with the explanatory note, greater use will be made of the Procedure, perhaps overcoming one of the explanations for the failure of contracting parties to make use of the ICC Pre-Arbitral Referee Rules which serve a similar purpose in respect of ICC arbitrations.[83]

---

effect"); Blumenthal v. Merrill Lynch, Pierce, Fenner & Smith, Inc., 910 F.2d 1049, 1054 (2d Cir. 1990) ("[w]here an injunction has been issued and it turns out that prompt arbitration is available, the enjoined party is that much more able to have the injunction promptly reconsidered"); Sauer-Getriebe KG v. White Hydraulics, Inc. 715 F.2d 348, 351 (7th Cir. 1983) *cert. den.* 464 U.S. 1070 (1984) (injunction was justified "[s]ince [the plaintiff] seeks only an injunction pending arbitration").

[80] This characterization is given by WIPO. *Proposed WIPO Emergency Relief Rules*, WIPO ARBITRATION COUNCIL, Third Meeting, Geneva, November 27, 1996 (Document ARB/AC/III/96/3), Para. 5, p. 3. (EDITOR'S NOTE: The WIPO Emergency Relief Rules are expected to be approved in December 1999.)

[81] WIPO EMERGENCY RELIEF RULES, Article IX(a).

[82] *See* note 80 *supra*.

[83] *See* Hans Smit, *Provisional Relief in International Arbitration: The ICC and Other Proposed Rules*, 1 AM. REV. INT'L ARB. 388 (1990).

B. *The Effect of the Procedure on Other WIPO Rules*

The WIPO Arbitration Rules apply *mutatis mutandis* to the Procedure, but the Procedure specifically excludes the application of several important WIPO Arbitration Rules.[84]

C. *Relationship of the Procedure to Other Proceedings*

The philosophy of the Procedure, as expressed in Article III, is to allocate the power to grant interim relief to a tribunal constituted in response to a Request for Arbitration under the WIPO Arbitration Rules or Expedited Arbitration Rules pursuant to Article 46, but to reserve to the Emergency Arbitrator appointed in accordance with the Procedure the power to act prior to that time when a Request for Relief under the Emergency Rules is initiated or the arbitration tribunal is constituted. Article III(b)(i) empowers the Emergency Arbitrator to act from the time first appointed until the tribunal is constituted, and Article III(b)(ii) provides for the power of an Emergency Arbitrator to act under circumstances where a Request for Relief is initiated after a Request for Arbitration has been received but before the tribunal is constituted. In either circumstance the power of the Emergency Arbitrator to make interim awards, or modify interim awards, is lost when the tribunal is constituted.

The Procedure also anticipates the possibility that resort to the national courts, or the initiation of a non-WIPO arbitration, might occur after a Request for Relief under the Emergency Rules has been received. Article III(a) provides that an Emergency Arbitrator appointed pursuant to the Procedure "shall retain power to make an award and to modify it" in these circumstances. This language suggests that the Procedure is not available, and interim relief cannot be obtained through an Emergency Arbitrator, when resort to a national court, or initiation of a non-WIPO arbitration, occurs prior to the time a Request for Relief under the Emergency Rules is filed. If this is the proper interpretation of Article III(a), this provision has the effect of allowing a party to circumvent the contractually stipulated Procedure, and thus defeat the power of the Emergency Arbitrator, by seeking interim relief from a national court before the other party has an opportunity to file a Request for Relief under the Emergency Rules.

D. *Who Renders Emergency Relief Orders and Awards*

The normal WIPO procedure contemplates the significant involvement of the parties in the process of constituting the arbitration tribunal.[85] The Emergency Rules, in contrast, make no provision for the involvement of the parties in selecting the Emergency Arbitrator in default of agreement on the arbitrator in advance of transmission of a Request for Relief to the WIPO Center. Rather, the arbitrator is selected by the WIPO Center from among those individuals whose names appear on a published list. The list is composed by the Center, and the only specifically identified

---

[84] WIPO EMERGENCY RELIEF RULES, Article I(b) (final draft, 1996).

[85] WIPO ARBITRATION RULES, Articles 15–19.

qualification for inclusion on the list is a commitment by the listed individual to be available on 24-hours notice. Doubtless there are other qualifications which the Center will impose in compiling the list, and in making the appointments, but the essential characteristics and qualifications of potential Emergency Arbitrators will not be known until the first list is published and the first Emergency Arbitrators begin to be appointed.

The Procedure specifies that the Center will act on the appointment "promptly."[86] In practice the parties can probably expect to receive notice of appointment within a few days of the transmittal of a Request for Relief to the Center. The parties then have *24 hours* from notice of appointment to lodge a challenge, and *24 hours* to reply to a challenge. The appointment will thus appear almost *a fait accompli* to parties accustomed to the more leisurely process in normal arbitrations for lodging challenges. Perhaps this result was specifically desired by the drafters, fully intended as a means to eliminate the possibilities of undue delay in the treatment of a request for interim relief through the challenge process.

Absent the consent of the parties, or as required by a court, the Emergency Arbitrator may not participate in the arbitral proceedings as a member of the tribunal.[87] The Emergency Arbitrator is empowered to render interim relief up to the composition of the tribunal, and then retires from service with respect to the subject matter.

E.   *The Paperwork Of The Procedure*

The initiation of a request for interim relief under the Emergency Rules commences with the lodging of a Request for Relief with the WIPO Arbitration Center.[88] The Request for Relief is to include the names and pertinent communication and address details of the parties,[89] copies of the pertinent agreements, a "concise" statement of the relevant facts, a statement of the rights of the parties to be preserved and the interim relief sought, a "concise" statement of the harm expected if relief is not granted, an explanation of why the relief requested is urgently needed, the evidence justifying the grant of interim relief including copies of documents and statements, and observations on whether a hearing is necessary and the time, date and place proposed for the hearing.[90] The party initiating the Request for Relief is instructed to "exercise good faith" in not withholding facts, circumstances or documents "known to it or in its possession that would be material to the decision."[91] If the application is *ex parte* the claimant is required to include reasons why notice "would involve a real risk that

---

[86] WIPO EMERGENCY RELIEF RULES, Article VII(b).

[87] WIPO EMERGENCY RELIEF RULES, Article IX.

[88] WIPO EMERGENCY RELIEF RULES, Article IV(a).

[89] WIPO EMERGENCY RELIEF RULES, Article IV(c)(i). The reference to "other communication references" should probably be understood to refer to e-mail.

[90] WIPO EMERGENCY RELIEF RULES, Article IV(c).

[91] WIPO EMERGENCY RELIEF RULES, Article IV(d).

the purpose of the Procedure would be defeated.''[92] American lawyers will find that these submission obligations bear a passing resemblance to the requirements of an application for a temporary restraining order in a state or federal court.[93]

The respondent is given 60 hours to respond to the Request for Relief. That response is to take the form of an Answer to the Request for Relief containing a reply to the particulars of the Request for Relief.[94] The evidence upon which the respondent relies, including documents and statements, in opposition to the Request for Relief, and the respondent's own claim for interim relief, if any, are also to be submitted to the Center, either separately or within the Answer, within the 60-hour time period.[95]

F. *Rapid Notification of the Award or Order*

The Procedure contemplates that the Emergency Arbitrator will render a ruling within 24 hours of the termination of any hearing, and in any event within the shortest time possible.[96] The time period for the notification of the award or order may be extended by the WIPO Center on its own motion or at the request of the Emergency Arbitrator.[97]

G. *Scope of an Emergency Arbitrator's Power*

Under the Emergency Relief Rules the Emergency Arbitrator has power to ''make any award that the Emergency Arbitrator considers urgently necessary to preserve the rights of the parties.''[98] In particular, the Emergency Arbitrator may

(i)   issue an interim injunction or restraining order prohibiting the commission or continued commission of an act or course of conduct by a party;

(ii)   order the performance of a legal obligation by a party;

(iii) order the payment of an amount by one party to the other party or to another person;

(iv)   order any measure necessary to establish or preserve evidence or to ascertain the performance of a legal obligation by a party;

(v)   order any measure necessary for the conservation of any property;

(vi)   fix an amount of damages to be paid by a party for breach of the award under such condition as the Emergency Arbitrator considers appropriate.

While the Emergency Arbitrator is empowered to make ''any award'' that power is constrained by the requirement that the Emergency Arbitrator render only awards that are ''urgently necessary.'' The award itself must be one which ''preserve[s] the rights of the parties.''

---

[92] WIPO EMERGENCY RELIEF RULES, Article XIII(b).

[93] *See* Horning, *supra* note 1.

[94] WIPO EMERGENCY RELIEF RULES, Article V(a).

[95] WIPO EMERGENCY RELIEF RULES, Article V(b).

[96] WIPO EMERGENCY RELIEF RULES, Article XII(a).

[97] WIPO EMERGENCY RELIEF RULES, Article XII(b).

[98] WIPO EMERGENCY RELIEF RULES, Article XI(a).

H. *Security and Conditions to an Emergency Award*

The Procedure gives the Emergency Arbitrator ample power to protect the legitimate interests of the party subjected to the interim award.[99] The posting of security for the damages sustained, and the requirement that the party seeking the award promptly initiate WIPO arbitration under the regular Rules, are specifically spelled out. The only specified limitation on the conditions which may be attached to the award is that they be "appropriate."

I. *Ex Parte Requests for Relief and Orders*

Article XIII provides for the possibility of relief *ex parte* "where notice to the Respondent would involve a real risk that the purpose of the procedure would be defeated." The necessity for and the benefit of this provision are obvious.

In international arbitrations it may be difficult to obtain judicial confirmation and enforcement of an *ex parte* award. Article V(1)(b) of the New York Convention permits a court to refuse to enforce an award, at the request of the party against whom it is invoked, if "[t]he party against whom the award is invoked was not given proper notice of the appointment of the arbitrator or of the arbitration proceedings or was otherwise unable to present his case." This would seem to encompass *ex parte* awards, which by their very nature are rendered without notice of the appointment, without advance notice of the proceedings, and in any event without the opportunity to present evidence prior to the rendition of the interim relief award. To surmount this possible limitation on the utility of the Procedure, the term "award," used in respect of the *inter partes* aspects of the Procedure, is replaced with the term "order." The *ex parte* order has a contractual effect on the parties, but whether it is otherwise enforceable under the New York Convention is a debatable issue.[100]

CONCLUSION

The Expert Group and the WIPO Arbitration Council have undertaken a comprehensive review of the rules for interim relief. The result, Article 46, appears well adapted to the peculiar requirements of intellectual property arbitration. Article 46, in providing the tribunal with broad powers while at the same time indicating the potential to condition interim relief on the posting of full security against the harm to be sustained by the distrained party during the interim period, seems a particularly

---

[99] "The Emergency Arbitrator may make the award subject to such conditions as the Emergency Arbitrator considers appropriate. In particular the Emergency Arbitrator may

    (i)   require, having regard to any agreement between the parties, that a party commence arbitration proceedings on the merits of the dispute within a designated period of time; or

    (ii)   require that a party in whose favor an award is made provide adequate security."

WIPO EMERGENCY RELIEF RULES, Article XI(c).

[100] *Proposed WIPO Emergency Relief Rules*, WIPO ARBITRATION COUNCIL, Third Meeting, Geneva, November 27, 1996 (Document ARB/AC/III/96/3), Para. 10, p. 3.

welcome innovation. The thorny problem of national court recognition and enforcement of interim relief remains, but by the same token WIPO has built into the Rules the flexibility which an arbitration tribunal may require to aid a party in securing national court enforcement of the arbitration tribunal's interim orders and awards.

The WIPO Emergency Relief Rules represent a new frontier in arbitration. Considerable thought has been given to creating procedures which will command the attention of international business. Time and further debate will demonstrate whether this evolution of arbitration practice and procedure is particularly well adapted to affording intellectual property owners reasonable emergency protection of their rights through the arbitration process.

DISCLOSURE OF TRADE SECRETS AND OTHER CONFIDENTIAL INFORMATION

Article 52

Hans Smit*

Article 52

(a)   For the purposes of this Article, confidential information shall mean any information, regardless of the medium in which it is expressed, which is

(i)   in the possession of a party,

(ii)   not accessible to the public,

(iii) of commercial, financial or industrial significance, and

(iv) treated as confidential by the party possessing it.

(b)   A party invoking the confidentiality of any information it wishes or is required to submit in the arbitration, including to an expert appointed by the Tribunal, shall make an application to have the information classified as confidential by notice to the Tribunal, with a copy to the other party. Without disclosing the substance of the information, the party shall give in the notice the reasons for which it considers the information confidential.

(c)   The Tribunal shall determine whether the information is to be classified as confidential and of such a nature that the absence of special measures of protection in the proceedings would be likely to cause serious harm to the party invoking its confidentiality. If the Tribunal so determines, it shall decide under which conditions and to whom the confidential information may in part or in whole be disclosed and shall require any person to whom the confidential information is to be disclosed to sign an appropriate confidentiality undertaking.

(d)   In exceptional circumstances, in lieu of itself determining whether the information is to be classified as confidential and of such nature that the absence of special measures of protection in the proceedings would be likely to cause serious harm to the party invoking its confidentiality, the Tribunal may, at the request of a party or on its own motion and after consultation with the parties, designate a confidentiality advisor who will determine whether the information is to be so classified, and, if so, decide under which conditions and to whom it may in part or in whole

---

* Stanley H. Fuld Professor of Law and Director, Center for International Arbitration and Litigation Law, Columbia University.

be disclosed. Any such confidentiality advisor shall be required to sign an appropriate confidentiality undertaking.

(e)   **The Tribunal may also, at the request of a party or on its own motion, appoint the confidentiality advisor as an expert in accordance with Article 55 in order to report to it, on the basis of the confidential information, on specific issues designated by the Tribunal without disclosing the confidential information either to the party from whom the confidential information does not originate or to the Tribunal.**

52.01.   *The Scope of Article 52*

Article 52 deals with the protection in arbitration of information that is confidential before it is disclosed. It differs in this respect from the information covered by Articles 73–76 that is confidential because it is disclosed in arbitration. Article 52 provides protection additional to that provided by Articles 73–76.

Protection under Article 52 can be obtained only by order of the Tribunal. Protection under Articles 73–76 attaches by operation of the Rules themselves. Confidentiality can also be secured by a special agreement between the parties. In fact, the parties may well prefer to enter into a special confidentiality agreement and thus to avoid the procedure prescribed in Article 52. Such an agreement does not bind the arbitrators, but the parties may request the arbitrators to accede to it, which, in most cases, the arbitrators will readily do.

52.02.   *The Purpose of Article 52*

The purpose of Article 52 is to provide a procedure pursuant to which, through the intervention of the Tribunal, trade secrets and secret know-how is protected from improper disclosure. It authorizes the Tribunal to issue a protective order similar to that issued by a court.

52.03.   *The Secret Know-How Covered*

Paragraph (a) of Article 52 defines the confidential information to which the procedures prescribed by Article 52 apply. It may be questioned whether it was necessary or desirable to provide this definition. After all, the party seeking the special protection afforded by Article 52 must obtain an order from the Tribunal, and the Tribunal must therefore decide whether, in the particular case presented, a protective order should issue and can take into account in this context whether and to what extent the information concerned deserves special protection. In any event, the definition in paragraph (a) should be given the broadest possible construction in order to avoid the Tribunal's finding that special protection is appropriate, but cannot be given since the information to be protected does not come within the reach of paragraph (a).

52.04.   *The Procedure to be Followed*

A party wishing to obtain a protective order must make a reasoned application, on notice, to the Tribunal detailing the information it seeks to have classified. The

Tribunal shall then determine whether and under what conditions the information is to be classified. It may also assign this task to a special master ("confidentiality advisor"), who may also be appointed as an expert pursuant to Article 55 to report on special issues without disclosing the confidential information.

52.05.   The Requirement of "Serious Harm"

The Tribunal may order special measures of protection only if disclosure "would be likely to cause serious harm" to the party seeking the protection. This requirement should be construed in the context of the individual case. As a general proposition, the Tribunal should decide to what extent the special protection demanded would do disservice to the public interest in having the information disclosed. Since arbitration under the WIPO Rules is generally subject to a fair measure of confidentiality, the public interest in disclosure is attenuated in any event. It would therefore seem that the special protection prescribed by Article 52 should be granted as soon as the person seeking the protection demonstrates a reasonable interest in obtaining it and would therefore suffer serious harm if it were not accorded.

52.06.   The "Confidentiality Advisor" Under Paragraph (d)

Article 52(d) provides for the appointment of a confidentiality advisor to make the determination whether the special protection sought is to be accorded. The reasons for which the Tribunal may decide to substitute someone else for itself to make this determination are not clear. It may be that the subject is so technically complex that the Tribunal is unable to make the determination itself. Another reason, advanced by the drafters of the WIPO Rules, is that the Tribunal may wish to protect against disclosure by (party-appointed) arbitrators by limiting disclosure of the trade secrets only to the confidentiality advisor. The way paragraph (d) is drafted, it does not appear to allow the Tribunal, after it has received the decision of the confidentiality advisor, in any way to modify the decision of the confidentiality advisor. That being so, it would appear appropriate for the Tribunal to reserve that power when it assigns to a confidentiality advisor the task of making a decision pursuant to paragraph (d).

52.07.   The "Confidentiality Advisor" Under Paragraph (e)

Paragraph (e) opens the possibility of the Tribunal's appointing the "confidentiality advisor" as an expert under Article 55 to report on specific issues without disclosing the confidential information on which the advisor's report is based to the opposing party or the Tribunal. It would seem that this avenue should be taken only in the most exceptional cases. For accepting a report and deciding a matter on information provided by one party that is not disclosed to the other may be argued to be contrary to fundamental notions of due process. Of course, by agreeing to arbitration under the WIPO Rules, a party has agreed to this procedure, but the possibility is not excluded that a court, asked to enforce the award, will rule that this agreement conflicts with fundamental notions of due process and is therefore unenforceable.

AWARDS AND OTHER DECISIONS

Articles 59 to 66

*Christopher S. Gibson**

I. GENERAL OBSERVATIONS

The hallmark of the WIPO Arbitration Rules might be their comprehensive undertaking to incorporate a number of the important lessons that have been learned over time in international arbitration. This is coupled with several innovative provisions (*e.g.*, emergency interim relief rules) tailored to address issues arising in intellectual property disputes. The Rules include features — such as specifying that the parties' choice of law will be construed as excluding reference to a state's conflict of laws rules — that are now recognized as good practice, and preferred in most cases. In the past, practitioners would have had to include such terms in the arbitration clause (making for a long and complex clause, likely to be viewed as unwieldy in the context of the contemplated transaction) to achieve the relative clarity and efficiency of an arbitration conducted under the WIPO Rules.

The WIPO Arbitration Rules help the parties using them to be aware of and to avoid some of the pitfalls that have made international arbitration unjustifiably costly, complex and lengthy, and that have produced results that were uncertain and out of sync with one or another of the parties' expectations.

Most fundamentally, the WIPO Rules are conscientiously tuned to maximize the possibility that an award rendered in an arbitration conducted under them will be valid and enforceable. Parties choosing international arbitration should not be put to the risk of spending substantial sums for a private adjudication forum that yields no enforceable result. Many of the above refinements are reflected in the rules in Chapter V, entitled Awards and Other Decisions, reviewed in this part. In Chapter V, the WIPO Rules treat as a group the various aspects of rendering an award, including the law to be applied; the decision-making process of the arbitral tribunal for obtaining an award; the form and substance of the award; the notification and timing for delivery of the award and its effective date; corrections to the award and/or requests for additional awards; settlements and consent awards; appeals; and specific elements that routinely present themselves such as currency and interest.

---

* Christopher Gibson is a Senior Legal Officer of the WIPO Arbitration and Mediation Center; formerly in the San Francisco office of Pillsbury, Madison & Sutro, practicing in commercial international litigation and arbitration; B.A., University of Chicago; M.P.P., Kennedy School of Government, Harvard University; J.D., Boalt School of Law, University of California at Berkeley.

II. DISCUSSION OF SPECIFIC ARTICLES

A. *The Law to be Applied*

Laws Applicable to the Substance of the Dispute, the Arbitration and Arbitration Agreement

Article 59

(a)   The Tribunal shall decide the substance of the dispute in accordance with the law or rules of law chosen by the parties. Any designation of the law of a given State shall be construed, unless otherwise expressed, as directly referring to the substantive law of that State and not to its conflict of laws rules. Failing a choice by the parties, the Tribunal shall apply the law or rules of law that it determines to be appropriate. In all cases, the Tribunal shall decide having due regard to the terms of any relevant contract and taking into account applicable trade usages. The Tribunal may decide as *amiable compositeur* or *ex aequo et bono* only if the parties have expressly authorized it to do so.

(b)   The law applicable to the arbitration shall be the arbitration law of the place of arbitration, unless the parties have expressly agreed on the application of another arbitration law and such agreement is permitted by the law of the place of arbitration.

(c)   An Arbitration Agreement shall be regarded as effective if it conforms to the requirements concerning form, existence, validity and scope of either the law or rules of law applicable in accordance with paragraph (a), or the law applicable in accordance with paragraph (b).

59.01. *Summary of Contents*

Article 59 of the WIPO Arbitration Rules carefully distinguishes the law(s) that may be applicable to the substance of the dispute (the substantive law), to the arbitration (the *lex arbitri*) and to the arbitration agreement. In Article 59, the WIPO Rules attempt to provide a set of precise and clarifying rules for approaching these elements which often involve complex conflict of laws issues. It should be observed at the outset, however, that to the extent any of the provisions under Article 59 come into conflict with a mandatory law applicable to the arbitration, the WIPO Rules expressly recognize the mandatory law will prevail.[1]

59.02. *Substantive Law to be Applied*

In accordance with the principle of party autonomy in international arbitration, it is well-established that the parties may choose for themselves the law applicable to

---

[1] The WIPO Rules, Article 3(a), provide, "[T]hese Rules shall govern the arbitration, except that, where any of these Rules is in conflict with a provision of the law applicable to the arbitration from which the parties cannot derogate, that provision shall prevail."

their contract, that is, the "substantive law."[2] Although it is commonly accepted as good practice to specify the substantive law that will govern in case of a dispute, parties nevertheless often fail to make any choice. Unless they can agree on the choice of substantive law at the time a dispute arises, the failure to have chosen when contracting may lead to application of a system of law which is inappropriate to the subject matter covered by the contract and to the intentions of the parties. The process of determining the substantive law to be applied may itself lead to extenuating litigation involving a digressing conflict of laws analysis also upsetting the parties' intent.

Therefore, the parties at the time of contracting should choose the substantive law to be applied and when doing so, should also consider that (i) the system of law selected is adequately developed in regard to the issues that may arise in relation to the contract; (ii) if a particular municipal law is chosen, it will permit arbitration of the disputes that may be anticipated to arise in relation to the contract (subject matter arbitrability); and (iii) the conflict of laws principles of the legal system chosen should be excluded so that *that* system is in fact applied to the substance of the dispute.[3]

Article 59(a) of the WIPO Rules sets forth the provisions for the choice of law applicable to the substance of a dispute. It provides in relevant part that the "Tribunal shall decide the substance of the dispute in accordance with the law or rules of law chosen by the parties." The major arbitration rules contain similar provisions.[4] Article 59(a) also includes a reference to "rules of law" that may be applied. This reflects the possibility that the parties will choose, not a national (or municipal) law to govern the contract (this is the traditional approach), but a broader scope of law including general principles of law, *lex mercatoria*, and/or provisions of multinational conventions. Indeed, "rules of law" may be selected by the parties as the sole source of law governing the contract, or as a supplementing source of law to be referenced in addition to the national law chosen.[5] Such rules of law may be selected if the parties are unable to agree on the application of any particular national law. In the view of

---

[2] The "substantive law" is also known as the "governing law," the "applicable law" or the "proper law" of the contract. It is the law that governs the interpretation and validity of the contract, the rights and obligations of the parties thereunder, the mode of performance and the consequences for any breach. ALAN REDFERN & MARTIN HUNTER, LAW AND PRACTICE OF INTERNATIONAL COMMERCIAL ARBITRATION 96, 99 n.1 (2d ed. 1991). In many contracts, the substantive law provision appears as a stand-alone term, not as part of the arbitration clause. *See* WIPO RULES, Art. 9(iii).

[3] These points were made in a discussion paper by Charles R. Ragan of Pillsbury, Madison & Sutro, dated January 23, 1997. His comparisons of the most updated versions of the major arbitration rules were extremely helpful to the preparation of my comments in this section.

[4] *See* AAA INTERNATIONAL ARBITRATION RULES OF 1997 [hereinafter AAA RULES], Art. 28; ICC RULES OF ARBITRATION OF 1998 [hereinafter ICC RULES], Art. 17(1); LCIA RULES OF 1998 [hereinafter, LCIA RULES], Art. 22.3; UNCITRAL ARBITRATION RULES [hereinafter UNCITRAL RULES], Art. 33(1).

[5] This point was made by Dr. Marc Blessing in his paper, "Choice of Substantive Law in Arbitration," presented at the IBA Conference in Berlin, October 23, 1996. The AAA Rules (Art. 28(1)), the LCIA Rules (Art. 22.3) and the ICC Rules (Art. 17(1)) all made reference to "rules of law," whereas the UNCITRAL Rules (Art. 33(1)) do not.

some practitioners, the "rules of law" approach is the preferred alternative, while others view such a choice as providing "fuzzy standards" for decision.

Article 59(a) in its second sentence does some of the work that, previously, was usually implemented in the arbitration clause itself, specifying that "[a]ny designation of the law of a given State shall be construed, unless otherwise expressed, as directly referring to the substantive law of that State *and not to its conflict of laws rules.*"[6] (Emphasis added.) This phrase makes clear that the substantive law chosen, not some other law derived from a conflict of laws analysis, will in fact be the law applicable to issues involving the interpretation and validity of the contract, the rights and obligations of the parties thereunder, its performance, and the consequences for breach. The phrase reflects a new consensus that complicated conflict of laws analyses may often upset the expectations of the parties by leading to unpredictable and legally uncertain rules.[7]

The WIPO Rules also provide for the circumstance that the parties fail to select the applicable law. "Failing a choice by the parties, the Tribunal shall apply the law or rules of law that it determines to be appropriate." Under the Rules the arbitrators will have flexibility to determine the proper substantive law to be applied.[8] The conventional approach has been to select a national system of law by applying the relevant "conflict" rules of private international law.[9]

The third sentence of Article 59(a) adds that "[i]n *all* cases, the Tribunal shall decide having due regard to the terms of any relevant contract and taking into account applicable trade usages." (Emphasis added.) A similar provision appears in the UNCITRAL Rules and in the AAA and ICC Rules. Thus, the contract itself should serve as the starting point (and perhaps ending point) for determining most if not all of the issues that may be in dispute. In practice, arbitral tribunals may sometimes reach a decision on the merits without any detailed reference to a system of law or to any legal document other than the contract between the parties.

---

[6] *See supra* note 3 and accompanying text. A typical clause might provide that the agreement will be governed by, and any decision by arbitrator(s) will be rendered in accordance with, the substantive laws of the State of California, *without regard to its choice-of-law rules.*

[7] The possibility that the parties *can* choose the substantive law without reference to that law's conflict of laws principles is a direct recognition that no mandatory rule of law should overrule this exclusion. *Cf., e.g.,* NTPC v. Singer (AIR 1993 SC 998) (Indian court ruled that foreign award could not be enforced in India if the parties had agreed that Indian law was the substantive law to be applied; this decision was criticized and the relevant section of Indian law mandating the same was recently deleted by the Indian Arbitration and Conciliation (Second) Ordinance 1996)).

[8] A very similar formulation appears in the UNCITRAL Rules (Art. 33(1)) and in the rules of the AAA (Art. 28(1)), ICC (Art. 17(1)) and LCIA (Art. 22.3).

[9] For a time, the most widely accepted criterion for attributing a choice of law to the parties, in the absence of an express choice, was based on the parties' choice of forum. It was assumed they intended the law of that country to apply to the substance of their disputes. Now, however, there is recognition that the choice of place may be for reasons other than applicable law, such as neutral and convenient venue, good facilities for arbitration, etc. Thus, choice of forum is now viewed merely as one connecting factor which may be considered by the arbitral tribunal. REDFERN & HUNTER, *supra* note 2, at 123–24.

The importance of custom and usage are recognized in Article 59(a): if there are ambiguities in certain disputed terms, the WIPO Rules allow the arbitrators to take into account trade usages. Some practitioners have suggested, however, that, rather than help, reference to trade usages might generate problems.[10] The trade usage may be different from the substantive law chosen by the parties; by agreeing to the WIPO Rules, the parties may have, without intending to do so, modified the law chosen to govern the contract.

Finally, the WIPO Rules make clear that the arbitral tribunal may decide as *amiable compositeur* or *ex aequo et bono only* if the parties have expressly authorized it to do so. While proceeding on this basis may enhance a tribunal's power to find an equitable solution to a dispute (which, for example, would not necessarily have to be grounded on a strict legal interpretation of the contract), parties would also have to accept that there is great difficulty appealing against an award of *amiable compositeur*, so long as the tribunal has acted with procedural regularity and fairness. In any event, the necessity of deciding on an equitable basis may be low; as an alternative, the arbitral tribunal has freedom under the WIPO Rules to suggest at appropriate times that the parties explore settlement.[11]

59.03. Law Applicable to the Arbitration

In Article 59(b), the WIPO Rules provide that the law applicable to the arbitration will be the arbitration law of the place of arbitration, unless the parties have expressly agreed on the application of another arbitration law and such agreement is permitted by the law of the place of arbitration.[12] The rule codifies the norm that the law governing the arbitration (or *lex arbitri*), is usually that of the place of the arbitration (*i.e.*, recognizing the impact of the *situs*). The WIPO Rule signals clearly to the parties that the law of the place will apply, *unless the parties have expressly agreed on the application of another arbitration law.*

Agreeing on the application of another arbitration law, however, may complicate matters. Article 59(b) recognizes this, providing that the parties may agree on the application of another arbitration law only to the extent *"such agreement is permitted by the law of the place of arbitration."* (Emphasis added.) One might question why parties would wish to complicate the conduct of an arbitration in this way. Even where a law other than the law of the place of arbitration is chosen, the law of the place of arbitration will have some impact. First, some aspects of the law of the place of arbitration may be "mandatory" — applicable to the proceedings regardless of the governing law. Thus, if the parties decide that the federal procedural arbitration law of the United States (*i.e.*, the Federal Arbitration Act) will apply to an arbitration held in

---

[10] *See* U.S. Council Comments to the First Draft Revised ICC Rules (Document No. 420-350), dated January 22, 1997.

[11] WIPO RULES, Art. 65(a).

[12] None of the other major arbitration rules have previously included such a provision; however, the revision to the LCIA Rules has followed WIPO's lead and now includes an identical provision in Article 16.3.

Paris, this means the parties will have to concern themselves with two sets of procedural law — that of the Federal Arbitration Act as the chosen law, and that of France, to the extent that certain provisions of the French law are mandatory.

Second, the law of the place of arbitration will determine the extent to which the arbitration proceedings may be interrupted by parallel court proceedings. (The modern trend is to limit such interruptions.) Moreover, under the example above, a French court may be reluctant to give a ruling on United States procedural law.[13]

Nonetheless, there may be instances where concerns about the location of the arbitration might lead to a split between the location and the *lex arbitri* the parties wish to be applied. The WIPO Rules allow the parties flexibility to attempt to separate these two elements.

59.04. Law Establishing the Effectiveness of the Arbitration Agreement

Article 59(c) speaks to the validity of the arbitration agreement itself, and the law(s) that would be applied to test its legal effectiveness. The arbitration agreement will be considered "effective" if it conforms to the "requirements concerning form, existence, validity and scope" of the substantive law chosen under Article 59(a) "*or*" the law applicable to the arbitration under Article 59(b).

Article 59(c) recognizes that both the substantive law to be applied and/or the *lex arbitri* may impact upon the "form, existence, validity and scope" of the agreement.[14] In particular, the "scope" of the agreement to arbitrate may be judged under either system of law. For example, if the substantive law applied is from a jurisdiction in which certain antitrust or securities claims are not arbitrable,[15] this will limit the scope of the claims that can be brought under the arbitration agreement. If the law of the place of arbitration poses similar restrictions on "subject matter arbitrability," this too may limit the claims that can be joined in the arbitration if such strictures are mandatory. In sum, if the arbitration agreement covers matters incapable of being settled by arbitration, under the law of the agreement or under the law of the place of arbitration, the agreement may be at least partially ineffective since it will be unenforceable in this respect.[16] In Article 59(c) the WIPO Rules expressly recognize these potential limitations.

---

[13] Rejecting the principle of "territoriality," the state of Florida has expressly provided that arbitrations held in Florida may be conducted under foreign procedural law. REDFERN & HUNTER, *supra* note 2, at 92 & n. 78 (Sec. 684.05 of the Florida International Arbitration Act).

[14] Article 59(c) is in accordance with Article V(I)(a) of the 1958 New York Convention on the Recognition and Enforcement of Foreign Arbitral Awards [hereinafter New York Convention], which recognizes that an internationally effective arbitration agreement should be valid "under the law to which the parties have subjected it or, failing any indication thereon, under the law of the country where the award was made."

[15] "Each state may decide, in accordance with its own economic and social policy, which matters may be settled by arbitration and which may not." REDFERN & HUNTER, *supra* note 2, at 137.

[16] An award or a portion of it may be annulled on this basis. Further, recognition and enforcement of the award may be refused if the subject matter is not arbitrable under the law of the country or countries where enforcement is sought (*e.g.*, on grounds of economic or public policy). Therefore, at least three

One further aspect implicated by Article 59(c) is whether or not the original arbitration agreement must be in writing. The requirement is not contained in Article 59(c). However, the definition of ''Arbitration Agreement'' in Article 1,[17] as well as the specification in Article 9(iii) that the Request for Arbitration ''shall'' contain ''a copy of the Arbitration Agreement and, if applicable, any separate choice-of-law clause,'' would seem to imply that a written agreement is expected, if not required. Yet Article 59(c) sets forth the text for the ''effectiveness'' of the arbitration agreement. Rather than require a writing, Article 59(c) refers to the applicable requirements of the substantive law or the *lex arbitri*, even for matters concerning ''form'' of the agreement. In short, under this line of analysis, the extent to which a writing is required may be determined by reference to the substantive law or *lex arbitri*. In any event, the result is likely to be that a writing is required — for example, the *only* requirement of form imposed in respect of arbitration agreements under the international conventions is that the agreement should be in writing.[18]

B. *Issues Pertaining to Currency and Interest*

Currency and Interest

Article 60

    (a)   Monetary amounts in the award may be expressed in any currency.

    (b)   The Tribunal may award simple or compound interest to be paid by a party on any sum awarded against that party. It shall be free to determine the interest at such rates as it considers to be appropriate, without being bound by legal rates of interest, and shall be free to determine the period for which the interest shall be paid.

60.01. Summary of Contents

Article 60 deals with the issues of currency and interest, elements that routinely arise both in private international arbitration and in cases before international arbitral claims tribunals, but as to which the major arbitration rules have, until recently, been silent.[19]

---

different systems of law may be implicated: the law chosen as the substantive law to be applied to the contract; the law of the place of arbitration; and the law(s) of the country (or countries) where enforcement is sought.

[17] The ''Arbitration Agreement'' is defined in Article 1 of the WIPO Rules as ''an agreement by the parties to submit to arbitration all or certain disputes which have arisen or which may arise between them; an Arbitration Agreement may be in the form of an arbitration clause in a contract [most common] or in the form of a separate contract.''

[18] The New York Convention, Articles II(1) and (2), provides that the Contracting State will recognize an ''agreement in writing'' and this term is defined to include ''an arbitral clause in a contract or an arbitration agreement, signed by the parties or contained in an exchange of letters or telegrams.'' Would this definition covers e-mail?

[19] The one exception has been the LCIA Rules, which in Article 26.6 provide that awards may be expressed in any currency, and the Tribunal may order that simple or compound interest shall be paid by

60.02. Currency of the Award

The currency in which an award is rendered may make a significant difference to the parties to an international arbitration. In a case where more than one currency is involved, if sometime after the dispute arises one of the currencies substantially depreciates against the value of another, the potential exists for loss (or windfall) due to this fluctuation. The issue may frequently arise when doing business in countries where inflation runs rampant. If currency conversion is required, issues involving the proper date and rate of conversion are implicated.[20]

WIPO Article 60(a), addressing the currency of an award, reflects prevailing practice by leaving discretion to the arbitral tribunal to determine the appropriate currency for amounts awarded.[21] Unlike the ICC and UNCITRAL Rules (which have no similar provision), in Article 60(a) the WIPO Rules make this grant of discretion *express* so there can be no question about the arbitrators' authority in this area. Moreover, the WIPO formulation (along with the LCIA Rule) seems to have set a useful example: the revisions to the AAA International Arbitration Rules now include a similar provision on currency whereas previously they were silent on the topic.[22]

The WIPO formulation, that "[m]onetary amounts in the award may be expressed in any currency," differs slightly from the provision in the LCIA Rules: "An award

---

any party on any sum awarded at such rates as the Tribunal determines to be appropriate, without being bound by legal rates of interest imposed by any state court, in respect of any period which the Tribunal determines to be appropriate ending not later than the date upon which the award is complied with. *See also* former Article 16.5 of the 1985 Rules.

Article 60 of the WIPO Rules was apparently modelled, at least in part, on the LCIA provision.

[20] When currency conversion becomes an issue, the international practice, in the absence of a contractual provision specifying a particular rate, is that such conversions should be made at a rate so as to make the injured party whole and to avoid any windfall to the party in breach. The date used for conversion may depend on whether the currency of the loss has appreciated or depreciated relative to the currency of payment. Three dates are usually considered for determining the proper conversion rate. The first is the date on which the loss was incurred. In contractual cases, for example, that is usually the date of the breach. The second is the date the award is rendered. The third is the date on which payment under the award is made. In short, the conversion should be made at whichever date will best serve the ends of justice under the circumstances. *See* Joseph Gold, *The Restatement of the Foreign Relations Law of the United States (Revised) and International Monetary Law*, 22(1) INT'L LAW. 25 (1988); Hans Smit, *Judgments and Arbitral Awards in a Foreign Currency: A Means of Dealing with Currency Fluctuations in International Adjudication*, 7 AM. REV. INT'L ARB. 21 (1996).

[21] The most common type of award made in an international arbitration is one directing the payment of a sum of money by one party to another for losses suffered. This payment "is usually expressed in the currency of the contract." REDFERN & HUNTER, *supra* note 2, at 361. In situations where more than one currency may be implicated (such as large international development projects), unless the parties agree on the currency, the arbitral tribunal will normally hear argument as to the currency or currencies in which the award should be made (*id.*), the appropriate date(s) for establishing the conversion rate, and then determine the currency or currencies and exchange rate(s) that are most appropriate under the circumstances.

[22] AAA RULES, Art. 28(4). The AAA Rules, first promulgated in 1991 and based originally on the UNCITRAL Arbitration Rules, were reviewed and revised in 1996–97 under the auspices of a special Task Force chaired by David Rivkin.

may be expressed in any currency.'' While the LCIA construction is simpler, the WIPO language brings a degree of precision, impliedly recognizing that an award may render relief other than monetary in kind.

The AAA Rules take a slightly different approach, directing that ''[a] monetary award shall be in the currency or currencies of the contract unless the tribunal considers another currency more appropriate . . .'' This approach reflects the reality that, unless a party can raise good reasons for doing otherwise, the currency of the contract will usually control the question and be the currency of payment in the award. Such an approach has been acknowledged as advantageous because it ''honors the parties' choice of currencies in which to transact business and bear risks,'' and also ''avoids disputes over the selection of a conversion date.''[23] The AAA Rules thus recognize that a presumption exists in favor of the currency of the contract. The WIPO Rules, on the other hand, are silent on this presumption. It remains to be seen whether the AAA Rules' approach provides any advantage over the formulation in the WIPO Rules.

60.03. Interest on the Award

While the accrual of interest is accepted as an essential feature in most modern commercial lending relations, there are still jurisdictions (such as Saudi Arabia or Iran where Islamic law is applied) where the levying of interest is prohibited. If awarded in an international arbitration, given the length of time that may pass from the outset of the dispute until the time of payment, the element of interest may represent a significant component in the monetary aspect of the case.

The trend reflecting modern realities is that, at least in most commercial contexts, interest is generally allowed in amounts awarded as compensation or damages in order to compensate for the delay in payment to a claimant.[24] The Iran-United States Claims Tribunal, for example, has found that interest should be paid.[25] Even when it is

---

[23] Mitsui & Co., Ltd. v. Oceantrawl Corp., 906 F. Supp. 202, 203–04 (S.D.N.Y. 1995). *Mitsui* concludes that ''[e]ntry of judgment in the currency of the parties' transactions accords with principles of fairness and with the goal of making injured parties whole because it provides them with payment in the currency for which they have bargained.'' *Id.* at 204 (*citing* Opinion of Professor Hans Smit, Stanley H. Fuld Professor of Law, Columbia University, November 17, 1995, at 8–9).

[24] The basic principle of allowing interest has been expressed in different ways: interest is a component of damages; interest is an integral part of the ''just compensation'' owing to a successful claimant; interest is necessary to make the claimant economically whole; interest is an effort to restore the claimant as nearly as possible to the same position occupied before the injury was committed. The focus is on compensation to the claimant, not punishment for the respondent. *See, e.g.*, Norwegian Shipowners' Claims, 1 R.I.A.A. 307, 341 (1922) (refusal of compound interest). The assessment of interest does not depend on the conduct or culpability of either party; rather, the calculation of interest should, in line with the principles supporting its application (*i.e.*, compensation for the delay in payment), be neutral and mechanical..

[25] The Iran-United States Claims Tribunal, after reviewing the international practice with respect to interest concluded that ''two principles or guidelines, of general import, albeit of delicate implementation, can be deduced from the international practice.'' The first is that ''under normal circumstances, and

awarded, however, significant differences in approach may exist. For example, while interest may be awarded for contract claims, it may be refused for non-contractual tort claims.[26] In England, while the right to recover interest under the terms of a contract has long been recognized, the award of interest is otherwise discretionary. In Germany, on the other hand, interest must be awarded in accordance with specific rules found in the Civil or Commercial codes.[27] To further complicate the matter, in some jurisdictions the rules pertaining to the award of interest are viewed as procedural, while in others they are characterized as substantive. Would the law of the contract or the law of the place apply? Would problems occur if the award of interest is against the public policy of the place of enforcement (such as Saudi Arabia)?

Faced with the diversity reflected in national laws on the subject, it is not surprising that there is a lack of consensus as to whether arbitrators may award interest, and on what terms, in international commercial arbitrations. Thus, interest is not granted automatically and when it is, it displays considerable variety on the rate as well as the respective dates from which it runs and ends. Thus, the analysis should begin with whether or not interest is due under the terms of the contract and the law governing its interpretation. If interest is found to be due on this basis, it should normally be awarded.[28]

As in the case of the issue of currency, until very recently the major institutional rules did not speak to the issue of interest.[29] In keeping with the complexity of issues concerning interest, WIPO Article 60(b) preserves maximum flexibility for the arbitrators, yet clearly establishes their authority to grant interest when and on which terms they may consider appropriate.

The arbitrators *"may"* award interest; such an award is not mandatory. The interest awarded can be "simple or compound."[30] As noted, the possibilities that an

---

especially in commercial cases, interest is allocated on the amounts awarded as damages in order to compensate for the delay with which the payment to the successful party is made." And second, "the rate of interest must be reasonable, taking due account of all pertinent circumstances . . ." McCollough & Co. v. Ministry of Post, Telegraph & Telephone (Award No. 225-89-3 at 37–38, *reprinted in* 11 Iran-U.S. C.T.R. 3, 28–29).

These principles were found to hold despite recognition of the variety in the international practice with respect to interest. The Tribunal found that no single, uniform rule of law exists for interest. On the one hand, the Tribunal noted that most national jurisdictions apply statutory rates of interest. The system in the United States, for example, usually provides for the award of interest, and although the rates vary considerably depending on the applicable statute, the trend is toward application of rates comparable to commercial rates of interest. *Id.* at 27. On the other hand, since the Islamic revolution in Iran, Iranian law, like the law in other countries following Islamic principles, prohibits the award of any interest. *Id.*

[26] In many cases of general damages, such as damages for tort, interest is usually not allowed "probably on the by no means unreasonable basis that the award of damages is such as to take the delay and the appropriate compensation for it into account." F.H. Mann, *On Interest, Compound Interest, and Damages*, 101 LAW Q. REV. 30, 42 (1985).

[27] REDFERN & HUNTER, *supra* note 2, at 403.

[28] *Id.*

[29] That is, with the exception of the LCIA Rules, *see supra* note 19.

[30] For a general discussion on interest, *see* Martin Hunter and Volker Triebel, *Awarding Interest in International Arbitration*, 6(1) J. INT'L ARB. 7, 22 (1989). The authors suggest that just as in the case of

award may grant either simple or compound interest was first set forth expressly in the LCIA Rules.[31] While compound interest is offered by financial institutions, the concept has found only limited application in international arbitral awards. It *may* be awarded if the claimant can show that he has actually paid compound interest to his bank — or would have received compound interest had he invested the principal sum claimed. The 1997 AAA International Rules also contain a provision (Article 28(4)) allowing for simple or compound interest.

The arbitrators are "free" to determine the interest rate, "without being bound by legal rates of interest." This wording is similar to that in the LCIA Rules and is apparently an attempt to free the interest determination from the statutory rates that might normally apply to judgments. The AAA Rules, on the other hand, make no specific reference to the "legal" rates, but provide instead that "the tribunal may award such pre-award and post-award interest, simple or compound, as it considers appropriate, *taking into consideration the contract and applicable law.*"[32] (Emphasis added.) Under Article 60(b) the Tribunal is also "free" to determine the "period for which the interest shall be paid." While this formulation, too, is an attempt to vest discretion in the arbitral tribunal, it remains to be seen whether the provisions of the *lex arbitri* might restrict the tribunal's power. In some legal systems the power to award interest may be related to the question of the remedies the arbitral tribunal is permitted to grant under the law. The award may be set aside if the courts in the place of arbitration consider that the arbitral tribunal exceeded its powers under the law of that place, for example by awarding interest at an excessively high rate or for an impermissibly long period.[33]

C. *Process For Decision*

Decision-Making

Article 61
Unless the parties have agreed otherwise, where there is more than one arbitrator, any award, order or other decision of the Tribunal shall be made

---

many other issues, the determination of whether or not to award interest can give rise to "classical conflict of laws problems."

[31] *See* LCIA RULES OF 1985, Art. 16.5 (Art. 26.6 of the 1998 RULES).

[32] The Task Force involved in drafting the revised AAA International Arbitration Rules commented that it believed Article 60 of the WIPO Rules is more complicated than necessary, but that WIPO's language was useful in making clear the arbitrators' authority in the area. While this comment was directed generally to Articles 60 on currency and interest, the comment is likely to have been directed principally to 60(b) on interest. In comparison, the AAA Rule covers the subject in relative simplicity (omitting the express non-recourse to the "legal rate of interest").

[33] Hunter & Triebel, *supra* note 30, at 9. The law of the likely place of enforcement should also be taken into account. It is also suggested that, to maximize the possibility that an award of interest will be saved from annulment or unenforceability, the award should clearly distinguish between interest for pre- and post-award periods. *Id.* at 23.

by a majority. In the absence of a majority, the presiding arbitrator shall make the award, order or other decision as if acting as sole arbitrator.

61.01. Decision by Majority or Presiding Arbitrator

If the arbitral tribunal consists of more than one arbitrator, the process for reaching a decision will be more involved. While a sole arbitrator will necessarily decide alone, engaging in a solitary process for making the award, a tribunal with three members will require deliberations and, ultimately, voting "rules" for obtaining a decision on the award or other ruling in the absence of unanimity.

Once appointed and properly established, an arbitral tribunal is normally duty-bound to render a decision.[34] There are three principle ways in which that decision can be arrived at by a three-member tribunal: by unanimous vote; by majority vote; or by the presiding arbitrator alone if he or she is empowered to decide alone under the applicable rules.[35]

Obviously, if a unanimous decision is not achieved, one of the other two possibilities will come into play. Among the major institutional rules, however, there is a significant difference in how these two alternatives will come into play in the voting process for obtaining a decision. All of the major arbitration rules begin by providing that where more than one arbitrator has been appointed, the decision will be by majority.[36] Similarly, WIPO Article 61, in its first sentence, provides that where more than one arbitrator is involved, any decision of an arbitral tribunal "shall be made by a majority." The majority decision rule seems to stem from the simple premise that "two heads are usually better than one."

Satisfied that this premise will yield the most appropriate results, the UNCITRAL and AAA Rules stop right at this point and provide no further alternative decision method in the case a majority is not reached.[37] Under their respective formulations, the members of the arbitral tribunal *must* form a majority. If, for example, each of the three members has a slightly different view on a key issue such that each has staked out his or her own desired result, under the UNCITRAL and AAA Rules they nevertheless must continue to negotiate and compromise where needed until a majority is reached. The situation may be further complicated if there are multiple issues on which the three arbitrators cannot agree. Nevertheless, at least two of the arbitrators

---

[34] An arbitral tribunal has no authority to return a verdict of *non liquet*. REDFERN & HUNTER, *supra* note 2, at 490. *But cf.*, WIPO Article 65(c) providing that, even for reasons other than settlement, if the Tribunal determines that the arbitration has become "unnecessary or impossible," it has the power to issue an order terminating the arbitration.

[35] REDFERN & HUNTER, *supra* note 2, at 369–70.

[36] *See* AAA RULES, Art. 26(1); ICC RULES, Art. 25(1); LCIA RULES, Art. 26.3; UNCITRAL RULES, Art. 31(1).

[37] Article 26(1) of the AAA Rules provides that "[w]hen there is more than one arbitrator, any award, decision or ruling of the arbitral tribunal shall be made by a majority of the arbitrators."

Article 31(1) of the UNCITRAL Rules provides similarly that "[w]hen there are three arbitrators, any award or other decisions of the arbitral tribunal shall be made by a majority of the arbitrators."

will need to reconcile their views sufficiently to produce a majority. While placing trust in the majority principle, the process may also yield results that reflect a "compromise" solution.[38] Further, there is a risk that it is genuinely impossible to achieve a majority, in which case the parties will have spent substantial sums yet obtained no result.[39]

WIPO, like the ICC and LCIA Rules, in the second sentence of Article 61 provides that if no majority is reached, "the presiding arbitrator" will make the decision "as if acting as sole arbitrator." Not only does this term reduce the risk that no decision will be obtained, it substantially changes the dynamics of the deliberating process. In the most common situation where the parties have each appointed an arbitrator and these two have, in turn, selected the third arbitrator who will be the presiding member (*see* WIPO Rules Article 17(b)), both of the party-appointed arbitrators will be aware that if they cannot agree among themselves, or if either of them cannot persuade the presiding member to agree with his or her view of a particular issue, then the presiding member will be authorized to make the decision alone. Under this approach the pressure is not on the presiding arbitrator, but on the other arbitrators to join him in forming a majority. Given the presiding member's contingent authority to act alone, his or her views will carry additional weight in the deliberations. This system may reflect a degree of trust that the presiding arbitrator is likely to be the least partisan of the tribunal members. There is, however, at least some risk of a run-away presiding member with whom neither of the other two arbitrators can agree; although this arbitrator was not appointed by the parties, he or she may ultimately be making the award that will be binding on them.[40]

There are two other elements worth mentioning in the first sentence of Article 61. Unlike the other major arbitration rules, the first sentence in Article 61 begins with the introductory phrase that "Unless the parties have agreed otherwise," where more than one arbitrator is involved the decision will be by majority. The WIPO Rule thus contain an express acknowledgment of the parties' flexibility to establish a different

---

[38] As described by REDFERN & HUNTER with respect to the ICSID Arbitration Rules, which also provide *only* for majority voting, the "majority rule means that at least two of the three members of the arbitral tribunal *must* be prepared to agree with each other, whatever element of bargaining or compromise this might involve. *Id.*, *supra* note 2, at 368 (emphasis added).

[39] The arbitral tribunal has no authority to return a verdict of *non licet*; therefore, if it is impossible to form a majority, the proper course is for the tribunal to resign and replacement arbitrators to be appointed. *See* REDFERN & HUNTER, *supra* note 2, at 490.

[40] There is another instance in which the second sentence of Article 61 providing for decision by the presiding arbitrator may become involved. Under Article 35 (Truncated Tribunal), the WIPO Rules grant authority to the remaining two members of a tribunal to continue an arbitration if the third member, though properly notified and without good cause, fails to participate in the work of the tribunal. In this situation, it may be that the remaining two arbitrators ultimately cannot reach a consensus and thus, without the means of obtaining a majority, under Article 61 the presiding member would make the award. It is unclear if this result was envisioned by the rules. Thus, Article 61 can be read to address the contingency that, if for whatever reasons an arbitrator refuses to participate, the tribunal can still proceed.

voting procedure for reaching a decision.[41] The parties, for example, may wish to adopt an umpire procedure[42] or move to the majority rule approach (with no possibility of the presiding arbitrator deciding in the absence of a majority).

61.02. No Difference for Questions of Procedure

Finally, Article 61 provides that its terms apply to "any award, order or other decision of the Tribunal." The WIPO Rules thus make clear that the decision process applies to all types of decisions, including procedural rulings, made by the arbitral tribunal. Article 25 of the ICC Rules, on the other hand, applies only to the decision on the award.[43] The UNCITRAL Rules refer to "any award or other decisions" and the AAA Rules refer to "any award, decision or ruling;" however, both also have a term making the distinction that in regard to decisions or rulings on "questions of procedure," the presiding arbitrator may decide on his own in cases where there is no majority, where the arbitral tribunal so authorizes or where the parties agree.[44] The LCIA Rules also address procedural decisions in a separate article (Article 5.3), and go even further, giving the Chairman extensive powers over procedural matters, directing that where there is a three-member tribunal, "the Chairman may, after consulting the other arbitrators, make procedural rulings alone." Thus, the Chairman can exercise such powers whether or not a consensus (or majority) is achieved, and there need be no agreement by the parties to bring this about. All of these rules raise the problem of identifying those questions which are matters of "procedure" (for example, is a determination of the place of arbitration procedure?). The WIPO Rules avoid this problem altogether.

D. Form Of Award, Notification, Period for Delivery and Effective Date

Form and Notification of Awards

Article 62

(a)   The Tribunal may make preliminary, interim, interlocutory, partial or final awards.

(b)   The award shall be in writing and shall state the date on which it was made, as well as the place of arbitration in accordance with Article 39(a).

(c)   The award shall state the reasons on which it is based, unless the parties have agreed that no reasons should be stated and the law applicable to the arbitration does not require the statement of such reasons.

---

[41] The AAA Rules and the UNCITRAL Rules, both in their respective Articles 1(1), provide that their provisions may be modified by the parties in writing. Thus, under these rules the voting process for decision could also be amended by the parties.

[42] *E.g.*, the umpire becomes involved only if the party-appointed arbitrators cannot reach a joint decision.

[43] The ICC Rules do not specifically address the decision process for procedural matters when a three-member panel is constituted. *See* ICC RULES, Art. 15.

[44] *See* UNCITRAL RULES, Art. 31(2) and AAA RULES, Art. 26(2).

(d) The award shall be signed by the arbitrator or arbitrators. The signature of the award by a majority of the arbitrators, or, in the case of Article 61, second sentence, by the presiding arbitrator, shall be sufficient. Where an arbitrator fails to sign, the award shall state the reason for the absence of the signature.

(e) The Tribunal may consult the Center with regard to matters of form, particularly to ensure the enforceability of the award.

(f) The award shall be communicated by the Tribunal to the Center in a number of originals sufficient to provide one for each party, the arbitrator or arbitrators and the Center. The Center shall formally communicate an original of the award to each party and the arbitrator or arbitrators.

(g) At the request of a party, the Center shall provide it, at cost, with a copy of the award certified by the Center. A copy so certified shall be deemed to comply with the requirements of Article IV(1)(a) of the Convention on the Recognition and Enforcement of Foreign Arbitral Awards, New York, June 10, 1958.

62.01. Summary of Contents

Article 62 of the WIPO Rules addresses the formal requirements for awards and other rulings by the arbitral tribunal that should be satisfied to ensure their validity.

62.02. Types of Awards

Under Article 62(a) the arbitral panel may make "preliminary, interim, interlocutory, partial or final *awards*." (Emphasis added.) These can be helpful tools when used to address matters during the course of the proceedings that are susceptible of determination and which, once determined, may save time and money. Because all rulings of the tribunal are designated as a form of "award" (rather than order), it appears the WIPO Rules have attempted to achieve at least facial consistency with Article III of the New York Convention, providing that States will recognize "arbitral awards" as binding.

62.03. Form of Award

The requirements of form for an award are usually dictated by the arbitration agreement and the law of the arbitration (*lex arbitri*). While an arbitration clause may (out of caution) specify the form requirements for an award, it is not imperative to do so. All of the major arbitration rules include the form requirements. Under the ICC Rules, for example, the award itself is subject to the scrutiny of the International Court of Arbitration. The Court may "lay down modifications as to the form" and no award is to be signed by an arbitral tribunal "until it has been approved by the court as to its form."[45] The WIPO Rules are less overbearing in this regard, providing in Article

---

[45] ICC RULES, Art. 27.

62(e) that the "Tribunal may consult the Center with regard to matters of form, particularly to ensure the enforceability of the award."

There are normally five basic form requirements: the award must be in writing, reasoned, dated, signed and indicate the place of making. The WIPO Rules set forth all these requirements. Under Article 62(b) the award must be in writing and state the date and place of arbitration. Article 62(d) provides that the award must be signed by the arbitrator(s).[46] And Article 62(c) provides that "the award shall state the reasons on which it is based, unless the parties have agreed that no reasons should be stated *and* the law applicable to the arbitration does not require the statement of such reasons." (Emphasis added.) Given the conjunctive construction, even if the parties have agreed that no reasons should be stated, this will not be enough under the WIPO Rules if the law applicable to the arbitration would require a statement of reasons to obtain the award's validity.[47] Here, the WIPO Rules are geared toward producing an outcome, a written award, that will have the maximum potential of being enforceable wherever enforcement may be sought.

62.04. *Notification and Effective Date (Articles 62(f) and 64(b))*

Under Article 62(f), the arbitral tribunal is to communicate the award to the Center, not directly to the parties,[48] in the number of originals sufficient to provide one copy for each of the parties, the arbitrator(s) and the Center. The Center, in turn, formally communicates a copy of an original award to each of the parties and to the arbitrator(s). This formal delivery triggers the date on which the award will be considered "effective and binding on the parties."[49] The Center's involvement in formally communicating the award is useful and important because the time limit within which a party may apply to a court for recourse against the award often runs from the date of communication of the award. On request, the Center will provide a party with a certified copy of the award, deemed to comply with the requirements of Article IV(1)(a) of the New York Convention.[50]

---

[46] Article 62(d) also directs that signature by a majority of the arbitrators, or by the presiding member when there is no majority, is sufficient. Where an arbitrator fails to sign, the award must state the reasons for the absence of the signature. This requirement may be intended to ameliorate the situation of seeking to have the award recognized as valid and enforceable in a jurisdiction where the law requires that normally *all* arbitrators must sign an award in order for it to be valid.

[47] The movement internationally has been in favor of requiring that reasons be given for an award. *See* REDFERN & HUNTER, *supra* note 2, at 389–90. An exception is found in the AAA's domestically applied Commercial Rules of Arbitration which would permit an award without reasoning. Experience suggests, however, that parties to an award will be more likely to respect the award, and perhaps even to perform the obligations imposed therein without recourse to court, when the award provides reasons.

[48] *Cf.* UNCITRAL RULES, Art. 32.6: "Copies of the award signed by the arbitrators shall be communicated to the parties by the arbitral tribunal."

[49] WIPO RULES, Art. 64(b).

[50] The New York Convention provides in relevant part that to obtain recognition and enforcement, a party applying for the same must supply, *inter alia*, a "duly authenticated original award or a duly certified copy thereof." The other document normally required under the Convention is a certified copy of

62.05. Dissenting Opinions

The WIPO Rules say nothing about dissenting opinions. Normally, however, an arbitrator has the right to express an opinion in dissent unless some relevant provision of the *lex arbitri* prohibits it. Because the dissenting opinion does not form part of the award, the majority arbitrators (or the presiding member) are not under a duty to communicate the dissent to the WIPO Center.[51] Further, although the WIPO Rules suggest, by implication, that it is proper practice for the dissenting arbitrator to sign the majority award,[52] it may be unreasonable to expect an arbitrator to join in an award with which he or she strongly disagrees. It has been suggested that a *quid pro quo* for the dissenting arbitrator's signature on the majority award could be an agreement that the dissent will be annexed to the award and communicated with it to the parties.[53]

Time Period for Delivery of the Final Award

Article 63

(a)   The arbitration should, wherever reasonably possible, be heard and the proceedings declared closed within not more than nine months after either the delivery of the Statement of Defense or the establishment of the Tribunal, whichever event occurs later. The final award should, wherever reasonably possible, be made within three months thereafter.

(b)   If the proceedings are not declared closed within the period of time specified in paragraph (a), the Tribunal shall send the Center a status report on the arbitration, with a copy to each party. It shall send a further status report to the Center, and a copy to each party, at the end of each ensuing period of three months during which the proceedings have not been declared closed.

(c)   If the final award is not made within three months after the closure of the proceedings, the Tribunal shall send the Center a written explanation for the delay, with a copy to each party. It shall send a further explanation, and a copy to each party, at the end of each ensuing period of one month until the final award is made.

63.01. Time Period for Proceedings and Delivery of Award

Time limits are sometimes imposed on an arbitral tribunal to ensure a case is dealt with in an expeditious manner. Such rules may be imposed by agreement of the parties themselves, by the arbitral rules or by relevant law. The parties may have the best of intentions by including a strict time limit in an arbitration clause. Doing so, however,

---

the agreement to arbitrate. Art. IV(1)(b). The certified copies of the award and the arbitration agreement may also require translation if they are not already in the official language of the country in which enforcement is sought. Art. IV(a)(2).

[51] *See* WIPO RULES, Art. 62(f).

[52] *See* WIPO RULES, Art. 62(d).

[53] REDFERN & HUNTER, *supra* note 2, at 491.

can be counterproductive. If the time limit is a rigid and mandatory deadline, then when the limit is reached the mandate of the tribunal will end and it will no longer have jurisdiction to make a valid award. The time limit will need to be either observed or extended before it expires. A recalcitrant party, however, can intentionally delay the proceedings and refuse an extension in an attempt to frustrate the arbitration and generate grounds for the invalidity of an award rendered.

Thus, it is generally preferred practice that rigid time limits be avoided in the arbitration agreement. A non-mandatory provision should be enough to create the expectations and time pressure needed to move the proceedings (and arbitral tribunal) along.

63.02. *No Mandatory Time Limits in the WIPO Rules*

This is the approach adopted by the WIPO Rules in Articles 63(a)-(c). The WIPO Rules envision that an arbitration up to the issuance of the award may take up to *one year* from either the delivery of the Statement of Defense or the establishment of the arbitral Tribunal, whichever is later. The arbitration is to be heard, and the proceedings declared closed, *"wherever reasonably possible,"* within nine months of the Statement of Defense or appointment of the Tribunal. The final award should, *"wherever reasonably possible,"* be made *"within"* three months after the proceedings are declared closed.[54]

If these flexible deadlines are not met, the WIPO Rules provide that the arbitral tribunal must communicate the reasons for failure to the Center and to the parties. If the proceedings do not close within the nine-month period, the arbitral tribunal must provide a "status report" on the arbitration, and must continue to do so at the end of each ensuing three-month period.[55] If the award is not rendered within three months after the closure of the arbitration proceedings, the tribunal must send "a written explanation for the delay," and must continue to do so at the end of each ensuing month until the final award is made.[56] This approach builds in non-mandatory deadlines and allows the Center and the parties to monitor progress if the deadlines are not met, while avoiding the problems of mandatory deadlines.

E. *Waiver of Right to Appeal*

Effect of Award

Article 64

(a) By agreeing to arbitration under these Rules, the parties undertake to carry out the award without delay, and waive their right to any form of appeal or recourse to a court of law or other judicial authority, insofar as such waiver may validly be made under the applicable law.

---

[54] WIPO RULES, Art. 63(a).
[55] WIPO RULES, Art. 63(b).
[56] WIPO RULES, Art. 63(c).

(b) The award shall be effective and binding on the parties as from the date it is communicated by the Center pursuant to Article 62(f), second sentence.

64.01. Award's Binding Effect and Parties' Undertaking to Carry Out the Award Without Delay

A successful party in an international arbitration is entitled to expect that the award will be performed by the other party without delay. The arbitration agreement itself would be undermined if there was no implied duty that the parties will endeavor to carry out the award. Thus, while it is not strictly necessary to include an express provision to this effect, most international arbitration rules contain words to emphasize the binding nature of the award, as well as the commitment of the parties to carry it out without delay.[57]

Article 64 is consistent with the other major arbitration rules in this respect. By agreeing to the WIPO Rules, the parties agree to Article 64(a) providing that "the parties undertake to carry out the award without undue delay." Moreover, Article 64(b) confirms that the "award *shall* be effective and binding (emphasis added). These provisions, coupled with the provision for waiver of appeal discussed below, should make clear the parties' intention in this respect.

64.02. Right to Appeal Waived

One of the widely accepted purposes of arbitration is to achieve a final and binding determination of a dispute without unreasonable cost and delay. In countries where arbitration is favored, including those enforcing the New York Convention, court review of an arbitral award is extremely limited. An award will not be disturbed merely because the court thinks the arbitrators reached the wrong conclusion on a question of fact or law.[58]

In the past, if the parties wished to exclude the possibility of an appeal on the merits, it was wise to include such an express provision in the arbitration clause.[59] Now, however, the prevailing assumption, as reflected in the WIPO Rules, is that parties generally desire to restrict rights to appeal or to other recourse to courts other

---

[57] *See* AAA RULES, Art. 27(1); ICC RULES, Art. 28(6); LCIA RULES, Art. 26.9; UNCITRAL RULES, Art. 32(2). Most arbitral awards are in fact performed voluntarily. REDFERN & HUNTER, *supra* note 2, at 416.

[58] *See, e.g.*, Monscharsh v. Heily & Blase, 3 Cal. 4th 1, 28 (Cal. 1992) (award will not be overturned even when an error of law appears on the face of the award).

[59] The traditional practice in England, for example, was to subject errors of law to court review. Under the new Arbitration Act 1996, which came into force on January 31, 1997, Section 69 provides in relevant part that "*unless otherwise agreed by the parties,*" (emphasis added) a party to an arbitration may appeal to the court on a question of law arising from the award. The court may determine for itself whether to grant leave to appeal (*e.g.*, if the decision of the arbitral tribunal "is obviously wrong" or involves a question of "general public importance"). Further, an agreement to dispense with reasons for an award will be considered an agreement to exclude any appeal under Section 69. By agreeing to the WIPO Rules, a party now will be taken to have agreed that an appeal is excluded.

than for limited reasons such as those set forth in the New York Convention.[60] On the other hand, if the parties desire a wider scope of review and are willing to incur the additional time and cost for court proceedings following arbitration, and are also willing to have the (private) matters in the dispute subjected to public hearings, they should include an expression of this desire in the arbitration agreement (*e.g.*, by agreeing that for certain errors of fact or law, the parties consent to the jurisdiction of a particular court).[61]

By agreeing to arbitration under the WIPO Rules, the parties, through Article 64(a), will be deemed to have waived their right to an appeal or recourse to a court or other judicial authority.[62] With such a provision in the Rules, it is no longer imperative that the parties include in the arbitration clause a term specifically excluding appeal. However, the parties may waive only *"to the extent that such a waiver is valid under the applicable law."* (Emphasis added.)

This form of wording carries with it the implication that the waiver of all forms of appeal is not always permissible, and the impact of the law of the place of arbitration must be considered.[63]

---

[60] Under the New York Convention, Article V, a foreign award *may* be denied enforcement only if a party furnishes proof that: (i) the parties lacked capacity; (ii) arbitration agreement is invalid; (iii) there was inadequate notice; (iv) the matter arbitrated was outside the scope of the arbitration agreement or was not otherwise arbitrable; (v) the arbitral tribunal was not properly constituted in accordance with the parties' agreement or the law of the place of arbitration; (vi) the award is not binding or has been set aside by the courts where it was rendered; or (vii) the award is against public policy.

[61] *See* discussion paper of C. Ragan, *supra* note 3, at 17–18. If the parties wish to have such an appeal heard in the United States federal courts, they should be aware there is an open question as to whether such a provision will be considered valid, or a violation of the principle that federal courts are courts of limited jurisdiction, which jurisdiction can be conferred only by the U.S. Congress and not by private parties. *See* Chicago Typographical Union v. Chicago Sun-Times, 935 F.2d 1501, 1505 (7th Cir. 1991) (Posner, J.) (federal jurisdiction cannot be created by contract); Baravati v. Josephthal, Lyon & Ross, Inc., 28 F.3d 704, 706 (7th Cir. 1994) (same). *But cf.* Lapine Technology Corp. v. Kyocera Corp., 130 F.3d 884, 888 (9th Cir. 1997) (federal courts must honor an agreement where "the parties have indisputably contracted for heightened judicial scrutiny of the arbitrators' award"); Gateway Technologies, Inc. v. MCI Telecommunications Corp., 64 F.3d 993, 997 (5th Cir. 1995) (parties can agree to expand scope of judicial review).

[62] Note, however, that concerning interim measures of protection or security for claims and costs, Article 46(d) of the WIPO Rules provides in pertinent part that a request for such relief addressed to a judicial authority "shall not be deemed incompatible with the Arbitration Agreement."

[63] Thus, despite the language in Article 64(a), parties may still attempt to use the appeals process as a tactic simply to postpone the day on which payment is due, so that one of the purposes of international arbitration — the speedy resolution of disputes — is defeated. *See, e.g.*, Chromalloy Aeroservices v. Arab Republic of Egypt, 937 F. Supp. 907, 913 (D.D.C. 1996) (doctrine of international comity does not require deference to decision of Egyptian Court of Appeal nullifying arbitration award, where there was an exclusion of any right to appeal in the contract and the award was otherwise valid).

F. *Settlement, Consent Orders and Termination*

Settlement or Other Grounds for Termination

Article 65

(a) The Tribunal may suggest that the parties explore settlement at such times as the Tribunal may deem appropriate.

(b) If, before the award is made, the parties agree on a settlement of the dispute, the Tribunal shall terminate the arbitration and, if requested jointly by the parties, record the settlement in the form of a consent award. The Tribunal shall not be obliged to give reasons for such an award.

(c) If, before the award is made, the continuation of the arbitration becomes unnecessary or impossible for any reason not mentioned in paragraph (b), the Tribunal shall inform the parties of its intention to terminate the arbitration. The Tribunal shall have the power to issue such an order terminating the arbitration, unless a party raises justifiable grounds for objection within a period of time to be determined by the Tribunal.

(d) The consent award or the order for termination of the arbitration shall be signed by the arbitrator or arbitrators in accordance with Article 62(d) and shall be communicated by the Tribunal to the Center in a number of originals sufficient to provide one for each party, the arbitrator or arbitrators and the Center. The Center shall formally communicate an original of the consent award or the order for termination to each party and the arbitrator or arbitrators.

65.01. Settlement

Under the WIPO Rules, the arbitral tribunal has authority to suggest at appropriate times that the parties explore settlement.[64] While all of the major arbitration rules expressly provide that arbitral tribunals may make consent awards (or awards on agreed terms),[65] this provision authorizing the tribunal to suggest settlement is unique to the WIPO Rules. The role of the arbitral tribunal has thus been somewhat expanded from that of a private adjudicator to a more involved role, though something less than that akin to the role of a mediator.[66] The WIPO Rules provide no guidance as to *how* the arbitral panel would communicate the suggestion that the parties explore settlement. How would the panel do so without giving indications of how it viewed the

---

[64] WIPO RULES, Art. 65(a).

[65] AAA RULES, Art. 29; ICC RULES, Art. 26; LCIA RULES, Art. 26.8; UNCITRAL RULES, Art. 34.

[66] In fact, there has been lively debate as to whether or not it is wise that the person serving as a mediator should, in turn, be allowed to serve as an arbitrator in a subsequent arbitration if the mediation fails. The WIPO Mediation Rules provide in Article 20 that ''[u]nless required by a court of law *or authorized in writing by the parties*, the mediator shall not act in any capacity whatsoever . . . in any pending or future proceedings, whether judicial, arbitral or otherwise, relating to the subject matter of the dispute.'' (Emphasis added)

merits? On the other hand, some judges do give preliminary views on certain matters submitted before them as a means of encouraging the parties to consider settlement.

65.02. Termination and Consent Award

Article 65 in sub-parts (b) and (c) gives the arbitral tribunal power to terminate the arbitration proceedings. The tribunal may do so in the case of a settlement, in which case it is also authorized *"if requested jointly by the parties"* to record the settlement in a consent award. The WIPO Rules also give the arbitral tribunal power to terminate the proceedings if "the continuation of the arbitration becomes unnecessary or impossible for any reason not mentioned in paragraph [65](b)." This could happen, for example, if one of the parties ceased to exist, if the parties failed to make required deposits in respect of costs, or if the claimant failed to take some step ordered by the arbitral panel.[67] If a consent award and/or order for termination of the proceedings are issued, they must be signed in accordance with the requirements applicable to any other award (in Article 62(d)) and communicated to the WIPO Center in the same manner.[68]

G. Award Corrections and Additional Awards

Correction of the Award and Additional Award

Article 66

(a)   Within 30 days after receipt of the award, a party may, by notice to the Tribunal, with a copy to the Center and the other party, request the Tribunal to correct in the award any clerical, typographical or computational errors. If the Tribunal considers the request to be justified, it shall make the correction within 30 days after receipt of the request. Any correction, which shall take the form of a separate memorandum, signed by the Tribunal in accordance with Article 62(d), shall become part of the award.

(b)   The Tribunal may correct any error of the type referred to in paragraph (a) on its own initiative within 30 days after the date of the award.

(c)   A party may, within 30 days after receipt of the award, by notice to the Tribunal, with a copy to the Center and the other party, request the Tribunal to make an additional award as to claims presented in the arbitral proceedings but not dealt with in the award. Before deciding on the request, the Tribunal shall give the parties an opportunity to be heard. If the Tribunal considers the request to be justified, it shall, wherever reasonably possible, make the additional award within 60 days of receipt of the request.

66.01. Correction of the Award and Request for Additional Award(s)

Article 66 deals with requests for corrections to an award and/or requests for an additional award. Under Article 66 sub-parts (a) and (b), either the parties or the

---

[67] *See* REDFERN & HUNTER, *supra* note 2, at 492.

[68] WIPO RULES, Art. 65(d).

arbitral tribunal will have 30 days in which to correct any clerical, typographical or computational errors in the award. In the case of the parties, they must make a request to the tribunal, which will be granted if it is "justified." While the tribunal can make a "correction" on its own initiative, it cannot, under Article 66(c), make an additional award of its own initiative.

On this issue, the position under the different sets of arbitration rules varies. The LCIA, AAA and ICC Rules all contain provisions for the correction of an award.[69] While the LCIA and ICC Rules, like the WIPO Rules, provide that a correction can be made either on the request of a party or the initiative of the tribunal, the AAA Rules allow for a correction only on the parties' request, if it is justified.

The LCIA Rules, like the WIPO Rules, also provide for the making of an additional award, "as to claims that were presented in the arbitral proceedings but not dealt with in the award," on request of the parties.[70] In such case, the WIPO Rules specify that the tribunal "shall" give the parties an opportunity to be heard before deciding whether the request is justified. The LCIA Rules provide only for "notice" to the other party or parties that the request for an additional award has been made. Further, while the LCIA Rules provide that the tribunal "shall" make the additional award within 60 days if it views the request as justified, the WIPO Rules provide that an additional award should be made within 60 days "wherever reasonably possible." Both the AAA and ICC Rules contain no provisions for additional awards.

66.02. No Interpretation of Awards

Finally, the WIPO Rules, like the AAA and LCIA Rules, contain no provision authorizing the parties to request, or the tribunal to issue, an interpretation of the award. The UNCITRAL and ICC Rules, however, do authorize the parties to request an interpretation. Under the UNCITRAL Rules, the tribunal is to provide such an interpretation in writing within 45 days of the request.[71] The ICC Rules allow the other party a short time, "normally not exceeding 30 days," to comment on the request for interpretation, and the tribunal then has 30 more days to submit its decision if it decides to interpret the award.[72] The allowance of an interpretation, however, raises some problematic issues. Will there be fresh deliberations by the arbitrators to produce the "interpretation?" What if they cannot agree? What if the matter involved would make a substantial difference in the performance of the award? If the arbitrators could not agree, would this undermine the award itself? Perhaps because the finality of the award may itself be undermined, the WIPO Rules have omitted such a provision.

---

[69] AAA RULES, Art. 30; LCIA RULES, Art. 27; ICC RULES, Art. 29.

[70] WIPO RULES, Art. 66(c); LCIA RULES, Art. 27.3.

[71] UNCITRAL RULES, Art. 35.

[72] ICC RULES, Art. 29(2).

FEES AND COSTS

Articles 67 to 72

Erik Wilbers*

I. GENERAL

On January 20, 1995, the WIPO Arbitration and Mediation Center (the Center) organized in Geneva, in collaboration with the Swiss Arbitration Association (ASA), a Conference on Rules for Institutional Arbitration and Mediation. On that occasion, the Director of the Center, Dr. Francis Gurry, presented a paper on fees and costs explaining the general background to the approach taken by WIPO and summing up the advantages and disadvantages of the various options as expressed in the cost provisions of different arbitral institutions.[1] The present article seeks to complement that comparative summary by providing a more detailed textual analysis of, and practical guidance to, each of the WIPO Rules relating to fees and costs.

Perhaps the most important requirements regarding arbitration fees and costs are transparency and cohesiveness of the relevant provisions and a reasonable level of fees. The WIPO provisions, including the Schedules of Fees, represent a modern balance between the interests of users, the position of the arbitrators, and the role of the administering authority. The structure of the WIPO Rules on fees and costs is straightforward and follows the logical order of the proceedings.

At the outset of the procedure, the Claimant is to pay a flat, relatively modest registration fee to the Center (Article 67; Schedule of Registration Fees). Following the Claimant's submission of the Request for Arbitration, it must pay a further fee to the Center (Article 68). Subject to a maximum amount (which, again, is relatively low), this administration fee is calculated on the basis of the amount of the claim (Schedule of Administration Fees). An administration fee, again on an *ad valorem* basis, is payable also by a Respondent who files a counterclaim (Article 68). The Center fixes the third component of the procedural costs, the fees of the arbitrators, within the minimum and maximum ranges indicated by the Schedule of Arbitrators'

---

* Erik Wilbers, a national of The Netherlands (1958), is a Senior Counselor at the WIPO Arbitration and Mediation Center, World Intellectual Property Organization, Geneva. Following studies in The United States and The Netherlands, Mr. Wilbers was a research fellow at the Max Planck Institute for Intellectual Property Law in Munich. Before joining WIPO in 1996, he practiced with the law firm of Clifford Chance in Amsterdam, was on the legal staff of the Iran-United States Claims Tribunal in The Hague, and headed a division of the Compensation Commission of the United Nations Security Council dealing with claims arising from the Gulf War. Mr. Wilbers has written and spoken on a variety of legal subjects, including arbitration and intellectual property.
[1] Francis Gurry, *Fees and Costs*, Conference on Rules for Institutional Arbitration and Mediation 91–102 (Geneva, January 20, 1995).

Fees, and in consultation with the parties and the arbitrators (Article 69; Schedule of Arbitrators' Fees).

To secure payment of the arbitrators' fees and the other costs of arbitration, the Center determines a deposit, which the parties must in principle bear in equal parts (Article 70). The Center may require supplementary deposits in the course of the arbitration. At the end of the procedure, the arbitrators' fees and the other costs of arbitration determined by the Center are recorded in the award and, if they are still outstanding, are debited from the deposit (Article 71). The award further contains the Tribunal's allocation of these costs and of the registration and administration fees between the parties (Article 71). Also, the Tribunal may determine and allocate the legal expenses incurred by the parties in presenting their case (Article 72).

II. DISCUSSION OF SPECIFIC ARTICLES

A. *Fees of the Center*

Article 67

(a) The Request for Arbitration shall be subject to the payment to the Center of a registration fee, which shall belong to the International Bureau of WIPO. The amount of the registration fee shall be fixed in the Schedule of Fees applicable on the date on which the Request for Arbitration is received by the Center.

(b) The registration fee shall not be refundable.

(c) No action shall be taken by the Center on a Request for Arbitration until the registration fee has been paid.

(d) If a Claimant fails, within 15 days after a second reminder in writing from the Center, to pay the registration fee, it shall be deemed to have withdrawn its Request for Arbitration.

Article 67(a) provides that the Request for Arbitration shall be subject to the payment to the Center of a registration fee, which shall belong to the International Bureau of WIPO and which shall be fixed in the Schedule of Fees applicable on the date of receipt of the Request by the Center.

The registration fee is the first component of what may be termed the procedural costs, which should be distinguished from the parties' costs. Within the procedural costs, the registration fee is the first element of the costs of the arbitral institution, *i.e.*, the fees of the Center.

The explanation of what the fee covers follows from the term "registration fee" itself, as well as the provision of Article 67(c) and the separate provisions of Article 68 concerning payment of an administration fee. The registration fee entitles the Claimant to file a Request for Arbitration and to have the Center undertake initial action upon such Request.

The Article does not state expressly that it is the Claimant who must pay the registration fee. This follows from the fact that it is the Claimant who, pursuant to

Article 6, transmits the Request for Arbitration. It also follows from the provision of Article 67(d).

Unlike the system for the payment of administrative fees, the Rules do not contain a parallel provision also subjecting the submission of a counterclaim by the Respondent to the payment to the Center of a registration fee. By paying the registration fee, the Claimant may be deemed to commence the arbitral process also for the Respondent.

The provision that the fee shall belong to the International Bureau merely reflects the Center's status as forming part of the Secretariat of WIPO, also called the International Bureau.

In light of its function, the registration fee, unlike the administration fee payable pursuant to Article 68, does not increase if the Claimant increases the amount of its claim in the course of the proceedings.

As a further difference from the system for payment of the administration fee, Article 67 does not provide for the Center to notify the Claimant of the amount of the registration fee payable. Until the Center has received the Request for Arbitration or otherwise been contacted, such notification is impossible. However, the Claimant may itself ascertain the level of the registration fee payable on the basis of the Schedule of Fees as one of only three flat fee amounts provided therein.

Reflecting the more advanced stage of the procedure, Articles 68(a) and 70(c), dealing respectively with the administration fee and the deposit for the costs of arbitration, specify a payment period of 30 days. The deadline for payment of the registration fee follows from the provision of Article 67(d); reference is made to the observations made with regard thereto.

Article 67(b) provides that the registration fee shall not be refundable.

The Article does not contain any exceptions, and simply clarifies that under no circumstances will a paid registration fee be refunded. In practice, those circumstances will usually be the settlement of the case, causing the withdrawal of the Request for Arbitration by the Claimant, or, if the arbitration has gotten underway, the withdrawal of the case by the parties.

Article 67(c) provides that no action shall be taken by the Center on a Request for Arbitration until the registration fee has been paid.

Rather than attempting to specify the various types of action which the Center will not take, this Article makes clear generally that the Center will not act on a Request for Arbitration until the registration fee has been paid. However, even in the absence of such payment, by virtue of Article 7, the Center's receipt of the Request for Arbitration triggers the date of commencement of the arbitration, primarily for the purpose of determining the suspension of the running period of any applicable statute of limitations. Even in the absence of payment, therefore, the Center will, pursuant to Article 8, inform the parties of its receipt of the Request for Arbitration and of the date of commencement of the arbitration. Another such exception to the strict letter of Article 67(c) are the Center's payment reminders implied by Article 67(d).

For the purpose of determining the date of commencement of a time limit, the Rules contain provisions on the receipt of notices or other communications. With regard to receipt of payments, the provisions leave some room for practical interpretation. Article 67(a), while referring to payment rather than receipt thereof, would entitle the Center to await the actual arrival of the registration fee in its account. Of course, the Center may in its discretion decide to act on confirmation by the paying bank that it has transferred the funds.

Article 67(d) provides that a Claimant who fails to pay the registration fee within 15 days after a second written reminder from the Center shall be deemed to have withdrawn its Request for Arbitration.

The Article implies that the Center is obliged to send at least two written reminders to a Claimant who fails to pay the registration fee. The Article leaves to the discretion of the Center when, following receipt of the Request for Arbitration, to send the first of these reminders, and when to follow up with a second. In practice, it appears reasonable that the Center will observe at least the 15-day period of this Article for these purposes also, if not a 30-day period similar to that foreseen under Article 68(a) for payment of the administration fee and under Article 70(c) for payment of the deposit for the costs of arbitration.

One effect of the Claimant's deemed withdrawal of its Request for Arbitration may be to terminate the suspension of the running period of any applicable statute of limitations. Also, the withdrawal releases the Center from any obligation to undertake action in the case. Likewise, in the absence of a Request for Arbitration, there is no case for the Respondent to answer.

In practice, given the modest amount of the registration fee and the pressure which the Claimant will want to exert on the Respondent, the scenario foreseen in this Article may primarily materialize in the event of a settlement of the case.

Schedule of Fees

The Schedule of Fees, which was established in 1994 and remains valid, provides the calculation basis and amounts of the registration fee. The Schedule also contains a number of explanatory Notes.

The registration fee is calculated as a flat fee by reference to the amount of the claim, both amounts expressed in United States dollars. If the amount of the claim is up to $1,000,000, the registration fee is $1,000; between $1,000,001 and $10,000,000, it is $2,000; and over $10,000,000, it is $3,000.

Unlike the system for calculating the administration fee and the arbitrators' fees, these registration fee amounts are not cumulative, *i.e.*, the fee is either $1,000, or $2,000, or $3,000.

Subject to two exceptions, the determination of the registration fee does not take into account interest claims. The first exception is where the claim consists only of interest, such as a claim for the interest (but not the principal) due on a loan; and the second exception occurs where the interest claim exceeds the main claim, in which case it replaces the latter as the basis for the fee calculation.[2]

It is the policy of the Center that where the arbitration was preceded, pursuant to the combined procedure under WIPO Rules, by an unsuccessful mediation of the dispute, the Center will credit the registration fee paid for the mediation (which has a lower minimum but higher maximum registration fee than arbitration) against the registration fee payable for the arbitration.

Note 1 to the schedule of fees provides that where the amount of the claim is not specified at the time the Request for Arbitration is submitted, a registration fee of $1,000 is payable, subject to adjustment when the Statement of Claim is filed.

This solution, which offers a presumption that the amount claimed is in the lower of the brackets mentioned, allows the arbitration to commence even if the amount of the claim has not been expressed. It accommodates the provision of Article 9(v), which states that the Request for Arbitration shall contain an indication of any amount claimed ''to the extent possible.''

It follows from the Schedule of Fees that the adjustment could never lead to a registration fee in excess of $3,000. Because the system provides for a flat registration fee, it has not been necessary to add a Note recording this cap similar to Note 3 in the Schedule of Fees dealing with the administration fee.

Note 2 to the schedule of fees provides for the possibility that the claim is not for a monetary amount, in which case a registration fee of $1,000 is payable, subject to such adjustment as the Center considers to be appropriate upon examination of the Request for Arbitration or the Statement of Claim.

This solution, which offers a presumption that the equivalent amount is in the lower of the brackets mentioned, allows the arbitration to commence even if the claim is not for a monetary amount. While theoreticians may submit that any claim can be quantified in monetary terms, many types of claim are conceivable that are not normally so expressed. For example, the Claimant may seek an award ordering the Respondent to publish a rectification.

The Note leaves the final determination of the fee to the discretion of the Center. While the Center is to consider the Request for Arbitration or the Statement of Claim, the Center may determine the fee which it finds ''appropriate in the circumstances.'' In practice, this requires the Center to determine an appropriate value for the claim, which is the more direct wording used to guide the Center's determination of the arbitrators' fees.

Again, it follows from the Schedule of Fees that such determination could never lead to a registration fee in excess of $3,000 and, because of the flat fee structure, no need has been found to add a Note recording this cap.

---

[2] *Id.* at 94.

Further observations on the Center's determination of fees for claims not seeking a monetary amount are made in the context of the Notes relating to the Schedule of Arbitrators' Fees.

Note 3 to the schedule of fees provides that amounts of claims expressed in currencies other than United States dollars shall, for the purpose of calculating the registration fee, be converted to United States dollar amounts on the basis of the official United Nations exchange rate prevailing on the date of submission of the Request for Arbitration.

This provision creates an objective standard for the calculation of the registration fee payable if the amount claimed has not been expressed in United States dollars. It should eliminate differences of opinion which might otherwise arise in such cases between the Claimant and the Center.

The official United Nations exchange rate is used by United Nations organizations as the calculation basis for such purposes as payments to employees and third parties, and determination of membership dues. The rate is fixed monthly and published by the United Nations Secretariat in New York.

The fact that the applicable rate is that prevailing on the date of submission of the Request for Arbitration implies that a Claimant's late payment of the fee could not affect the level of the amount itself.

Article 68

(a)   **An administration fee, which shall belong to the International Bureau of WIPO, shall be payable by the Claimant to the Center within 30 days after the commencement of the arbitration. The Center shall notify the Claimant of the amount of the administration fee as soon as possible after receipt of the Request for Arbitration.**

(b)   **In the case of a counter-claim, an administration fee shall also be payable by the Respondent to the Center within 30 days after the date on which the counter-claim referred to in Article 42(c) is made. The Center shall notify the Respondent of the amount of the administration fee as soon as possible after receipt of notification of the counter-claim.**

(c)   **The amount of the administration fee shall be calculated in accordance with the Schedule of Fees applicable on the date of commencement of the arbitration.**

(d)   **Where a claim or counter-claim is increased, the amount of the administration fee may be increased in accordance with the Schedule of Fees applicable under paragraph (c), and the increased amount shall be payable by the Claimant or the Respondent, as the case may be.**

(e)   **If a party fails, within 15 days after a second reminder in writing from the Center, to pay any administration fee due, it shall be deemed to have withdrawn its claim or counter-claim, or its increase in claim or counter-claim, as the case may be.**

(f)   The Tribunal shall, in a timely manner, inform the Center of the amount of the claim and any counter-claim, as well as any increase thereof.

Article 68(a) provides that an administration fee, which shall belong to the International Bureau of WIPO, shall be payable by the Claimant to the Center within 30 days after the commencement of the arbitration, and that the Center shall notify the Claimant of the amount of such fee as soon as possible after receipt of the Request for Arbitration.

The administration fee is the second component of the procedural costs. Within the procedural costs, it is, after the registration fee, the second and final element of the costs of the arbitral institution, *i.e.*, the fees of the Center.

As discussed above, the registration fee entitles the Claimant to file a Request for Arbitration and to have the Center undertake initial action upon such Request. The administration fee covers all further action which the Claimant may expect from the Center until the arbitration has come to an end.[3]

While the commencement of the arbitration presumes payment of the registration fee, the reverse may apply to the administration fee: its payment normally presumes the commencement of the arbitration, and the time limit for its payment runs from that moment.

Again, the provision that the fee shall belong to the International Bureau merely reflects the Center's status as forming part of the WIPO Secretariat.

The provision that the Center shall notify the Claimant of the administration fee payable as soon as possible after the receipt by the Center of the Request for Arbitration aims to avoid as much as possible a reduction in practice of the 30-day period for payment. While an alternative approach might have let such time period commence as of the Center's notification of the Claimant, nothing should in practice prevent an informed Claimant from itself performing the calculation of the applicable administration fee without awaiting notification.

Unlike Article 67 with respect to the registration fee, Article 68 does not provide that the administration fee shall be nonrefundable. Indeed, since the administration fee is charged to cover the Center's involvement in the arbitration until delivery of the

---

[3] The services provided by the Center include: the processing of the initial written statements prior to the establishment of the Tribunal; the exercise of the power to extend certain time limits under Article 4(g); the appointment of arbitrators where the parties themselves either do not appoint the arbitrators or fail to exercise a right to appoint an arbitrator within the prescribed time limits; the determination of the fees of arbitrators; the determination of the amount of, and the administration of, deposits for costs from each party; the determination of the place of arbitration, where the parties themselves do not agree upon it; the constitution, where necessary, of an *ad hoc* committee of the WIPO Consultative Commission to rule on the challenge or replacement of an arbitrator; the monitoring of certain time limits; the processing of the award; the provision, where the arbitration takes place in Geneva, of a hearing room, party rooms and an arbitrators' room; and the Center's communication expenses in respect of the arbitration. *Id.* at 93–94.

final award, earlier settlement of the case may give rise to a complete or partial refund of this fee.[4]

Article 68(b) provides that an administrative fee shall also be payable by a Respondent who has submitted a counterclaim, within 30 days of its filing date. The Center shall notify the Respondent of the amount payable as soon as possible after its receipt of notification of the counterclaim.

The Respondent need not pay a registration fee, but does have to pay an administration fee if it files a counterclaim. This requirement obviously is not intended (nor is it likely) to deter a Respondent from making such filing. Instead, it reflects the probability that, as a result of the introduction of a counterclaim, the proceedings increase not only in value, but, in all likelihood, also in complexity, duration and cost.

The Article is basically a parallel provision to that of Article 68(a) with respect to the submission of a Request for Arbitration, with two distinctions. Where Article 68(a) refers to the notification of the Claimant after the Center's receipt of the Request for Arbitration, provision (b) refers to notification of the Respondent after the Center's receipt "of notification" of the counterclaim. This formulation reflects the fact that the arbitral Tribunal will usually have been constituted before the Respondent files a counterclaim, in which case the Tribunal will notify the Center.

The second, more nominal difference is that the Article does not expressly state that the administration fee payable by the Respondent shall belong to the International Bureau of WIPO. It may be considered obvious, however, that this clarification applies to any payment of fees owed to the Center.

Again, the provision that the Center shall notify the Respondent as soon as possible is intended to avoid to the extent possible a reduction in practice of the 30-day period for payment. While, as an alternative possibility, this Article also could have let the period commence with the Center's notification, the Respondent may also take the calculation of the administration fee upon itself without awaiting such notice.

Article 68(c) provides that the administration fee shall be calculated in accordance with the Schedule of Fees applicable on the date of commencement of the arbitration.

The previously noted fact that payment of the administration fee normally presumes the commencement of the arbitration allows the fee to be set on the basis of the Schedule of Fees applicable on the date of such commencement.

---

[4] The Center's refund policy is based on the following principles: If settlement occurs after the submission of the Request for Arbitration but before the establishment of the Tribunal, the administration fee will not be payable, or, if already paid, will be refunded. If settlement occurs after the Tribunal has been established, at least one-third of the administration fee will be payable, or, if already paid, will be retained by the Center. The precise amount, if any, over and above this one-third will depend on the circumstances of the case, including the stage to which the proceedings have progressed and the administrative functions performed by the Center. *Id.* at 94–95.

Article 68(d) provides that, where a claim or counterclaim is increased, the amount of the administration fee may be increased in accordance with the Schedule of Fees applicable under paragraph (c), which increased amount shall be payable by the Claimant or the Respondent, as the case may be.

As indicated by the Schedule of Fees, the level of the administration fee payable by the Claimant is determined by reference to the amount claimed, and the administration fee payable by the Respondent depends on the amount counterclaimed. It follows that, as provided by this Article, any increase in the amount claimed and/or counterclaimed (sometimes one party's increase is in reaction to an increase introduced by the other) may also cause an increase in the corresponding administrative fee. This contrasts with the approach followed with regard to the registration fee, which, as noted, is unaffected by any increase in the claim.

The provision states that the amount of the administrative fee "may" be increased. This provides the Center with a measure of discretion, for example where the amount of the increase of the (counter)claim is relatively insignificant. (Even if the Article would have contained mandatory (i.e., "shall") wording, the Center presumably might still, within limits of procedural equality, have the option of waiving fees payable to itself.)

The Article refers to an increase in the claim or counterclaim, but does not contain a similar provision providing for a reduction of fees in case of a decrease in the claim or counterclaim. An increase is expected to affect the complexity and duration of the arbitration to a larger relative extent than would a decrease. In addition, it may deter the filing of frivolous (counter)claims.

The reference to Article 68(c) implies that the Schedule of Fees applicable to the increase is that which is valid on the date of commencement of the arbitration. This prevents the possibility that the administration fee would become determined by changes in the Schedule of Fees taking effect between the date of commencement of the arbitration and the increase in the claim and/or counterclaim.

Since the initial administration fee is likely to have been paid by the time of the increase in the claim and/or counterclaim, the reference to the "increased amount" in practice may also be read as the "amount of the increase."

Articles 68(a) and (b) specify the initial period within which the original administration fee must be paid. Reflecting, in most cases, the more advanced stage of the procedure, the initial period for payment of an increase in the administration fee has been left open. In practice, a period of 30 days such as foreseen in Articles 68(a) and (b) may apply here as well.

Similarly, where Articles 68(a) and (b) expressly provide for the Center to notify the party of the amount of the administration fee payable, such notification may be considered implied in Article 68(d), given also the reference in Article 68(e) to written reminders from the Center.

Article 68(e) provides that if a party fails, within 15 days after a second written reminder from the Center, to pay any administration fee due, it shall be deemed to have withdrawn its claim or counterclaim, or the increase thereof, as the case may be.

In principle, the Claimant's deemed withdrawal of its claim may trigger Article 65(c), which deals with the situation where the continuation of the arbitration becomes unnecessary or impossible for reasons other than settlement. One question which may thereby arise is the effect of such withdrawal on the proceedings if the Respondent has submitted a counterclaim.

The Respondent's deemed withdrawal of its counterclaim eliminates the need for the Claimant to reply to the counterclaim.

A deemed withdrawal of the increase in the claim or counterclaim removes the need for the other party to address the increase.

Another effect of the withdrawal of part or all of a (counter)claim is that it may terminate the suspension of the running period of any applicable statute of limitations.

The provision implies that the Center is obliged to send at least two written reminders to a party who fails to pay the administration fee. Strict application of this provision would have the two reminders follow, *i.e.*, not include, the first notification referred to in Articles 68(a) and (b).

Article 68(e) leaves it to the discretion of the Center to determine the period between the first and the second reminder. In practice, it appears reasonable that the Center will observe at least the 15-day period of this Article for this purpose also, if not the 30-day initial period for payment foreseen under Article 68(a).

Like Article 67(c), Article 68(e) refers to payment rather than receipt thereof. A practical interpretation suggests that a party has missed the deadline for payment if the Center has not received payment within the stipulated period.

By the time of the deemed withdrawal of the claim or counterclaim, the Center may have incurred costs in relation to the case, prompting the question whether, and to what extent, the administration fee remains payable. A similar question may apply to any arbitrators' fees which may have arisen, as well as costs incurred by the other party. The determinations on these points may be recorded in the Tribunal's termination order.

Article 68(f) provides that the Tribunal shall timely inform the Center of the amount of the claim and any counterclaim, as well as any increase thereof.

The prompt notification by the Tribunal of the amount of the claim and of the counterclaim, and of any increase thereof, allows the Center to determine and charge the administration fee, and to do so without undue delay.

Of course, it is possible that the Request for Arbitration, or the Statement of Claim which may be filed with it, allows the Center to determine the administration fee before the arbitral Tribunal has been constituted. In such a case, which has actually been foreseen by Article 68(a), separate notification by the Tribunal would merely serve the purpose of confirmation. The same situation may apply to determination of the administrative fee payable by the Respondent, whose Answer to the Request may already contain an indication of the amount of its counterclaim.

Schedule of Fees

The Schedule of Fees, which was established in 1994 and continues to be valid, provides the calculation basis and minimum and maximum amounts of the administration fee. The Schedule also contains a number of explanatory Notes.

Like the registration fee, the administration fee is calculated by reference to the amount of the claim or counterclaim. However, unlike the system used to determine the registration fee, the administrative fee calculation makes use of a regressive percentage scale. All amounts are expressed in United States dollars.

The minimum administration fee is $1,000, payable for a (counter)claim of up to $100,000. The next bracket is that from $100,001 to $1,000,000, in which case the fee is $1,000 plus 0.40% of the amount in that bracket. The next bracket runs from $1,000,001 to $5,000,000, with a fee of $4,600 plus 0.20% of the amount in that bracket. The next bracket is that between $5,000,001 to $20,000,000, corresponding to a fee of $12,600 plus 0.10% of the amount above $5,000,000. Finally, if the (counter)claim exceeds $20,000,000, the administration fee comes to $27,600 plus 0.05% of the amount above $20,000,000, provided that the maximum fee payable is $35,000.

Like the calculation of the registration fee, the determination of the administration fee does not take into account (counter)claims for interest, subject to two exceptions. The first exception is where the (counter)claim consists only of interest, such as a (counter)claim for the interest (but not the principal) due on a loan; the second exception occurs where the interest (counter)claim exceeds the main (counter)claim, in which case it replaces the latter as the basis for the fee calculation.[5]

Note 1 provides that where a claim or counterclaim is not for a monetary amount, the Center shall determine an appropriate administration fee.

Determination of the administration fee is thus left to the discretion of the Center, although the cap set by Note 3 implies that such discretion cannot lead to an administration fee higher than $35,000. In practice, the Center will be required to determine an appropriate value for the claim, which is the more direct wording used for the determination of the arbitrators' fees.

There is no need for an initial fixed administration fee which may then be adjusted, because, unlike at the stage where a registration fee is due, the arbitration has already commenced and the record may even include the Statement of Claim.

Further observations on the Center's determination of fees for claims not seeking a monetary amount are made in the context of the Notes relating to the Schedule of Arbitrators' Fees.

---

[5] *Id.* at 94.

Note 2 provides that the percentage figures provided in the Schedule are applied to each successive part of the amount of the (counter)claim.

An example of this system, commonly used for income tax calculations, is where the amount of the claim is $1,000,000: $1,000 is payable for the first $100,000 of the claim, and the 0.40% is subsequently applied to the remaining $900,000, adding up to a total administration fee of $4,600.

Note 3 specifies the amount of $35,000 as the maximum administration fee payable.

This maximum (much higher, of course, than the maximum registration fee) is reached if the total amount of the (counter)claim is $34,800,000. Any adjustment of this maximum, for example for an arbitration which proves to be very lengthy or requires an exceptional degree of involvement on the part of the Center, would need to be agreed with the parties.

Note 4 provides that amounts of (counter)claims expressed in currencies other than United States dollars shall, for the purpose of calculating the administration fee, be converted to United States dollar amounts on the basis of the official United Nations exchange rate prevailing on the date of submission of the (counter)claim.

This provision is similar to that relating to conversion for the purpose of determining the registration fee and, *mutatis mutandis*, the observations made with regard to the latter apply.

B.   *Fees of the Arbitrators*

Article 69

(a)   The amount and currency of the fees of the arbitrators and the modalities and timing of their payment shall be fixed, in accordance with the provisions of this Article, by the Center, after consultation with the arbitrators and the parties.

(b)   The amount of the fees of the arbitrators shall, unless the parties and arbitrators agree otherwise, be determined within the range of minimum and maximum fees set out in the Schedule of Fees applicable on the date of the commencement of the arbitration, taking into account the estimated time needed by the arbitrators for conducting the arbitration, the amount in dispute, the complexity of the subject-matter of the dispute, the urgency of the case and any other relevant circumstances of the case.

Article 69(a) provides that the amount and currency of the fees of the arbitrators and the modalities and timing of their payment shall be fixed, in accordance with the provisions of this Article, by the Center, after consultation with the arbitrators and the parties.

The first two components of the procedural costs (which, as noted, may be distinguished from the parties' costs) relate to the fees of the Center. This Article addresses the third component: the arbitrators' fees. These cover the professional time and expertise which the arbitrators have invested in the arbitration, but do not include their out-of-pocket expenses, which are dealt with in Article 71.

Article 69(a) establishes the Center's authority and duty to determine the fees of the arbitrators. In exercising this mandate, the Center acts as a buffer between the parties and the arbitrators, thus avoiding the need for the parties and the arbitrators to engage in direct fee negotiations that might strain their relations.[6] Of course, the provision does require the Center to consult them prior to deciding on the fees.

The provision's place within the Fees and Costs chapter as well as its references to the timing of the arbitrators' payment and, in Article 69(b), to the estimated time needed by the arbitrators, confirm that the arbitrators' fees are fixed at the outset of the proceedings. Reference is made to the further observations made on the subject in connection with Article 71(a).

Within the confines of Article 69(a)'s implicit reference to the provisions of Article 69(b), this Article leaves substantial flexibility for the Center to make its determination. For example, whereas the Schedules of Fees and the registration and administration fees are in United States dollars, the arbitrators' fees may be set in a different currency, thus allowing the Center to take into account the nationalities, locations and other circumstances involved.

Another example of the discretion afforded by the Article relates to the timing of payment, implying the possibility of partial payment at various stages of the arbitration. This installment option has become increasingly common, particularly for lengthy arbitrations or arbitrations that are time-intensive for the arbitrators even in earlier phases of the proceedings.

The discretion inherent in the broad term ''modalities'' of payment may not be interpreted to suggest an authority on the part of the Center to apportion the costs between the parties; Article 71(c) reserves this decision to the Tribunal.

Article 69(b) provides that the amount of the arbitrators' fees shall, unless the parties and arbitrators agree otherwise, be determined within the range of minimum and maximum fees set out in the Schedule of Fees applicable on the date of the commencement of the arbitration, taking into account the estimated time needed by the arbitrators for conducting the arbitration, the amount in dispute, the complexity of the subject matter of the dispute, the urgency of the case and any other relevant circumstances of the case.

Where Article 69(a) states that the Center, in determining the arbitrators' fees, must observe the provisions of Article 69(b), the latter allows for a certain discretion for the Center, subject to two stipulations: unless otherwise agreed between the parties and the arbitrators, the Center's determination must fall within the ranges provided by the Schedule of Fees to which Article 69(b) refers in its turn, and it must take into account the factors enumerated in Article 69(b).

---

[6] *Id.* at 95.

The Schedule of Fees serves various functions. A primary function, which it shares with fee systems for private practitioners, is to contribute to the predictability and stability of the costs of the arbitration. First of all, this is important to parties. There are at least two moments when they may wish to assess their cost exposure: when they decide whether to provide for arbitration in their contract, and, if they do, under which rules; and when they decide whether to commence arbitration once a dispute has arisen. The Schedule of Arbitrators' Fees is more important in this respect than the Schedules of Fees for the registration and administration fees, because the arbitrators' fees normally are a much larger component of the procedural costs, and are more difficult to assess than the less discretionary registration and administration fees. Thus, a clear and reasonable framework such as the Schedule of Arbitrators' Fees helps parties to choose and to enter into arbitration; it allows comparison and prevents any discretion from being exercised in an arbitrary fashion.

Of course, predictability of the arbitrators' fees is useful not only for the parties, but also for the arbitrators themselves. It allows them to assess the direct return on their investment of time and effort in the case if they accept appointment.

In providing that the fees can only be set outside the limits of the Schedule through the agreement of the parties and the arbitrators, the Article provides them with the flexibility to establish a different fee basis. For example, the parties may agree with the arbitrators that they will be remunerated in accordance with time spent.

The Schedule is a practical mechanism guiding the Center's determination, providing an objective basis for its decision vis-à-vis the parties and the arbitrators as well as ensuring a degree of consistency. Article 69(b)'s listing of factors which the Center must thereby take into account provides a certain amount of discretion to the Center. The list of factors is broad, and the Center may take into account ''any other relevant circumstances'' which it wishes to consider. Parties are often already familiar with the listed factors, because they are generally reflected in most legal fees. Among the listed factors, the estimated time needed by the arbitrators for conducting the arbitration is the one most likely to involve serious consultation with the arbitrators.

The fact that the applicable Schedule of Fees is that which is valid on the date of the commencement of the arbitration implies that the timing of the determination of the fees does not affect their level.

Where a case is settled before delivery of the final award, the amount of fees payable to the arbitrators will be determined in accordance with the circumstances of the case. The right to such a fee will only arise after the transmission to the Tribunal of the file in accordance with Article 37. Should settlement occur after the transmission of the file, the fees due to the arbitrators will be determined having regard to the stage at which settlement occurs and to the work already performed, for example through preparatory conferences, file study, and procedural actions.[7]

---

[7] *Id.* at 97.

Schedule of Fees

The Schedule of Fees, which was established in 1994 and remains in effect, provides the basis for calculating the arbitrators' fees. The Schedule also contains a number of explanatory Notes.

Like the registration and administration fees, the arbitrators' fees are calculated by reference to the amount of the (counter)claim, and like the system for determining the administration fee, the calculation makes use of a regressive percentage scale.

Unlike the registration and administration fee schedules, application of the Schedule of Arbitrators' Fees does not provide one particular amount, but instead indicates a minimum and a maximum per claim bracket.

A further feature particular to the Schedule of Arbitrators' Fees is that these amounts differ according to whether the Tribunal consists of a sole arbitrator or of three persons. The amounts and percentages applying to a three-person Tribunal are generally two and a half times those which apply to a sole arbitrator. The fact that the ratio is two and a half, and not three, reflects the sharing of work and responsibility among the arbitrators; this consideration follows indirectly from Note 6.

The minimum fee is $2,000 for a sole arbitrator and $5,000 for a three-person Tribunal. On the other end of the Schedule, the open-ended final bracket, for claims over $25,000,000, provides for a maximum fee for a sole arbitrator of $308,500 plus 1.00% of the amount above $25,000,000, and a maximum fee for a three-person Tribunal of $771,250 plus 2.50% of the amount above $25,000,000.

Like the calculation of the registration fee and the administration fee, the determination of the arbitrators' fees does not take into account (counter)claims for interest, subject to two exceptions. The first exception is where the (counter)claim consists only of interest, such as a (counter)claim for the interest (but not the principal) due on a loan; the second exception where the (counter)claimed interest exceeds the main (counter)claim, in which case it replaces the latter as the basis for the fee calculation.[8]

Note 1 provides that, for the purpose of calculating the amount of claims, the value of any counterclaim is added to the amount of the claim.

Pursuant to Article 68, each of the Claimant and the counterclaimant must advance an administration fee in accordance with the amount of the (counter)claim. By contrast, the Schedule of Arbitrators' Fees is not concerned with the question which party is to pay, but rather with the total amount of the arbitrators' fees. Since this amount is to reflect the importance and complexity of the case (of which its financial value is often considered a reliable indicator), the amount of the claim and the counterclaim are to be added for purposes of calculating the arbitrators' fees.

---

[8] *Id.*

Note 2 provides that, for the purpose of calculating the minimum and maximum amounts of the arbitrators' fees, the percentage figures are applied to each successive part of the whole amount of claims.

This Note expresses the same principle as that which applies to the calculation of the administration fee, which system is also commonly used for income tax calculations. The "whole amount of claims" refers to the total amount of the claim and the counterclaim.

Note 3 provides that where a claim or counterclaim is not for a monetary amount, the Center shall, in consultation with the arbitrators and the parties, determine an appropriate value for the claim or counterclaim for the purpose of determining the arbitrators' fees.

The Note covers various scenarios. It may be that the claim is not for a monetary amount, but that the counterclaim is; or that the counterclaim is not for a monetary amount, but the claim is; or that neither the claim nor the counterclaim are for a monetary amount. These variations require the Center to assess the value of the (counter)claim.

It is also conceivable that part of the claim (or counterclaim) is for a monetary amount, and part of the claim is not; for example, a party may claim for damages as well as for the publication of a rectification. Whether the Center would determine the fees on the basis of such a partially quantified claim, or would rather make a full valuation of the claim for this purpose, will likely depend on the nature of the non-monetary component of the claim.

Two differences exist between the provisions relating to the determination of the registration and administration fees where the (counter)claim is not for a monetary amount, and the provision relating to the arbitrators' fees where the (counter)claim has not been quantified. First, whereas the provisions relating to the registration and administration fees refer to the determination of those fees which the Center considers to be appropriate, this Note specifies that the Center shall determine an appropriate value for the (counter)claim. Because, on the basis of the value thus established, the Center has discretion to determine the arbitrators' fees within the applicable range in the Schedule, the end effect of both formulas is the same.

The second, less nominal difference lies in the Center's obligation, for purposes of determining the arbitrators' fees, to consult the arbitrators and the parties. As to consulting the Tribunal, while the Center will normally determine the registration fee before the Tribunal has been constituted, the Tribunal may exist by the time the Center determines the administration fee. As to consulting the parties, this possibility theoretically exists both with regard to the registration fee and with regard to the administration fee. The consultation obligation nevertheless is only foreseen for the determination of the arbitrators' fees, because they form by far the largest component of the procedural costs and, unlike the registration and administration fees, directly affect the position of the arbitrators. Also, the Schedule of Arbitrators' Fees has many more brackets than the Schedules relating to the registration fee and the administration fee, so that, in the context of the arbitrators' fees, the incorrect assessment of the amount of the (counter)claim would be more likely to have an impact upon the resulting fees. In the end, of course, the decision is still up to the Center.

Note 4 provides that amounts of (counter)claims expressed in currencies other than United States dollars shall, for the purpose of calculating the arbitrators' fees, be converted to United States dollar amounts on the basis of the official United Nations exchange rate prevailing on the date of submission of the (counter)claim.

This provision is similar to those relating to conversion for the purpose of determining the registration and administration fees; and, *mutatis mutandis,* the observations made with regard thereto apply.

Note 5 provides that the amounts and percentage figures specified in the Schedule of Fees for a three-person Tribunal represent the total fees payable to such a Tribunal, and not the fees payable to each arbitrator. The Note further provides that such fees shall be distributed among the three persons in accordance with the unanimous decision of those three persons, and that, in the absence of such a decision, the distribution shall be 40 percent for the presiding arbitrator, and 30 percent for each of the other two arbitrators.

The first part of the Note records what is also implied by the relationship in the Fee Schedule between the fees payable to a sole arbitrator and those payable to a three-person Tribunal, which are two and a half times as high. For the Center to follow the decision of the Tribunal, there are no conditions other than that the decision be unanimous. The chances for the Tribunal to reach a unanimous decision may be best at the outset of the arbitration, when the arbitrators discuss the schedule of the case and their respective workloads, but a more informed decision may also be taken at a later stage.

In the event that the arbitrators do not reach unanimous agreement, the Note provides a distribution key. There will be little risk that such a fixed determination may induce an arbitrator who has contributed little to the proceedings to block any decision that would grant him or her less than 30 percent. Moreover, any such possibility is outweighed by the importance, both for the Center and for the arbitrators, of having an objective standard guaranteeing predictable and consistent determinations. In fact, the absence of such a key would undermine the benefits of having a Schedule of Fees.

It is difficult to fix percentage shares that will do justice to the particulars of each and every case. In some cases, a Chairman who is unable to claim reimbursement of the costs of engaging the services of a research or drafting assistant may feel entitled to more than 40 percent. On the other hand, all members of the Tribunal are expected to invest a considerable amount of time and effort, and many would consider a share of less than 30 percent unacceptable. Thus, the distribution key contained in this Note must be seen as a generally reasonable standard. Moreover, timely discussions with and among the arbitrators will usually prevent any serious issues from arising.

Note 6 provides that where, by the agreement of the parties, a number of arbitrators other than one or three is appointed to a Tribunal, the scale of minimum and maximum fees for the Tribunal shall be determined by the Center. The Note further provides that this scale shall be so determined by multiplying the scale for a sole arbitrator by the number of arbitrators reduced by a factor that takes account of the sharing of work and responsibility among the arbitrators.

The appointment of a number of arbitrators other than one or three is a relatively rare occurrence, and the practical application of this Note will therefore be limited. This is all the more so because Article 18 provides for the joint appointment of an arbitrator in case of multiple Claimants or Respondents.

Where the Note mentions the scale of fees, this implies a reference not only to the percentages, but also to the absolute base amounts contained in the Schedule of Fees.

As is the case, implicitly, with the fee determination for a three-person Tribunal, the starting point for the calculation is the scale for a sole arbitrator. Given the even greater sharing of work and responsibility for Tribunals of more than three arbitrators, the relative ratio for such Tribunals will likely be different than the multiplier applying to a three-person Tribunal. On the other hand, the Tribunal's determination will need to reflect the fact that, however the duties may be shared, each arbitrator, by virtue of his or her position as a Tribunal member, has an individual responsibility. Also, it is not inconceivable that, if the appointment as arbitrator would become significantly less interesting from a financial point of view, the proceedings themselves at some point might begin to suffer as a result.

C. *Deposits*

Article 70

(a) Upon receipt of notification from the Center of the establishment of the Tribunal, the Claimant and the Respondent shall each deposit an equal amount as an advance for the costs of arbitration referred to in Article 71. The amount of the deposit shall be determined by the Center.

(b) In the course of the arbitration, the Center may require that the parties make supplementary deposits.

(c) If the required deposits are not paid in full within 30 days after receipt of the corresponding notification, the Center shall so inform the parties in order that one or other of them may make the required payment.

(d) Where the amount of the counter-claim greatly exceeds the amount of the claim or involves the examination of significantly different matters, or where it otherwise appears appropriate in the circumstances, the Center in its discretion may establish two separate deposits on account of claim and counter-claim. If separate deposits are established, the totality of the deposit on account of claim shall be paid by the Claimant and the totality of the deposit on account of counter-claim shall be paid by Respondent.

(e)   **If a party fails, within 15 days after a second reminder in writing from the Center, to pay the required deposit, it shall be deemed to have withdrawn the relevant claim or counter-claim.**

(f)   **After the award has been made, the Center shall, in accordance with the award, render an accounting to the parties of the deposits received and return any unexpended balance to the parties or require the payment of any amount owing from the parties.**

Article 70(a) provides that, upon receipt of notification from the Center of the establishment of the Tribunal, the Claimant and the Respondent shall each deposit an equal amount as an advance for the costs of arbitration referred to in Article 71, the amount of such deposit to be determined by the Center.

Article 71(a) clarifies that the costs of arbitration consist of the fees of the arbitrators, their properly incurred expenses, the cost of expert and other assistance required by the Tribunal, and other necessary expenses such as the cost of hearing facilities. Thus, as further confirmed by the wording of Article 71(c), the Center's fees are not included in the costs of arbitration.

The purpose of requiring an advance payment of such costs is twofold. First, the deposit functions as security for the parties' liability for the costs incurred in the proceedings. Second, such a deposit allows certain payments and reimbursements to be made already in the course of the proceedings, such as the payment of an advance installment (which possibility is implied by Article 69(a)) of the arbitrators' fees. Furthermore, although more an effect than a purpose of the provision, the prompt and full payment of a deposit, more than the payment of the registration and administration fees, serves to indicate the serious intentions of the parties.

The deposit becomes payable upon notification of the establishment of the Tribunal. As implied by Article 23, this refers to the moment when all the arbitrators have accepted appointment. The registration and administration fees become payable at an earlier stage; they are usually not difficult to determine, and they serve to involve the Center and to fund its expenses, a significant portion of which will be incurred before the establishment of the Tribunal. The timing set out in Article 70(a) reflects that, by contrast, most of the costs of arbitration are incurred, and can only be assessed, after the Tribunal has been established. In particular, the Center needs to consult the members of the Tribunal, whose fees account for a large part of the costs of arbitration for which the deposit is made.

The Center's obligation to notify the parties of the establishment of the Tribunal follows from Article 23(c). The provision of Article 70(a) implies that, together with such notification, the Center inform the parties of the deposit to be made. In practice, however, nothing prevents the Center, which may for example require more time to consult the Tribunal, from notifying the parties of the establishment of the Tribunal first and then determining and notifying the deposit.

In determining the amount of the deposit, the Center will attempt to make a first estimate of the costs of arbitration as itemized in Article 71(a). As part of this estimate, the Center will assess the likelihood and cost level of expert and other advice. The Center's assessment of the arbitrators' fees will take account of the criteria set out in Article 69(b).

The Claimant and the Respondent shall deposit an equal amount, because, by entering into the arbitration agreement, each has committed itself to the arbitral process and should participate in financing that process until the Tribunal has issued its award, including a decision on costs.[9] This arrangement also reflects the absence of a presumption as to the outcome of the case. Unless otherwise determined in accordance with Article 70(d), the deposit to be made by each party need not bear a relationship to the amount of the claim and the counterclaim, nor to whether or not a counterclaim has been filed.

The Center has indicated that it will consider the possibility of deposits being paid in installments in appropriate circumstances.[10]

Article 70(b) provides that in the course of the arbitration, the Center may require that the parties make supplementary deposits.

This Article provides some flexibility to let the amount of the deposit generally keep track of the actual costs of the proceedings. Such flexibility may help to limit the parties' initial exposure, and it enables adjustments to be made where the cost assessment made at the outset of the arbitration is rendered inaccurate by events in the course of the arbitration. Examples of such events are the filing of a counterclaim; the increase or amendment of a claim; the Tribunal's decision to engage external assistance on certain issues; the need to hold additional meetings or hearings; or the replacement of a Tribunal member.

In view of such factors, an increase of the deposit in the course of the arbitration is neither uncommon nor unreasonable. Nevertheless, a conservative cost estimate at the outset of the procedure may help prevent, or at least delay, later deposit increases. On the other hand, parties will not want the Center to exaggerate in erring on the side of caution.

The Article allows for supplementary deposits. It does not provide for a possible downward adjustment (*i.e.*, a refund in the course of the proceedings) of the deposit, for example in case part of the claim, or the counterclaim, is withdrawn, or if the initially anticipated need for expert assistance does not materialize. The absence of such a provision reflects the primary function of the deposit, which is to provide sufficient security for the costs of arbitration, rather than to constitute an exact approximation thereof at every stage of the proceedings. The deposit constitutes an advance for the eventual costs, making it unlikely that events will occur that actually justify a decrease of the deposit (such events are if anything more likely to delay or to prevent the need for a supplementary deposit).

---

[9] *Id.* at 98.
[10] *Id.* at 99.

Article 70(c) provides that if the required deposits are not paid in full within 30 days after receipt of the corresponding notification, the Center shall so inform the parties in order that one or other of them may make the required payment.

Considering the fact that the deposits only become payable after the Tribunal has been constituted, the possibility exists that, by the time the 30-day period has lapsed without full payment of the deposits, the arbitrators will have commenced work and incurred expenses on the case. In practice, the Center and the Tribunal may ensure that the arbitration does not get seriously underway until the deposits have been received. Against this background, Article 70(c) aims to prevent a party from sabotaging the proceedings by withholding payment of its deposit share.

Although this provision refers to payment rather than receipt thereof, a practical interpretation dictates that the Center will await the actual receipt of the deposits. Of course, the Center in its discretion may decide to act on transfer confirmation by the paying bank.

The paragraph makes clear that partial payment will not suffice. This applies in two senses: except where payment in installments has been agreed, it will not do for a party to pay less than the full amount of its deposit; nor is it sufficient if one party pays its full deposit but the other party does not pay its deposit, or fails to pay in full.

It follows from this provision that if one party has paid, but the other has not, the Center will not only notify the party in default, but also the party who has paid. Based on the Article's provision that the outstanding payment may be made by one or other of the parties, the paying party may thus decide whether it will advance the deposit actually due by the other party. This may be in the interest of the Claimant, or, in rare instances, even in the interest of a Respondent who has filed a counterclaim or is otherwise determined to see the case through. If a party advances the share of the other party, it will be reimbursed in the event that this debtor later pays its deposit.

If supplementary deposits are to be made in the course of the arbitration, a party who has advanced all or part of the other party's earlier deposit is not credited for this extra payment; it must still pay its own full share of the supplementary deposit. On the other hand, if the other party wins the case, the advance made by the first party may be deducted from the amount awarded against that party; likewise, if the advancing party wins an award against the defaulting party, the cost award may take the advance into account.

Article 70(d) provides that, where the amount of the counterclaim greatly exceeds the amount of the claim or involves the examination of significantly different matters, or where it otherwise appears appropriate in the circumstances, the Center in its discretion may establish two separate deposits on account of claim and counterclaim. This provision further provides that if separate deposits are established, the totality of the deposit on account of claim shall be paid by the Claimant and the totality of the deposit on account of counterclaim shall be paid by the Respondent.

In order to discourage the introduction of artificial or inflated counterclaims, Article 70(d) entitles the Center to establish separate accounts in the event of a significant imbalance in terms of amount and subject matter between the claim and the much larger or very different counterclaim. More generally, this provision provides the discretion to establish separate accounts whenever the Center considers this appropriate under the circumstances; some might argue that this should include the event of a much larger but seemingly undocumented claim.

The terminology suggests that the imbalance must be obvious; the counterclaim may be disproportionate in amount, or may raise issues or facts unrelated to the substance of the claim. This requirement of a clear distinction facilitates the Center's task of determining when the provision applies. Moreover, one of the parties may alert the Center to the perceived existence of an imbalance in the sense of the Article.

The establishment of separate deposits implies that the determination of the deposits, and thus the security provided by the parties, reflects the particulars of the counterclaim as compared to the claim. Thus, Article 70(d) allows the Center to vary the basic principle of deposit equality laid down in Article 70(a). This is further confirmed by the requirement that the Claimant pay the full claim deposit, and the Respondent pay the full counterclaim deposit.

The latter requirement does not exclude the possibility, implied by Article 70(c), that a party pay the other party's deposit; this option may apply also where separate deposits have been established.

Article 70(e) provides that if a party fails to pay the required deposit within 15 days after a second reminder in writing from the Center, it shall be deemed to have withdrawn the relevant claim or counterclaim.

Article 70(e), which follows up on the provision of Article 70(c), logically applies to all forms of deposit regulated in Article 70: the equal deposits, any supplementary deposits, and separate deposits. It mirrors the provision of Article 68(e) relating to the payment of the administration fee, and, *mutatis mutandis*, most of the observations made with regard to that provision apply: the consequences of the deemed withdrawal, the number and timing of the Center's reminders, and the meaning of payment.

Interpretation in light of Article 70(c) suggests that the Center will send each reminder (at least in copy) to both parties, and that each party may, in reaction to any of these reminders, rectify the other party's failure to pay.

Article 70(f) provides that after the award has been made, the Center shall, in accordance with the award, render an accounting to the parties of the deposits received and return any unexpended balance to the parties or require the payment of any amount owing from the parties.

In providing for an accounting, the return of any unexpended balance, and the payment of owing amounts, Article 70(f) implies that the Center shall debit the costs of arbitration from the deposits made pursuant to Article 70. Article 71(b) expressly confirms this.

The statement in this provision that the Center shall act "in accordance with the award" indicates that the accounting, return and additional payment are to be based on the amount of the arbitration costs which the Tribunal, pursuant to Article 71(a), has fixed in the award.

Article 70(f) leaves open the question whether the accounting, return and additional payment are, additionally, to take account of the Tribunal's apportionment of such costs pursuant to Article 71(c). The purpose of the deposits and final payments is primarily to cover the costs of arbitration, rather than to settle the costs score between the parties. Thus, if any amount is owing to cover the costs of arbitration, the Center could request both parties to make up for the balance, regardless of any apportionment; Article 71(b), which deals with the debiting from the deposits, actually precedes the provision dealing with apportionment, Article 71(c). (The principle of Article 70(c) could thereby apply: a victorious (counter)claimant may make the other party's final payment.) Given the fact that the costs of arbitration have already been covered, it is less likely that the return of an unexpended balance would not take account of the apportionment decision.

The Center will endeavor to determine the initial, and, if necessary, supplementary deposits in such a way as to cover the full costs of arbitration and to limit the incidence of outstanding cost exposure after the award has been made. However, where the deposits are insufficient, the Center as administering authority should normally be able to procure payment of any final amounts owing. Article 62(f) provides that the Tribunal shall communicate its award to the Center, and it is the Center that, pursuant to the same provision, formally communicates the original award to each party. The Article does not specify any time frame for this communication, which would allow the Center, where appropriate, to withhold the award pending receipt of final payment.

An important element of the WIPO deposit scheme, not contained in the Rules but recorded in other publications of the Center, is that the Center will credit parties for any interest accruing on their deposits. While such a policy may seem obvious, it is not, in fact, followed by every administering authority.

D. *Award of Costs of Arbitration*

Article 71
(a) **In its award, the Tribunal shall fix the costs of arbitration, which shall consist of:**
    (i)   **the arbitrators' fees,**
    (ii)   **the properly incurred travel, communication and other expenses of the arbitrators,**
    (iii)   **the costs of expert advice and such other assistance required by the Tribunal pursuant to these Rules, and**
    (iv)   **such other expenses as are necessary for the conduct of the arbitration proceedings, such as the cost of meeting and hearing facilities.**
(b) **The aforementioned costs shall, as far as possible, be debited from the deposits required under Article 70.**

(c) The Tribunal shall, subject to any agreement of the parties, apportion the costs of arbitration and the registration and administration fees of the Center between the parties in the light of all the circumstances and the outcome of the arbitration.

Article 71(a) provides that, in its award, the Tribunal shall fix the costs of arbitration, which shall consist of: (i) the arbitrators' fees, (ii) the properly incurred travel, communication and other expenses of the arbitrators, (iii) the costs of expert advice and such other assistance required by the Tribunal pursuant to the Rules; and (iv) such other expenses as are necessary for the conduct of the arbitration proceedings, such as the cost of meeting and hearing facilities.

Article 71(a) does not grant the Tribunal authority to determine the costs of arbitration, but primarily concerns the Tribunal's recording thereof in the award, which serves to finalize these costs. In implementing this provision, the Tribunal acts in consultation with the Center. The Tribunal's duty to fix the costs in the award is limited to the costs of arbitration; the fees of the Center are of a different nature, having been established by the Center and having been paid at an earlier stage.

As to the individual components of the arbitration costs listed in this provision, as noted, the arbitrators' fees are set by the Center on the basis of the Schedule of Fees and in consultation with the arbitrators and the parties, and the amounts so determined are recorded in the award. In exceptional cases, if the Center's initial determination pursuant to Article 69(a) reasonably requires reconsideration in light of the development of the case, the Center may (always in consultation with the arbitrators and the parties and, unless these have agreed otherwise, on the basis of the Schedule of Fees) adapt such fees for purposes of the award.

As previously observed, the fees of the arbitrators do not include their out-of-pocket expenses. Article 71(a) refers to the most common of these expenses: travel (understood in a broad sense to include, for example, accommodation costs) and communication expenses (such as telephone and telefax charges, nowadays reduced considerably as a result of the advent of e-mail). Article 71(a) poses the important condition that, for such expenses to be reimbursable, they must have been properly incurred. This allows the Center to scrutinize claimed expenses, not only for their actual incidence, but also for their reasonableness under the circumstances, and to reduce or disallow certain items that do not pass this test.

The second cost component of Article 71(a), the costs of expert advice, will usually be determined by the Tribunal when it engages such assistance. The Tribunal's determination normally takes account of the observations of the parties and may form part of the terms of reference of the expert established pursuant to Article 55.

The provision also allows for costs of assistance other than expert advice, but this is not an open-ended formula: to be covered, such assistance must have been required by the Tribunal pursuant to the Rules. Thus, unless otherwise agreed by the parties, the costs of secretarial and drafting assistance engaged by the Tribunal in principle does not fall under the costs permitted by Article 71.

Reflecting the fact that each case may involve different types of expenses particular to the circumstances of the case, the listing of Article 71 is not exhaustive. The main limitation expressed in this connection is that the expenses must be necessary for the conduct of the arbitration proceedings. While this condition unavoidably entails a measure of subjectivity, it implies a stricter test than would such terms as ''appropriate'' or ''conducive'' to the arbitration.

By way of example of other necessary expenses, the Article mentions the cost of meeting and hearing facilities. As noted, for arbitrations under the WIPO Rules that are held at WIPO in Geneva, the Center provides, without extra charge, suitably equipped facilities (a hearing room, a retiring room for the Tribunal, and a room for each party). Additional services, such as interpretation and secretarial assistance, are payable at cost.

Article 71(b) provides that the costs mentioned in Article 71(a) shall, as far as possible, be debited from the deposits required under Article 70.

Reference is made to the comments made concerning Article 70(f) with regard to the debiting of the arbitration costs from the deposits required under Article 70. The reference to the costs mentioned in Article 71(a) is not merely to the cost categories enumerated therein, but to the actual costs of arbitration as fixed by the Tribunal in the award. The provision that such debits shall be made to the extent possible refers to the situation where the costs of arbitration exceed the amounts on deposit.

Article 71(c) provides that the Tribunal shall, subject to any agreement of the parties, apportion the costs of arbitration and the registration and administration fees of the Center between the parties in the light of all the circumstances and the outcome of the arbitration.

This simply worded provision records the Tribunal's important mandate to apportion the costs of arbitration and the fees of the Center between the parties. Thus, while the registration fee is paid by the Claimant, the administration fee is paid by each party in accordance with its (counter)claim, and the starting point of the deposits is that both parties make equal payment, this provision allows the actual final costs to be allocated between the parties. The term apportionment does not exclude any options: both parties may have to bear complementing shares; or a single party may have to pay the entire costs.

The title of Article 71(c) refers to the costs of arbitration, because it is mainly these that the provision regulates. Article 71(c) additionally encompasses the fees of the Center, which, although normally much lower, form part of a party's costs like the costs of arbitration. In its listing of the cost components that may be apportioned, this provision may be read in conjunction with Article 72.

In recognition of the specific nature of every case, the provision refers to allocation in the light of all the circumstances, leaving the allocation decision to the discretion of the Tribunal. Importantly, the only form of more specific guidance concerns the outcome of the arbitration, which Article 71(c) singles out as a factor to be taken into account by the Tribunal. If the Tribunal follows the ground rule that costs follow the event, the apportionment will be more or less proportionate to the outcome of the case.[11]

Article 71(c) clarifies that the Tribunal's apportionment shall respect any cost division that may have been agreed between the parties. In practice, where such prior agreement exists, it may record that the parties shall bear the fees and costs in equal parts, or that the party who substantially prevails will be reimbursed by the other party.

E. *Award of Costs Incurred by a Party*

Article 72
In its award, the Tribunal may, subject to any contrary agreement by the parties and in the light of all the circumstances and the outcome of the arbitration, order a party to pay the whole or part of reasonable expenses incurred by the other party in presenting its case, including those incurred for legal representatives and witnesses.

Article 72 provides that, in its award, the Tribunal may, subject to contrary agreement by the parties and in the light of all the circumstances and the outcome of the arbitration, order a party to pay the whole or part of reasonable expenses incurred by the other party in presenting its case, including those incurred for legal representatives and witnesses.

In extending the Tribunal's authority to apportion costs to the parties' legal expenses, this provision complements the provision of Article 71(c). These two provisions have certain points in common and differ in a number of other respects.

Article 72 recognizes that a party's costs of presenting its case may constitute the largest cost component of the arbitration. From the point of view of a prevailing party (and, depending on the fee arrangements, its lawyers), a satisfactory outcome of the case will include the possibility of recouping as much as possible such legal expenses.

Where Article 71(c) provides that the Tribunal shall apportion the costs mentioned therein, Article 72 states that the Tribunal "may" apportion the legal expenses. Furthermore, where Article 71(c) does not mention the possibility of allocating less than full costs, Article 72 expressly allows for the apportionment of the whole or part of legal expenses. These differences reflect the fact that reimbursement of direct procedural costs such as the costs of arbitration is awarded more frequently, and in larger proportions, than reimbursement of legal fees, a tendency shared by court decisions in many jurisdictions.

The discretion to award less than the full legal expenses is also reflected in the Article's condition that such expenses be reasonable. This condition allows the Tribunal, in fixing and apportioning legal expenses, to disallow claims to the extent

---

[11] Other factors generally cited to merit consideration in the allocation decision include the conduct of the parties in the arbitration, in particular any occurrence of undue delay in the presentation of a party's case, and the question whether the arbitration concerns issues on which reasonable persons could in good faith disagree. *Id.* at 101.

that these are perceived to be based on overcharging or on fee arrangements otherwise inappropriate to the particulars of the arbitration.

While Article 72 clarifies that the costs of presenting a case include those of legal representatives and witnesses, it does not purport to provide an exhaustive list of allowable cost categories. In this respect as well, Article 72 does not tie the hands of the Tribunal, which may, for example, consider whether to award costs of in-house representation or expertise.

Article 72 subjects the Tribunal's determination to contrary agreement between the parties. Similar to the reference in Article 71(c), this means that the parties may agree on a particular apportionment formula.

Finally, in connection with Article 72, it may be noted that Article 46(b), which "Ken-Ren"[12] provision forms part of the chapter regulating the Conduct of the Arbitration, allows the Tribunal, if it considers it to be required by exceptional circumstances and at the request of a party, to order a party to provide security for the other party's expenses in presenting its case.

---

[12] *See* Coppée-Lavalin SA/NV v. Ken-Ren Chemicals and Fertilizers Ltd.; Voest-Alpine v. Ken-Ren Chemicals and Fertilizers Ltd., H.L., [1994] 2 All E.R. 449.

CONFIDENTIALITY

Articles 73 to 76

*Hans Smit**

I. GENERAL OBSERVATIONS

A. *The Confidentiality of Arbitration Generally*

1. *Legal basis.*   Confidentiality has long been touted as one of the advantages of arbitration. However, until recently, institutional rules generally did not provide for confidentiality. The ICC Rules were the exception. They provided, and in Article 6 of Appendix I and Article 1 of Appendix II, continue to provide, for confidentiality, but only for the proceedings before the Court itself, not for the proceedings before the arbitral tribunals. This situation changed as the result of amendments to the ICC Rules and those of the London Court of International Arbitration that entered into effect on January 1, 1998. The LCIA Rules provide in Article 30 for the confidentiality of arbitral proceedings. The ICC Rules provide for more differentiated treatment: Article 21 (3) provides that "persons not involved in the proceedings" shall not be admitted to the hearings except with the approval of the tribunal and the parties; and Article 20 (7) authorizes the Tribunal to take the appropriate measures to protect trade secrets and confidential information.

Although there is a widely-held view that arbitration is confidential, in the absence of a specific provision in the arbitration agreement or the institutional rules, the legal basis for a requirement of confidentiality is unclear. Indeed, until relatively recently, the subject of confidentiality in arbitration did not engage the sustained interest of either the courts or the scholars. A change came with a case decided in Australia by the High Court of Justice, *Esso v. Plowman.*[1] In this case, one of the parties refused to participate in a projected arbitration unless it was assured that the proceedings before the arbitral tribunal would be confidential. The dispute involved the delivery of minerals to a utility, and its outcome could affect the price charged to the utility's customers. The plaintiff in the court proceedings sought a declaration that the arbitral proceedings would be confidential. The Ministry of Energy opposed the application. Experts in arbitration from all around the world submitted opinions for both sides. The Court ruled that the information sought by the Minister of Energy could not be withheld on the basis of confidentiality. An entire issue of *Arbitration International*[2] collecting both the judicial rulings and the experts' opinions, was devoted to the

---

* Stanley H. Fuld Professor of Law and Director, Center for International Arbitration and Litigation Law, Columbia University.

[1] Esso Australia Resources Ltd. v. Plowman, [1995] 128 A.L.R. 391.

[2] 11(3) ARB. INT'L (1995).

subject. All experts who submitted opinions to the Australian court agreed that arbitration was, to some extent, confidential, but there was a great measure of disagreement about its legal basis. Confidentiality was argued by some to be inherent in the institution of arbitration; others discerned an implied condition of confidentiality premised on usage and trade custom; while still others opined that there was no obligation of confidentiality.

2. *Reach.* There also appears to be a lack of unanimity as to the scope of the requirement of confidentiality that may exist. In the Australian case, the Court ruled that confidentiality could not stand in the way of a requirement of disclosure imposed by a governmental agency in the exercise of its legitimate functions, but leading experts had opined differently. It would appear that, even assuming there is a rule of confidentiality, it may be limited in a number of respects. The limitations may be imposed by law, such as the law requiring a person to testify in legal proceedings or to provide disclosure in statutorily defined cases. Disclosure may also be argued to be permissible when required by fiduciary obligations owed to shareholders or for the protection of one's rights or interests.

3. *Persons affected.* Distinctions may also be made, depending on the person who is alleged to be bound by an obligation to maintain confidentiality. The different persons involved in arbitration may be held to different obligations, depending on their role in the arbitral process. Clearly, a party or one of its employees may be in a position different from that of the administering institution, an arbitrator, an expert, or a witness.

4. *Temporal aspect.* The requirement of confidentiality may also vary with the time at which disclosure is sought. For example, it may operate differently depending on whether disclosure is sought during the arbitration or thereafter. The increasing frequency of the publication of arbitration awards bears testimony to this.

5. *The nature of the disclosure.* Finally, the requirement of confidentiality may vary with the nature of the disclosure sought. For example, it may be that it does not violate a rule of confidentiality to disclose the existence of an arbitration, while it may violate the rule to disclose particulars about the proceedings. This is recognized by the WIPO Rules which, in Articles 73, 74 and 75 deal separately with disclosure of the existence of an arbitration, disclosure of particulars of the proceedings, and disclosure of the award.

6. *The need for an institutional rule.* Clearly, therefore, a great many different factors may bear on determining whether confidentiality is required in a particular situation, and it may be difficult to address in a written rule the many different circumstances that may occur. It might therefore be deemed preferable to let the courts and the arbitrators deal with the problems as they occur. And the parties could be left to work out confidentiality agreements in particular cases as the need for confidentiality might present itself in those cases in which they might not wish to leave resolution of questions of confidentiality to the courts or arbitrators. However, that solution could not satisfactorily provide for confidentiality at the beginning of the arbitration, before

the Tribunal can act when the parties do not agree on confidentiality. Quite significantly, until recently, the major institutions had refrained from introducing written rules on the subject.[3] The analysis of the WIPO Rules that follows may provide a clearer answer as to the desirability of formulating written rules and their adequacy in dealing with issues of confidentiality in differing contexts.

B. *The Approach of the WIPO Rules*

1. The WIPO rules seek to deal with the subject of confidentiality in comprehensive fashion. They do so by dealing separately with disclosure of the existence of arbitration (Article 73), disclosures made during the arbitration (Article 74), confidentiality of the award (Article 75), and confidentiality to be observed by the arbitrator and the Center (Article 76). They also specify on whom the obligation to maintain confidentiality is imposed — namely, the parties (Articles 73–75), witnesses (Article 74(b)), and the arbitrator and the Center (Article 76). Furthermore, they deal with the scope of the obligation in all the articles in Chapter VII and focus on the time at which disclosure is made. Finally, they deal separately, in Article 52, with the protection of trade secrets. Clearly, they represent an ambitious attempt to deal with the subject in adequate detail. As already indicated, in this respect the WIPO Rules are truly unique.

C. *The Desirable Reach of Confidentiality Rules*

1. The detailed treatment in the WIPO Rules of the confidentiality of the various aspects of arbitration raises two questions: First, to what extent is confidentiality in arbitration appropriate; and second, to what extent is it assured in the absence of contractual provisions or institutional rules. Of course, the answer to the first question will influence that to the second.

2. Before seeking to answer these questions, it should be determined what the concept of confidentiality seeks to cover. As a general rule, arbitration proceedings are private and not accessible to the public at large.[4] To that extent, they may be said to be confidential. But that is not the only aspect that the concept of confidentiality in arbitration is generally assumed to cover. In its most comprehensive form, it treats all aspects of the arbitral process as protected from disclosure. It is clear, however, that such an extreme notion of confidentiality in arbitration is not acceptable. A more modulated concept must be found that properly accommodates the public need for transparency of proceedings that may affect others than the persons that participate in the arbitration and the interests of the participants to preserve the privacy of, or to disclose, their proceedings. When that balancing is performed, it becomes readily

---

[3] As already indicated, the LCIA Rules now provide, in Article 30, for the confidentiality of arbitral proceedings, while Article 21(3) of the ICC Rules deals only with admission of outsiders to hearings.

[4] WIPO RULES, Art. 53(c), AAA RULES, Art. 21(4), ICC RULES, Art. 21(3), and LCIA RULES, Art. 19(4).

apparent that there must be significant limitations on a notion of confidentiality that shrouds the arbitral process in secrecy. Indeed, as will be discussed below, the WIPO Rules expressly recognize that there are such limitations. The crucial question is what they are and how far they should extend.

The Australian case, *Esso v. Plowman*, provides a good example of the limitations on the confidentiality of arbitration proceedings by ruling that it cannot be pleaded as an excuse for not providing information to a governmental authority that needs the information adequately to discharge its public functions. When the public interest in knowing what utilities pay for the minerals they use in generating electricity is involved, the private interest of the parties to keep their proceedings secret is of attenuated significance. Indeed, it should be stressed that the relative importance of making arbitration proceedings transparent and that of the parties to keep their proceedings secret or to disclose them may vary with the particular element of the arbitral process with respect to which disclosure is sought. Thus, for example, once an award has been rendered, the public interest in disclosing it becomes particularly pressing. After all, publication of awards serves a variety of public interests: It provides an insight into how society resolves disputes; it holds arbitrators publicly responsible for their decisions; it contributes to the development of the law by disclosing to the world at large the rules arbitrators apply to international disputes and by exposing their decisions to critical analysis; and it enables arbitrators in subsequent cases to draw guidance and inspiration from decisions others made in comparable cases. Indeed, the increasing frequency with which the ICC International Court of Arbitration publishes its awards, and the great measure of attention these awards receive from the commentators, counsel, and arbitrators in subsequent cases, bear telling testimony to the significant public interest that is served by publication of international awards. But what may be the compelling considerations in the determination of whether and to what extent arbitral awards should be confidential, do not necessarily apply when the question is whether the existence of the arbitration or particulars concerning the proceedings should be kept confidential.[5]

Another significant problem is at what stage of disclosure the applicable confidentiality requirement attaches. For example, while it may be that publication of an award with the names of the parties and other particulars that are likely to identify them may breach a requirement of confidentiality, publication of an award after deletion of the identifying particulars may not. The analysis of Articles 73–76 of the WIPO Rules that follows will focus on these considerations.

D.   *Is Chapter VII Exhaustive?*

Since Chapter VII of the WIPO Rules deals with confidentiality in great detail, it would appear that a disclosure that is not prohibited by this Chapter is permitted. For it

---

[5] *See generally,* Hans Smit, Plowman v. Esso Australia Resources Ltd: *Confidentiality in Arbitration*, 2 AM. REV. INT'L ARB. 490 (1991); Hans Smit, *Confidentiality in Arbitration*, 6 AM. REV. INT'L ARB. 61 (1995).

would make little sense to regulate confidentiality in such detail and, at the same time, leave room for the argument that confidentiality reigns in cases not covered by the Chapter.

E. *Confidentiality Agreements*

If the parties wish to obtain confidential treatment in cases not covered by Chapter VII, they can do so by entering into a special confidentiality agreement or by requesting that the arbitrators, in the exercise of their powers to regulate the procedure before the tribunal, provide for such treatment. It is quite usual for a party to make a request for such treatment in international arbitration, and international arbitral tribunals quite commonly issue orders requiring confidential treatment. An advantage of such an order or agreement is that it can deal effectively with the specifics of the confidential treatment desired. Of course, when such an agreement or order is contemplated, the parties must address the question of how such an agreement or order is to be enforced.

F. *Enforcement of Confidentiality*

Parties intent upon assuring confidentiality should consider how it is to be enforced. During the arbitration, the arbitrators may issue appropriate orders which can be judicially enforced. However, if confidentiality is prescribed by a separate agreement, the arbitrators may not have the requisite authority, unless the confidentiality agreement gives them that authority. And because an order to be issued by the arbitrators would again need judicial enforcement when disobeyed, it might be preferable to provide not for arbitral, but for judicial, enforcement in such an agreement.

A possible solution, offering the best of two worlds, would leave it to the party seeking enforcement to go to the arbitrator or the court. Whether such a unilateral arbitration clause is enforceable must be decided under the general law relating to unilateral arbitration clauses. The prevailing view appears to be that they are enforceable, but there certainly is no dearth of support for the opposite view.[6] If, in the case considered here, the unilateral clause would be regarded as invalid because of lack of mutuality or for any other reason, it would appear appropriate to leave the party with access to court only, even though in other cases the clause might be converted into a bilateral arbitration clause.

Once the final award has been rendered and the tribunal is *functus officio*, it would appear preferable in the general run of cases to leave enforcement of the confidentiality order or agreement to the courts. This will avoid the necessity of constituting a new tribunal for adjudicating confidentiality issues alone. However, it might also be argued that the original arbitration clause covers non-compliance with the confidentiality

---

[6] *See* Doctor's Associates, Inc. v. Distajo, 66 F.3d 438 (2d Cir. 1995), *cert. denied,* 116 S. Ct. 1352 (1996) and Lopez v. Plaza Fireman Co., Case No. 95-C-7567, 1996 U.S. Dist. Lexis 5566 (N.D. Ill. 1996).

order and can provide the basis for a new arbitration on that question. Of course, prevoyant parties will also define in the confidentiality agreement or order the sanctions for disobedience.

G.   *Breach of Confidentiality as a Ground for Annulment of an Award*

In a decision that has attracted attention and condemnation in equal measure, the Stockholm City Court, on September 10, 1998,[7] annulled an international arbitration award rendered in Sweden on the grounds that one of the parties had published an interlocutory award on the issue of arbitral competence, that this breached its obligation of confidentiality, and that this breach was fundamental, warranted termination of the arbitration agreement, and deprived the arbitral tribunal of jurisdiction. The Swedish Svea Court of Appeal reversed this decision.[8] It ruled that the particular disclosure complained of, if a breach, did not warrant avoidance of the arbitration clause.

The Swedish courts' decisions appear subject to well-founded criticism. First, there appears to be no authority whatsoever for the view that a breach of confidentiality may warrant avoiding the whole arbitration agreement. In the second place, the questions of whether publication of the interlocutory award constituted a breach of the arbitration agreement and whether this breach was so fundamental as to warrant avoidance of the arbitration agreement should clearly have been left for decision by the arbitrators. The arbitration clause gave the arbitrators authority to resolve all disputes arising "by reason of" the agreement and the question raised fell squarely within the tribunal jurisdiction. The complaining party had in fact raised the same pleas before the arbitral tribunal, which had rejected them. The Swedish courts should have accepted the arbitral ruling rather than review it *de novo*. Second, the Swedish courts applied Swedish law in resolving these questions, although the parties had selected Austrian law, including the New York Convention, as the applicable law. Third, the Stockholm City Court endorsed a concept of confidentiality of unparalleled and unqualified reach by ruling that confidentiality covers all aspects of the arbitral process and that any breach was a fundamental one. In the process, it rejected the argument that the applicable ECE Rules provided only for confidentiality of the hearings and paid no attention to the prevailing view that, of all of the elements of the arbitral process, awards have the least respectable claim to confidentiality.

The proper approach appears to be that no breach of any confidentiality requirement can ever be regarded as being so fundamental as to warrant avoidance of the arbitration agreement. Until this position is firmly established, drafters of an arbitration agreement would do well to consider specifying that no breach of any requirement of confidentiality will warrant avoidance of the arbitration agreement.

---

[7] Bulgarian Foreign Trade Bank Ltd. v. A.I. Trade Finance Inc. (Stockholm City Ct. 1998), *reproduced in* 13(11) INT'L ARB. REP. at A-1 (1998).

[8] A.I. Trade Finance Inc. v. Bulgarian Foreign Trade Bank (Svea App. 1999), *reproduced in* 14(4) INT'L ARB. REP. at A-1 (1999).

II. ARTICLE 73: CONFIDENTIALITY OF THE EXISTENCE OF THE ARBITRATION

Article 73

(a) **Except to the extent necessary in connection with a court challenge to the arbitration or an action for enforcement of an award, no information concerning the existence of an arbitration may be unilaterally disclosed by a party to any third party unless it is required to do so by law or by a competent regulatory body, and then only**

> **(i)** **by disclosing no more than what is legally required, and**
>
> **(ii)** **by furnishing to the Tribunal and to the other party, if the disclosure takes place during the arbitration, or to the other party alone, if the disclosure takes place after the termination of the arbitration, details of the disclosure and an explanation of the reason for it.**

(b) **Notwithstanding paragraph (a), a party may disclose to a third party the names of the parties to the arbitration and the relief requested for the purpose of satisfying any obligation of good faith or candor owed to that third party.**

73.01. *Summary of Contents of Article 73*

Article 73(a) imposes on the parties an obligation not to disclose "information concerning the existence of an arbitration" to "any third party," except in two cases. The first is that this information may be disclosed "to the extent necessary in connection with a court challenge to the arbitration or an action for enforcement of an award;" and the second is that the disclosure may be made if required "by law or by a competent regulatory body." Subparagraphs (i) and (ii) of Article 73(a) further define the particulars that may be disclosed and the notice to be given to the other parties to the arbitration. Paragraph (b) provides for an exception to all of paragraph (a). It permits a party to disclose to a third party the names of the parties and the relief requested in order to satisfy "any obligation of good faith or candor owed to that third party."

Read in its entirety, Article 73 therefore prohibits a party to disclose to a third party "information concerning the existence of an arbitration," subject to three exceptions: first, a party may disclose this information to the extent necessary to challenge the arbitration in court or in an action for enforcement of the award; second, a party may disclose this information in discharging an "obligation of good faith or candor;" and third, the further specifications contained in subparagraphs (i) and (ii) apply.

73.02. *The Substantive Reach of Article 73*

Article 73 prohibits the disclosure of "information concerning the existence of an arbitration." The fair import of this prohibition would appear to be that any information that would indicate the existence of the arbitration is precluded. Normally, the disclosure of the existence of an arbitration involves the identification of the subject matter of the dispute and the circumstance that it is being arbitrated. But it may be questioned whether Article 73 forbids the disclosure of so limited a measure of information. After all, the mere disclosure that a particular type of dispute is being arbitrated would not normally have any potentially unfavorable effect, as long as the parties to the dispute are not identified. Of course, Article 73 is addressed to a party and a party that discloses the existence of an arbitration may thereby indicate that it is a party to the arbitration and thus provide an identifying particular. However, that inference is not necessarily warranted, because others may also have learned of the circumstance that a particular dispute is being arbitrated. In most cases, it may not make a difference how far the prohibition reaches, because a party that makes the disclosure may frequently benefit from one of the exceptions for which Article 73 provides. But when this is not the case, the problem remains. Since the private interest in maintaining confidentiality to such an extreme extent would generally appear attenuated and there is a significant public interest in disseminating knowledge about the resolution of disputes, a case can be made for permitting disclosure of arbitrations that stops short of providing identifying particulars.

73.03. The Personal Reach of Article 73

The prohibition of Article 73 is addressed only to a party to the arbitration and forbids only unilateral disclosure. Accordingly, a disclosure by all parties appears permitted. But what if more than one, but less than all parties, make the disclosure? In that case, the disclosure is not unilateral and may be regarded as permitted, especially when the disclosure is made by parties that are opponents in the arbitration.

Although Article 73 speaks only of disclosure by "a party," the term should reasonably include the representatives of a party, including its counsel, employees and other agents in the proceedings. The same is not true of a witness or expert. Article 74(b) deals specifically with the obligation of confidentiality of a witness and limits its reach to disclosure regulated by Article 74. Disclosure regulated by Article 73 is therefore not affected by the extension of the reach of Article 74 to witnesses. It might be argued that the second sentence of Article 74(b), which makes a party responsible for the maintenance of confidentiality to the same degree as that required by a party with respect to "other information obtained in the arbitration," also imposes on a witness a requirement of confidentiality in regard to the existence of the arbitration. However, the information concerned is only that information to which the witness is given access "in order to prepare the witness's testimony." This phrase appears to denote information that bears on the witness's testimony and not information of the mere existence of the arbitration. In fact, if the drafters intended to impose an obligation of confidentiality on a witness, they could easily have done so more directly by insertion in Article 73 of a provision similar to Article 74(b).

On the other hand, if a witness were permitted to disclose the existence of the arbitration, a party who wished to disclose it could easily avoid application of Article 73 by encouraging a friendly witness to disclose the existence of the arbitration.

To close this loophole, Article 73 should be read to somehow identify a witness of a party with the party itself and thus to preclude a witness from disclosing the existence of the arbitration.

Of course, the witness can be bound to secrecy by an appropriate confidentiality agreement. A party seeking this type of confidentiality would therefore act prudently by seeking such an agreement.

The obligation of confidentiality imposed on the Center and the arbitrator by Article 76 is more broadly formulated. It appears to cover also the existence of the arbitration. *See* Section 76.02 *infra*.

73.04. The Definition of "Any Third Party"

Article 73 applies only to disclosures made to "any third party." Article 73 does not contain a provision similar to the first sentence of Article 74(b), which provides that "for the purposes of this Article, a witness called by a party shall not be considered a party." It would therefore seem that a witness is a third party for the purpose of applying Article 73 and that the existence of an arbitration may not be disclosed to a witness. But this would appear to make little sense, since it will normally not be possible to attract and prepare a witness without disclosing that the witness's testimony is sought for an existing arbitration. And since Article 74(b) is based on the premise that a party may prepare a witness for his or her testimony, it is necessarily based on the assumption that a witness may be told by a party about the existence of the arbitration.

Also necessarily implied in the provisions of Chapter VII is the assumption that the arbitrators, secretaries of the tribunal, transcribers of the proceedings, translators and staff members of the Center are not to be regarded as "third parties." Indeed, it might have been preferable if the rules had defined a "third party" as someone not involved in the arbitration in any capacity and had imposed on the appropriate party, the tribunal, or the Center an obligation to ensure the confidentiality that was deemed appropriate.

73.05. The First Exception

The confidentiality requirement imposed by Article 73 does not attach when and "to the extent necessary in connection with a court challenge to the arbitration or an action for enforcement of an award." This provision is based on the commonsensical notion that a party cannot be prevented from addressing a court with an action or application relating to the arbitration. However, the circumstances identified by Article 73(a) are unduly limited. A court may be addressed in connection with an arbitration in circumstances other than those specified in Article 73(a).

For example, a party may address a court for assistance in the arbitration by way of interim relief. Article 46(d) makes explicit provision for such an application. The tribunal or a party may also seek the assistance of a court to compel the testimony or production of evidence by a party or non-party. Some arbitration laws specifically provide for such assistance. In all of these circumstances, the prohibition embodied in Article 73(a) should not apply. This result may be achieved by a teleological interpretation of Article 73 and by regarding the two situations specifically identified as merely illustrative of the more general principle that any application to a court may disclose the existence of the arbitration to that court as long as such disclosure is relevant to the action brought or application submitted. The more relaxed standard of "reliance" rather than that of "necessity" stated in Article 73(a) can be applied by reading Article 73(a) as leaving it to the party seeking the relief in court to determine whether disclosure is necessary.

Article 73(a) also provides that the disclosure may be made "to the extent" necessary. Here again, this qualification should not be read as imposing an unduly restrictive requirement. The party making the disclosure should normally be the judge of the extent to which disclosure is desirable and its judgment in this regard should be reviewed only under a standard that accords proper deference to a party's view as to how much of the arbitration is to be disclosed to the court.

73.06.   The Second Exception

A party may also disclose the existence of an arbitration when "it is required to do so by law or by a competent regulatory body." Article 73(a) thus makes clear, as it necessarily must, that any requirement of confidentiality imposed by it must give way to a conflicting requirement to disclose imposed by law. The addition of the requirement of disclosure to a competent regulatory body as an exception serves the purpose of making clear that disclosure is proper even when not required directly by law, but by a regulatory body that exercises its functions pursuant to law. Indeed, the qualification that the body be regulatory may be too narrow. Any official body, properly constituted in accordance with law, should be included. For example, disclosure should be permitted to an official investigatory body or a legislative committee without compelling such a body to resort to the issuance of a subpoena.

73.07.   The Requirements of Subparagraphs (i) and (ii) Generally

It is not clear whether the provisions contained in subparagraphs (i) and (ii) of Article 73(a) apply only to the second exception or to both exceptions to the requirement of confidentiality imposed by Article 73. Since the exceptions are part of a single sentence, it could be argued that they apply to both exceptions. On the other hand, if it had been the intention to apply them to both exceptions, a more straightforward provision, starting with the prohibition and then reciting the two exceptions, with their modalities, would have been the more obvious way of achieving this result. Furthermore, in the case of the first exception, there would be no need to make disclosure to the other party which, under generally prevailing due process notions, would have to be informed of the court proceedings in any event. In addition, the requirement of subparagraph (i) that the disclosure must be limited to "what is legally required'' is less suitable in the context of an application to a court, for the party making the application is not required by law to make it and, once that party makes the application, it should be free to disclose whatever it deems useful.

73.08. The Requirement of Subparagraph (i)

Subparagraph (i) permits disclosure of "no more than what is legally required." Since it limits disclosure of "information concerning the existence of an arbitration," it is not readily apparent how a party disclosing only the existence of the arbitration could disclose more than what is legally required. Of course, the second exception (as well as the first one, for that matter) could have been made an exception to all obligations of confidentiality imposed by Chapter VII, and in that case the further qualification in subparagraph (i) (and subparagraph (ii) for that matter) would have made greater sense. But since it was not, it is not clear how one could disclose only information concerning the existence of an arbitration required by law or a competent official body and, at the same time, disclose "more than what is legally required." In any event, the notion that a person who discloses information compatibly with the provisions of Chapter VII should disclose no more than reasonably necessary to serve the purposes for which disclosure is permitted should apply across the board.

73.09. The Requirement of Subparagraph (ii)

Subparagraph (ii) of Article 73(a) requires that the party making the disclosure inform the other parties of the details of, and the reasons for, the disclosure. The same information must be given to the tribunal if the disclosure takes place before the termination of the arbitration.

Insofar as subparagraph (ii) requires that the specified information be given "to the other party," it most probably refers to all parties to the arbitration other than the one making the disclosure, and not only to opposing parties. Compliance with this requirement will enable the party that believes the disclosure to be unauthorized to seek appropriate relief. It will also enable it to determine to what extent the disclosure is compatible with Article 73.

Subparagraph (ii) requires that the party making the disclosure provide "details of this disclosure." These words should be construed to serve their apparent aim, which is to enable the other parties and the tribunal or court that may be asked to evaluate the propriety of the disclosure to make the proper evaluation.

Viewed from that perspective, they require the disclosing party to inform the other parties and the tribunal of both the contents of the disclosure made and the manner and circumstances in which it was made. And the explanation required to be furnished should provide the reasons that will enable the parties and the tribunal to determine to what extent the disclosure was permitted.

73.10. The Overall Exception of Article 73(b)

Paragraph(b) of Article 73 provides for an exception to all of paragraph (a). Even a disclosure that would run afoul of paragraph (a) in any of its elements is permitted "for the purpose of satisfying any obligation of good faith or candor" owed to a third party. But, in that event, the disclosure must be limited to "the names of the parties to the arbitration and the relief requested."

73.11.   The Purpose of Article 73(b)

The apparent purpose of Article 73(b) is to permit a party to disregard an otherwise applicable confidentiality requirement imposed by Article 73 when it has an obligation "of good faith or candor" to do so. The quoted words appear to have a considerable reach, but may nevertheless be too limited. In the first place, it may well be argued that a party should be able to disregard otherwise applicable confidentiality requirements, whether imposed by Article 73 or Articles 74 or 75, when "good faith or candor" so require. Secondly, it may equally well be argued that in appropriate cases "good faith or candor" should justify disclosure of the particulars of an arbitration when it is made in the good faith pursuit of one's own interests. A simple example may illustrate all three of these points.

An arbitration has been commenced to invalidate a license under an allegedly invalid patent; around the same time, similar arbitrations relating to the same patent have been commenced before other arbitral tribunals, and the licensor is a wholly-owned subsidiary of another company. It may not be clear whether in this situation the law imposes an obligation of good faith or candor, but the licensor should be free to make the disclosure it deems appropriate to its parent in the pursuit of proper relations with its parent. In addition, a party may wish to communicate to a tribunal in a related case the details of an arbitration in which it is involved. It may not be required by an obligation of good faith or candor to do so, but it may well wish to do so in seeking to protect its own interests, avoid the possibility of conflicting determinations, and promote efficiency in adjudication, all of which are entirely proper purposes. Furthermore, in both of these cases, a party should normally be free to disclose more than merely the names of the parties and the relief requested if it is adequately to pursue its legitimate interest or to discharge its fiduciary obligations.

In addition, a party involved in an arbitration may wish to inform third parties of the existence of the arbitration, even though it is not obligated to do so. It may do so to demonstrate to third parties its preparedness to take appropriate action to protect its interests. It should reasonably be free to do so, even when it has no obligation to that effect.

III.   ARTICLE 74: CONFIDENTIALITY OF DISCLOSURES MADE DURING THE ARBITRATION

Article 74

(a)   **In addition to any specific measures that may be available under Article 52, any documentary or other evidence given by a party or a witness in the arbitration shall be treated as confidential and, to the extent that such evidence describes information that is not in the public domain,** shall not be used or disclosed to any third party by a party whose access to that information arises exclusively as a result of its participation in the arbitration for any purpose without the consent of the parties or order of a court having jurisdiction.

(b)   For the purposes of this Article, a witness called by a party shall not be considered to be a third party. To the extent that a witness is given access to evidence or other information obtained in the arbitration in order to prepare the witness's testimony, the party calling such witness shall be responsible for the maintenance by the witness of the same degree of confidentiality as that required of the party.

74.01.   The Scope of Article 74

Article 74 deals with the confidentiality of "any documentary or other evidence given by a party or a witness." Article 74(a) requires that this evidence may not be disclosed by a party to a third party as long as it "is not in the public domain." But it applies only to a party "whose access to that information arises exclusively as a result of its participation in the arbitration." Evidence that meets these specifications may not be disclosed "for any purpose" without the consent of the parties or a court order.

Article 74(b) provides for an exception to Article 74(a) by providing that a witness is not to be considered a third party insofar as Article 74 is concerned, but that, if a witness is given "access to evidence or other information obtained in the arbitration in order to prepare the witness's testimony, the party calling such the witness" must ensure that the witness maintain "the same degree of confidentiality as that required of the party."

74.02.   The Confidential Information Covered by Article 74(a)

Article 74(a) declares confidential "any documentary or other evidence given . . . in the arbitration," but prohibits its use or disclosure only if it is not in the public domain. This distinction appears to be inadvertent, and it would appear that only evidence that is not in the public domain should be regarded as confidential.

74.03.   The Party That Is Subject to the Obligation of Confidentiality

The duty of non-use or non-disclosure rests only on a party "whose access to that information arises exclusively as a result of its participation in the arbitration." Stated more directly, the requirement of confidentiality applies only to the evidence specified that is not in the public domain and that could not be obtained otherwise than in the arbitration. The apparent purpose of this paragraph is to prohibit disclosure of information that is not in the public domain and could be obtained only in the arbitration. For if it can be obtained from other sources, the access to it does not arise exclusively from the participation in the arbitration. As a consequence, even if the information was obtained in the arbitration, it is not confidential unless it could have been obtained only in the arbitration. This limitation may pose some problems, for most information obtained in an arbitration may also be obtained by a third party from other sources, such as the witness him or herself, especially if the witness is friendly. As a practical matter, therefore, only information provided by a witness produced by an opponent who would not have been willing to provide it to the party making the disclosure is confidential under this provision.

74.04.   The Purpose for which Disclosure is Prohibited

Article 74(a) provides straightforwardly that the disclosure it covers is prohibited "for any purpose" unless the parties agree or a court orders otherwise. It is not clear why the exceptions provided for in Article 73 do not also apply when the information sought is that covered by Article 74. Of course, since paragraph (b) permits disclosure to a witness, the prohibition of Article 74, insofar as the persons to whom disclosure may be made, is less extensive. But, nevertheless, it may be necessary to disclose the information covered by Article 74(a) when required by law or a competent official body. When that is the case, the applicable law will no doubt override the provisions of Article 74. Disclosure required by fiduciary obligations should similarly displace the prohibition of Article 74. But whether the disclosure forbidden by Article 74 may be made by a party in the good faith pursuit of its legitimate interests is not clear.

Article 74(a) permits disregard of its confidentiality requirement only with the consent of the parties or pursuant to court order. It would have been preferable if paragraph (a) had also permitted the tribunal to grant dispensation. Since Article 38(a) provides that the tribunal may conduct the arbitration in such manner as it considers appropriate, the tribunal may, in an appropriate case, be persuaded to issue an order of dispensation from the requirement of Article 74(a), even if the disclosure is not required by law or an official body pursuant to law.

74.05.   The Treatment of Witnesses Under Article 74

Article 74(b) provides that for "the purposes of this Article, a witness called by a party shall not be considered to be a third party." This provision is designed to permit a party that wishes to call a witness to provide that person with information that otherwise would be shielded from disclosure by Article 74(a). While the underlying idea is sound, its technical elaboration in the Rules is subject to question. First of all, it would appear that a party should be able to tell a witness everything about the arbitration that is likely to prepare the witness for his or her testimony. To that extent, the rule laid down in Article 74(a) (first sentence) should also apply to Articles 73 and 75. Second, as written, Article 74(b) applies only to witnesses called by a party. But what is the position when a party, upon interviewing the witness and having informed him or her of the arbitration and the subject of the proposed testimony, decides not to call the witness or when, in the end, because of time pressures or for other reasons, the party does not call the witness? A reasonable interpretation of Article 74(a) is to read the word "called" as "intending to be called."

The second sentence of Article 74(b) provides indirectly for what could more properly have been achieved directly. It imposes on the party calling the witness responsibility for the maintenance by the witness of the same degree of confidentiality as that required of the party. Read literally, it imposes an obligation on the party, while its object should be to impose obligations both on the party and the witness. As written, Article 74(b) provides for recourse only against the party and makes the party responsible for the conduct of the witness. However, a party saddled with this responsibility would act prudently by extracting from the witness an enforceable promise to maintain confidentiality, of which the other parties to the arbitration are named third-party beneficiaries. A party that does so can reasonably be argued to have done everything to discharge its responsibility under Article 74(b).

But what is the situation if the witness were to refuse making the requisite pledge? Is the party calling the witness responsible when the witness subsequently discloses information that is confidential? If the witness is in the employ of the party, he or she may be under an implied obligation to accede to a confidentiality agreement. But when this is not the case, a party cannot force a witness to enter into such an agreement. Must, in that case, the party refrain from calling the witness or can the tribunal relieve the party of its responsibility for the witness's maintaining the requisite confidentiality? Here again, the tribunal's inherent authority to assure the proper conduct of the arbitration acknowledged by Article 38(a) should enable the tribunal to tailor an order appropriate in the circumstances. If this were not the case, it would be most desirable to execute, at the beginning of the arbitration, a special confidentiality agreement addressing all the issues that may arise under the WIPO Rules. In actual international arbitration practice, the disclosure by witnesses of what might be regarded as confidential aspects of arbitration proceedings has not created significant problems. However, the detailed provisions of the WIPO Rules render it appropriate for the drafters of arbitration clauses and the arbitrators to address at an early time the problems that may arise.

IV. ARTICLE 75: CONFIDENTIALITY OF THE AWARD

Article 75
The award shall be treated as confidential by the parties and may only be disclosed to a third party if and to the extent that
(i)   the parties consent, or
(ii)   it falls into the public domain as a result of an action before a national court or other competent authority, or
(iii) it must be disclosed in order to comply with a legal requirement imposed on a party or in order to establish or protect a party's legal rights against a third party.

75.01.   The Special Treatment of the Award
Article 75 contains special provisions regarding the obligation of the parties to maintain the confidentiality of the award. Article 76 imposes a similar, although not identical, obligation on the Center and the arbitrators. The thrust of Article 75 is to prohibit disclosure of the award to a third party except in three identified cases.

75.02.   Article 75 Deals With Disclosure of the Award by a Party to a Third Party

Since Article 75 regulates disclosure of the award by a party to a third party, the same questions that arise as to the proper definitions of these terms under Articles 73 and 74 also arise under Article 75. *See* Section *73.04 supra.*

75.03.   The Three Exceptions

A party may disclose an award to a third party in the three situations specified in subparagraphs (i), (ii) and (iii) of Article 75.

The first exception is that the parties may consent to the disclosure. As a consequence, witnesses and experts who testify on the assumption that the arbitration proceedings are confidential may find subsequently that their evidence, to the extent it is embodied in the award, is disclosed. If they want to guard against that, a separate confidentiality agreement is required.

The second exception attaches when, as the result of an attack in court or before a competent authority, the award becomes public. It should be noted that the permissibility of disclosure under this subparagraph depends on the law of the court or authority in which the award is attacked. If that law does not provide for public access, the award remains secret, unless any of the other exceptions apply.

The third exception permits disclosure by a party who is legally required to make it or who seeks to protect or establish a right against a third party. The first alternative deals with the situation in which the applicable law requires a party to make disclosure. This may be a law requiring persons to testify in court proceedings, a law requiring that disclosure be made to public authorities, or any other law requiring disclosure. It should be noted that this law is not necessarily the law applicable to the merits of the dispute, the arbitration agreement, or the arbitration proceedings: It is the law of the place where the disclosure is required to be made. As a consequence, an American party to an arbitration conducted in Tokyo may be required to disclose the award to the American Securities and Exchange Commission when the applicable American law requires it to do so.

The second leg of the alternative stated in subparagraph (iii) of Article 75 permits disclosure by a party in order to establish or to protect that party's right against a third party. This exception differs from those contained in Article 73 and Article 76(a). Article 73 does not, in terms, grant an exception in order to establish or protect a right against a third party. And Article 76 permits disclosure of the award by the Center or an arbitrator only in connection with an action relating to the award or as required by law. As already indicated, a good argument can be made for the view that disclosure may be made in the good faith pursuit of one's legitimate interests. *See* Section 73.11 *supra.*

Under Article 75 as written, it may even be questioned whether a party may disclose an award in an attack on the award itself. For in such an attack the party does not seek to protect its rights against a third party as required by subparagraph (iii), nor can the party benefit from subparagraph (ii) because under that provision the award may be disclosed only after it has been attacked. Nevertheless, so untoward a result cannot have been intended. A party should be able to disclose an award when it attacks it in court or other competent body. This conclusion may be justified by reading the term "third party" in subparagraph (iii) to include one's opponent, by reading subparagraph (ii) to permit, by implication, disclosure of the award in an action before a national court or other competent authority, or by reading the words "information concerning the existence of an arbitration" in Article 73(a) as including information about the award. All of these readings appear strained, but the conclusion to which they lead is so appropriate that the strain is sufferable.

However, as written, Article 75 does not permit disclosure that serves to promote a party's economic or other interests rather than to protect its legal rights. Thus, for example, under Article 75 as written, a wholly-owned subsidiary might not be permitted to disclose to its parent an award rendered against it. A different conclusion can be reached only by giving the concept of protecting one's legal rights against a third party an unusually broad interpretation.

V. ARTICLE 76: MAINTENANCE OF CONFIDENTIALITY BY THE CENTER AND ARBITRATOR

Article 76

(a) Unless the parties agree otherwise, the Center and the arbitrator shall maintain the confidentiality of the arbitration, the award and, to the extent that they describe information that is not in the public domain, any documentary or other evidence disclosed during the arbitration, except to the extent necessary in connection with a court action relating to the award, or as otherwise required by law.

(b) Notwithstanding paragraph (a), the Center may include information concerning the arbitration in any aggregate statistical data that it publishes concerning its activities, provided that such information does not enable the parties or the particular circumstances of the dispute to be identified.

76.01. The Scope of Article 76

Article 76 deals with the confidentiality to be maintained by the Center and the arbitrator. Their obligation of confidentiality covers "the arbitration, the award, and, to the extent that they describe information that is not in the public domain, any documentary or other evidence disclosed during the arbitration." These are fairly much the same aspects of the arbitral process that are dealt within Articles 73, 74 and 75.

The general obligation of confidentiality imposed by Article 76 is subject to three exceptions: Disclosure is permitted (1) "to the extent necessary in connection with a court action relating to the award," or (2) "as otherwise required by law," or (3) as prescribed in paragraph (b), to the extent necessary to provide statistical information published by the Center.

*76.02. The Reach of the Obligation of Confidentiality Under Article 76
Compared with that Under Articles 73–75*

The description of the reach of the obligation of confidentiality in Article 76 is similar to, but not identical with, that specified in Articles 73–75. It would appear, however, that the differences in description are not intended to entail differences in substance.

Article 76 provides that the obligation of confidentiality covers "the arbitration," while Article 73 speaks of "the existence of an arbitration." It may be thought that the term "arbitration" is broader and covers all aspects of the arbitration, but that notion is dispelled by the separate mention of "the award" and "evidence disclosed during the arbitration," the subjects dealt with separately in Articles 74 and 75. Clearly, the mention of the additional aspects of the arbitration would have been unnecessary if they had already been included in the term "arbitration." The more plausible reading is that Article 76 covers the same three subjects as those dealt with separately in Articles 73, 74 and 75. And while it is true that Article 76 speaks more briefly of "documentary or other evidence disclosed during the arbitration that is not in the public domain," while Article 74 imposes the further requirement that the obligation of confidentiality attaches only if the party involved had access to it "exclusively as a result of its participation in the arbitration," it would appear reasonable to assume that Article 76 does not impose an obligation of confidentiality either with respect to information that the Center or the arbitrators may have derived from other sources.

76.03. The Exceptions Provided for in Article 76(a)

Disclosure of the award may be made under Article 76 "to the extent necessary in connection with a court action relating to the award." Usually, of course, an action relating to the award is brought by one of the parties. One would therefore expect that the parties would be relieved of their obligation of confidentiality when they bring such an action. However, as indicated, Article 75 does so, if at all, only indirectly. *See* Section 75.03 *supra*. On the other hand, the Center and arbitrators will be engaged in judicial proceedings relating to an award only in exceptional cases. The first exception provided for in Article 76(a) is therefore unlikely to find frequent application.

Nor are there likely to be many instances in which disclosure of an award by the arbitrators, WIPO, or the Center is required by law, as provided for in the second exception.

76.04. The Exception of Article 76(b)

Paragraph (b) of Article 76 provides for the Center a limited exception from the obligation of confidentiality imposed by paragraph (a). It may publish statistical information about its activities as long as this information does not identify the dispute or the parties. The WIPO Rules thus forswear publication of the awards rendered under its auspices, unless the parties agree otherwise. Indeed, Article 76, in terms, does not even permit publication of an award with the consent of the parties. Only Article 75 does so, but it is limited to disclosure to "a third party." Even if the Center is regarded as a third party, it does not necessarily follow that it may publish the award. However, the better view is that Article 75 should be construed to permit it.

Article 76 represents a policy decision. It permits the interests of private parties to outweigh the interests of society at large in making arbitration more transparent. It would seem that a better middle ground could have been found. In times when arbitral awards are published with ever increasing frequency and the ICC International Court of Arbitration steadily publishes awards deprived of their identifying characteristics, the Center might have been authorized to publish sanitized awards after having given the parties an opportunity to comment on, but not to preclude, publication. Publication of such awards would be of immeasurable help to arbitrators faced with the resolution of novel questions, promote consistency in adjudication, and subject arbitral awards to constructive criticism by the legal profession and the public at large.

76.05. *Disclosure by Arbitrators in Related Arbitrations*

As written, Article 76 appears to prohibit an arbitrator from disclosing any information relating to the arbitration to arbitrators in a related arbitration. Since existing rules frequently make it impossible for the institution or the arbitrators to order the parties in related matters to consolidate their cases before one panel, a party intent on promoting efficiency of adjudication and consistency of adjudication will frequently appoint the same arbitrators in related cases. The advantages of doing so are obvious, and, if all parties cooperate, it will be possible to select the same panel in all related cases. However, Article 76 would appear to create a serious obstacle to this practice. Of course, if all parties cooperate in selecting the same arbitrators, they will normally agree to relieve the arbitrators of their obligation of confidentiality in their mutual relations. But what if one of the parties, moved by considerations other than efficiency of adjudication and avoidance of inconsistent determination, selects different arbitrators in related cases? In that situation, that party's arbitrator is not attuned to what is happening in the related arbitration and the non-cooperative party is likely to claim that the arbitrator appointed in both arbitrations will make disclosures about the related arbitration that are forbidden by Article 76. And since the common arbitrator cannot help but bring what he or she learns in one arbitration to bear on what happens in the related arbitration, the prohibition of Article 76 would appear to make it advisable not to permit the arbitrator to serve in the related arbitration. Since the exceptions provided for in Article 76 do not appear to be applicable, Article 76 would then become a tool for a party in its efforts to keep related arbitrations apart and thus to gain more than one bite at the apple. To prevent this from happening, it would have been desirable to permit the arbitral tribunals to decide to what extent and under what conditions information obtained by an arbitrator in one arbitration may be disclosed in another. After all, courts have the power to provide for this, and there is no good reason for denying arbitral tribunals the same authority.

76.06.   Disclosure by Arbitrators in Court Actions

Article 76 permits disclosure "to the extent necessary in connection with a court action relating to the award." The disclosure may be of "the arbitration, the award, and . . . any documentary or other evidence disclosed during the arbitration." Typically, such disclosure is made by a party bringing a court action relating to the award. Article 73 permits a party to disclose the existence of the arbitration for this purpose, and Article 75 does the same for the award. There is, however, a question with respect to evidence given in an arbitration. Article 74 permits this to be disclosed pursuant to a court order, while Article 76 permits such disclosure "in connection with a court action relating to the award." The latter provision, on its face, is considerably broader than Article 74. Article 76 permits the arbitrator, the party less likely to be asked to make this disclosure, to make it when necessary in a court action relating to the award, while Article 74 requires a court order. Of course, it makes little sense to require a party bringing an action relating to an award to elicit a court order permitting disclosure of the evidence by that party before it brings the action. This can hardly have been the intention of the rulemakers. They used the phrase "in connection with" a court action in Articles 73 and 76, and it would appear reasonable to read Articles 74 and 75 as imposing the same requirement.

A significant question, already raised above (*see* Section 73.02 *supra*), is whether there is a difference of substance between disclosure of "the existence of an arbitration" regulated by Article 73 and disclosing information concerning "the arbitration" regulated by Article 76. The latter provision might be construed as permitting disclosure of any aspect of the arbitration in connection with a court action relating to the award. If so construed, it would permit arbitrators to disclose particulars about the deliberations among the arbitrators. This has happened in the past and should most definitely be proscribed. Article 76, although lacking the requisite precision, should nevertheless be construed as doing so.

MISCELLANEOUS ARTICLES

Articles 77 and 78

*Hans Smit**

I. GENERAL OBSERVATIONS

1.   This Chapter deals with two subjects that are extraneous to the processing of an arbitration. It provides in Article 77 for exclusion of liability of the arbitrators, WIPO, and the Center, and in Article 78 for a waiver of any claim for defamation based on utterances in preparation for, or in the course of, an arbitration. While the applicable law of defamation may regard the conduct covered by these provisions as not actionable in any event, the rulemakers apparently deemed it prudent contractually to regulate these subjects. These provisions raise two questions: first, do they effectively eliminate liability when it would be imposed under otherwise applicable law; and, second, to what extent may otherwise applicable law exclude liability beyond that excluded by this Chapter.

2.   The effort of this Chapter is to address the substantive obligations of the arbitrators, WIPO, the Center, and the parties resulting from their participation in the arbitral process. It naturally raises the question why exclusion of liability and waiver of defamation were the only subjects addressed in this Chapter. In particular, it might be argued that this Chapter would have provided the appropriate ambiance for setting forth all affirmative obligations the participants in the arbitral process would incur by their participation.

II.   ARTICLE 77: EXCLUSION OF LIABILITY

Article 77
Except in respect of deliberate wrongdoing, the arbitrator or arbitrators, WIPO and the Center shall not be liable to a party for any act or omission in connection with the arbitration.

77.01.   The Elements of the Exclusion
Article 77 excludes liability ''to a party for any act or omission in connection with the arbitration,'' except for deliberate wrongdoing. The liability excluded is only that of the arbitrators, WIPO, and the Center, to a party. Article 77 does not affect the liability of an arbitrator to the Center or WIPO. Also, liability is excluded only for an act or omission in connection with the arbitration.

---

* Stanley H. Fuld Professor of Law and Director, Center for International Arbitration and Litigation Law, Columbia University.

77.02.   The Reach of "In Connection With"

The phrase "in connection with" would appear to limit the exclusion of liability to acts or omissions in the course of participation in the process of arbitrating a dispute. An arbitrator who negligently injures a party outside of the arbitral venue cannot plead Article 77 as an excuse, even though the injury would not have occurred if he had not participated in the arbitration. The purpose of Article 77 is to shield an arbitrator, WIPO, and the Center from liability that they might otherwise incur because of their participation in the arbitral process.

77.03.   The Liability of The Arbitrator

Undoubtedly of the most practical importance is the exclusion by Article 77 of the liability of the arbitrator. As already indicated, in the absence of deliberate wrongdoing, the exclusion attaches only for acts or omissions in connection with the arbitration. *See* 77.02 *supra*. Most importantly, Article 77 does not exclude liability for "deliberate wrongdoing." The meaning of this term is not clear on its face. Does it describe wrongdoing that is deliberate or doing a wrong deliberately? In other words, does the arbitrator have to commit a wrong while knowing that it is a wrong? Favoring the broadest possible exclusion of liability is the construction that makes the exception apply only when the arbitrator knows that what he or she is doing is wrong. For it will normally be very difficult to establish that an arbitrator deliberately did something that he or she knew to be wrong. On the other hand, showing that what an arbitrator did deliberately was wrong will normally be considerably easier and might well deprive an arbitrator of the exclusion of liability in a case in which, under applicable law, no liability would attach and then raise the question of whether Article 77 extends, rather than limits, an arbitrator's liability. All of these questions would be avoided by a provision that would exclude the arbitrator's liability to the extent permitted by applicable law.

In its present version, Article 77 raises the interesting question of whether it provides relief against an arbitrator who, for improper reasons, fails to discharge his or her duties to the end of the arbitration. A good example is that of the arbitrator who seeks to resign during, or even at the very end of, the arbitration in order to frustrate its progress. Doing so is wrong, should be known by the arbitrator to be wrong, and since it is done deliberately, should expose him or her to liability. It may be that such conduct would not be actionable under applicable law. In that case, if Article 77 should be interpreted affirmatively to impose liability, it would produce a worthwhile result. It would also make clear the arbitrator's obligation properly to discharge the duties of an arbitrator and to carry the arbitration to its end.

77.04.   Who Determines the Arbitrator's Liability

The WIPO Rules are part and parcel of the agreement between the parties to arbitrate their disputes, and the arbitrators, when they accept their commission, become part of that agreement. Does that mean that, when an arbitrator breaches the agreement, his or her liability is to be settled in arbitration? Surely, the recommended

WIPO arbitration clause is sufficiently broad to encompass such a dispute, and the arbitrator may be argued to have acceded to it by accepting his or her appointment. On the other hand, it is unlikely that the parties and the arbitrators contemplated, and therefore intended, this construction, one of the advantages of which would be to keep disputes of this kind in a neutral forum rather than in the court of a particular state. In any event, if the dispute is to go to arbitration, it should go to a separate panel constituted as between the parties to that dispute.

III.   ARTICLE 78: WAIVER OF DEFAMATION

Article 78
The parties and, by acceptance of appointment, the arbitrator agree that any statements or comments, whether written or oral, made or used by them or their representatives in preparation for or in the course of the arbitration shall not be relied upon to found or maintain any action for defamation, libel, slander or any related complaint, and this Article may be pleaded as a bar to any such action.

78.01.   The Thrust of Article 78.
The apparent purpose of Article 78 is to exclude liability for defamation for any statement made by the arbitrators and the parties or their counsel in, or in the preparation for, the arbitration. It is to be noted that Article 78 specifically mentions the representatives of the parties, a mention that is omitted in Articles 73–75. The specific mention in Article 78 may invite the argument that the omission in Articles 73–75 is deliberate and that the latter Articles are not addressed to counsel. As already indicated, that argument should be rejected. It would deprive Articles 73–75 of most of their significance. *See* 73.03, 74.03, and 75.02 *supra.*[1]

Essentially, Article 78 excludes liability for defamation committed in the arbitration. To make clear that any claim that in substance is one for defamation is excluded, its text speaks of "defamation, libel, slander or any related complaint." Of course, defamation encompasses both libel and slander, and when the text speaks of "related complaint," it probably means "similar" or related in kind, so that a claim for intentional infliction of emotional distress is included.

Article 78 overlaps to a certain extent Article 77 which, except for deliberate wrongdoing, excludes arbitral liability for acts or omissions in connection with the arbitration. However Article 77 excepts deliberate wrongdoing, while Article 78 does not, and Article 78 covers statements "in preparation for or in the course of the arbitration," while Article 77 covers acts or omissions "in connection with the arbitration." Since it is difficult to see why a difference should be made in defining the relationship to the arbitration, the quoted language should be given the same meaning as covering acts or omissions by parties or arbitrators as participants in the arbitration.

---

[1] *See* Hans Smit, *Confidentiality, supra* at 233.

However, Article 78 should prevail over Article 77 insofar as it shields from liability statements that might be regarded as "deliberate wrongdoing."

78.02.   The Relevance of Otherwise Applicable Law.

Article 78 entitled "Waiver of Defamation" provides that statements made in preparation for, or in the course of the arbitration, shall not be relied on or support an action for defamation "or related complaint" and that it may be pleaded as a bar to any such action. One may wonder why this Article does not straightforwardly exclude liability for defamation committed in an arbitration. Perhaps the rulemakers assumed that they could not do so, but there is no good reason for their being able to exclude liability in Article 77 and their not being able to do so in Article 78. In any event, this Article affects only the parties and the arbitrators. The claims of others offended by defamatory statements in an arbitration are not affected. They will have such claims as the law may give them. In addition, it may be questioned whether defamatory statements that are actionable under the otherwise applicable law cease to be so by virtue of Article 78. Whether Article 78 will have this effect will depend on the applicable law, and, more particularly, on whether it permits exclusion of liability for defamatory statements that are not privileged or qualifiedly privileged under the applicable law. Indeed, the net effect of Article 78 cannot be more than to exclude liability for defamation to the extent permitted by applicable law. Article 78 could more simply and directly have so provided.

As it is, the text of Article 78 is rather prolix. It provides that the arbitrators agree "by acceptance of appointment." The Rules do not elsewhere indicate the basis for obligations they impose on arbitrators. Nor was it necessary to distinguish between "statements" and "comments" or to distinguish between making or using a statement. Similarly, simply excluding liability for the statements declared not actionable would have had the same effect as providing that the non-actionable statements cannot support a claim for relief and that Article 78 may be pleaded as a bar.

78.03.   The Limited Personal Reach of Article 78

Article 78 addresses only the liability for defamation of arbitrators, parties, and the representatives of parties. It properly includes the representatives of the parties. Although Articles 73–76 do not do so, it would appear proper to consider them also included, on a par with the parties, in those Articles.

The exclusion of liability extends also to statements made "in preparation for" the arbitration. The quoted words differ from the words "in connection with" used in Articles 73, 76, and 77. They make clear that statements made after the arbitration are not affected by Article 78.

It should be stressed that, although Article 78 deals only with the arbitrators and the parties and their representatives, other persons, such as witnesses and experts, who make defamatory statements in the course of an arbitration, may benefit from exclusion of liability for such statements under applicable law.

APPENDIX

WIPO ARBITRATION RULES

(Effective from October 1, 1994)

CONTENTS

I. GENERAL PROVISIONS

Abbreviated Expressions

Article 1

In these Rules:

"Arbitration Agreement" means an agreement by the parties to submit to arbitration all or certain disputes which have arisen or which may arise between them; an Arbitration Agreement may be in the form of an arbitration clause in a contract or in the form of a separate contract;

"Claimant" means the party initiating an arbitration;

"Respondent" means the party against which the arbitration is initiated, as named in the Request for Arbitration;

"Tribunal" includes a sole arbitrator or all the arbitrators where more than one is appointed;

"WIPO" means the World Intellectual Property Organization;

"Center" means the WIPO Arbitration Center, a unit of the International Bureau of WIPO;

Words used in the singular include the plural and vice versa, as the context may require.

Scope of Application of Rules

Article 2

Where an Arbitration Agreement provides for arbitration under the WIPO Arbitration Rules, these Rules shall be deemed to form part of that Arbitration Agreement and the dispute shall be settled in accordance with these Rules, as in effect on the date of the commencement of the arbitration, unless the parties have agreed otherwise.

Article 3

(a) These Rules shall govern the arbitration, except that, where any of these Rules is in conflict with a provision of the law applicable to the arbitration from which the parties cannot derogate, that provision shall prevail.

(b) The law applicable to the arbitration shall be determined in accordance with Article 59(b).

Notices, Periods of Time

Article 4

(a) Any notice or other communication that may or is required to be given under these Rules shall be in writing and shall be delivered by expedited postal or courier service, or transmitted by telex, telefax or other means of telecommunication that provide a record thereof.

(b) A party's last-known residence or place of business shall be a valid address for the purpose of any notice or other communication in the absence of any notification of a change by that party. Communications may in any event be addressed to a party in the manner stipulated or, failing such a stipulation, according to the practice followed in the course of the dealings between the parties.

(c) For the purpose of determining the date of commencement of a time-limit, a notice or other communication shall be deemed to have been received on the day it is delivered or, in the case of telecommunications, transmitted in accordance with paragraphs (a) and (b) of this Article.

(d) For the purpose of determining compliance with a time-limit, a notice or other communication shall be deemed to have been sent, made or transmitted if it is despatched, in accordance with paragraphs (a) and (b) of this Article, prior to or on the day of the expiration of the time limit.

(e) For the purpose of calculating a period of time under these Rules, such period shall begin to run on the day following the day when a notice or other communication is received. If the last day of such period is an official holiday or a non-business day at the residence or place of business of the addressee, the period is extended until the first business day which follows. Official holidays or non-business days occurring during the running of the period of time are included in calculating the period.

(f) The parties may agree to reduce or extend the periods of time referred to in Articles 11, 15(b), 16(b), 17(b), 17(c), 18(b), 19(b)(iii), 41(a) and 42(a).

(g) The Center may, at the request of a party or on its own motion, extend the periods of time referred to in Articles 11, 15(b), 16(b), 17(b), 17(c), 18(b), 19(b)(iii), 67(d), 68(e) and 70(e).

Documents Required to Be Submitted to the Center

Article 5

(a) Until the notification by the Center of the establishment of the Tribunal, any written statement, notice or other communication required or allowed under Articles 6 to 36 shall be submitted by a party to the Center and a copy thereof shall at the same time be transmitted by that party to the other party.

(b) Any written statement, notice or other communication so sent to the Center shall be sent in a number of copies equal to the number required to provide one copy for each envisaged arbitrator and one for the Center.

(c) After the notification by the Center of the establishment of the Tribunal, any written statements, notices or other communications shall be submitted by a party directly to the Tribunal and a copy thereof shall at the same time be supplied by that party to the other party.

(d)   The Tribunal shall send to the Center a copy of each order or other decision that it makes.

II.   COMMENCEMENT OF THE ARBITRATION

Request for Arbitration

Article 6

The Claimant shall transmit the Request for Arbitration to the Center and to the Respondent.

Article 7

The date of commencement of the arbitration shall be the date on which the Request for Arbitration is received by the Center.

Article 8

The Center shall inform the Claimant and the Respondent of the receipt by it of the Request for Arbitration and of the date of the commencement of the arbitration.

Article 9

The Request for Arbitration shall contain:

(i)   a demand that the dispute be referred to arbitration under the WIPO Arbitration Rules;

(ii)   the names, addresses and telephone, telex, telefax or other communication references of the parties and of the representative of the Claimant;

(iii)   a copy of the Arbitration Agreement and, if applicable, any separate choice-of-law clause;

(iv)   a brief description of the nature and circumstances of the dispute, including an indication of the rights and property involved and the nature of any technology involved;

(v)   a statement of the relief sought and an indication, to the extent possible, of any amount claimed;

(vi)   any appointment that is required by, or observations that the Claimant considers useful in connection with, Articles 14 to 20.

Article 10

The Request for Arbitration may also be accompanied by the Statement of Claim referred to in Article 41.

Answer to the Request

Article 11

Within 30 days from the date on which the Respondent receives the Request for Arbitration from the Claimant, the Respondent shall address to the Center and to the

Claimant an Answer to the Request which shall contain comments on any of the elements in the Request for Arbitration and may include indications of any counter-claim or set-off.

Article 12

If the Claimant has filed a Statement of Claim with the Request for Arbitration pursuant to Article 10, the Answer to the Request may also be accompanied by the Statement of Defense referred to in Article 42.

Representation

Article 13

(a)   The parties may be represented by persons of their choice, irrespective of, in particular, nationality or professional qualification. The names, addresses and telephone, telex, telefax or other communication references of representatives shall be communicated to the Center, the other party and, after its establishment, the Tribunal.

(b)   Each party shall ensure that its representatives have sufficient time available to enable the arbitration to proceed expeditiously.

(c)   The parties may also be assisted by persons of their choice.

III.   COMPOSITION AND ESTABLISHMENT OF THE TRIBUNAL

Number of Arbitrators

Article 14

(a)   The Tribunal shall consist of such number of arbitrators as has been agreed by the parties.

(b)   Where the parties have not agreed on the number of arbitrators, the Tribunal shall consist of a sole arbitrator, except where the Center in its discretion determines that, in view of all the circumstances of the case, a Tribunal composed of three members is appropriate.

Appointment Pursuant to Procedure Agreed Upon by the Parties

Article 15

(a)   If the parties have agreed on a procedure of appointing the arbitrator or arbitrators other than as envisaged in Articles 16 to 20, that procedure shall be followed.

(b)   If the Tribunal has not been established pursuant to such procedure within the period of time agreed upon by the parties or, in the absence of such an agreed period of time, within 45 days after the commencement of the arbitration, the Tribunal shall be established or completed, as the case may be, in accordance with Article 19.

Appointment of a Sole Arbitrator

Article 16

(a)   Where a sole arbitrator is to be appointed and the parties have not agreed on a procedure of appointment, the sole arbitrator shall be appointed jointly by the parties.

(b)   If the appointment of the sole arbitrator is not made within the period of time agreed upon by the parties or, in the absence of such an agreed period of time, within 30 days after the commencement of the arbitration, the sole arbitrator shall be appointed in accordance with Article 19.

Appointment of Three Arbitrators

Article 17

(a)   Where three arbitrators are to be appointed and the parties have not agreed upon a procedure of appointment, the arbitrators shall be appointed in accordance with this Article.

(b)   The Claimant shall appoint an arbitrator in its Request for Arbitration. The Respondent shall appoint an arbitrator within 30 days from the date on which it receives the Request for Arbitration. The two arbitrators thus appointed shall, within 20 days after the appointment of the second arbitrator, appoint a third arbitrator, who shall be the presiding arbitrator.

(c)   Notwithstanding paragraph (b), where three arbitrators are to be appointed as a result of the exercise of the discretion of the Center under Article 14(b), the Claimant shall, by notice to the Center and to the Respondent, appoint an arbitrator within 15 days after the receipt by it of notification by the Center that the Tribunal is to be composed of three arbitrators. The Respondent shall appoint an arbitrator within 30 days after the receipt by it of the said notification. The two arbitrators thus appointed shall, within 20 days after the appointment of the second arbitrator, appoint a third arbitrator, who shall be the presiding arbitrator.

(d)   If the appointment of any arbitrator is not made within the applicable period of time referred to in the preceding paragraphs, that arbitrator shall be appointed in accordance with Article 19.

Appointment of Three Arbitrators in Case of Multiple Claimants or Respondents

Article 18

(a)   Where
    (i)   three arbitrators are to be appointed,
    (ii)   the parties have not agreed on a procedure of appointment, and
    (iii)   the Request for Arbitration names more than one Claimant, the Claimants shall make a joint appointment of an arbitrator in their Request for Arbitration. The appointment of the second arbitrator and the presiding arbitrator shall,

subject to paragraph (b) of this Article, take place in accordance with Article 17(b), (c) or (d), as the case may be.

    (b)   Where

        (i)   three arbitrators are to be appointed,

        (ii)   the parties have not agreed on a procedure of appointment, and

        (iii)   the Request for Arbitration names more than one Respondent, the Respondents shall jointly appoint an arbitrator. If, for whatever reason, the Respondents do not make a joint appointment of an arbitrator within 30 days after receiving the Request for Arbitration, any appointment of the arbitrator previously made by the Claimant or Claimants shall be considered void and two arbitrators shall be appointed by the Center. The two arbitrators thus appointed shall, within 30 days after the appointment of the second arbitrator, appoint a third arbitrator, who shall be the presiding arbitrator.

    (c)   Where

        (i)   three arbitrators are to be appointed,

        (ii)   the parties have agreed upon a procedure of appointment, and

        (iii)   the Request for Arbitration names more than one Claimant or more than one Respondent, paragraphs (a) and (b) of this Article shall, notwithstanding Article 15(a), apply irrespective of any contractual provisions in the Arbitration Agreement with respect to the procedure of appointment, unless those provisions have expressly excluded the application of this Article.

Default Appointment

Article 19

    (a)   If a party has failed to appoint an arbitrator as required under Articles 15, 17 or 18, the Center shall, in lieu of that party, forthwith make the appointment.

    (b)   If the sole or presiding arbitrator has not been appointed as required under Articles 15, 16, 17 or 18, the appointment shall take place in accordance with the following procedure:

        (i)   The Center shall send to each party an identical list of candidates. The list shall comprise the names of at least three candidates in alphabetical order. The list shall include or be accompanied by a brief statement of each candidate's qualifications. If the parties have agreed on any particular qualifications, the list shall contain only the names of candidates that satisfy those qualifications.

        (ii)   Each party shall have the right to delete the name of any candidate or candidates to whose appointment it objects and shall number any remaining candidates in order of preference.

        (iii)   Each party shall return the marked list to the Center within 20 days after the date on which the list is received by it. Any party failing to return a marked list within that period of time shall be deemed to have assented to all candidates appearing on the list.

(iv)   As soon as possible after receipt by it of the lists from the parties, or failing this, after the expiration of the period of time specified in the previous sub-paragraph, the Center shall, taking into account the preferences and objections expressed by the parties, invite a person from the list to be the sole or presiding arbitrator.

(v)   If the lists which have been returned do not show a person who is acceptable as arbitrator to both parties, the Center shall be authorized to appoint the sole or presiding arbitrator. The Center shall similarly be authorized to do so if a person is not able or does not wish to accept the Center's invitation to be the sole or presiding arbitrator, or if there appear to be other reasons precluding that person from being the sole or presiding arbitrator, and there does not remain on the lists a person who is acceptable as arbitrator to both parties.

(c)   Notwithstanding the provisions of paragraph (b), the Center shall be authorized to appoint the sole or presiding arbitrator if it determines in its discretion that the procedure described in that paragraph is not appropriate for the case.

Nationality of Arbitrators

Article 20

(a)   An agreement of the parties concerning the nationality of arbitrators shall be respected.

(b)   If the parties have not agreed on the nationality of the sole or presiding arbitrator, such arbitrator shall, in the absence of special circumstances such as the need to appoint a person having particular qualifications, be a national of a country other than the countries of the parties.

Communication between Parties and Candidates for Appointment as Arbitrator

Article 21

No party or anyone acting on its behalf shall have any *ex parte* communication with any candidate for appointment as arbitrator except to discuss the candidate's qualifications, availability or independence in relation to the parties.

Impartiality and Independence

Article 22

(a)   Each arbitrator shall be impartial and independent.

(b)   Each prospective arbitrator shall, before accepting appointment, disclose to the parties, the Center and any other arbitrator who has already been appointed any circumstances that might give rise to justifiable doubt as to the arbitrator's impartiality or independence, or confirm in writing that no such circumstances exist.

(c)   If, at any stage during the arbitration, new circumstances arise that might give rise to justifiable doubt as to any arbitrator's impartiality or independence, the arbitrator shall promptly disclose such circumstances to the parties, the Center and the other arbitrators.

Availability, Acceptance and Notification

Article 23

(a)   Each arbitrator shall, by accepting appointment, be deemed to have undertaken to make available sufficient time to enable the arbitration to be conducted and completed expeditiously.

(b)   Each prospective arbitrator shall accept appointment in writing and shall communicate such acceptance to the Center.

(c)   The Center shall notify the parties of the establishment of the Tribunal.

Challenge of Arbitrators

Article 24

(a)   Any arbitrator may be challenged by a party if circumstances exist that give rise to justifiable doubt as to the arbitrator's impartiality or independence.

(b)   A party may challenge an arbitrator whom it has appointed or in whose appointment it concurred only for reasons of which it becomes aware after the appointment has been made.

Article 25

A party challenging an arbitrator shall send notice to the Center, the Tribunal and the other party, stating the reasons for the challenge, within 15 days after being notified of that arbitrator's appointment or after becoming aware of the circumstances that it considers give rise to justifiable doubt as to that arbitrator's impartiality or independence.

Article 26

When an arbitrator has been challenged by a party, the other party shall have the right to respond to the challenge and shall, if it exercises this right, send, within 15 days after receipt of the notice referred to in Article 25, a copy of its response to the Center, the party making the challenge and the arbitrators.

Article 27

The Tribunal may, in its discretion, suspend or continue the arbitral proceedings during the pendency of the challenge.

Article 28

The other party may agree to the challenge or the arbitrator may voluntarily withdraw. In either case, the arbitrator shall be replaced without any implication that the grounds for the challenge are valid.

Article 29

If the other party does not agree to the challenge and the challenged arbitrator does not withdraw, the decision on the challenge shall be made by the Center in accordance with its internal procedures. Such a decision is of an administrative nature and shall be final. The Center shall not be required to state reasons for its decision.

Release from Appointment

Article 30

At the arbitrator's own request, an arbitrator may be released from appointment as arbitrator either with the consent of the parties or by the Center.

Article 31

Irrespective of any request by the arbitrator, the parties may jointly release the arbitrator from appointment as arbitrator. The parties shall promptly notify the Center of such release.

Article 32

At the request of a party or on its own motion, the Center may release an arbitrator from appointment as arbitrator if the arbitrator has become *de jure* or *de facto* unable to fulfill, or fails to fulfill, the duties of an arbitrator. In such a case, the parties shall be offered the opportunity to express their views thereon and the provisions of Articles 26 to 29 shall apply *mutatis mutandis*.

Replacement of an Arbitrator

Article 33

(a) Whenever necessary, a substitute arbitrator shall be appointed pursuant to the procedure provided for in Articles 15 to 19 that was applicable to the appointment of the arbitrator being replaced.

(b) In the event that an arbitrator appointed by a party has either been successfully challenged on grounds which were known or should have been known to that party at the time of appointment, or has been released from appointment as arbitrator in accordance with Article 32, the Center shall have the discretion not to permit that party to make a new appointment. If it chooses to exercise this discretion, the Center shall make the substitute appointment.

(c)   Pending the replacement, the arbitral proceedings shall be suspended, unless otherwise agreed by the parties.

Article 34

Whenever a substitute arbitrator is appointed, the Tribunal shall, having regard to any observations of the parties, determine in its sole discretion whether all or part of any prior hearings are to be repeated.

Truncated Tribunal

Article 35

(a)   If an arbitrator on a three-person Tribunal, though duly notified and without good cause, fails to participate in the work of the Tribunal, the two other arbitrators shall, unless a party has made an application under Article 32, have the power in their sole discretion to continue the arbitration and to make any award, order or other decision, notwithstanding the failure of the third arbitrator to participate. In determining whether to continue the arbitration or to render any award, order or other decision without the participation of an arbitrator, the two other arbitrators shall take into account the stage of the arbitration, the reason, if any, expressed by the third arbitrator for such non-participation, and such other matters as they consider appropriate in the circumstances of the case.

(b)   In the event that the two other arbitrators determine not to continue the arbitration without the participation of a third arbitrator, the Center shall, on proof satisfactory to it of the failure of the arbitrator to participate in the work of the Tribunal, declare the office vacant, and a substitute arbitrator shall be appointed by the Center in the exercise of the discretion defined in Article 33, unless the parties otherwise agree.

Pleas as to the Jurisdiction of the Tribunal

Article 36

(a)   The Tribunal shall have the power to hear and determine objections to its own jurisdiction, including any objections with respect to form, existence, validity or scope of the Arbitration Agreement examined pursuant to Article 59(b).

(b)   The Tribunal shall have the power to determine the existence or validity of any contract of which the Arbitration Agreement forms part or to which it relates.

(c)   A plea that the Tribunal does not have jurisdiction shall be raised not later than in the Statement of Defense or, with respect to a counter-claim or a set-off, the Statement of Defense thereto, failing which any such plea shall be barred in the subsequent arbitral proceedings or before any court. A plea that the Tribunal is exceeding the scope of its authority shall be raised as soon as the matter alleged to be beyond the scope of its authority is raised during the arbitral proceedings. The Tribunal may, in either case, admit a later plea if it considers the delay justified.

(d)   The Tribunal may rule on a plea referred to in paragraph (c) as a preliminary question or, in its sole discretion, decide on such a plea in the final award.

(e)   A plea that the Tribunal lacks jurisdiction shall not preclude the Center from administering the arbitration.

IV.   CONDUCT OF THE ARBITRATION

Transmission of the File to the Tribunal

Article 37

The Center shall transmit the file to each arbitrator as soon as the arbitrator is appointed.

General Powers of the Tribunal

Article 38

(a)   Subject to Article 3, the Tribunal may conduct the arbitration in such manner as it considers appropriate.

(b)   In all cases, the Tribunal shall ensure that the parties are treated with equality and that each party is given a fair opportunity to present its case.

(c)   The Tribunal shall ensure that the arbitral procedure takes place with due expedition. It may, at the request of a party or on its own motion, extend in exceptional cases a period of time fixed by these Rules, by itself or agreed to by the parties. In urgent cases, such an extension may be granted by the presiding arbitrator alone.

Place of Arbitration

Article 39

(a)   Unless otherwise agreed by the parties, the place of arbitration shall be decided by the Center, taking into consideration any observations of the parties and the circumstances of the arbitration.

(b)   The Tribunal may, after consultation with the parties, conduct hearings at any place that it considers appropriate. It may deliberate wherever it deems appropriate.

(c)   The award shall be deemed to have been made at the place of arbitration.

Language of Arbitration

Article 40

(a)   Unless otherwise agreed by the parties, the language of the arbitration shall be the language of the Arbitration Agreement, subject to the power of the Tribunal to determine otherwise, having regard to any observations of the parties and the circumstances of the arbitration.

(b)   The Tribunal may order that any documents submitted in languages other than the language of arbitration be accompanied by a translation in whole or in part into the language of arbitration.

Statement of Claim

Article 41

(a)   Unless the Statement of Claim accompanied the Request for Arbitration, the Claimant shall, within 30 days after receipt of notification from the Center of the establishment of the Tribunal, communicate its Statement of Claim to the Respondent and to the Tribunal.

(b)   The Statement of Claim shall contain a comprehensive statement of the facts and legal arguments supporting the claim, including a statement of the relief sought.

(c)   The Statement of Claim shall, to as large an extent as possible, be accompanied by the documentary evidence upon which the Claimant relies, together with a schedule of such documents. Where the documentary evidence is especially voluminous, the Claimant may add a reference to further documents it is prepared to submit.

Statement of Defense

Article 42

(a)   The Respondent shall, within 30 days after receipt of the Statement of Claim or within 30 days after receipt of notification from the Center of the establishment of the Tribunal, whichever occurs later, communicate its Statement of Defense to the Claimant and to the Tribunal.

(b)   The Statement of Defense shall reply to the particulars of the Statement of Claim required pursuant to Article 41(b). The Statement of Defense shall be accompanied by the corresponding documentary evidence described in Article 41(c).

(c)   Any counter-claim or set-off by the Respondent shall be made or asserted in the Statement of Defense or, in exceptional circumstances, at a later stage in the arbitral proceedings if so determined by the Tribunal. Any such counter-claim or set-off shall contain the same particulars as those specified in Article 41(b) and (c).

Further Written Statements

Article 43

(a)   In the event that a counter-claim or set-off has been made or asserted, the Claimant shall reply to the particulars thereof. Article 42(a) and (b) shall apply *mutatis mutandis* to such reply.

(b)   The Tribunal may, in its discretion, allow or require further written statements.

Amendments to Claims or Defense

Article 44

Subject to any contrary agreement by the parties, a party may amend or supplement its claim, counter-claim, defense or set-off during the course of the arbitral proceedings, unless the Tribunal considers it inappropriate to allow such amendment having regard to its nature or the delay in making it and to the provisions of Article 38(b) and (c).

Communication Between Parties and Tribunal

Article 45

Except as otherwise provided in these Rules or permitted by the Tribunal, no party or anyone acting on its behalf may have any *ex parte* communication with any arbitrator with respect to any matter of substance relating to the arbitration, it being understood that nothing in this paragraph shall prohibit *ex parte* communications which concern matters of a purely organizational nature, such as the physical facilities, place, date or time of the hearings.

Interim Measures of Protection; Security for Claims and Costs

Article 46

(a)   At the request of a party, the Tribunal may issue any provisional orders or take other interim measures it deems necessary, including injunctions and measures for the conservation of goods which form part of the subject-matter in dispute, such as an order for their deposit with a third person or for the sale of perishable goods. The Tribunal may make the granting of such measures subject to appropriate security being furnished by the requesting party.

(b)   At the request of a party, the Tribunal may, if it considers it to be required by exceptional circumstances, order the other party to provide security, in a form to be determined by the Tribunal, for the claim or counter-claim, as well as for costs referred to in Article 72.

(c)   Measures and orders contemplated under this Article may take the form of an interim award.

(d)   A request addressed by a party to a judicial authority for interim measures or for security for the claim or counter-claim, or for the implementation of any such measures or orders granted by the Tribunal, shall not be deemed incompatible with the Arbitration Agreement, or deemed to be a waiver of that Agreement.

Preparatory Conference

Article 47

The Tribunal may, in general following the submission of the Statement of Defense, conduct a preparatory conference with the parties for the purpose of organizing and scheduling the subsequent proceedings.

Evidence

Article 48

(a)   The Tribunal shall determine the admissibility, relevance, materiality and weight of evidence.

(b)   At any time during the arbitration, the Tribunal may, at the request of a party or on its own motion, order a party to produce such documents or other evidence as it considers necessary or appropriate and may order a party to make available to the Tribunal or to an expert appointed by it or to the other party any property in its possession or control for inspection or testing.

Experiments

Article 49

(a)   A party may give notice to the Tribunal and to the other party at any reasonable time before a hearing that specified experiments have been conducted on which it intends to rely. The notice shall specify the purpose of the experiment, a summary of the experiment, the method employed, the results and the conclusion. The other party may by notice to the Tribunal request that any or all such experiments be repeated in its presence. If the Tribunal considers such request justified, it shall determine the timetable for the repetition of the experiments.

(b)   For the purposes of this Article, "experiments" shall include tests or other processes of verification.

Site Visits

Article 50

The Tribunal may, at the request of a party or on its own motion, inspect or require the inspection of any site, property, machinery, facility, production line, model, film, material, product or process as it deems appropriate. A party may request such an inspection at any reasonable time prior to any hearing, and the Tribunal, if it grants such a request, shall determine the timing and arrangements for the inspection.

Agreed Primers and Models

Article 51

The Tribunal may, where the parties so agree, determine that they shall jointly provide:

(i)   a technical primer setting out the background of the scientific, technical or other specialized information necessary to fully understand the matters in issue; and

(ii)   models, drawings or other materials that the Tribunal or the parties require for reference purposes at any hearing.

Disclosure of Trade Secrets and Other Confidential Information

Article 52

(a)   For the purposes of this Article, confidential information shall mean any information, regardless of the medium in which it is expressed, which is
   (i)   in the possession of a party,
   (ii)   not accessible to the public,
   (iii)   of commercial, financial or industrial significance, and
   (iv)   treated as confidential by the party possessing it.

(b)   A party invoking the confidentiality of any information it wishes or is required to submit in the arbitration, including to an expert appointed by the Tribunal, shall make an application to have the information classified as confidential by notice to the Tribunal, with a copy to the other party. Without disclosing the substance of the information, the party shall give in the notice the reasons for which it considers the information confidential.

(c)   The Tribunal shall determine whether the information is to be classified as confidential and of such a nature that the absence of special measures of protection in the proceedings would be likely to cause serious harm to the party invoking its confidentiality. If the Tribunal so determines, it shall decide under which conditions and to whom the confidential information may in part or in whole be disclosed and shall require any person to whom the confidential information is to be disclosed to sign an appropriate confidentiality undertaking.

(d)   In exceptional circumstances, in lieu of itself determining whether the information is to be classified as confidential and of such nature that the absence of special measures of protection in the proceedings would be likely to cause serious harm to the party invoking its confidentiality, the Tribunal may, at the request of a party or on its own motion and after consultation with the parties, designate a confidentiality advisor who will determine whether the information is to be so classified, and, if so, decide under which conditions and to whom it may in part or in whole be disclosed. Any such confidentiality advisor shall be required to sign an appropriate confidentiality undertaking.

(e)   The Tribunal may also, at the request of a party or on its own motion, appoint the confidentiality advisor as an expert in accordance with Article 55 in order to report to it, on the basis of the confidential information, on specific issues designated by the Tribunal without disclosing the confidential information either to the party from whom the confidential information does not originate or to the Tribunal.

Hearings

Article 53

(a) If either party so requests, the Tribunal shall hold a hearing for the presentation of evidence by witnesses, including expert witnesses, or for oral argument or for both. In the absence of a request, the Tribunal shall decide whether to hold such a hearing or hearings. If no hearings are held, the proceedings shall be conducted on the basis of documents and other materials alone.

(b) In the event of a hearing, the Tribunal shall give the parties adequate advance notice of the date, time and place thereof.

(c) Unless the parties agree otherwise, all hearings shall be in private.

(d) The Tribunal shall determine whether and, if so, in what form a record shall be made of any hearing.

Witnesses

Article 54

(a) Before any hearing, the Tribunal may require either party to give notice of the identity of witnesses it wishes to call, as well as of the subject matter of their testimony and its relevance to the issues.

(b) The Tribunal has discretion, on the grounds of redundance and irrelevance, to limit or refuse the appearance of any witness, whether witness of fact or expert witness.

(c) Any witness who gives oral evidence may be questioned, under the control of the Tribunal, by each of the parties. The Tribunal may put questions at any stage of the examination of the witnesses.

(d) The testimony of witnesses may, either at the choice of a party or as directed by the Tribunal, be submitted in written form, whether by way of signed statements, sworn affidavits or otherwise, in which case the Tribunal may make the admissibility of the testimony conditional upon the witnesses being made available for oral testimony.

(e) A party shall be responsible for the practical arrangements, cost and availability of any witness it calls.

(f) The Tribunal shall determine whether any witness shall retire during any part of the proceedings, particularly during the testimony of other witnesses.

Experts Appointed by the Tribunal

Article 55

(a) The Tribunal may, after consultation with the parties, appoint one or more independent experts to report to it on specific issues designated by the Tribunal. A copy of the expert's terms of reference, established by the Tribunal, having regard to any observations of the parties, shall be communicated to the parties. Any such expert shall be required to sign an appropriate confidentiality undertaking.

(b)　Subject to Article 52, upon receipt of the expert's report, the Tribunal shall communicate a copy of the report to the parties, which shall be given the opportunity to express, in writing, their opinion on the report. A party may, subject to Article 52, examine any document on which the expert has relied in such a report.

(c)　At the request of a party, the parties shall be given the opportunity to question the expert at a hearing. At this hearing, the parties may present expert witnesses to testify on the points at issue.

(d)　The opinion of any expert on the issue or issues submitted to the expert shall be subject to the Tribunal's power of assessment of those issues in the context of all the circumstances of the case, unless the parties have agreed that the expert's determination shall be conclusive in respect of any specific issue.

Default

Article 56

(a)　If the Claimant, without showing good cause, fails to submit its Statement of Claim in accordance with Article 41, the Tribunal shall terminate the proceedings.

(b)　If the Respondent, without showing good cause, fails to submit its Statement of Defense in accordance with Article 42, the Tribunal may nevertheless proceed with the arbitration and make the award.

(c)　The Tribunal may also proceed with the arbitration and make the award if a party, without showing good cause, fails to avail itself of the opportunity to present its case within the period of time determined by the Tribunal.

(d)　If a party, without showing good cause, fails to comply with any provision of, or requirement under, these Rules or any direction given by the Tribunal, the Tribunal may draw the inferences therefrom that it considers appropriate.

Closure of Proceedings

Article 57

(a)　The Tribunal shall declare the proceedings closed when it is satisfied that the parties have had adequate opportunity to present submissions and evidence.

(b)　The Tribunal may, if it considers it necessary owing to exceptional circumstances, decide, on its own motion or upon application of a party, to re-open the proceedings it declared to be closed at any time before the award is made.

Waiver

Article 58

A party which knows that any provision of, or requirement under, these Rules, or any direction given by the Tribunal, has not been complied with, and yet proceeds with the arbitration without promptly recording an objection to such non-compliance, shall be deemed to have waived its right to object.

V. AWARDS AND OTHER DECISIONS

Laws Applicable to the Substance of the Dispute, the Arbitration and the Arbitration Agreement

Article 59

(a)   The Tribunal shall decide the substance of the dispute in accordance with the law or rules of law chosen by the parties. Any designation of the law of a given State shall be construed, unless otherwise expressed, as directly referring to the substantive law of that State and not to its conflict of laws rules. Failing a choice by the parties, the Tribunal shall apply the law or rules of law that it determines to be appropriate. In all cases, the Tribunal shall decide having due regard to the terms of any relevant contract and taking into account applicable trade usages. The Tribunal may decide as *amiable compositeur* or *ex aequo et bono* only if the parties have expressly authorized it to do so.

(b)   The law applicable to the arbitration shall be the arbitration law of the place of arbitration, unless the parties have expressly agreed on the application of another arbitration law and such agreement is permitted by the law of the place of arbitration.

(c)   An Arbitration Agreement shall be regarded as effective if it conforms to the requirements concerning form, existence, validity and scope of either the law or rules of law applicable in accordance with paragraph (a), or the law applicable in accordance with paragraph (b).

Currency and Interest

Article 60

(a)   Monetary amounts in the award may be expressed in any currency.

(b)   The Tribunal may award simple or compound interest to be paid by a party on any sum awarded against that party. It shall be free to determine the interest at such rates as it considers to be appropriate, without being bound by legal rates of interest, and shall be free to determine the period for which the interest shall be paid.

Decision-Making

Article 61

Unless the parties have agreed otherwise, where there is more than one arbitrator, any award, order or other decision of the Tribunal shall be made by a majority. In the absence of a majority, the presiding arbitrator shall make the award, order or other decision as if acting as sole arbitrator.

Form and Notification of Awards

Article 62

(a)   The Tribunal may make <u>preliminary</u>, <u>interim</u>, <u>interlocutory</u>, <u>partial</u> or <u>final</u> awards.

(b)   <u>The award shall be in writing and shall state the date on which it was made,</u> as well as the place of arbitration in accordance with Article 39(a).

(c)   <u>The award shall state the reasons on which it is based,</u> unless the parties have agreed that no reasons should be stated and <u>the law applicable to the arbitration does not require the statement of such reasons.</u>

(d)   <u>The award shall be signed by the arbitrator or arbitrators.</u> The signature of the award by a majority of the arbitrators, or, in the case of Article 61, second sentence, by the presiding arbitrator, shall be sufficient. Where an arbitrator fails to sign, <u>the award shall state the reason for the absence of the signature.</u>

(e)   The Tribunal may consult the Center <u>with regard to matters of form,</u> particularly <u>to ensure the enforceability of the award.</u>

(f)   The award shall be communicated by the Tribunal to the Center in a number of originals sufficient to provide one for each party, the arbitrator or arbitrators and the Center. The Center shall formally communicate an original of the award to each party and the arbitrator or arbitrators.

(g)   At the request of a party, the Center shall provide it, at cost, with a copy of the award certified by the Center. A copy so certified shall be deemed to comply with the requirements of Article IV(1)(a) of the Convention on the Recognition and Enforcement of Foreign Arbitral Awards, New York, June 10, 1958.

Time Period for Delivery of the Final Award

Article 63

(a)   The arbitration should, wherever reasonably possible, be heard and the proceedings declared closed within not more than nine months after either the delivery of the Statement of Defense or the establishment of the Tribunal, whichever event occurs later. The final award should, wherever reasonably possible, be made within three months thereafter.

(b)   If the proceedings are not declared closed within the period of time specified in paragraph (a), the Tribunal shall send the Center a status report on the arbitration, with a copy to each party. It shall send a further status report to the Center, and a copy to each party, at the end of each ensuing period of three months during which the proceedings have not been declared closed.

(c)   If the final award is not made within three months after the closure of the proceedings, the Tribunal shall send the Center a written explanation for the delay, with a copy to each party. It shall send a further explanation, and a copy to each party, at the end of each ensuing period of one month until the final award is made.

Effect of Award

Article 64

(a)   By agreeing to arbitration under these Rules, the parties undertake to carry out the award without delay, and waive their right to any form of appeal or recourse to a court of law or other judicial authority, insofar as such waiver may validly be made under the applicable law.

(b)   The award shall be effective and binding on the parties as from the date it is communicated by the Center pursuant to Article 62(f), second sentence.

Settlement or Other Grounds for Termination

Article 65

(a)   The Tribunal may suggest that the parties explore settlement at such times as the Tribunal may deem appropriate.

(b)   If, before the award is made, the parties agree on a settlement of the dispute, the Tribunal shall terminate the arbitration and, if requested jointly by the parties, record the settlement in the form of a consent award. The Tribunal shall not be obliged to give reasons for such an award.

(c)   If, before the award is made, the continuation of the arbitration becomes unnecessary or impossible for any reason not mentioned in paragraph (b), the Tribunal shall inform the parties of its intention to terminate the arbitration. The Tribunal shall have the power to issue such an order terminating the arbitration, unless a party raises justifiable grounds for objection within a period of time to be determined by the Tribunal.

(d)   The consent award or the order for termination of the arbitration shall be signed by the arbitrator or arbitrators in accordance with Article 62(d) and shall be communicated by the Tribunal to the Center in a number of originals sufficient to provide one for each party, the arbitrator or arbitrators and the Center. The Center shall communicate an original of the consent award or the order for termination to each party and the arbitrator or arbitrators.

Correction of the Award and Additional Award

Article 66

(a)   Within 30 days after receipt of the award, a party may, by notice to the Tribunal, with a copy to the Center and the other party, request the Tribunal to correct in the award any clerical, typographical or computational errors. If the Tribunal considers the request to be justified, it shall make the correction within 30 days after receipt of the request. Any correction, which shall take the form of a separate memorandum, signed by the Tribunal in accordance with Article 62(d), shall become part of the award.

(b) The Tribunal may correct any error of the type referred to in paragraph (a) on its own initiative within 30 days after the date of the award.

(c) A party may, within 30 days after receipt of the award, by notice to the Tribunal, with a copy to the Center and the other party, request the Tribunal to make an additional award as to claims presented in the arbitral proceedings but not dealt with in the award. Before deciding on the request, the Tribunal shall give the parties an opportunity to be heard. If the Tribunal considers the request to be justified, it shall, wherever reasonably possible, make the additional award within 60 days of receipt of the request.

VI. FEES AND COSTS

Fees of the Center

Article 67

(a) The Request for Arbitration shall be subject to the payment to the Center of a registration fee, which shall belong to the International Bureau of WIPO. The amount of the registration fee shall be fixed in the Schedule of Fees applicable on the date on which the Request for Arbitration is received by the Center.

(b) The registration fee shall not be refundable.

(c) No action shall be taken by the Center on a Request for Arbitration until the registration fee has been paid.

(d) If a Claimant fails, within 15 days after a second reminder in writing from the Center, to pay the registration fee, it shall be deemed to have withdrawn its Request for Arbitration.

Article 68

(a) An administration fee, which shall belong to the International Bureau of WIPO, shall be payable by the Claimant to the Center within 30 days after the commencement of the arbitration. The Center shall notify the Claimant of the amount of the administration fee as soon as possible after receipt of the Request for Arbitration.

(b) In the case of a counter-claim, an administration fee shall also be payable by the Respondent to the Center within 30 days after the date on which the counter-claim referred to in Article 42(c) is made. The Center shall notify the Respondent of the amount of the administration fee as soon as possible after receipt of notification of the counter-claim.

(c) The amount of the administration fee shall be calculated in accordance with the Schedule of Fees applicable on the date of commencement of the arbitration.

(d) Where a claim or counter-claim is increased, the amount of the administration fee may be increased in accordance with the Schedule of Fees applicable under paragraph (c), and the increased amount shall be payable by the Claimant or the Respondent, as the case may be.

(e)   If a party fails, within 15 days after a second reminder in writing from the Center, to pay any administration fee due, it shall be deemed to have withdrawn its claim or counter-claim, or its increase in claim or counter-claim, as the case may be.

(f)   The Tribunal shall, in a timely manner, inform the Center of the amount of the claim and any counter-claim, as well as any increase thereof.

Fees of the Arbitrators

Article 69

(a)   The amount and currency of the fees of the arbitrators and the modalities and timing of their payment shall be fixed, in accordance with the provisions of this Article, by the Center, after consultation with the arbitrators and the parties.

(b)   The amount of the fees of the arbitrators shall, unless the parties and arbitrators agree otherwise, be determined within the range of minimum and maximum fees set out in the Schedule of Fees applicable on the date of the commencement of the arbitration, taking into account the estimated time needed by the arbitrators for conducting the arbitration, the amount in dispute, the complexity of the subject-matter of the dispute, the urgency of the case and any other relevant circumstances of the case.

Deposits

Article 70

(a)   Upon receipt of notification from the Center of the establishment of the Tribunal, the Claimant and the Respondent shall each deposit an equal amount as an advance for the costs of arbitration referred to in Article 71. The amount of the deposit shall be determined by the Center.

(b)   In the course of the arbitration, the Center may require that the parties make supplementary deposits.

(c)   If the required deposits are not paid in full within 30 days after receipt of the corresponding notification, the Center shall so inform the parties in order that one or other of them may make the required payment.

(d)   Where the amount of the counter-claim greatly exceeds the amount of the claim or involves the examination of significantly different matters, or where it otherwise appears appropriate in the circumstances, the Center in its discretion may establish two separate deposits on account of claim and counter-claim. If separate deposits are established, the totality of the deposit on account of claim shall be paid by the Claimant and the totality of the deposit on account of counter-claim shall be paid by the Respondent.

(e)   If a party fails, within 15 days after a second reminder in writing from the Center, to pay the required deposit, it shall be deemed to have withdrawn the relevant claim or counter-claim.

(f)   After the award has been made, the Center shall, in accordance with the award, render an accounting to the parties of the deposits received and return any unexpended balance to the parties or require the payment of any amount owing from the parties.

Award of Costs of Arbitration

Article 71

(a)   In its award, the Tribunal shall fix the costs of arbitration, which shall consist of:

   (i)   the arbitrators' fees,

   (ii)   the properly incurred travel, communication and other expenses of the arbitrators,

   (iii)   the costs of expert advice and such other assistance required by the Tribunal pursuant to these Rules, and

   (iv)   such other expenses as are necessary for the conduct of the arbitration proceedings, such as the cost of meeting and hearing facilities.

(b)   The aforementioned costs shall, as far as possible, be debited from the deposits required under Article 70.

(c)   The Tribunal shall, subject to any agreement of the parties, apportion the costs of arbitration and the registration and administration fees of the Center between the parties in the light of all the circumstances and the outcome of the arbitration.

Award of Costs Incurred by a Party

Article 72

In its award, the Tribunal may, subject to any contrary agreement by the parties and in the light of all the circumstances and the outcome of the arbitration, order a party to pay the whole or part of reasonable expenses incurred by the other party in presenting its case, including those incurred for legal representatives and witnesses.

VII.   CONFIDENTIALITY

Confidentiality of the Existence of the Arbitration

Article 73

(a)   Except to the extent necessary in connection with a court challenge to the arbitration or an action for enforcement of an award, no information concerning the existence of an arbitration may be unilaterally disclosed by a party to any third party unless it is required to do so by law or by a competent regulatory body, and then only

   (i)   by disclosing no more than what is legally required, and

   (ii)   by furnishing to the Tribunal and to the other party, if the disclosure takes place during the arbitration, or to the other party alone, if the disclosure takes place after the termination of the arbitration, details of the disclosure and an explanation of the reason for it.

(b) Notwithstanding paragraph (a), a party may disclose to a third party the names of the parties to the arbitration and the relief requested for the purpose of satisfying any obligation of good faith or candor owed to that third party.

Confidentiality of Disclosures Made During the Arbitration

Article 74

(a) In addition to any specific measures that may be available under Article 52, any documentary or other evidence given by a party or a witness in the arbitration shall be treated as confidential and, to the extent that such evidence describes information that is not in the public domain, shall not be used or disclosed by a party whose access to that information arises exclusively as a result of its participation in the arbitration to any third party for any purpose without the consent of the parties or order of a court having jurisdiction.

(b) For the purposes of this Article, a witness called by a party shall not be considered to be a third party. To the extent that a witness is given access to evidence or other information obtained in the arbitration in order to prepare the witness's testimony, the party calling such witness shall be responsible for the maintenance by the witness of the same degree of confidentiality as that required of the party.

Confidentiality of the Award

Article 75

The award shall be treated as confidential by the parties and may only be disclosed to a third party if and to the extent that

(i)   the parties consent, or

(ii) it falls into the public domain as a result of an action before a national court or other competent authority, or

(iii) it must be disclosed in order to comply with a legal requirement imposed on a party or in order to establish or protect a party's legal rights against a third party.

Maintenance of Confidentiality by the Center and Arbitrator

Article 76

(a) Unless the parties agree otherwise, the Center and the arbitrator shall maintain the confidentiality of the arbitration, the award and, to the extent that they describe information that is not in the public domain, any documentary or other evidence disclosed during the arbitration, except to the extent necessary in connection with a court action relating to the award, or as otherwise required by law.

(b)   Notwithstanding paragraph (a), the Center may include information concerning the arbitration in any aggregate statistical data that it publishes concerning its activities, provided that such information does not enable the parties or the particular circumstances of the dispute to be identified.

VIII.   MISCELLANEOUS

Exclusion of Liability

Article 77

Except in respect of deliberate wrongdoing, the arbitrator or arbitrators, WIPO and the Center shall not be liable to a party for any act or omission in connection with the arbitration.

Waiver of Defamation

Article 78

The parties and, by acceptance of appointment, the arbitrator agree that any statements or comments, whether written or oral, made or used by them or their representatives in preparation for or in the course of the arbitration shall not be relied upon to found or maintain any action for defamation, libel, slander or any related complaint, and this Article may be pleaded as a bar to any such action.

SCHEDULE OF FEES

(All amounts are in United States dollars)

Fees of the Center

I. Registration Fee (Article 67, WIPO Arbitration Rules)

Amount of Claim	Registration Fee
Up to $1,000,000	$1,000
$1,000,001 to $10,000,000	$2,000
Over $10,000,000	$3,000

Notes

1. Where the amount of the claim is not specified at the time of submitting the Request for Arbitration, a registration fee of $1,000 shall be payable, subject to adjustment when the Statement of Claim is filed.

2. Where a claim is not for a monetary amount, a registration fee of $1,000 shall be payable, subject to adjustment. The adjustment shall be made by reference to the registration fee that the Center, upon examination of the Request for Arbitration or the Statement of Claim, determines to be appropriate in the circumstances.

3. The amount of claims expressed in currencies other than United States dollars shall, for the purposes of calculating the registration fee, be converted to amounts expressed in United States dollars on the basis of the official United Nations exchange rate prevailing on the date of submission of the Request for Arbitration.

II. Administration Fee (Article 68, WIPO Arbitration Rules)

Amount of Claim or Counter-Claim	Administration Fee
Up to $100,000	$1,000
$100,001 to $1,000,000	$1,000 + 0.40% (of the amount above $100,000)
$1,000,001 to $5,000,000	$4,600 + 0.20% (of the amount above $1,000,000)
$5,000,001 to $20,000,000	$12,600 + 0.10% (of the amount above $5,000,000)
Over $20,000,000	$27,600 + 0.05% (of the amount above $20,000,000 up to a *maximum* administration fee of $35,000)

SCHEDULE OF FEES (continued)

Notes

1. Where a claim or counter-claim is not for a monetary amount, the Center shall determine an appropriate administration fee.
2. For the purpose of calculating the administration fee, the percentage figures are applied to each successive part of the amount of claim or counter-claim. For example, if the amount of claim is $5,000,000, the administration fee would be calculated as follows:

$100,000		$1,000
$900,000 (difference between $100,000 and $1,000,000)	0.40%	$3,600
$4,000,000 (difference between $1,000,000 and $5,000,000)	0.20%	$8,000
$5,000,000		$12,600

3. The maximum administration fee payable is $35,000.
4. The amounts of claims or counter-claims expressed in currencies other than United States dollars shall, for the purposes of calculating the administration fee, be converted to amounts expressed in United States dollars on the basis of the official United Nations exchange rate prevailing on the date of submission of the claim or of the counter-claim, respectively.

Arbitrators' Fees
(See Table, page 288)

Notes

1. For the purpose of calculating the amount of claims, the value of any counter-claim is added to the amount of the claim.
2. For the purpose of calculating the minimum and maximum amounts of the arbitrators' fees, the percentage figures are applied to each successive part of the whole amount of claims. For example, if the amount of claim is $1,500,000, the minimum fees for a sole arbitrator would be calculated as follows:

SCHEDULE OF FEES (continued)

$100,000		$2,000
$400,000 (difference between $100,000 and $500,000)	2.00%	$8,000
$500,000 (difference between $500,000 and $1,000,000)	1.50%	$7,500
$500,000 (difference between $1,000,000 and $1,500,000)	1.00%	$5,000
$1,500,000		$22,500

3. Where a claim or counter-claim is not for a monetary amount, the Center shall, in consultation with the arbitrators and the parties, determine an appropriate value for the claim or counter-claim for the purpose of determining the arbitrators' fees.

4. The amounts of claims or counter-claims expressed in currencies other than United States dollars shall, for the purpose of determining the arbitrators' fees, be converted to amounts expressed in United States dollars on the basis of the official United Nations exchange rate prevailing on the date of submission of the claim or of the counter-claim, respectively.

5. The amounts and percentage figures specified in the Table for a three-person Tribunal represent the total fees payable to such a Tribunal, and not the fees payable to each arbitrator. Such fees shall be distributed between the three persons in accordance with the unanimous decision of those three persons. In the absence of such a decision, the distribution shall be 40 per cent for the presiding arbitrator, and 30 per cent for each of the other two arbitrators.

6. Where, by the agreement of the parties, a number of arbitrators other than one or three is appointed to a Tribunal, the scale of minimum and maximum fees for the Tribunal in question shall be determined by the Center. That scale shall be so determined by multiplying the scale for a sole arbitrator by the number of arbitrators reduced by a factor that takes account of the sharing of work and responsibility among the arbitrators.

Arbitrators' Fees
(Article 69, WIPO Arbitration Rules)

Amount of Claims	Fees			
	Minimum		Maximum	
	Sole Arbitrator	Three-person Tribunal	Sole Arbitrator	Three-person Tribunal
Up to $100,000	$2,000	$5,000	10.00%	25.00%
$100,001 to $500,000	$2,000 + 2.00% (of the amount above $100,000)	$5,000 + 5.00% (of the amount above $100,000)	$10,000 + 4.00% (of the amount above $100,000)	$25,000 + 10.00% (of the amount above $100,000)
$500,001 to $1,000,000	$10,000 + 1.50% (of the amount above $500,000)	$25,000 + 3.75% (of the amount above $500,000)	$26,000 + 3.50% (of the amount above $500,000)	$65,000 + 8.75% (of the amount above $500,000)
$1,000,001 to $2,000,000	$17,500 + 1.00% (of the amount above $1,000,000)	$43,750 + 2.50% (of the amount above $1,000,000)	$43,500 + 2.00% (of the amount above $1,000,000)	$108,750 + 5.00% (of the amount above $1,000,000)
$2,000,001 to $5,000,000	$27,500 + 0.75% (of the amount above $2,000,000)	$68,750 + 1.90% (of the amount above $2,000,000)	$63,500 + 1.50% (of the amount above $2,000,000)	$158,750 + 3.75% (of the amount above $2,000,000)
$5,000,001 to $10,000,000	$50,000 + 0.50% (of the amount above $5,000,000)	$125,750 + 1.25% (of the amount above $5,000,000)	$108,500 + 1.00% (of the amount above $5,000,000)	$271,250 + 2.50% (of the amount above $5,000,000)
$10,000,001 to $25,000,000	$75,000 + 0.30% (of the amount above $10,000,000)	$188,250 + 0.75% (of the amount above $10,000,000)	$158,500 + 1.00% (of the amount above $10,000,000)	$396,250 + 2.50% (of the amount above $10,000,000)
Over $25,000,000	$120,000 + 0.25% (of the amount above $25,000,000)	$300,750 + 0.65% (of the amount above $25,000,000)	$308,500 + 1.00% (of the amount above $25,000,000)	$771,250 + 2.50% (of the amount above $25,000,000)

WIPO EXPEDITED ARBITRATION RULES*
(Effective from October 1, 1994)

CONTENTS

---

* EDITOR'S NOTE: Text in bold indicates where the WIPO Arbitration Rules have been modified.

I. GENERAL PROVISIONS

Abbreviated Expressions

Article 1

In these Rules:

"Arbitration Agreement" means an agreement by the parties to submit to arbitration all or certain disputes which have arisen or which may arise between them; an Arbitration Agreement may be in the form of an arbitration clause in a contract or in the form of a separate contract;

"Claimant" means the party initiating an arbitration;

"Respondent" means the party against which the arbitration is initiated, as named in the Request for Arbitration;

"Tribunal" means the arbitrator;

"WIPO" means the World Intellectual Property Organization;

"Center" means the WIPO Arbitration Center, a unit of the International Bureau of WIPO;

Words used in the singular include the plural and vice versa, as the context may require.

Scope of Application of Rules

Article 2

Where an Arbitration Agreement provides for arbitration under the WIPO *Expedited* Arbitration Rules, these Rules shall be deemed to form part of that Arbitration Agreement and the dispute shall be settled in accordance with these Rules, as in effect on the date of the commencement of the arbitration, unless the parties have agreed otherwise.

Article 3

(a)   These Rules shall govern the arbitration, except that, where any of these Rules is in conflict with a provision of the law applicable to the arbitration from which the parties cannot derogate, that provision shall prevail.

(b)   The law applicable to the arbitration shall be determined in accordance with Article 59(b).

Notices, Periods of Time

Article 4

(a)   Any notice or other communication that may or is required to be given under these Rules shall be in writing and shall be delivered by expedited postal or courier service, or transmitted by telex, telefax or other means of telecommunication that provide a record thereof.

(b)   A party's last-known residence or place of business shall be a valid address for the purpose of any notice or other communication in the absence of any notification of a change by that party. Communications may in any event be addressed to a party in the manner stipulated or, failing such a stipulation, according to the practice followed in the course of the dealings between the parties.

(c)   For the purpose of determining the date of commencement of a time-limit, a notice or other communication shall be deemed to have been received on the day it is delivered or, in the case of telecommunications, transmitted in accordance with paragraphs (a) and (b) of this Article.

(d)   For the purpose of determining compliance with a time-limit, a notice or other communication shall be deemed to have been sent, made or transmitted if it is despatched, in accordance with paragraphs (a) and (b) of this Article, prior to or on the day of the expiration of the time limit.

(e)   For the purpose of calculating a period of time under these Rules, such period shall begin to run on the day following the day when a notice or other communication is received. If the last day of such period is an official holiday or a non-business day at the residence or place of business of the addressee, the period is extended until the first business day which follows. Official holidays or non-business days occurring during the running of the period of time are included in calculating the period.

(f)   The parties may agree to reduce or extend the periods of time referred to in **Articles 11, 14(b), 43(a), 53(b) and 55(a).**

(g)   The Center may, at the request of a party or on its own motion, extend the periods of time referred to in **Articles 11, 14(b), 43(a), 53(b), 55(a), 67(d), 68(e) and 70(e).**

(h) The Center may, in consultation with the parties, reduce the period of time referred to in Article 11.

Documents Required to Be Submitted to the Center

Article 5

(a)   Until the notification by the Center of the establishment of the Tribunal, any written statement, notice or other communication required or allowed under Articles 6 to 36 shall be submitted by a party to the Center and a copy thereof shall at the same time be transmitted by that party to the other party.

(b)   Any written statement, notice or other communication so sent to the Center shall be sent in the number of copies required to provide one copy for the envisaged arbitrator and one for the Center.

(c)   After the notification by the Center of the establishment of the Tribunal, any written statements, notices or other communications shall be submitted by a party directly to the Tribunal and a copy thereof shall at the same time be supplied by that party to the other party.

(d)   The Tribunal shall send to the Center a copy of each order or other decision that it makes.

II.   COMMENCEMENT OF THE ARBITRATION

Request for Arbitration

Article 6

The Claimant shall transmit the Request for Arbitration to the Center and to the Respondent.

Article 7

The date of commencement of the arbitration shall be the date on which the Request for Arbitration is received by the Center.

Article 8

The Center shall inform the Claimant and the Respondent of the receipt by it of the Request for Arbitration and of the date of the commencement of the arbitration.

Article 9

The Request for Arbitration shall contain:

(i)   a demand that the dispute be referred to arbitration under the WIPO *Expedited* Arbitration Rules;

(ii)   the names, addresses and telephone, telex, telefax or other communication references of the parties and of the representative of the Claimant;

(iii)   a copy of the Arbitration Agreement and, if applicable, any separate choice-of-law clause;

(iv)   **[sub-paragraph not used];**

(v)   **[sub-paragraph not used];**

(vi)   **any observations that the Claimant considers useful in connection with Articles 14 and 20.**

Article 10

The Request for Arbitration shall be accompanied by the Statement of Claim in conformity with Article 41(b) and (c).

Answer to the Request

Article 11

Within 20 days from the date on which the Respondent receives the Request for Arbitration from the Claimant or within ten days from the date of the appointment of the Tribunal, whichever event occurs later, the Respondent shall

address to the Center and to the Claimant an Answer to the Request which shall contain comments on any of the items in the Request for Arbitration.

Article 12

The Answer to the Request shall be accompanied by the Statement of Defense in conformity with Article 42(b) and (c).

Representation

Article 13

(a)   The parties may be represented by persons of their choice, irrespective of, in particular, nationality or professional qualification. The names, addresses and telephone, telex, telefax or other communication references of representatives shall be communicated to the Center, the other party and, after its establishment, the Tribunal.

(b)   Each party shall ensure that its representatives have sufficient time available to enable the arbitration to proceed expeditiously.

(c)   The parties may also be assisted by persons of their choice.

III.   COMPOSITION AND ESTABLISHMENT OF THE TRIBUNAL

Sole Arbitrator

Article 14

(a)   The Tribunal shall consist of a sole arbitrator, who shall be appointed jointly by the parties.

(b)   If the appointment of the sole arbitrator is not made within 15 days after the commencement of the arbitration, the sole arbitrator shall be appointed by the Center.

Article 15

[Article not used]

Article 16

[Article not used]

Article 17

[Article not used]

Article 18

[Article not used]

Article 19

[Article not used]

Nationality of Arbitrator

Article 20

(a) An agreement of the parties concerning the nationality of the arbitrator shall be respected.

(b) If the parties have not agreed on the nationality of the arbitrator, the arbitrator shall, in the absence of special circumstances such as the need to appoint a person having particular qualifications, be a national of a country other than the countries of the parties.

Communication Between Parties and Candidates for Appointment as Arbitrator

Article 21

No party or anyone acting on its behalf shall have any *ex parte* communication with any candidate for appointment as arbitrator except to discuss the candidate's qualifications, availability or independence in relation to the parties.

Impartiality and Independence

Article 22

(a) The arbitrator shall be impartial and independent.

(b) The prospective arbitrator shall, before accepting appointment, disclose to the parties and the Center any circumstances that might give rise to justifiable doubt as to the arbitrator's impartiality or independence, or confirm in writing that no such circumstances exist.

(c) If, at any stage during the arbitration, new circumstances arise that might give rise to justifiable doubt as to the arbitrator's impartiality or independence, the arbitrator shall promptly disclose such circumstances to the parties and the Center.

Availability, Acceptance and Notification

Article 23

(a) The arbitrator shall, by accepting appointment, be deemed to have undertaken to make available sufficient time to enable the arbitration to be conducted and completed expeditiously.

(b) The prospective arbitrator shall accept appointment in writing and shall communicate such acceptance to the Center.

(c) The Center shall notify the parties of the establishment of the Tribunal.

Challenge of Arbitrator

Article 24

(a)   The arbitrator may be challenged by a party if circumstances exist that give rise to justifiable doubt as to the arbitrator's impartiality or independence.

(b)   A party may challenge an arbitrator whom it has appointed or in whose appointment it concurred only for reasons of which it becomes aware after the appointment has been made.

Article 25

A party challenging the arbitrator shall send notice to the Center, the Tribunal and the other party, stating the reasons for the challenge, within seven days after being notified of that arbitrator's appointment or after becoming aware of the circumstances that it considers give rise to justifiable doubt as to that arbitrator's impartiality or independence.

Article 26

When the arbitrator has been challenged by a party, the other party shall have the right to respond to the challenge and shall, if it exercises this right, send, within seven days after receipt of the notice referred to in Article 25, a copy of its response to the Center, the party making the challenge and the arbitrator.

Article 27

The Tribunal may, in its discretion, suspend or continue the arbitral proceedings during the pendency of the challenge.

Article 28

The other party may agree to the challenge or the arbitrator may voluntarily withdraw. In either case, the arbitrator shall be replaced without any implication that the grounds for the challenge are valid.

Article 29

If the other party does not agree to the challenge and the challenged arbitrator does not withdraw, the decision on the challenge shall be made by the Center in accordance with its internal procedures. Such a decision is of an administrative nature and shall be final. The Center shall not be required to state reasons for its decision.

Release from Appointment

Article 30

At the arbitrator's own request, the arbitrator may be released from appointment as arbitrator either with the consent of the parties or by the Center.

Article 31

Irrespective of any request by the arbitrator, the parties may jointly release the arbitrator from appointment as arbitrator. The parties shall promptly notify the Center of such release.

Article 32

At the request of a party or on its own motion, the Center may release the arbitrator from appointment as arbitrator if the arbitrator has become *de jure* or *de facto* unable to fulfill, or fails to fulfill, the duties of an arbitrator. In such a case, the parties shall be offered the opportunity to express their views thereon and the provisions of Articles 26 to 29 shall apply *mutatis mutandis*.

Replacement of Arbitrator

Article 33

(a)   Whenever necessary, a substitute arbitrator shall be appointed pursuant to the procedure provided for in Article **14** that was applicable to the appointment of the arbitrator being replaced.

(b)   **[Paragraph not used]**

(c)   Pending the replacement, the arbitral proceedings shall be suspended, unless otherwise agreed by the parties.

Article 34

Whenever a substitute arbitrator is appointed, the Tribunal shall, having regard to any observations of the parties, determine in its sole discretion whether all or part of any prior hearings are to be repeated.

Article 35

[Article not used]

Pleas as to the Jurisdiction of the Tribunal

Article 36

(a)   The Tribunal shall have the power to hear and determine objections to its own jurisdiction, including any objections with respect to form, existence, validity or scope of the Arbitration Agreement examined pursuant to Article 59(b).

(b)   The Tribunal shall have the power to determine the existence or validity of any contract of which the Arbitration Agreement forms part or to which it relates.

(c)   A plea that the Tribunal does not have jurisdiction shall be raised not later than in the Statement of Defense or, with respect to a counter-claim or a set-off, the Statement of Defense thereto, failing which any such plea shall be barred in the subsequent arbitral proceedings or before any court. A plea that the Tribunal is exceeding the scope of its authority shall be raised as soon as the matter alleged to be beyond the scope of its authority is raised during the arbitral proceedings. The Tribunal may, in either case, admit a later plea if it considers the delay justified.

(d)   The Tribunal may rule on a plea referred to in paragraph (c) as a preliminary question or, in its sole discretion, decide on such a plea in the final award.

(e)   A plea that the Tribunal lacks jurisdiction shall not preclude the Center from administering the arbitration.

IV.   CONDUCT OF THE ARBITRATION

Transmission of the File to the Tribunal

Article 37

The Center shall transmit the file to the arbitrator as soon as the arbitrator is appointed.

General Powers of the Tribunal

Article 38

(a)   Subject to Article 3, the Tribunal may conduct the arbitration in such manner as it considers appropriate.

(b)   In all cases, the Tribunal shall ensure that the parties are treated with equality and that each party is given a fair opportunity to present its case.

(c)   The Tribunal shall ensure that the arbitral procedure takes place with due expedition. It may, at the request of a party or on its own motion, extend in exceptional cases a period of time fixed by these Rules, by itself or agreed to by the parties.

Place of Arbitration

Article 39

(a)   Unless otherwise agreed by the parties, the place of arbitration shall be decided by the Center, taking into consideration any observations of the parties and the circumstances of the arbitration.

(b)   The Tribunal may, after consultation with the parties, conduct hearings at any place that it considers appropriate. It may deliberate wherever it deems appropriate.

(c)   The award shall be deemed to have been made at the place of arbitration.

Language of Arbitration

Article 40

(a)   Unless otherwise agreed by the parties, the language of the arbitration shall be the language of the Arbitration Agreement, subject to the power of the Tribunal to determine otherwise, having regard to any observations of the parties and the circumstances of the arbitration.

(b)   The Tribunal may order that any documents submitted in languages other than the language of arbitration be accompanied by a translation in whole or in part into the language of arbitration.

Statement of Claim

Article 41

(a)   **[Paragraph not used]**

(b)   The Statement of Claim shall contain a comprehensive statement of the facts and legal arguments supporting the claim, including a statement of the relief sought.

(c)   The Statement of Claim shall, to as large an extent as possible, be accompanied by the documentary evidence upon which the Claimant relies, together with a schedule of such documents. Where the documentary evidence is especially voluminous, the Claimant may add a reference to further documents it is prepared to submit.

Statement of Defense

Article 42

(a)   **[Paragraph not used]**

(b)   The Statement of Defense shall reply to the particulars of the Statement of Claim required pursuant to Article 41(b). The Statement of Defense shall be accompanied by the corresponding documentary evidence described in Article 41(c).

(c)   Any counter-claim or set-off by the Respondent shall be made or asserted in the Statement of Defense or, in exceptional circumstances, at a later stage in the arbitral proceedings if so determined by the Tribunal. Any such counter-claim or set-off shall contain the same particulars as those specified in Article 41(b) and (c).

Further Written Statements

Article 43

(a)   In the event that a counter-claim or set-off has been made or asserted, the Claimant shall reply to the particulars thereof **within 20 days from the date on which the Claimant receives such counter-claim or set-off**. Article **42(b)** shall apply *mutatis mutandis* to such reply.

(b)   The Tribunal may, in its discretion, allow or require further written statements.

Amendments to Claims or Defense

Article 44

Subject to any contrary agreement by the parties, a party may amend or supplement its claim, counter-claim, defense or set-off during the course of the arbitral proceedings, unless the Tribunal considers it inappropriate to allow such amendment having regard to its nature or the delay in making it and to the provisions of Article 38(b) and (c).

Communication Between Parties and Tribunal

Article 45

Except as otherwise provided in these Rules or permitted by the Tribunal, no party or anyone acting on its behalf may have any *ex parte* communication with the arbitrator with respect to any matter of substance relating to the arbitration, it being understood that nothing in this paragraph shall prohibit *ex parte* communications which concern matters of a purely organizational nature, such as the physical facilities, place, date or time of the hearings.

Interim Measures of Protection; Security for Claims and Costs

Article 46

(a)   At the request of a party, the Tribunal may issue any provisional orders or take other interim measures it deems necessary, including injunctions and measures for the conservation of goods which form part of the subject-matter in dispute, such as an order for their deposit with a third person or for the sale of perishable goods. The Tribunal may make the granting of such measures subject to appropriate security being furnished by the requesting party.

(b)   At the request of a party, the Tribunal may, if it considers it to be required by exceptional circumstances, order the other party to provide security, in a form to be determined by the Tribunal, for the claim or counter-claim, as well as for costs referred to in Article 72.

(c)   Measures and orders contemplated under this Article may take the form of an interim award.

(d)   A request addressed by a party to a judicial authority for interim measures or for security for the claim or counter-claim, or for the implementation of any such measures or orders granted by the Tribunal, shall not be deemed incompatible with the Arbitration Agreement, or deemed to be a waiver of that Agreement.

Preparatory Conference

Article 47

The Tribunal may, in general following the submission of the Statement of Defense, conduct a preparatory conference with the parties for the purpose of organizing and scheduling the subsequent proceedings.

Evidence

Article 48

(a)   The Tribunal shall determine the admissibility, relevance, materiality and weight of evidence.

(b)   At any time during the arbitration, the Tribunal may, at the request of a party or on its own motion, order a party to produce such documents or other evidence as it considers necessary or appropriate and may order a party to make available to the Tribunal or to an expert appointed by it or to the other party any property in its possession or control for inspection or testing.

Experiments

Article 49

(a)   A party may give notice to the Tribunal and to the other party at any reasonable time before a hearing that specified experiments have been conducted on which it intends to rely. The notice shall specify the purpose of the experiment, a summary of the experiment, the method employed, the results and the conclusion. The other party may by notice to the Tribunal request that any or all such experiments be repeated in its presence. If the Tribunal considers such request justified, it shall determine the timetable for the repetition of the experiments.

(b)   For the purposes of this Article, ''experiments'' shall include tests or other processes of verification.

Site Visits

Article 50

The Tribunal may, at the request of a party or on its own motion, inspect or require the inspection of any site, property, machinery, facility, production line, model, film, material, product or process as it deems appropriate. A party may request such an inspection at any reasonable time prior to any hearing, and the Tribunal, if it grants such a request, shall determine the timing and arrangements for the inspection.

Agreed Primers and Models

Article 51

The Tribunal may, where the parties so agree, determine that they shall jointly provide:

(i)   a technical primer setting out the background of the scientific, technical or other specialized information necessary to fully understand the matters in issue; and

(ii)   models, drawings or other materials that the Tribunal or the parties require for reference purposes at any hearing.

Disclosure of Trade Secrets and Other Confidential Information

Article 52

(a)   For the purposes of this Article, confidential information shall mean any information, regardless of the medium in which it is expressed, which is
  (i)   in the possession of a party,
  (ii)   not accessible to the public,
  (iii)   of commercial, financial or industrial significance, and
  (iv)   treated as confidential by the party possessing it.

(b)   A party invoking the confidentiality of any information it wishes or is required to submit in the arbitration, including to an expert appointed by the Tribunal, shall make an application to have the information classified as confidential by notice to the Tribunal, with a copy to the other party. Without disclosing the substance of the information, the party shall give in the notice the reasons for which it considers the information confidential.

(c)   The Tribunal shall determine whether the information is to be classified as confidential and of such a nature that the absence of special measures of protection in the proceedings would be likely to cause serious harm to the party invoking its confidentiality. If the Tribunal so determines, it shall decide under which conditions and to whom the confidential information may in part or in whole be disclosed and shall require any person to whom the confidential information is to be disclosed to sign an appropriate confidentiality undertaking.

(d)   In exceptional circumstances, in lieu of itself determining whether the information is to be classified as confidential and of such nature that the absence of special measures of protection in the proceedings would be likely to cause serious harm to the party invoking its confidentiality, the Tribunal may, at the request of a party or on its own motion and after consultation with the parties, designate a confidentiality advisor who will determine whether the information is to be so classified, and, if so, decide under which conditions and to whom it may in part or in whole be disclosed. Any such confidentiality advisor shall be required to sign an appropriate confidentiality undertaking.

(e)   The Tribunal may also, at the request of a party or on its own motion, appoint the confidentiality advisor as an expert in accordance with Article 55 in order to report to it, on the basis of the confidential information, on specific issues designated by the Tribunal without disclosing the confidential information either to the party from whom the confidential information does not originate or to the Tribunal.

Hearings

Article 53

(a)   If either party so requests, the Tribunal shall hold a hearing for the presentation of evidence by witnesses, including expert witnesses, or for oral argument or for both. In the absence of a request, the Tribunal shall decide whether to hold such a hearing or hearings. If no hearings are held, the proceedings shall be conducted on the basis of documents and other materials alone.

(b) **If a hearing is held, it shall be convened within 30 days after the receipt by the Claimant of the Answer to the Request and the Statement of Defense. The Tribunal shall give the parties adequate advance notice of the date, time and place of the hearing. Except in exceptional circumstances, hearings may not exceed three days. Each party shall be expected to bring to the hearing such persons as necessary to adequately inform the Tribunal of the dispute.**

(c) Unless the parties agree otherwise, all hearings shall be in private.

(d) The Tribunal shall determine whether and, if so, in what form a record shall be made of any hearing.

(e) **Within such short period of time after the hearing as is agreed by the parties or, in the absence of such agreement, determined by the Tribunal, each party may communicate to the Tribunal and to the other party a post-hearing brief.**

Witnesses

Article 54

(a) Before any hearing, the Tribunal may require either party to give notice of the identity of witnesses it wishes to call, as well as of the subject matter of their testimony and its relevance to the issues.

(b) The Tribunal has discretion, on the grounds of redundance and irrelevance, to limit or refuse the appearance of any witness, whether witness of fact or expert witness.

(c) Any witness who gives oral evidence may be questioned, under the control of the Tribunal, by each of the parties. The Tribunal may put questions at any stage of the examination of the witnesses.

(d) The testimony of witnesses may, either at the choice of a party or as directed by the Tribunal, be submitted in written form, whether by way of signed statements, sworn affidavits or otherwise, in which case the Tribunal may make the admissibility of the testimony conditional upon the witnesses being made available for oral testimony.

(e) A party shall be responsible for the practical arrangements, cost and availability of any witness it calls.

(f) The Tribunal shall determine whether any witness shall retire during any part of the proceedings, particularly during the testimony of other witnesses.

Experts Appointed by the Tribunal

Article 55

(a) The Tribunal may, after consultation with the parties, appoint one or more independent experts to report to it on specific issues designated by the Tribunal. A copy of the expert's terms of reference, established by the Tribunal, having regard to any observations of the parties, shall be communicated to the parties. Any such expert shall be required to sign an appropriate confidentiality undertaking. **The terms of reference shall include a requirement that the expert report to the Tribunal within 30 days of receipt of the terms of reference**.

(b)   Subject to Article 52, upon receipt of the expert's report, the Tribunal shall communicate a copy of the report to the parties, which shall be given the opportunity to express, in writing, their opinion on the report. A party may, subject to Article 52, examine any document on which the expert has relied in such a report.

(c)   At the request of a party, the parties shall be given the opportunity to question the expert at a hearing. At this hearing, the parties may present expert witnesses to testify on the points at issue.

(d)   The opinion of any expert on the issue or issues submitted to the expert shall be subject to the Tribunal's power of assessment of those issues in the context of all the circumstances of the case, unless the parties have agreed that the expert's determination shall be conclusive in respect of any specific issue.

Default

Article 56

(a)   If the Claimant, without showing good cause, fails to submit its Statement of Claim in accordance with Article 10, the Tribunal shall terminate the proceedings.

(b)   If the Respondent, without showing good cause, fails to submit its Statement of Defense in accordance with Article 12, the Tribunal may nevertheless proceed with the arbitration and make the award.

(c)   The Tribunal may also proceed with the arbitration and make the award if a party, without showing good cause, fails to avail itself of the opportunity to present its case within the period of time determined by the Tribunal.

(d)   If a party, without showing good cause, fails to comply with any provision of, or requirement under, these Rules or any direction given by the Tribunal, the Tribunal may draw the inferences therefrom that it considers appropriate.

Closure of Proceedings

Article 57

(a)   The Tribunal shall declare the proceedings closed when it is satisfied that the parties have had adequate opportunity to present submissions and evidence.

(b)   The Tribunal may, if it considers it necessary owing to exceptional circumstances, decide, on its own motion or upon application of a party, to re-open the proceedings it declared to be closed at any time before the award is made.

Waiver

Article 58

A party which knows that any provision of, or requirement under, these Rules, or any direction given by the Tribunal, has not been complied with, and yet proceeds with the arbitration without promptly recording an objection to such non-compliance, shall be deemed to have waived its right to object.

V. AWARDS AND OTHER DECISIONS

Laws Applicable to the Substance of the Dispute, the Arbitration and the Arbitration Agreement

Article 59

(a)   The Tribunal shall decide the substance of the dispute in accordance with the law or rules of law chosen by the parties. Any designation of the law of a given State shall be construed, unless otherwise expressed, as directly referring to the substantive law of that State and not to its conflict of laws rules. Failing a choice by the parties, the Tribunal shall apply the law or rules of law that it determines to be appropriate. In all cases, the Tribunal shall decide having due regard to the terms of any relevant contract and taking into account applicable trade usages. The Tribunal may decide as *amiable compositeur* or *ex aequo et bono* only if the parties have expressly authorized it to do so.

(b)   The law applicable to the arbitration shall be the arbitration law of the place of arbitration, unless the parties have expressly agreed on the application of another arbitration law and such agreement is permitted by the law of the place of arbitration.

(c)   An Arbitration Agreement shall be regarded as effective if it conforms to the requirements concerning form, existence, validity and scope of either the law or rules of law applicable in accordance with paragraph (a), or the law applicable in accordance with paragraph (b).

Currency and Interest

Article 60

(a)   Monetary amounts in the award may be expressed in any currency.

(b)   The Tribunal may award simple or compound interest to be paid by a party on any sum awarded against that party. It shall be free to determine the interest at such rates as it considers to be appropriate, without being bound by legal rates of interest, and shall be free to determine the period for which the interest shall be paid.

Article 61

[Article not used]

Form and Notification of Awards

Article 62

(a) The Tribunal may make preliminary, interim, interlocutory, partial or final awards.

(b) The award shall be in writing and shall state the date on which it was made, as well as the place of arbitration in accordance with Article 39(a).

(c) The award shall state the reasons on which it is based, unless the parties have agreed that no reasons should be stated and the law applicable to the arbitration does not require the statement of such reasons.

(d) The award shall be signed by the arbitrator.

(e) The Tribunal may consult the Center with regard to matters of form, particularly to ensure the enforceability of the award.

(f) The award shall be communicated by the Tribunal to the Center in a number of originals sufficient to provide one for each party and one for the Center. The Center shall formally communicate an original of the award to each party and the arbitrator.

(g) At the request of a party, the Center shall provide it, at cost, with a copy of the award certified by the Center. A copy so certified shall be deemed to comply with the requirements of Article IV(1)(a) of the Convention on the Recognition and Enforcement of Foreign Arbitral Awards, New York, June 10, 1958.

Time Period for Delivery of the Final Award

Article 63

(a) The arbitration should, wherever reasonably possible, be heard and the proceedings declared closed within not more than **three months** after either the delivery of the Statement of Defense or the establishment of the Tribunal, whichever event occurs later. The final award should, wherever reasonably possible, be made within **one month** thereafter.

(b) If the proceedings are not declared closed within the period of time specified in paragraph (a), the Tribunal shall send the Center a status report on the arbitration, with a copy to each party. It shall send a further status report to the Center, and a copy to each party, at the end of each ensuing period of **one month** during which the proceedings have not been declared closed.

(c) If the final award is not made within **one month** after the closure of the proceedings, the Tribunal shall send the Center a written explanation for the delay, with a copy to each party. It shall send a further explanation, and a copy to each party, at the end of each ensuing period of one month until the final award is made.

Effect of Award

Article 64

(a) By agreeing to arbitration under these Rules, the parties undertake to carry out the award without delay, and waive their right to any form of appeal or recourse to a court of law or other judicial authority, insofar as such waiver may validly be made under the applicable law.

(b)   The award shall be effective and binding on the parties as from the date it is communicated by the Center pursuant to Article 62(f), second sentence.

Settlement or Other Grounds for Termination

Article 65

(a)   The Tribunal may suggest that the parties explore settlement at such times as the Tribunal may deem appropriate.

(b)   If, before the award is made, the parties agree on a settlement of the dispute, the Tribunal shall terminate the arbitration and, if requested jointly by the parties, record the settlement in the form of a consent award. The Tribunal shall not be obliged to give reasons for such an award.

(c)   If, before the award is made, the continuation of the arbitration becomes unnecessary or impossible for any reason not mentioned in paragraph (b), the Tribunal shall inform the parties of its intention to terminate the arbitration. The Tribunal shall have the power to issue such an order terminating the arbitration, unless a party raises justifiable grounds for objection within a period of time to be determined by the Tribunal.

(d)   The consent award or the order for termination of the arbitration shall be signed by the arbitrator and shall be communicated by the Tribunal to the Center in a number of originals sufficient to provide one for each party, the arbitrator and the Center. The Center shall communicate an original of the consent award or the order for termination to each party and the arbitrator.

Correction of the Award and Additional Award

Article 66

(a)   Within 30 days after receipt of the award, a party may, by notice to the Tribunal, with a copy to the Center and the other party, request the Tribunal to correct in the award any clerical, typographical or computational errors. If the Tribunal considers the request to be justified, it shall make the correction within 30 days after receipt of the request. Any correction, which shall take the form of a separate memorandum signed by the Tribunal, shall become part of the award.

(b)   The Tribunal may correct any error of the type referred to in paragraph (a) on its own initiative within 30 days after the date of the award.

(c)   A party may, within 30 days after receipt of the award, by notice to the Tribunal, with a copy to the Center and the other party, request the Tribunal to make an additional award as to claims presented in the arbitral proceedings but not dealt with in the award. Before deciding on the request, the Tribunal shall give the parties an opportunity to be heard. If the Tribunal considers the request to be justified, it shall, wherever reasonably possible, make the additional award within **30** days of receipt of the request.

VI. FEES AND COSTS

Fees of the Center

Article 67

(a)   The Request for Arbitration shall be subject to the payment to the Center of a registration fee, which shall belong to the International Bureau of WIPO. The amount of the registration fee shall be fixed in the Schedule of Fees applicable on the date on which the Request for Arbitration is received by the Center.

(b)   The registration fee shall not be refundable.

(c)   No action shall be taken by the Center on a Request for Arbitration until the registration fee has been paid.

(d)   If a Claimant fails, within 15 days after a second reminder in writing from the Center, to pay the registration fee, it shall be deemed to have withdrawn its Request for Arbitration.

Article 68

(a)   An administration fee, which shall belong to the International Bureau of WIPO, shall be payable by the Claimant to the Center within 30 days after the commencement of the arbitration. The Center shall notify the Claimant of the amount of the administration fee as soon as possible after receipt of the Request for Arbitration.

(b)   In the case of a counter-claim, an administration fee shall also be payable by the Respondent to the Center within 30 days after the date on which the counter-claim referred to in Article 42(c) is made. The Center shall notify the Respondent of the amount of the administration fee as soon as possible after receipt of notification of the counter-claim.

(c)   The amount of the administration fee shall be calculated in accordance with the Schedule of Fees applicable on the date of commencement of the arbitration.

(d)   Where a claim or counter-claim is increased, the amount of the administration fee may be increased in accordance with the Schedule of Fees applicable under paragraph (c), and the increased amount shall be payable by the Claimant or the Respondent, as the case may be.

(e)   If a party fails, within 15 days after a second reminder in writing from the Center, to pay any administration fee due, it shall be deemed to have withdrawn its claim or counter-claim, or its increase in claim or counter-claim, as the case may be.

(f)   The Tribunal shall, in a timely manner, inform the Center of the amount of the claim and any counter-claim, as well as any increase thereof.

Fees of the Arbitrator

Article 69

(a)   The amount and currency of the fees of the arbitrator and the modalities and timing of their payment shall be fixed, in accordance with the provisions of this Article, by the Center, after consultation with the arbitrator and the parties.

(b)   The amount of the fees of the arbitrator shall, unless the parties and arbitrator agree otherwise, be determined within the range of minimum and maximum fees set out in the Schedule of Fees applicable on the date of the commencement of the arbitration, taking into account the estimated time needed by the arbitrator for conducting the arbitration, the amount in dispute, the complexity of the subject-matter of the dispute, the urgency of the case and any other relevant circumstances of the case.

Deposits

Article 70

(a)   Upon receipt of notification from the Center of the establishment of the Tribunal, the Claimant and the Respondent shall each deposit an equal amount as an advance for the costs of arbitration referred to in Article 71. The amount of the deposit shall be determined by the Center.

(b)   In the course of the arbitration, the Center may require that the parties make supplementary deposits.

(c)   If the required deposits are not paid in full within **20** days after receipt of the corresponding notification, the Center shall so inform the parties in order that one or other of them may make the required payment.

(d)   Where the amount of the counter-claim greatly exceeds the amount of the claim or involves the examination of significantly different matters, or where it otherwise appears appropriate in the circumstances, the Center in its discretion may establish two separate deposits on account of claim and counter-claim. If separate deposits are established, the totality of the deposit on account of claim shall be paid by the Claimant and the totality of the deposit on account of counter-claim shall be paid by the Respondent.

(e)   If a party fails, within 15 days after a second reminder in writing from the Center, to pay the required deposit, it shall be deemed to have withdrawn the relevant claim or counter-claim.

(f)   After the award has been made, the Center shall, in accordance with the award, render an accounting to the parties of the deposits received and return any unexpended balance to the parties or require the payment of any amount owing from the parties.

Award of Costs of Arbitration

Article 71

(a)   In its award, the Tribunal shall fix the costs of arbitration, which shall consist of:

(i)   the arbitrator's fees,

(ii)   the properly incurred travel, communication and other expenses of the arbitrator,

(iii)   the costs of expert advice and such other assistance required by the Tribunal pursuant to these Rules, and

(iv)   such other expenses as are necessary for the conduct of the arbitration proceedings, such as the cost of meeting and hearing facilities.

(b)   The aforementioned costs shall, as far as possible, be debited from the deposits required under Article 70.

(c)   The Tribunal shall, subject to any agreement of the parties, apportion the costs of arbitration and the registration and administration fees of the Center between the parties in the light of all the circumstances and the outcome of the arbitration.

Award of Costs Incurred by a Party

Article 72

In its award, the Tribunal may, subject to any contrary agreement by the parties and in the light of all the circumstances and the outcome of the arbitration, order a party to pay the whole or part of reasonable expenses incurred by the other party in presenting its case, including those incurred for legal representatives and witnesses.

VII.   CONFIDENTIALITY

Confidentiality of the Existence of the Arbitration

Article 73

(a)   Except to the extent necessary in connection with a court challenge to the arbitration or an action for enforcement of an award, no information concerning the existence of an arbitration may be unilaterally disclosed by a party to any third party unless it is required to do so by law or by a competent regulatory body, and then only

(i)   by disclosing no more than what is legally required, and

(ii)   by furnishing to the Tribunal and to the other party, if the disclosure takes place during the arbitration, or to the other party alone, if the disclosure takes place after the termination of the arbitration, details of the disclosure and an explanation of the reason for it.

(b)   Notwithstanding paragraph (a), a party may disclose to a third party the names of the parties to the arbitration and the relief requested for the purpose of satisfying any obligation of good faith or candor owed to that third party.

Confidentiality of Disclosures Made During the Arbitration

Article 74

(a)   In addition to any specific measures that may be available under Article 52, any documentary or other evidence given by a party or a witness in the arbitration shall be treated as confidential and, to the extent that such evidence describes information that is not in the public domain, shall not be used or disclosed by a party whose access to that information arises exclusively as a result of its participation in the arbitration to any third party for any purpose without the consent of the parties or order of a court having jurisdiction.

(b)   For the purposes of this Article, a witness called by a party shall not be considered to be a third party. To the extent that a witness is given access to evidence or other information obtained in the arbitration in order to prepare the witness's testimony, the party calling such witness shall be responsible for the maintenance by the witness of the same degree of confidentiality as that required of the party.

Confidentiality of the Award

Article 75

The award shall be treated as confidential by the parties and may only be disclosed to a third party if and to the extent that
    (i)   the parties consent, or
    (ii)   it falls into the public domain as a result of an action before a national court or other competent authority, or
    (iii)   it must be disclosed in order to comply with a legal requirement imposed on a party or in order to establish or protect a party's legal rights against a third party.

Maintenance of Confidentiality by the Center and Arbitrator

Article 76

(a)   Unless the parties agree otherwise, the Center and the arbitrator shall maintain the confidentiality of the arbitration, the award and, to the extent that they describe information that is not in the public domain, any documentary or other evidence disclosed during the arbitration, except to the extent necessary in connection with a court action relating to the award, or as otherwise required by law.

(b)   Notwithstanding paragraph (a), the Center may include information concerning the arbitration in any aggregate statistical data that it publishes concerning its activities, provided that such information does not enable the parties or the particular circumstances of the dispute to be identified.

VIII.   MISCELLANEOUS

Exclusion of Liability

Article 77

Except in respect of deliberate wrongdoing, the arbitrator, WIPO and the Center shall not be liable to a party for any act or omission in connection with the arbitration.

Waiver of Defamation

Article 78

The parties and, by acceptance of appointment, the arbitrator agree that any statements or comments, whether written or oral, made or used by them or their representatives in preparation for or in the course of the arbitration shall not be relied upon to found or maintain any action for defamation, libel, slander or any related complaint, and this Article may be pleaded as a bar to any such action.

Schedule of Fees

(All amounts are in United States dollars)

Fees of the Center

1. Registration Fee (Article 67, WIPO Expedited Arbitration Rules)

Amount of Claim	Registration Fee
Up to $1,000,000	$1,000
$1,000,001 to $10,000,000	$2,000
Over $10,000,000	$3,000

Notes

1. Where the amount of the claim is not specified at the time of submitting the Request for Arbitration, a registration fee of $1,000 shall be payable, subject to adjustment **in the course of the proceedings**.
2. Where a claim is not for a monetary amount, a registration fee of $1,000 shall be payable, subject to adjustment. The adjustment shall be made by reference to the registration fee that the Center, upon examination of the Request for Arbitration or the Statement of Claim, determines to be appropriate in the circumstances.
3. The amount of claims expressed in currencies other than United States dollars shall, for the purposes of calculating the registration fee, be converted to amounts expressed in United States dollars on the basis of the official United Nations exchange rate prevailing on the date of submission of the Request for Arbitration.

2. Administration Fee (Article 68, WIPO Expedited Arbitration Rules)

Amount of Claim or Counter-Claim	Administration Fee
Up to $100,000	$1,000
$100,001 to $1,000,000	$1,000 + 0.40% (of the amount above $100,000)
$1,000,001 to $5,000,000	$4,600 + 0.20% (of the amount above $1,000,000)
$5,000,001 to $20,000,000	$12,600 + 0.10% (of the amount above $5,000,000)
Over $20,000,000	$27,600 + 0.05% (of the amount above $20,000,000 up to a *maximum* administration fee of $35,000)

SCHEDULE OF FEES (continued)

Notes

1. Where a claim or counter-claim is not for a monetary amount, the Center shall determine an appropriate administration fee.

2. For the purpose of calculating the administration fee, the percentage figures are applied to each successive part of the amount of claim or counter-claim. For example, if the amount of claim is $5,000,000, the administration fee would be calculated as follows:

$100,000		$1,000
$900,000 (difference between $100,000 and $1,000,000)	0.40%	$3,600
$4,000,000 (difference between $1,000,000 and $5,000,000)	0.20%	$8,000
$5,000,000		$12,600

3. The maximum administration fee payable is $35,000.

4. The amounts of claims or counter-claims expressed in currencies other than United States dollars shall, for the purposes of calculating the administration fee, be converted to amounts expressed in United States dollars on the basis of the official United Nations exchange rate prevailing on the date of submission of the claim or of the counter-claim, respectively.

Arbitrators' Fees
(See Table, page 288)

Notes

1. For the purpose of calculating the amount of claims, the value of any counter-claim is added to the amount of the claim.

2. For the purpose of calculating the minimum and maximum amounts of the arbitrator's fees, the percentage figures are applied to each successive part of the whole amount of claims. For example, if the amount of claim is $1,500,000, the minimum fees would be calculated as follows:

SCHEDULE OF FEES (continued)

$100,000		$2,000
$400,000 (difference between $100,000 and $500,000)	2.00%	$8,000
$500,000 (difference between $500,000 and $1,000,000)	1.50%	$7,500
$500,000 (difference between $1,000,000 and $1,500,000)	1.00%	$5,000
$1,500,000		$22,500

3. Where a claim or counter-claim is not for a monetary amount, the Center shall, in consultation with the arbitrator and the parties, determine an appropriate value for the claim or counter-claim for the purpose of determining the arbitrator's fees.

4. The amounts of claims or counter-claims expressed in currencies other than United States dollars shall, for the purpose of determining the arbitrators' fees, be converted to amounts expressed in United States dollars on the basis of the official United Nations exchange rate prevailing on the date of submission of the claim or of the counter-claim, respectively.

5. *[Note not used]*

6. *[Note not used]*

WIPO EMERGENCY RELIEF RULES

CONTENTS

Application of WIPO Arbitration Rules

Article I

(a) Except as varied by these provisions, the WIPO Arbitration Rules shall apply *mutatis mutandis* to the procedure for emergency interim relief under the provisions of this Annex (hereinafter called ''the Procedure'').

(b) Articles 4(a), 6 to 12, 14 to 19, 41 to 43 and 67 to 70 of the WIPO Arbitration Rules shall not apply to the Procedure.

Notices

Article II

All notices or other communications that may or are required to be given pursuant to the Procedure shall be in writing and shall be delivered in person or transmitted by telefax. Where a notice or other communication is transmitted by telefax, the original of such notice or other communication shall, at the same time, be sent by expedited postal or courier service.

Relationship to Other Arbitral Proceedings

Article III

(a) Subject to paragraph (b), if a party addresses a request to a judicial authority, or initiates another arbitration in relation to a dispute in respect of which a Request for Relief has been received by the Center, the Emergency Arbitrator appointed pursuant to the Request for Relief shall retain the power to make an award and to modify it.

(b) (i) If a party initiates an arbitration pursuant to the WIPO Arbitration Rules or the WIPO Expedited Arbitration Rules in relation to a dispute in respect of which a Request for Relief has been received by the Center, the Emergency Arbitrator appointed pursuant to the Request for Relief shall retain the power to make an award and to modify it until the date on which an arbitral tribunal is constituted in the arbitration pursuant to the WIPO Arbitration Rules or the WIPO Expedited Arbitration Rules.

(ii) A party that initiates an arbitration pursuant to the WIPO Arbitration Rules or the WIPO Expedited Arbitration Rules in relation to a dispute before transmitting a Request for Relief to the Center in respect of the same dispute shall be deemed to have waived its rights to request interim relief under the provisions of this Annex from the date on which an arbitral tribunal is constituted in the arbitration pursuant to the WIPO Arbitration Rules or the WIPO Expedited Arbitration Rules.

Request for Relief

Article IV

(a) A Claimant seeking emergency interim relief pursuant to the provisions of this Annex shall deliver or transmit a Request for Relief to the Center and to the Respondent.

(b)   In order to facilitate the necessary preparations on the part of the Center, prior to transmitting the Request for Relief, the Claimant shall, where possible, inform the Center in advance of its intention to transmit the Request for Relief and of the essence of the information that it intends to provide with the Request for Relief.

(c)   The Request for Relief shall contain or be accompanied by the following:

(i)   the names, addresses and telephone, telefax or other communication references of the parties and of the representative, if any, of the Claimant;

(ii)   a copy of the Arbitration Agreement and of the relevant parts of any contract of which it forms part;

(iii)   a concise statement of relevant facts and a statement of the rights to be preserved;

(iv)   a statement of the interim relief sought;

(v)   a concise statement of the harm expected to the Claimant if the interim relief is not granted and an explanation of why such relief is required urgently;

(vi)   evidence justifying the grant of the interim relief sought, including copies of documents and statements;

(vii)   any observations that the Claimant may wish to make on whether it wishes a hearing to be held, and, if so, the date, time and place thereof.

(d)   The Claimant shall exercise good faith in relation to the Request for Relief and shall not withhold facts, circumstances or documents known to it or in its possession that would be material to the decision of the Emergency Arbitrator on the interim relief sought.

Answer to the Request

Article V

(a)   Unless the Request for Relief is made *ex parte* pursuant to Article XIII, the Respondent shall, within 60 hours from the time at which it receives the Request for Relief from the Claimant, deliver or transmit to the Center and to the Claimant an Answer to the Request.

(b)   The Answer to the Request shall contain or be accompanied by the following, to be presented in as concise a manner as possible:

(i)   a reply to the particulars of the Request for Relief;

(ii)   any evidence upon which the Respondent relies including copies of documents and statements;

(iii)   any claim for interim relief by the Respondent.

(c)   If a claim for interim relief is made by the Respondent in accordance with paragraph (b)(iii), the Claimant shall reply to the particulars thereof. Paragraphs (a) and (b) shall apply *mutatis mutandis*.

Constitution of Standby Panel

Article VI

(a)   The Center shall constitute a standby panel of prospective arbitrators who are prepared to be available on 24 hours' notice to be appointed as an emergency arbitrator under the provisions of this Annex.

(b)   The Center shall publish the names of the members of the standby panel together with a statement of each member's qualifications and experience.

Appointment of the Emergency Arbitrator

Article VII

(a)   If the parties have agreed on a person to act as Emergency Arbitrator before the delivery or transmission of the Request for Relief, that person shall be appointed as Emergency Arbitrator.

(b)   Where the parties have not agreed on a person to act as Emergency Arbitrator before the delivery or transmission of the Request for Relief, or where a person that the parties have agreed will act as Emergency Arbitrator is unavailable to do so, the Center shall promptly proceed to appoint a member of the standby panel to act as Emergency Arbitrator.

Challenge of the Emergency Arbitrator

Article VIII

For the purpose of any challenge of the Emergency Arbitrator, the period of 15 days mentioned in Articles 25 and 26 of the WIPO Arbitration Rules shall be replaced by the period of 24 hours.

Disqualification from Acting in Related Proceedings

Article IX

Unless required by a court of law or authorized in writing by the parties, the Emergency Arbitrator shall not act in any capacity whatsoever, otherwise than as Emergency Arbitrator, in any pending or future proceedings, whether judicial, arbitral or otherwise, relating to the subject matter of the dispute.

Powers of the Emergency Arbitrator

Article X

(a)   The Emergency Arbitrator shall conduct the Procedure in such manner as the Emergency Arbitrator considers appropriate.

(b)   In particular, the Emergency Arbitrator may

(i)   proceed without a hearing and make an award where the Emergency Arbitrator considers that each party has had an opportunity to present its case;

(ii)   convene, on the shortest possible notice, the parties for the purpose of a hearing, whether in person, by telephone or by teleconference, at a time, date and place fixed by the Emergency Arbitrator;

(iii)   hear one party, and proceed to make an award in the absence of the other party, if the Emergency Arbitrator is satisfied that the other party has been given notice of the time, date and place of the hearing that was adequate, in view of the emergency nature of the Procedure, to enable that other party to be present; modify, in the event that a hearing is conducted and an award is made in the absence of a party, the time limit for the delivery or transmission of the Answer to the Request by that party, or convene a further hearing for the purpose of receiving further submissions.

Award

Article XI

(a)   The Emergency Arbitrator may make any award that the Emergency Arbitrator considers urgently necessary to preserve the rights of the parties.

(b)   In particular, the Emergency Arbitrator may

(i)   issue an interim injunction or restraining order prohibiting the commission or continued commission of an act or course of conduct by a party;

(ii)   order the performance of a legal obligation by a party;

(iii)   order the payment of an amount by one party to the other party or to another person;

(iv)   order any measure necessary to establish or preserve evidence or to ascertain the performance of a legal obligation by a party;

(v)   order any measure necessary for the conservation of any property;

(vi)   fix an amount of damages to be paid by a party for breach of the award under such conditions as the Emergency Arbitrator considers appropriate.

(c)   The Emergency Arbitrator may make the award subject to such conditions as the Emergency Arbitrator considers appropriate. In particular, the Emergency Arbitrator may

(i)   require, having regard to any agreement between the parties, that a party commence arbitration proceedings on the merits of the dispute within a designated period of time; or

(ii)   require that a party in whose favor an award is made provide adequate security.

Time Period for Delivery of the Award

Article XII

(a)   The Emergency Arbitrator shall make the award and communicate a copy thereof in the shortest time possible and, in any case, within 24 hours of the termination of any hearing.

(b)   At the request of the Emergency Arbitrator or on its own initiative, the Center may, in exceptional circumstances, extend the time limit set out in paragraph (a).

Ex Parte *Requests for Relief and Orders*

Article XIII

(a)   In exceptional circumstances, where notice to the Respondent would involve a real risk that the purpose of the Procedure would be defeated, the Claimant may deliver or transmit the Request for Relief to the Center without serving it on the Respondent.

(b)   A Request for Relief delivered or transmitted in accordance with paragraph (a) shall, in addition to the particulars required by Article IV, indicate the reasons why notice to the Respondent would involve a real risk that the purpose of the Procedure would be defeated.

(c)   Where satisfied that notice to the Respondent would involve a real risk that the purpose of the Procedure would be defeated, the Emergency Arbitrator may hear the Claimant and proceed to make an order in the absence of the Respondent. Such an order shall be made subject to the condition that the order, and such further documentation as the Emergency Arbitrator considers appropriate, be served on the Respondent in the manner and within the time ordered by the Emergency Arbitrator in order to enable the Respondent to be heard on the matter.

(d)   The provisions of this Annex shall apply *mutatis mutandis* to any procedure under this Article, it being understood that the provisions relating to an award shall so apply to an order made under this Article by the Emergency Arbitrator.

Deposit

Article XIV

(a)   The Request for Relief shall be subject to the payment by the Claimant to the Center of a deposit as an advance for the costs of the Procedure. The amount of the deposit shall be the amount fixed in the Schedule of Fees applicable on the date on which the Request for Relief is received by the Center.

(b)   No action shall be taken by the Center on a Request for Relief unless the deposit has been paid.

(c)   In the course of the Procedure, the Center may require a supplementary deposit.

(d)   After the award has been made, the Center shall, in accordance with the award, render an accounting of the deposits received and return any unexpended balance or require the payment of any amount owing.

(e)   In the case of a claim for interim relief by the Respondent, paragraphs (a) to (d) shall apply *mutatis mutandis*.

Administration Fee of the Center

Article XV

(a)   The Request for Relief shall also be subject to the payment by the Claimant to the Center of a non-refundable administration fee, which shall belong to the International Bureau of WIPO. No action shall be taken by the Center on a Request for Relief unless the administration fee has been paid by the Claimant.

(b)   In the case of a claim for interim relief by the Respondent, a non-refundable administration fee shall also be payable by the Respondent to the Center. The claim for interim relief shall not be receivable by the Emergency Arbitrator unless the administration fee has been paid by the Respondent.

(c)   The amount of the administration fee payable by the Claimant and, where applicable, the Respondent shall be the amount fixed in the Schedule of Fees applicable on the date on which the Request for Relief is received by the Center.

Fees of the Emergency Arbitrator

Article XVI

(a)   The amount and currency of the fees of the Emergency Arbitrator and the modalities and timing of their payment shall be fixed, in accordance with the provisions of this Article, by the Center.

(b)   The amount of the fees shall be calculated on the basis of the hourly indicative rate set out in the Schedule of Fees applicable on the date on which the Request for Relief is received by the Center, taking into account the complexity of the matter, the urgency of the case and any other relevant circumstances.

RECOMMENDED CONTRACT CLAUSES AND SUBMISSION AGREEMENTS

Future Disputes

RECOMMENDED WIPO ARBITRATION CLAUSE

"Any dispute, controversy or claim arising under, out of or relating to this contract and any subsequent amendments of this contract, including, without limitation, its formation, validity, binding effect, interpretation, performance, breach or termination, as well as non-contractual claims, shall be referred to and finally determined by arbitration in accordance with the WIPO Arbitration Rules. The arbitral tribunal shall consist of [three arbitrators][a sole arbitrator]. The place of arbitration shall be ... The language to be used in the arbitral proceedings shall be ... The dispute, controversy or claim shall be decided in accordance with the law of ..."

RECOMMENDED WIPO EXPEDITED ARBITRATION CLAUSE

"Any dispute, controversy or claim arising under, out of or relating to this contract and any subsequent amendments of this contract, including, without limitation, its formation, validity, binding effect, interpretation, performance, breach or termination, as well as non-contractual claims, shall be referred to and finally determined by arbitration in accordance with the WIPO Expedited Arbitration Rules. The place of arbitration shall be ... The language to be used in the arbitral proceedings shall be ... The dispute, controversy or claim shall be decided in accordance with the law of ..."

Existing Disputes

RECOMMENDED SUBMISSION AGREEMENT FOR WIPO ARBITRATION

"We, the undersigned parties, hereby agree that the following dispute shall be referred to and finally determined by arbitration in accordance with the WIPO Arbitration Rules:

[Brief description of the dispute]

"The arbitral tribunal shall consist of [three arbitrators] [a sole arbitrator]. The place of arbitration shall be ... The language to be used in the arbitral proceedings shall be ... The dispute shall be decided in accordance with the law of ..."

RECOMMENDED SUBMISSION AGREEMENT FOR WIPO EXPEDITED ARBITRATION

"We, the undersigned parties, hereby agree that the following dispute shall be referred to and finally determined by arbitration in accordance with the WIPO Expedited Arbitration Rules:

[Brief description of the dispute]

"The place of arbitration shall be . . . The language to be used in the arbitral proceedings shall be . . . The dispute shall be decided in accordance with the law of . . ."